Karl Korsch: Revolutionary Theory

Karl Korsch: Revolutionary Theory

Edited by Douglas Kellner

University of Texas Press, Austin & London

The publication of this book was assisted
by a grant from the Matchette Foundation

Library of Congress Cataloging in Publication Data

Korsch, Karl, 1889–1961.
  Karl Korsch: revolutionary theory.

  Includes bibliographical references.
  1. Communism—Collected works. 2. Revolutions
—Collected works. I. Kellner, Douglas, 1943–
HX271.K67 1977   335.43   76–56182
ISBN 0–292–74301–7

Copyright © 1974 by Europäische Verlagsanstalt Köln und Frankfurt;
copyright © 1977 by University of Texas Press

Printed in the United States of America

Contents

Acknowledgments

For helpful comments and criticisms of different drafts of the manuscript I would like to thank Barbara Barratt, Paul Breines, Steve Bronner, Andrew Giles-Peters, Cynthia Gardner, Harry O'Hara, Stuart Hersh, Paul Piccone, Jim Schmidt, Jim Watson, and especially Michael Buckmiller who provided much material and provocative criticism during a visit to the Korsch-Gerlach Archive in Hanover and who carefully read and criticized my introductory material. I would also like to thank the translators who put much labor-power into the task of rendering Korsch's sometimes prolix German into readable English: Andrew Giles-Peters and his colleagues in Australia, Karl-Heinz Otto and Heinz Schutte, and my friends Roy Jameson and Mark Ritter here in Austin.

Douglas Kellner

Karl Korsch: Revolutionary Theory

Korsch's Revolutionary Marxism

By Douglas Kellner

Karl Korsch is being increasingly recognized as one of the most interesting, neglected, and relevant political theorists of the century.[1] Korsch's early works contain reflections on workers' control and industrial democracy, focusing on the theme of the socialization of society. His essays on the transition to socialism and critique of both Social Democratic reformism and Soviet state socialism remain provocative contributions. He was one of the first to criticize the repressive turn of the Soviet Union under Stalin and developed a sharp critique of authoritarian communism. He also evolved a critique of Leninism, which he believed had become a fetter on the working-class movement that had to be removed to make possible a new era of revolution. Korsch was one of the most original and interesting proponents of revolutionary Marxism, and his analysis of "the crisis of Marxism" contains a challenging critique of the Marxian political theory and theory of revolution.

Korsch was also an early opponent of nazism and developed a theory of fascism and counterrevolution on a world-wide scale to explain the defeats of the working-class movement and their failure to follow the Marxian scenario. At the same time, he attempted to discover and elucidate other models of social change in syndicalism and anarcho-communism, and he studied the Paris Commune, the Russian Soviets, and the Spanish Collectives as alternative forms of industrial and agricultural organization. Further, Korsch was one of the first Western theorists to call attention to developments in the so-called Third World, which he perceived might be a locale for the sort of social revolution that had failed to materialize in Europe and America.

Korsch's works provide a privileged perspective through which to view and interpret the process of revolution and counterrevolution that has constituted the political dynamic of our beleaguered century. For Korsch was both an impassioned participant in the political struggles in Germany during the Weimar Republic and an illuminating interpreter of a fateful stretch of modern history. His writings provide an attempt to grasp his age in thought, to get a hold on historical reality through theory. Moreover, Korsch's theory was always geared toward political practice, toward showing the possibilities of and obstacles to radical social change; hence, his work provides a paradigm of the theorist of practice, of the political-theoretical activist. Although the triumph of nazism forced Korsch into an American exile that cut him off from participating in the central political events of the day, he continued to reflect upon and interpret the major movements of history. His essays in the 1930's and 1940's provide penetrating insights into the movement of contemporary history and brilliant critiques of theories which he felt offered a distorted and ideological picture of current history.

Korsch's interaction with his historical environment requires a detailed reconstruction of the historical events to which his writings were a response and an expression in order to provide the proper context to understand his work. In a 1954 review of a Bakunin anthology, Korsch complained, "Unfortunately they [Bakunin's writings] do not appear here in close connection with the historical conditions and concrete actions which entered into every theoretical concept of Bakunin. Without them, the living body of his 'thought in action' is transformed into a purely ideological system."[2] The same holds for Korsch. My introduction will attempt to elucidate the "close connection with the historical conditions and concrete action which entered into every theoretical concept" of Korsch, and to bring to life his "thought in action."

Notes

1. A complete edition of Korsch's works is being prepared in Germany, and translations of his major works are appearing in every European language. His works are being frequently discussed in Europe and there is a growing interest in his work in the United States. Two examples: Claudio Pozzoli, ed., *Uber Karl Korsch* (Frankfurt: Fisher, 1973), and the Korsch issue of *Telos* 26 (Winter 1975–76).

2. Karl Korsch, "A Bakunin Sampler," *Dissent* 1, no. 1 (Winter 1954): 110.

1. Korsch's Road to Marxian Socialism

Little is known of Korsch's early life.[1] He was born on August 15, 1886, in Todstedt, Germany, a small village southeast of Hamburg. He was one of six children in a middle-class family. The father rose from secretary in a city hall bureau to vice-president of a bank. He was well educated and had unfulfilled intellectual ambitions that were to be realized in an unexpected way by his son Karl. The mother, on the other hand, was not at all intellectual and was said to have maintained a rather untidy appearance and household. His wife Hedda Korsch's "Memories" contain the most detailed information on Korsch's family:

> Korsch came from a medium middle-class background. His father had been through secondary school, had taken the *Abitur*, and possessed great intellectual ambition. He was very interested in philosophy and wrote an enormous unpublished volume on the development of Leibnitz's theories of monads. He tried to put the whole of the cosmos into this philosophical system. It was his life's work and purely theoretical. The family came from East Prussia, from a farming background. But he wanted something more urban and intellectual. Soon after he married Teresa Raikovsky, Korsch's mother, they moved west to Todstedt. The father wanted to be closer to western culture, and he disliked the agricultural Junker environment in which they lived. Because although the Korsch family themselves had only a modest-sized farm, the big estates were all around them and his father had no interest in agriculture. His mother was totally unconcerned with intellectual matters and never read a thing. She was pretty and extremely temperamental: she cooked well when she was in a good humour, burnt everything when she was angry. She was terribly untidy and if there is one reason why Karl was so tidy it was because of his mother.[2]

The family moved to Meiningen in the Thuringen region when Karl was eleven, to provide better educational opportunities for the children. Karl entered the local school (*Gymnasium*) and did well in his studies. When he was eighteen he moved into an abandoned garden house where he read German literature and Kant—fleeing into nature and a higher aesthetic-philosophical world to escape from bourgeois reality: typical behavior of German youth fed up with their surroundings and in search of something more.[3] Michael Buckmiller, Korsch's biographer, suggests that Korsch began to put in question and oppose the society around him: "His oppositional stance to his parents and school grew quickly as he increasingly experienced the contradiction between beautiful sounding phrases and the harsh petty-bourgeois reality which surrounded him: the teachers who hammered with a Prussian cane the elevated moral values of German culture into the pupils' youthful heads and who were frequently themselves rather pathetic alcoholics; his father who in his leisure wrote lofty studies in natural philosophy on Leibnitz's theory of monads and who tried to lead a harmonious and healthy life guided by science, while in practice he led a self-dominating authoritarian regime and frequently beat his children."[4]

In 1906 and 1907 Korsch studied successively at Munich, Geneva, and Berlin to gain a broad foundation in philosophy and the humanities as background for his studies in law. Korsch entered the University of Jena in 1908 where he worked on a law degree and engaged in student politics. He joined a student group, the *Freie Studenten*,[5] which militated for a democratization and humanization of the University. Korsch was one of its most active members. He became editor of the student newspaper and organized lectures featuring socialist speakers, such as Edward Bernstein and Karl Liebknecht. The students arranged contacts with workers in the nearby Zeiss optical factory, which was presented as a model factory that shared profits with the workers, instituted workers' democracy, heavily financed the University, and built a culture center with lecture and theater rooms. Korsch published many articles in the student newspaper and actively participated in debates and lectures.[6] On a lecture tour he met Hedda Gagliardi whom he was to marry in 1913. Korsch graduated from the Jena law school summa cum laude superato in 1911.

During this period Korsch became attracted to socialism through his activities in the *Freie Studenten* group, his contact with local socialists and social reformers in the Zeiss optical factory, and his study of socialist literature. Hedda Korsch reports: "He was also a convinced socialist by the time of his last year in school. He looked around to see if there were any socialists among his school-mates, but he did not find any. He read a lot: I do not know when he first read Marx but I am inclined to think it was at school, because when he was a student he was an outspoken socialist—by conviction, although not a member of any organization."[7] The young Korsch had thus progressed from an attitude of withdrawal from, and individualistic opposition to, German society to a stance of reformist political activism. Like many intellectuals he was attracted to socialism but he saw socialism mainly as an ideal human society, and thus criticized the Social Democrats, who in his view only represented particular interests (the working class) and thus did not embrace "the whole future of the German nation."[8] Nonetheless, he supported the practice of the Social Democrats who "through social-political reforms . . . would introduce bearable conditions."[9] Socialism was indeed necessary in his view because the "capacity for culture" of a nation "depended upon whether it succeeded in eliminating a system of unlimited exploitation and domination by violence."[10]

The ideal of socialism for Korsch at this stage was not to be realized through parliamentary politics or trade union activity but through educating broad segments of the public to progressive ideas and the ideals of socialism. Korsch had thus overcome the romantic individualist tendencies of many German youth, but still had a highly idealistic vision of social change that was as much influenced by Kant as Marx.[11]

In 1912 Karl and Hedda went to England where he had received a grant to translate and write a commentary on a legal text of Sir Ernest Schuster.[12] The Korsches soon joined the Fabian society and became enthusiastic participants in its young people's group. Korsch published many articles on the Fabian activities and his experiences in England in the German journal Die Tat.[13] He was becoming an increasingly convinced advocate of socialism and, in an interesting article in 1912, he turned to a subject that was to be a life-long concern: the search for "The Socialist Formula for the Organization of a People's Economy." Korsch complained that the socialists had not yet found "an adequate formula for the construction and organization of a people's economy" that went beyond the demand for the "socialization of the means of production."[14] Already Korsch was criticizing the "leading dogmas of Marxism" and searching for practical, viable plans to carry through and realize socialism. He was sympathetic to Fabian proposals to gain public control of industry and their detailed plans to socialize society. Korsch believed that the Fabians' "marvelous undertaking" combined "observation, experiment, theoretical study, fantasy, and the power of judgment"; he urged German socialists to develop similar detailed plans to socialize German society.[15] Later he was to suggest that a Fabian society be developed in Germany and may have been instrumental in persuading his student and friend Felix Weil to finance the Frankfurt Institute for Social Research, which might have been modeled on the "Fabian Research Department."[16]

Interestingly, the qualities that Korsch praised in the Fabians were to become distinctive features of his own work. He praised the Fabians for their "sharp critique of the existing society and will to reform the future."[17] He also approved of their "utopian impatience," "knowledge of reality," and their "propensity toward the simple and the practical." He held the Fabians to be model democratic socialists and agreed with their educational goals, their efforts to create socialist consciousness, and their "propaganda by deed."[18] He believed that "The Fabian Society shares with German Marxism the conviction that economic and political socialism (the socialization of the means of production) will *come by itself* whether or not we as individuals endorse or oppose this development. They add to this theoretical insight, however, a very important *orientation of the will*. They wish to awaken the practical will to the position that with this unavoidable transformation of the human economy, a human culture, the ideal of humanity, will be demanded. And this ideal signifies the *higher development of the human race* ('Man and Superman')."[19] There is little doubt from a close reading of Korsch's early essays that he was heavily influenced by Fabian ideas. Although he was soon to turn from their reformism and idealism to Marxian revolutionary materialism, the Fabian spirit of practical political activism was to long remain a feature of Korsch's theory and practice.[20]

Korsch's Practical Socialism

When World War I broke out in 1914, Korsch's ideals of pacifism, social and political idealism, internationalism, and rationalism came up against an increasingly brutal and barbaric reality. Korsch returned to Germany and enlisted in the army, but remained true to his pacifist convictions throughout the war, refusing to bear arms even in the heat of battle. He was twice demoted for his refusal to obey orders, was wounded, and won the respect of his fellow soldiers for his convictions and bravery.[21] "It is," he wrote, "as if this quantitative increase in suffering had forced us to correctly perceive, feel, and experience the simple *qualitative* reality for the first time."[22] Despite his new insights into the utter barbarism of capitalism, Korsch did not fall into nihilistic pessimism and refused to surrender his ideals of a humanistic social order: "The simple difference today from our earlier position is that we do not yet feel satisfied with the highest and deepest of our strivings."[23]

Korsch's hopes for radical social change were given a dual impetus by the Russian Revolution of 1917 and the German revolution in 1918. The surprising collapse of the German military and political order and the mass uprising of sailors, soldiers, and workers in the councils organizations, convinced Korsch and others that the transition to socialism was on the historical agenda. Korsch's military unit was known as the "red company," and he participated in the founding of a "soldiers' council." The abdication of the Kaiser and the collapse of the old order signified for Korsch that "the presuppositions are created under which a new spirit can break into German politics that will make possible a fundamental transformation of the existing social order."[24]

In January 1919, Korsch was invited by Robert Wilbrandt to serve as an assistant in the socialist-dominated socialization commission, presided over by Karl Kautsky. Their task was to prepare recommendations for the socialization of the coal industry.[25] Korsch concentrated his energies at this time on working out a more general theory of socialization that would provide an adequate concept of socialism. In this situation, where it seemed that socialization was a real, indeed imminent, possibility in Germany, Korsch wrote a brochure, "What is Socialization?"[26] An immediate and practical urgency informs this essay, which was concerned with the burning question of the day: how can Germany be reconstituted on a socialist basis? Korsch was appalled at the lack of a socialist theory on these immensely practical and concrete questions: What is a socialist society? How does one organize the economy on socialist principles? What does socialization involve beyond nationalization of the means of production? Social Democrats, such as Kautsky and Bernstein, as well as the Spartacus League, had neglected such questions, thus manifesting, in Korsch's view, an "incomprehensible backwardness of socialist *theory* in regard to problems of practical realization."[27] Korsch intended his work to provide a "transitional program" which, through a system of "workers' councils," would begin the construction of socialism. Thus "What is Socialization?" was intended to fill a gap in socialist theory, and to address itself to the most important practical issue of the day. To those who think it was "utopian" or "idealistic" to expect a transition to socialism in Germany at the time, let us cite an account by E. H. Carr which indicates that socialist revolution was widely perceived to be a real possibility:

> Never had the call to world revolution as the staple of Soviet foreign policy seemed more clearly justified by its fruits. While the final blow that laid Germany low had been struck by others, there was evidence—which no Bolshevik was likely to overlook or underestimate—of the part played by Bolshevik propaganda in demoralizing the German armies. The civil population was in revolt against the horrors and privations of the war; the monarchy had fallen without a blow amid general execration; workers' and soldiers' councils on the Soviet pattern had been formed all over Germany, and the

Berlin council had created the counterpart of a Council of People's
Commissars; Germany had entered its "Kerensky period"; it seemed
inconceivable that, under the stimulus of Russian example and Russian encouragement, the parallel of the Russian revolution would
not be followed to the end. When Radek reached Berlin in December 1918 he had the impression that "nine-tenths of the workers
were taking part in the struggle against the government"; other ob-
servers took much the same view . . . both then and for more than
two years after, the imminence of proletarian revolution in Germany
continued to haunt many who feared it as well as the Bolsheviks
who hoped for it.[28]

In a series of articles in the early 1920's, Korsch grappled with the
central problems of socialization and confronted issues that were ignored
or suppressed by his Social Democratic contemporaries. The major problem in the construction of a socialist society is, he believed, that socialization involves two seemingly conflicting basic demands: first, in place of
the anarchy of the "free market" (which Korsch sarcastically remarked
is free mainly for capitalist exploiters), there will be a "planned administration of production and distribution through society."[29] Secondly, control from below (workers' control) and industrial democracy must be
inaugurated to carry out the liberation of labor and to provide a life more
worthy of human beings: "through the immediate introduction of this
control from below the entire realm of production is transformed from a
private affair of individual exploiters of production into the public affair
of all the participants of production; hence the 'wage-slaves' of the old
system will be transformed with a stroke into co-participating (*mitbestim-
menden*) 'working-citizens' of a socialist state (*sozialen Rechtsstaat*)."[30]
In attempting to carry through these two basic demands of socialization, certain problems arise which I shall call the contradictions of Socialist socialization. On one hand, Korsch stressed that "control from above"
—a central plan (requiring a central administration) to regulate the entire economy—is absolutely essential to implementing socialism.[31] On the
other hand, control from below—workers' control and participation in
decision-making procedures—is required to realize the radical demands
for the liberation of labor. Korsch formulated this contradiction in "What
is Socialization?" as the conflict between production and consumption:
between the production plants with their interests and the consuming
public with their interests. This is a genuine conflict of interests, for
abolishing the capitalists' right to own, exploit, and control the production process simultaneously raises (1) the workers' demand for division

of profits among themselves and control of the labor process and (2) the consumers' demand for their share of the revenues of production and public control over the production process. The task and challenge of socialism is to achieve a harmony, a balance, between these conflicting demands and interests to make possible "the most far-reaching *autonomy* and the simultaneous insertion of all individual economic units into a *planned economy*."[32]

Korsch showed that syndicalist and consumer cooperative projects of organizing individual production and consumer units will come into conflict with the general public interest. Different syndicalist groups advocated that the workers take over and socialize the industries in which they worked so that coal miners would own and control the coal mines, railroad workers the train system, and so on. There was a wide-spread consumer cooperative movement in Germany, France, and England that set up alternative consumer units and businesses of all sorts.[33] Korsch perceived that giving total autonomy to syndicalist-controlled production units and consumer cooperative units would create a series of conflicts of interest and would reproduce certain contradictions and competition of capitalism. Hence all production and consumer units must be coordinated and regulated by public organs and a central plan.[34] However, Korsch opposed with special vehemence state socialism and social technologies that equate socialism with a nationalization of the economy carried through by the state and controlled from above, thus failing to create workers' democracy or industrial autonomy.[35]

Korsch believed that the way to overcome these conflicting demands and interests is through instituting a system of workers' councils: "socialism requires workers' councils not only because it is socialistic, but because it is also democratic, because it wants participation of all the people and wants the best (*Auslese*) from everyone."[36] Only the councils, in Korsch's view, can fulfill Engels' demand for a total replacing of the capitalist economic order that rests on unfree labor by a " 'socially planned regulation of production according to the needs of the totality as well as every single individual.' "[37] The councils system would resolve the crucial problems in the construction of a socialist society: who can use the means of production and for what purpose? What and how much will be produced? How will production be organized? How will wages and profits be divided? How will commodities be distributed? Solving these problems requires what Korsch called "industrial autonomy" on the level of production, and consumers' associations representing the public as a whole that will help assess public demand and social needs. Hence a councils' system of production and consumer groups coordinated by a central plan responsive to the people will maximize production for social and individual need and maximize industrial and individual autonomy.

There will be inevitable problems of coordination and conflicts of interest but the councils system will provide a system of checks and balances in which consumer groups representing society as a whole, and workers' councils representing the workers in a given plant or industry will be organized in assemblies, meetings, and discussion groups on various levels to struggle with the problems of socialist socialization. As the people develop socialist consciousness there will be increasing cooperation and harmony between the various councils and it will be seen that the central plan and industrial autonomy, control from above and control from below, consumers' associations and workers' councils provide complementary organs of a socialist democracy.

Korsch's councils' system concept therefore contains a critique of both "state socialism" that attempts to implement socialism from above, and syndicalism that wishes to make the individual production units the sole organ of power in which the workers will own, control, and appropriate the profits for themselves. For whereas the first concept—by which the state owns everything—would be a form of state capitalism, the program of syndicalism—"the mines to the miners," "the railroads to the railway workers,"—would be a form of production capitalism. Against these conceptions, Korsch urges "pure community property for the totality of producers and consumers" to be administered by a councils' system.

The weakness of Korsch's theory of socialization lies in the political question of how this program is to be practically implemented. The difficulties are readily apparent in the last section of "What is Socialization?" called, significantly, "What Should We Do—Educating for Socialism." The last page contains the only discussion of the political means through which socialization is to be carried out. Korsch projected: (1) "political action" through state legislation and municipal ordinances; (2) developing cooperatives, and (3) economic action of the working class through collective bargaining, co-participation in management and the transformation of individual ownership through class struggle. Korsch concluded: "The logical continuation of these latter means of struggle is, in times of revolutionary fervor, the struggle to remove the capitalist enterpriser from control over the production process and to place him under the control of the totality of plant participants; today this struggle is being fought out in many individual plants according to the program of the Spartacus League. This last means holds no terror for those who affirm the ideal of socialism. It is not a means of socialization to be condemned on the basis of some kind of moral precept; not any more than political revolution is a morally objectionable means of political emancipation."[38] A contradiction emerges here between the sort of political action through parliamentary decree and municipal ordinance urged by the reformist Social Democrats and the revolutionary struggles urged by the Spartacus League. Korsch was not able to smooth over the contradictions between legal and illegal action, reformist political measures and revolutionary syndicalist labor struggles, between the parliamentary program of the Social Democrats and the radical workers' councils concept put forth by the Spartacus League and other leftist groups. Korsch didn't really take a stand with one side or another in "What is Socialization?" and his other early writings on socialization, and thus could not at this point envisage any concrete and practical political or economic strategy which would bring about the socialization process he so brilliantly outlined.

It should be noted that Korsch's concept of socialization is formulated as a "transitional program," or what Marx called the first stage of socialism (Korsch uses the term "first phase" of social or communal economy in several places in "What is Socialization?").[39] Hence he recognizes that in the first phase of socialization "private self-interest" and even aspects of a "market economy" will be operative and thus proposes "differentiated compensation for varying achievement." There are, moreover, some remnants of Fabian elitism and perhaps a bourgeois production-profit syndrome in some sections which urge that socialization utilize private self-interest "as motivation for the most profitable and prolific production possible even on a still greater scale of production"; that speak of "resurrecting the capitalist spirit" as "worker capitalism" after its elimination as "owner capitalism"; and that quote from Bernard Shaw to the effect that "the talented intellectual worker will be the last exploiter (*Ausbeuter*) of society."[40] But Korsch quickly adds: "Only gradually in autonomous production, decontaminated by the cessation of the class struggle between the capitalist 'haves' and the proletarian 'have-nots,' will that sense of community develop which is the prerequisite for the establishment of the second and higher phase of social economy, in which the working power of every individual, just as the material means of production, will be community property, whereby every individual contributes to social production according to their ability and in turn participates in the profits of communal production according to need."[41]

Korsch concludes by stressing that the development of socialist consciousness requires "a series of cultural and political measures which can be summarized by the term 'socialization of education.' "[42] In a 1919 article, "Die Politik im neuen Deutschland," Korsch argues that "socialization of the economy and socialization of education are in fact only two sides of the same process of transition from a private capitalist to a communal socialist economy. The transition itself is not important only and primarily for questions of production and consumption of material goods, but it is at the same time a cultural and spiritual affair of immense import."[43]

Korsch had been involved with educational reform both as a student and in England where he wrote several articles on education.[44] He now postulated a new socialist educational system grounded in an *Einheitsschule* where education (*Bildung*) "will be transferred from the privilege of a favored class into a communal good, social property of the totality."[45] Not only would education be extended to all classes in this conception, but the very nature and content of education would change to produce socialist consciousness: "The sort of school which wants to prepare the path for an evolving socialist community economy must already develop in itself the spirit of the new economic order." Above all, Korsch wanted "to combine education and material production to abolish the distinction between mental and material labor."[46] This in effect would abolish intellectuals as a separate class and would, as Gramsci envisioned, make every worker an intellectual in the sense that they would share in the general level of culture. Moreover, education would be more closely connected with industry and productivity: "on one hand, in all cases education of the older students in the higher classes would be connected with a limited amount of real material productive labor in industry and agriculture, while, on the other hand, even after one passed through school and college, there would still be accessible to the workers a continuing further education."[47]

Korsch also envisaged progressive education modeled on the "Freie Schulgemeinde" where his wife had once taught,[48] which would introduce co-education, non-hierarchical comradely relations between students and teachers, and would thus provide an organization of education parallel to the workers' councils' organization of industry: "the 'free schools' are aiming at autonomous education and must already be models in the present that realize in a pure form that which the 'free economic organizations' of a distant future can first universally become: places of work in which necessary labor serving the common good . . . will be performed out of love of the subject-matter and out of devotion to the community."[49]

The more immediate, pressing problem for intellectuals was, Korsch believed, to convince the people of the necessity now for socialism and to combat reactionary anti-socialist ideologies. Korsch postulated the need to develop a "new spirit of German politics" through rejecting the "hateful militarism" of the old Germany and cultivating a new spirit of freedom. This new all-pervasive freedom could only be created through a socialist reconstruction of the economy and education to increase the realm of autonomy in all areas of life. Korsch is taking the position here that he would reiterate in his 1930 reflections on *Marxism and Philosophy:* *"Socialism, both in its ends and in its means, is a struggle to realize freedom."*[50] He saw the demand for socialism as a task for "practical idealism" and talked in Kantian terms of a "duty" to construct socialism: "The duty toward socialization, toward the realization of socialism, stands before all other duties in Germany. It is identical with the duty to love your neighbor, identical with the duty of self-preservation. The historical task of practical socialism is to inexorably demand its fulfillment, to marshal together all spiritual powers in resolute action."[51]

Korsch called his theory at this time "practical socialism," which he defined as a third way between a purely intellectual socialism conceived as a "pure science" and a reformist socialist politics that eschews theory.[52] Practical socialism combines theory and practice in a dialectical unity. Practical socialism rejects the view that socialism automatically proceeds from economic development as a necessary and inevitable process, and stresses "conscious human activity (Marx's 'revolutionary praxis'). It holds that the presupposition, indeed the making possible, of socialist construction cannot dispense with a faith that moves mountains, a will to transform the world and creative human activity."[53] Korsch is stressing here the necessity of cultivating the subjective factors of revolutionary consciousness to make possible socialist revolution—a theme to which he will often return. The practical socialist should recognize that "capitalism is impossible in the future and that socialism does not come about by itself. Thus the practical socialist will direct all of his consciousness and endeavor, and put into motion all the powers of his thought and all the passion of his will, to begin and carry through socialist construction before it is too late."[54] In this way the practical socialist will adhere to "a socialism in which science, faith, and readiness for socialist action will be molded together in an inextricable unity. And that is practical socialism."[55]

Korsch's writings on socialization represent a transitional phase between his earlier Social Democratic/Fabian reformism and his move to Marxian revolutionary materialism. Indeed, it appears that at the time of writing "What is Socialization?" Korsch had but a simplistic understanding of the Marxian critique of political economy. With characteristic energy and enthusiasm, Korsch delved into an intense study of Marx in the early 1920's and praised the "Faustian knowledge of Marx" whom he characterized as that "Copernicanlike founder of the science of political economy."[56] Korsch had now truly begun his lifelong relationship with Marxism that would involve him in a series of fateful events.

As Korsch moved toward revolutionary Marxism, he developed a polemic against Social Democratic reformism which he believed had failed to perceive the primacy of production in the Marxian theory: that radical change must begin with the transformation of the *relations of production*, and that for Marx, "a fundamental restructuring of the social *relations of distribution* is simply impossible without a restructuring of the relations of production which are the foundation for all social relations."[57] Hence, "every serious social-political reform, every better and more just distribution of goods *within* a basically capitalistically organized economy is bound by *insurpassable limits*."[58] Moreover, Korsch came to believe that from a genuinely Marxist standpoint, socialization could not come about "through pure thought and the ideological will of talented social technicians," but rather only through revolutionary struggle; here he decisively moves away from his earlier Fabianism.[59] Later he criticized as "socialization opium" the projects of Hilferding, Kautsky, and others who wanted to leave socialization to functionaries of the Social Democratic government.[60] He concluded, "Only when from scientific knowledge we have deeply grasped the impossibility, the completely illusory character, of that seemingly so 'realistic' connection of a capitalistic production policy with a socialistic distribution policy can we become practical socialists."[61]

In the early 1920's, Korsch moved toward a revolutionary socialist position. This is clear in "Fundamentals of Socialization," translated in this anthology, which Rusconi describes as "the most important of this period," and "the first blueprint of Korsch's Marxism."[62] In this article, Korsch suggests that the working class movement has failed "to grasp the essentials of 'scientific socialism' in the specific sense layed down by Marx and Engels":[63] the primacy of revolutionary practice, "the identity of objectifying knowledge and activity," and the stress on revolutionary will, revolutionary phantasy, and revolutionary faith.[64] The deficiency of these subjective conditions of revolution and the lack of a decisive activist thrust in the working-class movement had momentous political implications. In explaining the failure to carry through a resolute and thoroughgoing transition to socialism in the November revolution, Korsch wrote: "It is by no means to be traced back to purely external coincidences that in the enormously fateful months after November, 1918, as the political power organization of the bourgeoisie collapsed and nothing external stood in the way of the transition from capitalism to socialism, that great hour nonetheless had to slip by unseized because the *social-psychological* presuppositions for its utilization were sorely lacking: a decisive *belief* in the immediate capacity for realization of the socialistic economic system which could have carried the masses onward was nowhere to be found, nor was there a clear knowledge of the nature of the first steps to be carried out."[65]

The deficit in the subjective conditions of revolution is at least in part attributed to a "backwardness of socialist theory." For Korsch, an important and neglected component of Marxism is what he calls concepts of realization which anticipate a new reality and posit historical alternatives. The future-oriented and practice-oriented thrust of Korsch's conception is strikingly expressed in the following passage:

> The concepts of realization arise out of a full knowledge of the economic and psychological totality and its perceivable tendencies of development. Through the concepts science anticipates the individual emerging social reality. Through their conscious anticipation of the coming these concepts also posit one of the realities through which the creative transformation from the old to the new forms of social and individual being can alone be accomplished. Scientific knowledge can of course take this particular form only in the creative fantasy of a revolutionary who has already previously carried out the transformation from the old to the new in his thought. And from the fact that Kautsky and all of those who stand close to him do not possess such creative, faithful revolutionary fantasy, we can explain their all too long denial of practical future-oriented thoughts. From this lack of revolutionary fantasy we may also explain the ghostliness of their programs of action and plans for socialization.[66]

In addition to Korsch's emphasis on the unity of revolutionary theory and practice and the importance of the subjective conditions of revolution, he stressed the need for revolutionary theory to concern itself with the "forms of socialist construction."[67] Korsch then discussed three concepts of socialization dominant at the time that were embedded in three complexes of "economic-historical realities" and actual socialization plans.[68] He argued that the superior concept of socialization is the one that posits the workers' councils as the authentic organ of socialism. Let us examine this position that equates socialization with the workers' councils—which defines the core of Korsch's political conception—in more detail.

Korsch and the Workers' Councils Movement

Korsch's earlier somewhat idealist and moralistic concept of socialism was to give way to an increasingly tough-minded concept of practical socialism under the twofold impact of his participation in the rise and decline of the workers' councils movement and his intensive study of Marx. During World War I, workers' councils spontaneously emerged in Germany from shop stewards' committees and strike committees, much as the Soviets had emerged from militant labor political-economic activity in Russia in 1905 and 1917.[69] The German unions and political parties were hampered in their activities both by irresolute bureaucratic leaders and by special laws that declared a state of siege (*Belagerungszustand*) and thus prohibited militant activity.[70] Groups of workers' councils emerged as alternative organs of protest and action against the war, and against the deteriorating economic-political-social situation, thus creating new forms of political struggle. In Berlin in June, 1916, 55,000 workers struck to protest the war, led by strike committees that were the seeds of the workers' councils. These groups continued to develop and mushroom throughout Germany. In a general strike in April, 1917, 300,000 workers participated, and in a general strike in January and February, 1918 over 500,000 workers participated, mobilized by the councils.[71] Throughout 1918 the military and economic-political situation in Germany rapidly deteriorated and a series of strikes and military insurrections culminated in the November uprisings in Berlin that forced the Kaiser to abdicate.[72] These events awakened sharp hopes and fervent militancy for a socialist workers' republic.

In this fluid and explosive situation Korsch first supported attempts led by the Social Democrats to socialize key German Industries, and then was drawn irresistably to the workers' councils movement. Indeed, Korsch was heavily influenced by the theorists of the councils movement and in turn contributed many articles to their journals.[73] It is interesting to note that the workers' councils theorist Ernst Däumig used the term "practical socialism" to describe the councils movement. The following passage from Däumig is extremely Korschian in its language and concepts and shows Korsch's deep kinship with the councils movement and its strong influence on his thought:

> The councils concept is in its pure and consequential application
> *practical socialism*. It should provide the possibilities to translate
> through the proletariat the teaching of socialist science as propagated
> by socialist parties into reality. The councils organization must be

constructed and extended according to these goals and tasks, and must receive their structure and completion in a councils system. Since the *councils organization* is the child of revolutionary epochs, it will never enter fixed and complete (*fix und fertig*) into beautifully paragraphed phrases, but will take its external form and tactical tasks according to the process of revolutionary development and the demands of the current revolutionary situation to which it *must conform*.[74]

The councils movement was at first almost unanimous in calling for the construction of a socialist republic of workers' councils and the abolition of capitalism. This radicalism in fact distinguishes the workers' councils from previous working-class organizations. Two contemporary accounts stress this point: "here lies an essential distinction between the workers' councils and previous forms of workers' organization: while the old economic and political organizations tie themselves to the conditions of the capitalist environment and the class state, and receive the laws of their movement from these, the working class seeks in the workers' councils new forms of means with which it posits the fully conscious task of definitely overcoming the capitalist economy and class state and at the same time building the foundation for the construction of the new."[75] And: "One should *not forget the revolutionary origin* of the councils conception in order to correctly understand it. All attempts to construct a councils organization in the framework of *bourgeois* society and on the foundation of *capitalist* production will either yield a distorted concept or will be obliterated by the *forward striving tendencies* of councils thought. A councils organization can only be related to proletarian socialist struggle that is determined to eliminate capitalist production and the state erected on it—even when it has a republican facade—and to put in its place socialist production and a self-administering public community."[76]

Korsch later argued that the demand for workers' councils expressed "in the first phase of the revolutionary movement in Germany the still very unclear and confused, but nevertheless very resolute and strong, will for social revolution."[77] The tremendous appeal of the councils showed that "the workers finally wanted to carry through in action an open and total break with that objectively long surpassed bourgeois conception of legality that every place of work is the private property of whatever owner and that every working person is seen as an instrument of labor (*Betriebsmittel*) bought by the owner."[78] The workers' councils were thus revolutionary organs inalterably opposed to the capitalist system. They demanded a complete break with the old system and demanded a new socialist order.

The central political question confronting the SPD leaders who nominally had taken over the reigns of government, and the militant workers in the councils movement who were the most powerful political force, was whether a parliamentary system or a workers' councils system should be constructed in Germany, or whether these organs could co-exist as "dual power."[79] Korsch did not in 1919–20 take a clear cut stand on this issue, although he was a firm supporter of the councils system. Possibly he believed, along with many other independent socialists, that dual power was possible, that the workers' councils and parliament could share state power.[80] This was to be an illusion with grave consequences for the SPD political leaders relentlessly consolidated power in the central government which they shared with the parliament, the military, the previous state functionaries, and other members of the former ruling class. Moreover, the unsuccessful Spartacus revolt, resulting in the deaths of militant radicals such as Karl Liebknecht and Rosa Luxemburg, as well as the violent suppression of councils governments in Bavaria, Bremen, Gotha, Halle, Leipzig, and elsewhere by government troops and the proto-fascist *Freikorps*, greatly weakened the revolutionary forces who wanted a councils socialist Republic.[81] Further, congresses of the councils movement in December, 1918, and October, 1920, voted for the creation of a parliament system that would in many ways supplant the councils, and the Social Democrat-dominated parliament quickly moved to weaken the power of the councils.[82] The parliamentary National Assembly in February, 1920 limited the power of the councils to an extreme degree and in effect destroyed the growth and impetus of the movement.

It seems that not only did the radical demands of the workers' councils movement threaten the domination of the former ruling class, but it also threatened the control of the labor movement by the parties and unions. Moreover, many of the members of the councils were party or union members (or leaders) themselves. This caused factionalism within the councils movement by the unions and parties and created divided loyalties that weakened the movement from within. Nonetheless, the concept of workers' councils as authentic organs of socialism was not to die and Korsch remained loyal to this concept throughout his life.

Korsch continually reflected on the intoxicating rise and depressing fall of the workers' councils movement and offered an analysis of the failure of the movement to achieve its goal of constructing a socialist republic.[83] While summarizing the recent history of the workers' councils movement, Korsch discerned three reasons for its failures: (1) the councils were coopted and controlled by the parties and the unions, rather than being autonomous organs of the workers, elected and controlled by the workers themselves for themselves; (2) the councils for the most part failed to exert real power and hence to replace or "control" the pre-revolutionary court and legal system, the military, the old governing bureaucracy, and other agents and institutions of the bourgeois system; thus the councils failed to become independent and dominant organs of people's power. Finally (3) the councils failed to assume both political and economic power and were confused as to their own function. Because it was not clear whether the councils were primarily political or economic organs, the parliamentary bureaucracy of the SPD could attempt to limit the councils to economic activity, while the old union bureaucracy could claim the councils had primarily political functions. In this way, "the government, the bourgeoisie, the SPD, the unions, and other open and hidden opponents of the councils system were able to play off against each other the economic and political tasks of the workers' councils."[84] The tragic failure of the workers' councils movement was thus in a sense rooted in a theoretical deficit: "there was little clarity over the essential tasks of the council dictatorship itself in the most well-known representatives of the revolutionary councils conception in Germany in the days after the November upheaval."[85] The law in the 1921 Weimar constitution that limited the councils to purely economic activity, and that was ratified by the councils congress itself, spelled for Korsch the end of the councils system as an instrument of revolution in Germany. Korsch sadly concluded: "Today there is no longer an independent councils movement in Germany . . . . Parliamentism, the party, and the union system have externally gained a full victory over the revolutionary 'councils system.' Hence, only subterraneously in the consciousness of the suffering masses, beside the thoughts of revolution, smoulders on the thought of the revolutionary councils system, smelted together in inseparable unity with the thought of revolution. On the day of revolutionary action, the councils will again rise like the phoenix from its ashes."[86]

Korsch was to return to the concept of workers' councils as the authentic organs of socialism throughout his life. He was one of the first to develop a neo-Marxist theory of revolutionary and democratic socialism, and thus provided a critique of the sort of state socialism, centralized bureaucracy, and new forms of domination that would develop in the Soviet Union. A problem in the Marxist theories of socialism dominant at the time was, Korsch believed, an over-evaluation of the role of the state in constructing socialism and de-emphasis on developing institutions that would put real power in the hands of the people. "State socialism," Korsch wrote, "will not be socialism at all."[87] The liberation of labor should proceed through the implementation of workers' control, and should be the work of the people themselves (and not the state, the party, or any other body). Hence, "only after the overcoming of the last remains of a formal-democratic *state-ideology* can the necessity of the workers' councils (*Räte*) for the construction of a classless and stateless socialist society be grasped in its innermost essence."[88]

The following passage well summarizes Korsch's position and shows why his concept of socialism is still of utmost relevance today:

> Socialization can first be achieved in a sense adequate to the actively working and productive class when the workers have become fully authorized participants in production on the way to direct socialization. None of the earlier socialist teachings that solely focus on the "political means" of liberating the working class from capitalist exploitation can bring us *the* socialism that working people desire. The striving of the masses for some sort of psychic equilibrium (*seelischen Ausgleich*) against the immense unfreedom of individual workers in large factories under the modern relations of production in large industries cannot be satisfied through a mere change of the employer; the single productive class of active workers will not as such be freer, their ways of life and labor will not be more worthy of a human being, through replacing the bosses installed by the owners of private capital by officials installed by the state government or a community administration. Thus in the consciousness of a large circle of workers the earlier socialist teaching is being put aside which began with the slogan, seize the "political power" in the state and then decree the "transition of the means of production to the whole public" through legal means—thus essentially in the forms of nationalization and communalization—this model is being replaced by a completely different conception of what is essential to the "socialization" demanded by modern socialism. One can say that today no socialist plan, no matter how it looks, will be acknowledged as a satisfactory fulfillment of the idea of socialization that does not carry, in one form or another, the notion of a broadly conceived "industrial democracy": the concept of the direct control and administration of every branch of industry, in which every single business is managed by the community of participating workers, and through organs determined by themselves. When "socialization" is demanded today, the word no longer merely invokes the universal and abstract demand for the transfer of the means of production into the possession of the whole public. Rather the demand for socialization today has solidified into the more concrete demand that

the transfer of the means of production into public property takes
place in such a way that everywhere the masses of workers themselves will receive the administration of their places of work, or at
least will receive the decisive part of the control of this administration.[89]

The subsequent rise of state socialism, both in the Soviet bloc and in
those countries where Social Democrats won state power, showed the
problems involved in the construction of a party-bureaucratic apparatus
which produced new forms of domination and failed to contribute to the
liberation of the working class. Korsch offers as an alternative to these
models of socialism an attractive democratic libertarian model, hence the
great interest in Korsch's ideas today.

In view of Korsch's early position on the primacy of workers' councils
in the construction of socialism and his critique of state socialism, it may
appear highly surprising that his turn toward Marxism and revolutionary
socialism took the form of an enthusiastic embrace of Leninism and the
Soviet Union as the model of socialism. Actually Korsch's orthodox Communist interlude would be a relatively brief one (1921–1926) and he
would emerge from his period of fervent Leninism as one of the leading
left-oppositionalists who again championed the workers' councils as the
authentic organs of socialism, criticizing the Leninist concepts of the party
and state which he had temporarily defended.

On the basis of Korsch's concept of socialization rooted in workers'
councils, his courageous opposition to Stalinism, and his brilliant critique
of Leninism and Marxism, there has arisen a legend that Korsch was the
paradigm of the left-oppositionalist libertarian socialist. It has been
alleged—falsely as we shall see—that Korsch had deep reservations about
entering the Communist party and that from the beginning of his involvement in the Communist movement, Korsch opposed the dominant policies of the German and Soviet Communists from a left-oppositionalist
position; that Korsch engaged in oppositionalist activity against the Communist International (Comintern) by participating in a left offensive
against Bolshevism at the Comintern World Congress in 1924; and,
finally, that Korsch began in the early 1920's developing a heretical
theoretical current which opposed a critical, dialectical Hegelian or Western Marxism to Communist (Marxist-Leninist) orthodoxy.

The true story of Karl Korsch's adventures with communism is far more
complicated and convoluted than the Korsch legend would have it. In the
following pages I would like to clear away the many myths which have
surrounded and occluded Korsch's theory and practice. I shall show, first,

why Korsch became a Leninist and unstintingly defended the Bolshevization of the German Communist party in his writings 1920–1925. We
shall then see how the myth arose that during this period Korsch was an
anti-Bolshevizer, and shall see that Korsch's special version of the philosophy of praxis which I call his "revolutionary historicism" underlies both
his support of Leninism and the Soviet Union, and his later critical, oppositionalist position. I shall then show how and why Korsch became a
left-oppositionalist and will reconstruct the progress through which he
became an anti-Leninist. In my view, Korsch's contribution to radical
social theory does not lie simply in being a left-oppositionalist who provides a model of negation and critical theory, nor does his critique of
Leninism consist in an abstract rejection of Leninist theory and practice.
Rather, Korsch reveals the limits of Leninism, and its failure as a model
of revolution for the West, by living through the Leninist experience
and painfully criticizing it from within, before he could "cut the umbilical
cord of Leninism," and evolve his oppositionalist position. For Korsch
identified with Leninism from the early 1920's to 1927, involved himself deeply in Leninist theory and practice, and then developed a critique
of Leninist theory from experience of the failure of Leninist practice in
Germany and the Soviet Union. Let us now examine the strange and
tragic story of Korsch's involvement with the Communist movement in
the 1920's.

Notes

1. The most detailed account of Korsch's life and thought is found in
Michael Buckmiller's "Marxismus als Realität," in Pozzoli, *Uber Karl Korsch*
(hereafter "Marxismus"), and his dissertation, *Karl Korsch und das Problem
der materialistischen Dialektik* (Hannover: Soak-Verlag, 1976) (hereafter
Karl Korsch). My Korsch interpretation is much indebted to Buckmiller's
work and to discussion with him in Hannover in the summer of 1975. Some
interesting biographical material is found in the interview with Hedda Korsch,
"Memories of Karl Korsch," *New Left Review* 76 (November–December
1972): 34–35.
2. Hedda Korsch, "Memories," pp. 35–36.
3. Buckmiller, *Karl Korsch*, pp. 6ff.
4. Ibid., pp. 6–7. All translations from the German are my own.
5. Buckmiller deals in detail with "the political and social changes at the
turn of the century and the formation of the German Free Students movement"
in ibid., pp. 7–19.

6. Korsch's student articles, which deal with the free student organization, women's liberation, and proposals for university and law school reform, are discussed in detail by Buckmiller in ibid., pp. 19–59.

7. Hedda Korsch, "Memories," p. 37.

8. Karl Korsch, "Die Stellung der Arbeiterinnen im Erwerbsleben," in *Jenaer Hochschulzeitung*, December 15, 1908.

9. Karl Korsch, "Japanische Arbeitsverhältnisse," in *Jenaer Hochschulzeitung*, January 20, 1909.

10. Ibid.

11. Buckmiller attempts to show how both the content and form of argumentation in the young Korsch were influenced by Kant in *Karl Korsch*.

12. Hedda Korsch, "Memories," p. 38.

13. Korsch published around twenty-one articles and reviews in *Die Tat* from 1912 to 1920. For a discussion of *Die Tat* and its publisher, Eugene Diederichs, see George Mosse, *The Crisis of German Ideology* (New York: Grosset and Dunlap, 1971), pp. 52ff. Hedda Korsch discusses the Diederichs circle with whom the Korsches were acquainted in Jena in "Memories," p. 38.

14. Karl Korsch, "Die sozialistische Formel für die Organization der Volkswirtschaft," *Die Tat* 4, no. 9 (December 1912); reprinted in Karl Korsch, *Politische Texte* (Frankfurt: Europäische Verlagsanstalt, 1974), p. 17.

15. Korsch, *Politische Texte*, pp. 20–21.

16. It has been claimed that, "originally, Weil had wanted his teacher, Karl Korsch, to be the head of the Institute." G. L. Ulmen, "Wittfogel's Science of Society," *Telos* 24 (Summer 1975):85. I discuss Korsch's influence on Weil and his probable role in the founding of the Institute for Social Research in "The Frankfurt School Revisited," *New German Critique* 4 (Winter 1975).

17. Karl Korsch, "Die Fabian Society," *Die Tat* 4, no. 8 (November 1912): 423.

18. Ibid., p. 425.

19. Ibid., p. 426.

20. A more detailed discussion of Korsch's Fabianism is found in Buckmiller's *Karl Korsch*, pp. 60ff. The Fabians were earlier an influence on Edward Bernstein when he lived in England, and in a sense the father of Social Democratic revisionism never escaped from Fabian reformism. Engels criticized Bernstein's "Fabian *Schwärmerei*" and sarcastically characterized the Fabians in a letter to Sorge as "a band of do-gooders who have enough sense to perceive the unavoidability of social revolution, but who cannot entrust this gigantic task to the crude proletariat alone, and therefore have the custom of putting themselves at the top; anxiety before revolution is their basic principle. They are the 'cultivated ones' (*Gebildeten*) par excellence." *Marx-Engels Werke* (Berlin: Dietz Verlag, 1968), 39:8.

21. Hedda Korsch's account of this period is fascinating; see "Memories," pp. 39–40.

22. Karl Korsch, "Akademisch-Soziale Monatsschrift," *Die Tat* 9, no. 11 (February 1918): 974.

23. Ibid., p. 975.

24. Karl Korsch, "Die Politik im neuen Deutschland," in Korsch, ed., *Der Geist der neuen Volksgemeinschaft* (Berlin: Zentrale für Heimatdienst, 1919), p. 63.

25. Nothing came out of their work and the commission was dissolved in April. Korsch made no contribution to the proceedings. Wilbrandt was a university socialist who influenced Korsch's concept of socialization and his initial reading of Marxism. See Karl Korsch, "Robert Wilbrandts 'Sozialismus,' " *Die Tat* 11, no. 10 (January 1920): 782–787.

26. Karl Korsch, *Was ist Sozialisierung?* (Hannover: Freies Deutschland Verlag, 1919), translated by Frankie Denton and Douglas Kellner as "What Is Socialization?" *New German Critique* 6 (Fall 1975): 60–81.

27. Karl Korsch, "Grundsätzliches über Sozialisierung," *Der Arbeiterrät* 2, no. 3 (January 1919): 900–911; translated in this anthology as "Fundamentals of Socialization," by Roy Jameson and Douglas Kellner.

28. E. H. Carr, *The Bolshevik Revolution, 1917–1923* (London: Penguin, 1971), 3:105–106.

29. Karl Korsch, "Die Sozialisierungsfrage vor und nach der Revolution," *Der Arbeiterrät* 1, no. 19 (1919), reprinted in *Schriften zur Sozialisierung* (Frankfurt: Europaische Verlag, 1969), p. 53.

30. Ibid., pp. 53–54.

31. Ibid.

32. Karl Korsch, "Fundamentals of Socialization."

33. The cooperative movement in Europe is discussed in detail by Bernstein in *Evolutionary Socialism* (New York: Schocken Books, 1961), pp. 109–135 and 186–189. Bernstein approves of the cooperative movement as a genuine step toward socialization, but notes Marx and Engels' ambivalence toward consumer cooperatives.

34. See Korsch's essay "Das sozialistische und das syndikalistische Sozialisierungsprogramm," *Der Sozialist*, June 28, 1915, pp. 402–405, reprinted in *Schriften zur Sozialisierung*, where he criticizes those anarchistic tendencies that want to do away immediately with the state and all forms of social control and authority.

35. Korsch, "Fundamentals of Socialization."

36. Ibid.

37. Ibid.

38. Korsch, "What Is Socialization?"

39. Ibid.

40. Ibid.

41. Ibid.

42. Ibid.

43. Korsch, "Die Politik im neuen Deutschland," p. 65.

44. Paul Breines makes the interesting suggestion that there is a connection between interest in radical education and a certain kind of leftist politics: "Not a few German so-called 'ultra-lefts' had backgrounds and/or professional experience in childhood education, for example, Alice Rühle, the wife of Otto Rühle. In the 1930's and after, Karl Korsch and Hedda Korsch were associated with ultra-left or council Communist groups. The basis for such connections is probably the idea of education for revolution as distinct from the idea of management of revolution," in "Korsch's Road to Marx," *Telos* 26 (Winter 1975–1976): 44. I might add that Hedda Korsch published several essays on child education and socialization in the *International* in 1924–1925 when Karl was editor. Both Karl and Hedda were active in councils schools in Jena in the early 1920's and later in the Karl Marx Schule in Berlin. Hedda Korsch continued working on educational reform during their years in exile in the United States and taught education courses at Wheaton College in Massachusetts. One might also refer here to Gramsci's work on education, culture, and the intellectuals, and Lukács' early emphasis on *Bildung*; on the latter theme, see James Schmidt, "Lukács' Concept of Proletarian Bildung," in *Telos* 24 (Spring 1975): 2–40. A comparison of the theories of education, culture, and the task of intellectuals in Gramsci, Korsch, and Lukács would make an interesting project.

45. Korsch, "Die Politik im neuen Deutschland," p. 70.

46. Ibid.

47. Korsch, "What Is Socialization?"

48. See Buckmiller, *Karl Korsch*, pp. 144–145.

49. Korsch, "Die Politik im neuen Deutschland," p. 71.

50. Karl Korsch, *Marxism and Philosophy*, Introduction by Fred Halliday (New York: Monthly Review Press, 1971) p. 144.

51. Karl Korsch, "Praktischer Sozialismus," *Die Tat* 11, no. 10 (January 1920). Reprinted in Karl Korsch, *Kommentare zur Deutschen 'Revolution' und ihrer Niederlage* (The Netherlands: Rotdruck, 1972), p. 26 (page references to reprint).

52. Ibid., p. 20.

53. Ibid., p. 21.

54. Ibid., p. 26.

55. Ibid., p. 24.

56. Korsch, "Fundamentals of Socialization."

57. Karl Korsch, "Sozialismus und soziale Reform," *Der Arbeiterrät* 2, no. 3 (January 1920): 7–9, reprinted in *Schriften zur Sozialisierung*, p. 40.

58. Ibid.

59. Korsch, "Fundamentals of Socialization."

60. Karl Korsch, "Der 18 Brumaire des Hugo Stinnes," reprinted in *Kommentare zur Deutschen 'Revolution.'*

61. Korsch, "Praktischer Sozialismus," p. 24.

62. Gian Rusconi, "Introduction to 'What Is Socialization?' " *New German Critique* 6 (Fall 1975) : 55, 57.

63. Korsch, "Fundamentals of Socialization."

64. Ibid.

65. Ibid.

66. Ibid.

67. Ibid.

68. Ibid.

69. For an account of the development of the Soviets in Russia, see Oscar Anweiler, *The Soviets, 1905–1921* (New York: Pantheon, 1975), and Peter Racheloff, "Soviets and Factory Committees in the Russian Revolution," *Radical America* 8, no. 6 (November–December 1974).

70. For an account of the German Revolution and workers' councils' movement see Richard Müller, *Vom Kaiserreich zur Republik* (Berlin: Malik, 1924–1925). Documents describing the councils' ideas and action are found in Dieter Schneider and Rudolf Kuda, *Arbeiterräte in der Novemberrevolution* (Frankfurt: Suhrkavip, 1973), and Charles Burdick and Ralph Lutz, *The Political Institutions of the German Revolution* (New York: Praeger, 1966). Peter von Oertzen, *Betriebsräte in der Novemberrevolution* (Dusseldorf: Droste, 1963), gives a good account of the councils' movement and Korsch's participation in it. Brian Peterson reviews a large number of recent German books on the workers' council movement, in "Workers' Councils in Germany, 1918–1919," *New German Critique* 4 (Winter 1975) : 113–124.

71. Schneider and Kuda, *Arbeiterräte*, pp. 16ff., and Burdick and Lutz, *Political Institutions*, pp. 1ff.

72. Schneider and Kuda, *Arbeiterräte*, pp. 21ff. Burdick and Lutz publish fascinating documents that portray the German government's reaction to the events that forced the Kaiser to abdicate, *Political Institutions*, pp. 17ff.

73. Many of Korsch's articles appeared in the councils' journal *Der Arbeiterrät*.

74. Ernst Däumig, "Der Rätegedanke und seine Verwirklichung," in Schneider and Kuda, *Arbeiterräte*, pp. 69–70.

75. Richard Seidel, "Die Gewerkschaftsbewegung und das Rätesystem," in Schneider and Kuda, *Arbeiterräte*, p. 25.

76. Däumig, "Der Rätegedanke," p. 69.

77. Karl Korsch, *Arbeitsrecht für Betriebsräte* (Frankfurt: Europaische Verlag, 1968), p. 108.

78. Ibid., p. 109.

79. For a discussion of the political situation, see Ruth Fisher, *Stalin and German Communism* (Cambridge: Harvard University Press), 1948, pp. 63–73; and Peterson, "Workers' Councils."

80. This seems to be the position Korsch takes in "What Is Socialization?"

although he also supports the "direct action" advocated by the Spartacus group in certain situations.

81. Fisher, *German Communism*, pp. 88–116.

82. Documents recording discussions and resolutions made at the Councils Congresses are collected in Burdick and Lutz, *Political Institutions*.

83. Karl Korsch, "Wandlungen des Problems der politischen Arbeiterräte in Deutschland," reprinted in *Politische Texte*.

84. Ibid., p. 26.

85. Ibid.

86. Ibid., p. 32.

87. Korsch, "Fundamentals of Socialization."

88. Ibid.

89. This passage is reproduced word for word in both "Die Sozial-isierungsfrage vor und nach der Revolution" and "Das sozialistische und das syndikalistische Sozialisierungsprogramm," and thus can be taken to be a favored programmatic summary of Korsch's position. Both are reprinted in *Schriften zur Sozialisierung*, pp. 52–53 and 55–56.

2. Korsch and Communism

In the summer of 1919, Korsch left Berlin for Jena where he was active in the workers' councils movement and then the communist movement. He completed his *Habilitationsschrift* and became a professor in the law faculty of the University of Jena.[1] He also contributed articles to leftist journals and newspapers, helped form a councils school, and gave many lectures to workers, students, and citizen groups.[2] After the attempt of counterrevolutionaries to seize state power in the Kapp putsch in March 1920—which was averted by a remarkable general strike that forced the reactionaries to capitulate[3]—Korsch saw the real dangers of counter-revolution and the need for a more resolute and militant left.

Korsch joined the USPD in autumn, 1919, when it was clear that the Social Democrats had no intention of radicalizing or carrying through the November Revolution.[4] The USPD—the Independent Socialist party—had split from the Social Democratic party (SPD) in 1917 as a socialist anti-war coalition, and included people from all political wings of the SPD: from Rosa Luxemburg (left) to Karl Kautsky (center) to Edward Bernstein (right). With such a diverse ideological spectrum the USPD was incapable of developing a unified politics due to the incompatible factions in its membership. Nonetheless, its numbers grew rapidly as a result of disgust with the "Kaiser socialism" of the SPD, and the USPD became an increasingly important political force.[5]

Korsch became increasingly active in the USPD and quickly radicalized his political position. In a party discussion on December 9, 1919, he criticized the Social Democrats' call for a national assembly and new constitution, which would in no way satisfy the demands of the workers and would, Korsch argued, serve to restore the old bourgeois order. He compared this parliamentary procedure with the Russian revolution.[6] His increased radicalization was evident in a new emphasis on the general strike as the supreme revolutionary tactic, and on resolute revolutionary struggle. In a speech three days before the Kapp putsch Korsch approvingly cited Bebel's motto: " 'As long as I breathe and speak and write . . . I shall remain the deadly foe of this bourgeois society and state, so as to undermine the conditions of its existence, and if I can to destroy it.' "[7]

After the Kapp putsch, the USPD and Communist party (KPD) both refused to participate in a workers' government and urged the formation of a workers' council republic. Korsch supported this position, placing primary emphasis now on "direct action of the masses, thus economic struggle," and called for "the organization of armed proletarian struggle."[8] Korsch's revolutionism was now thoroughgoing. However, the wide-spread radicalization process that briefly exploded after the Kapp putsch had been again exploited by the SPD and coopted by their parliamentary, reformist politics. Thus there was a debate within the USPD whether they should now fuse with the Communist party and join the Third International. The German historian of the USPD, Krause, sums up the debate as follows: "Since the objective conditions for revolution were 'mature,' then there must be a new, more radical organization found. Here the Soviets in Russia offered an example that appeared to be successful and by the very fact that it still existed, attracted many people."[9] Korsch adopted this position and urged a merger of the USPD with the KPD to form a new, stronger revolutionary organization on the Bolshevik model. Thus at the USPD convention in Halle on October, 1920, Korsch supported the majority decision to join the German Communist party and to accept the "twenty-one conditions" for entering the Communist International recently set forth by the Comintern.[10] This merger was to link disastrously together the fate of the German and Soviet parties and would result in the eventual control of the German Communist party by the Russians.

There are many legends concerning Korsch's attitude toward joining the KPD and his activities within the party which require clarification to help dispel the Korsch myth. Korsch's former student and later German editor, Erich Gerlach, erroneously claimed that "Korsch was originally an opponent of the uniting of the USPD with the KPD because of the '21 conditions' demanded by Moscow (for joining the Communist International), which called for a conspiratorial organization-apparatus beside the party. He saw an opening here for the fall of party democracy."[11] The claim is repeated by the German editor of another Korsch anthology and by two of Korsch's American editors.[12] Korsch's wife Hedda ratifies the myth: "He attended the USPD conference in 1920 when the party split and the majority opted for fusion with the Communists. Korsch went with the majority although he had great reservations about the 21 points that the Comintern had laid down. But it was the same as when we discussed his going back to Germany from London: he did not want to be a member of a small sect, but thought he should be where the masses were and he believed that the German workers were going Communist.

His main reservation about the 21 points concerned the centralized discipline from Moscow, the degree of dependence on the Russian party that they implied."[13]

As we shall see, Korsch did not have great reservations about accepting the twenty-one conditions or joining the Communist party. Rather, Gerlach, Hedda Korsch, and others were projecting Korsch's later critique of the domination of the German Communist party by the Soviet Union onto an earlier phase when there was, first, no evidence that the Soviets had the intention of exerting a repressive hegemony over their German comrades, who had enjoyed almost total autonomy in party affairs; nor, secondly, is there any evidence in Korsch's writings at the time that he feared this occurrence. Indeed, it can be shown that Korsch was at the time, and was to remain until 1925, an unambiguous champion of the Soviet Union, Leninism, and the Bolshevization of the KPD; in a series of 1920 articles Korsch supported "the immediate and unconditional acceptance and the speedy carrying through of the entrance conditions to the Third International."[14] In these articles, mostly published in the Thuringen communist newspaper *Neue Zeitung*, Korsch argued that "the Bolshevik movement is of decisive importance for the world revolution," and took a consistently positive position toward the Soviet Union, while criticizing the USPD leadership for its negative or mistrustful attitude toward the Soviet Revolution.[15] Korsch cited Rosa Luxemburg's idea that the "fatherland of the proletariat is the socialist international," and argued that it was imperative to join the Third International and defend in every way the Soviet Revolution, for "if Russia loses the revolution, then all is also lost in Germany."[16] Moreover, Korsch did not see entry into the KPD and the twenty-one conditions as a threat to party democracy. He believed that one must place the twenty-one conditions "in the context of the basic propositions [of the Comintern Second World Congress] and then one's hesitations will disappear. . . . democracy within the organization which the Third International has affirmed remains thoroughly preserved. . . . In the stages of intensified civil war the illegal organization must have the possibility to eliminate traitors without further ado."[17] Against the objection that joining the Communist party would splinter the USPD, Korsch argued that there were too many positions from left to right in the USPD, and that the splintering would bring forth a clearer revolutionary line that would make for a more efficacious organization and politics. Further, Korsch feared that if the USPD did not merge with the KPD that the left in the USPD would merge with the ultra-leftist KAPD—a move that he did believe would harmfully splinter the left.[18] In a caucus choosing delegates to the party convention in Halle that would decide on merging with the KPD, Korsch's entry resolution won. Hence at the USPD conference, Korsch supported completely the resolution to join with the Communist party and join the Third International.

Korsch's basic reason for joining the Communist party was his belief that Germany was in a revolutionary situation, and that it was imperative to create a revolutionary organization along the lines of the centralized, highly disciplined Bolshevik party: "When we have this conception, then we can only place ourselves on the side of the Bolsheviks."[19] Korsch believed that the Bolsheviks had created an efficacious revolutionary organization which had proved itself successful in the Russian Revolution, while the German parties had failed to carry through a socialist revolution because they lacked the proper revolutionary organization, theory and strategy. With these convictions Korsch entered into his Leninist period in which he was to emerge as one of the leaders of the German Communist party and one of the most articulate defenders of its policies and the Russian Revolution.

Korsch's Revolutionary Historicism

Korsch immersed himself in a study of the basic texts of Marx, Engels, and Lenin, and became one of the foremost Marx experts in Germany. His reading and interpretation of Marx was closely connected with his political work, and his essays were intended to present the basic ideas of Marxism to workers and party militants in a clear and compelling form.[20] He also lectured on Hegel at the law school in Jena, concluding that the Hegelian dialectical method was the theoretical core of Marxism. Although Korsch saw the Hegelian dialectic as providing the *form* of the Marxist theory, its *content* derived from the actual working-class struggles.[21] Korsch continually referred to Marx's dictum in the *Communist Manifesto* that "Communism, for us, is not a state of things to be established nor an ideal to which reality must adapt itself; we call communism the actual movement which transforms existing conditions."[22] In "15 Theses on Scientific Socialism," Korsch writes: "1. Scientific socialism (socialism as science) is the theoretical expression of the proletarian movement. This signifies: a) It is not a thing for itself (bourgeois 'presuppositionless' or 'pure' science or philosophy) but is a *component* of a real process, a 'movement,' or more precisely: an 'action,' the action of the 'oppressed class,' the 'proletariat' . . . b) It is a particular component of this movement, something special within this whole: the theoretical expression, science."[23]

Korsch was developing a radically historicist version of Marxism that derived both the content and form of ideology and theory from its "material and economic foundation."[24] In *Marxism and Philosophy* he approvingly cites Hegel's dictum that "philosophy can be nothing but *'its own epoch comprehended in thought'*,"[25] and then proceeds to dialectically relate both Hegel's and Marx's philosophy to the revolutionary struggles of the bourgeoisie and the proletariat, respectively, which were, in Korsch's view, reflected in the philosophies of the two masters of nineteenth century thought. Korsch's position here is what I call *revolutionary historicism* which roots revolutionary theory in the revolutionary movement and its class struggles.[26] He wished to demonstrate "the connections between the 'intellectual movement' of the period and the 'revolutionary movement' that was contemporary with it."[27] Hegel was read as the philosopher of the revolutionary bourgeoisie and his philosophy was connected with its revolutionary struggles:

> Hegel wrote that in the philosophic systems of this fundamentally revolutionary epoch, "revolution was lodged and expressed as if in the very form of their thought." Hegel's accompanying statements make it quite clear that he was not talking of what contemporary bourgeois historians of philosophy like to call a revolution in thought —a nice, quiet process that takes place in the pure realm of the study and far away from the crude realm of real struggles. The greatest thinker produced by bourgeois society in its revolutionary period regarded a "revolution in the form of thought" as an objective component of the total social process of a real revolution.[28]

Korsch was convinced that there was an inner connection between German idealism and Marxism on the grounds that both were expressions of the same revolutionary process:

> Since the Marxist system is the theoretical expression of the revolutionary movement of the proletariat, and German idealist philosophy is the theoretical expression of the revolutionary movement of the bourgeoisie, they must stand intellectually and historically (i.e. ideologically) in the same relation to each other as the revolutionary movement of the proletariat as a class stands to the revolutionary movement of the bourgeoisie, in the realm of social and political practice. There is one unified historical process of his-

torical development in which an "autonomous" proletarian class movement emerges from the revolutionary movement of the third estate, and the new materialist theory of Marxism "autonomously" confronts bourgeois idealist philosophy. All these processes affect each other reciprocally. The emergence of Marxist theory is, in Hegelian-Marxist terms, only the "other side" of the emergence of the real proletarian movement; it is both sides together that comprise the concrete totality of this historical process. This dialectical approach enables us to grasp the four different trends we have mentioned—the revolutionary movement of the bourgeoisie, idealist philosophy from Kant to Hegel, the revolutionary class movement of the proletariat, and the materialist philosophy of Marxism—as four moments of a single historical process.[29]

Korsch's defense of the importance of philosophy and his claim that understanding the relation between Marxism and philosophy requires grasping the Hegelian roots of Marxism has given rise to the interpretation of *Marxism and Philosophy* as a classic of "Hegelian Marxism," and has led to the picture of Korsch as one of the creators of a current that was in opposition to the dominant Marxist orthodoxy.[30] What has not been perceived is the extent to which Korsch believed he was merely restoring Marxist orthodoxy. Further, he saw himself as part of a philosophical front with Lenin and Luxemburg, representing a position of revolutionary socialism against the reformist Marxism of the Second International. The publication of Lukács' *History and Class Consciousness*, which attempts to synthesize Lenin and Luxemburg into a dialectical and revolutionary Marxist theory, could only strengthen Korsch's conviction that they—himself, Lukács, Lenin, and Luxemburg—represented genuine Marxism and constituted a theoretical-political front against Social Democratic revisionism.

Marxism and Philosophy begins with a quote from Lenin's 1922 essay "On the Significance of Militant Materialism": " 'We must organize a systematic study of the Hegelian dialectic from a materialist standpoint.' "[31] Korsch thus sees himself and Lenin as "materialist dialecticians" who both appreciate the dialectical nature of genuine Marxism and perceive its Hegelian roots. Korsch then provides an interpretation of the relation between Hegel and Marx and Marxism and Philosophy and concludes by noting

the peculiar parallelism between the two problems of Marxism and Philosophy and Marxism and State. It is well known that the latter, as Lenin says in *State and Revolution*, 'hardly concerned the

major theoreticians and publicists of the Second International.' This
raises the question: if there is a definite connection between the
abolition of the State and the abolition of the philosophy, is there
also a connection between the neglect of these two problems by the
Marxists of the Second International? The problem can be posed
more exactly. Lenin's bitter criticism of the debasement of Marxism
by opportunism connects the neglect of the problem of the State by
the Marxists of the Second International to a more general context. Is this context also operative in the case of Marxism and
philosophy? In other words, is the neglect of the problem of philosophy by the Marxists of the Second International also related to
the fact that *problems of revolution in general hardly concerned
them*?"[32]

The italicized quotation is from Lenin's *State and Revolution*; this is, of
course, Lenin's constantly reiterated critique of the Second International
which Korsch takes up here and radicalizes.

Korsch next works out his famous periodization of Marxism into (1)
the creative works of Marx and Engels; (2) the degeneration of Marxism in the Second International; and (3) the restoration of genuine Marxism by Luxemburg and Lenin:

What theoreticians like Rosa Luxemburg in Germany and Lenin in
Russia have done, and are doing, in the field of Marxist theory is to
liberate it from the inhibiting traditions of the Social Democracy of
the second period. They thereby answer the practical needs of the
new revolutionary stage of proletarian class struggle, for these traditions weighed "like a nightmare" on the brain of the working
masses whose objectively revolutionary socioeconomic position no
longer corresponded to these revolutionary doctrines. The apparent
revival of original Marxist theory in the Third International is
simply a result of the fact that in a new revolutionary period not
only the workers' movement itself, but the theoretical conceptions
of communists which express it, must assume an explicitly revolutionary form. This is why large sections of the Marxist system,
which seemed virtually forgotten in the final decades of the nineteenth century, have now come to life again. It also explains why
the leader of the Russian Revolution could write a book a few
months before October in which he stated that his aim was "in the
first place to *restore* the correct Marxist theory of the State." Events
themselves placed the question of the dictatorship of the proletariat
on the agenda as a practical problem. When Lenin placed the same

question theoretically on the agenda at a decisive moment, this was an early indication that the internal connection of theory and practice within revolutionary Marxism had been consciously re-established.[33]

Marxism and Philosophy was intended to provide a restoration of the philosophical dimension of Marxism and the importance of ideological struggle for revolutionary practice, much as Lenin has restored the political dimension of Marxism and the importance of revolutionary political struggle. Marxist theories had fallen victim, Korsch believed, to a "transcendental underestimation of ideology," and had failed to perceive the need for a critique of ideology and change of consciousness. For Korsch, "no really dialectical materialist conception of history (certainly not that of Marx and Engels) could cease to regard philosophical ideology, or ideology in general, as a material component of general sociohistorical reality—that is, a real part which had to be grasped in materialist theory and overthrown by materialist practice."[34] Ideology for Korsch is not only conceived as a theory that expresses the ideas of the ruling class but is to be grasped as a constituent of consciousness. Consciousness arises from the social life-process and in turn is a real component of that process. Hence a theory of revolution must take seriously the critique of ideology and change of consciousness. Korsch wanted to develop a theory of total revolution that "would restore the correct and full sense of Marx's theory. . . . a theory of social revolution that comprises all areas of society as a totality."[35] This project required a restoration of the philosophical dimension of Marxism and stress on the importance of ideological struggle as a component of revolution, as well as renewed reflection on Hegel and dialectics.

I have stressed the generally underestimated role that Lenin played in Korsch's problematic and the extent to which he believed his project is continuous with the positions of Leninism. We have noted that Korsch believed that the restoration of genuine Marxism began with Lenin and have shown the parallel which Korsch perceived between Lenin's and his own project. The brilliant section of *Marxism and Philosophy* where Korsch developed his dialectical theory of social revolution, and his concept of ideology critique and struggle, can also be read as a project totally consistent with Leninism, in the sense that Lenin also stressed the importance of ideological struggle in his theory of hegemony and in countless speeches and essays where he characterized Marxism as a weapon in the struggle against bourgeois ideology. In a way, Korsch conceived the relationship between Marx and Lenin in a parallel manner to the relation between Marx and Hegel—Lenin, like Marx, expressing a further stage of revolutionary struggle in his work. But here Korsch was operating with an idealized concept of Lenin which had little in common with either the historical Lenin or the Lenin who was being deified and re-tooled by the apologists for Soviet Marxism in Moscow.[36] Most of Lenin's works were not yet available in Europe and Korsch was no doubt unfamiliar with Lenin's *Materialism and Empirio-criticism*, which contained a crude and dogmatic philosophical materialism, copy theory of knowledge and perception, and correspondence theory of truth which had little in common with Korsch's dialectical conception of Marxism.[37] Moreover, Korsch was unaware that at the very moment he was penning *Marxism and Philosophy*, Soviet ideologists were concocting an ideological brew which they would label Marxism-Leninism and would relentlessly oppose to the Lukács-Korsch brand of Marxism.[38] But these events constitute the next chapter of our story and at this point Korsch's Lenin is the successful politician of the Bolshevik revolution and the revolutionary theorist whose theories were an integral component of the revolutionary process in Russia, which achieved the coveted unity of theory and practice that was the mark of genuine revolutionary theory for Korsch.

Korsch's interpretation of the relation between Marx and Hegel, his appraisal of the importance of philosophy and ideological struggle for socialist revolution, his periodization of Marxism which applies the historical materialist method to the history of Marxism, and his commitment to Leninism can all best be grasped in the context of his revolutionary historicism. Korsch stresses the historical rootedness of all ideas, consciousness, ideology, and revolutionary theory in a specific socioeconomic environment (this principle was later generalized by Korsch into the principle of historical specificity, which is akin to Gramsci's "absolute historicism"). The task of theory is in this view to conceptualize the interconnectedness of all ideas, institutions, and socioeconomic realities within the social totality and to describe the mediations which connect, for example, a philosophy to its socio-historical conditions. Here it should be noted that Korsch is not as sophisticated or brilliant a dialectician as Lukács, the members of the Frankfurt school, or even Gramsci.[39] In fact, Korsch is much more interested in the political consequences of theoretical activity than in the strictly philosophical components of his theory. Korsch is indeed much more of a political theorist with a strong activist bent than a philosopher. He is above all interested in developing a revolutionary theory and in defining the relationship of revolutionary theory to political practice and the historical reality in which both are rooted. For Korsch the task of revolutionary theory is to grasp conceptually the historical situation and to construct a political theory from this situation which will then provide an instrument of revolutionary change. A genuinely revolutionary theory is rooted in a revolutionary movement whose struggles, needs, and goals produce the theory, which in turn demonstrates its truth or efficacy in practice. A revolutionary theory is therefore to be judged according to its ability to mediate practice, to serve as an instrument of radical change, to serve the interests of the liberation of the working class. At the time Korsch believed that Marxism was the authentic expression of proletarian struggle from the time of the 1848 revolutions up to the present day, and that Leninism was the currently actual form of Marxism that expressed contemporary revolutionary struggles. Interestingly, this historicist position which sees theory as the consciousness of historical reality—this demand for an identity between theory and reality, and theory and practice—would provide the basis for his later critique of Leninism and Marxism itself.

Korsch was attempting to grasp and develop the revolutionary core of the Marxist teaching and to defend Marxism against revisionist distortions. One series of articles, including "The Marxist Dialectic" and "On Materialist Dialectic," translated in this anthology, contain crystal-clear distillations of the Marxist theory and show Korsch's ability to grasp the essence of the subject matter at issue—a characteristic that was to distinguish Korsch's theoretical practice. Another series of articles attempts to demolish leading bourgeois falsifications of Marxism and to critique competing communist interpretations.[40] These articles reveal a sharp critical acumen, as well as a sarcastic polemical bent.

In addition to his work in Marxist theory, Korsch was also busy lecturing on law in the University of Jena and was attempting to develop a Marxist legal theory, grounded in a theory of workers' rights and the legal structure of factory committees.[41] The main fruit of these labors was *Arbeitsrecht für Betriebsräte* published in 1922.[42] Korsch saw the workers' struggle for labor laws and legal rights and protection as an integral part of the process of radical social change that had been neglected by previous Marxist theoreticians. He wished to institutionalize the workers' councils as organs of participatory democracy which could be used as instruments of workers' power in the transition to socialism. The activistic component of his thought comes out in his concept of "legal action" (*juristische Aktion*)—an example of the sort of "intellectual action" (*geistige Aktion*) which in *Marxism and Philosophy* he defended as an integral part of revolutionary practice.[43] Korsch was developing a dialectical theory of revolution in which ideological struggle required socialist theories of ideology, law, and philosophy, as well as

political and economic theories. The problem was that "In an epoch
where in all realms of social life two classes confront each other antago-
nistically . . . in the sphere of law neither the old purely bourgeois standpoint of private law can be legitimately maintained unchanged (i.e., that
which conceives the labor relation as a private affair of those concerned
which rests on a free contract), nor can the new purely proletarian standpoint of social law (that sees the labor relation as a purely communal
relation that grounds social working-together)."[44] To resolve this problem, Korsch wanted to develop a clear distinction between bourgeois and
socialist legal theories, and to begin introducing socialist conceptions in
the present society as part of the revolutionary process. Korsch warns,
however, that "legal action" should not be seen as a substitute for class
struggle, but rather as a complement to economic action such as strikes
and political action.[45] Events were in fact to soon give him a chance to
participate in a series of political actions that would plunge him into the
center of the Communist movement.

Korsch and the Comintern

At the time when Korsch was working on the problems of Marxism and
philosophy he was also heavily involved in Communist politics. He lived
in the house where the local Thuringen Communist newspaper, the *Neue
Zeitung*, was published and frequently participated in party meetings.
He continuously reflected on the political-economic developments in Germany and wrote many articles on the subject. In 1923–24 Korsch analyzed the stabilization of monopoly capitalism in Germany through the
policies of Hugo Stinnes. Stinnes and his robber baron colleagues were
attempting to consolidate their economic power through concentration
and monopolization of key German industries, and were using the state
to protect and further their interests.[46] Korsch supported the Communist
position that in view of the capitalist offensive against the workers, a
united front policy was needed that would aim at "seizing material
goods" and "constituting a workers' government."[47] He attended the
Eighth Party Congress of the KPD in Leipzig in January 1923 and sided
with Brandler and the "right-center" majority who sought a united front
with the Social Democrats to fight the growing counterrevolution. At
this conference Korsch criticized as "undialectical" the left position of
Fisher and Maslow who rejected the united front policy and urged putting mass-supported armed struggle, and the slogan of the "dictatorship
of the proletariat," on the top of the agenda.[48] Again, we see the fallacy

of simply labelling Korsch a left-oppositionalist and see the need for a careful study of a complex period. We shall see that up until the middle of 1925 Korsch—far from being a left-oppositionalist—followed the mainstream policy and tactics of the KPD and Comintern which he both accepted and defended.

In 1923 the German economic situation grew progressively worse as inflation raged and food strikes broke out all over the land. The Weimar government appeared incapable of dealing with the massive economic crisis and growing political unrest. To add to the explosiveness of the situation both the right and left were arming their supporters to prepare for combat. Korsch was in charge of drilling local members of the KPD to form a proletarian army (*Hundertschaften*). It appeared that any day new revolutionary uprisings would emerge and after much debate the Russian leaders of the Comintern ordered the KPD to prepare for civil war.[49] The opportunity for armed confrontation with the ruling powers soon arrived. On October 10, 1923, the SPD and KPD formed a coalition government in Saxony and three days later they united in Thuringen to form a workers' government. Korsch was named justice minister in Thuringen and began an active political career that was to place him at the center of German politics for the next several years. The new coalition government demanded arms for the workers to protect the government from the danger of invasion by fascist troops from Bavaria. They put out a program calling for, among other things, the nationalization of heavy industry, the regulation of foreign commerce, setting up control commissions and new laws to protect workers, control of the police, and exclusion of reactionaries from public posts. The bourgeoisie panicked.[50]

Although the workers' governments in Saxony and Thuringen were legal constitutional governments formed according to Weimar parliamentary law, the Weimar Reichs government, with the complicity of the SPD, sent the Reichs army into central Germany and threatened to dissolve the Saxony government on the pretext that they refused to abolish their red armies.[51] Korsch called the workers to assemble for armed struggle to protect their government as they had done against the Kapp putsch.[52] He and others called for a general strike and barricades against the advancing government troops. The SPD leaders refused to take this course of action, however, and Brandler and other right-center leaders of the KPD hesitated to recommend any decisive action. As a result, when the Reichswehr arrived, the workers' governments in Saxony and Thuringen collapsed and Reichs troops occupied the region. Korsch was forced to go underground and could only safely emerge when an amnesty was granted. The period of active revolutionary struggle in Germany was now over and the counterrevolutionary forces were to increase their hegemony and prepare the way for the triumph of fascism.

The debacle of workers' government marked the end of a working-class offensive and began a period of capitalist stabilization. Korsch, as always, drew theoretical-political conclusions from these events. He and the majority of militants in the KPD decided that coalitions with the hopelessly reformist Social Democrats were impossible and decided that a Leninist-type party and tactics were needed to create an efficacious revolutionary movement in Germany. Korsch began a period of thoroughly dogmatic Leninism in which he tried to apply the Leninist theory and practice in every way possible to the situation in Germany. Korsch now sided with the new "left" leadership of Maslow and Fisher, who at the Frankfurt Party Day in April, 1924, urged developing a Leninist line for struggle for state power and urged as the goal the dictatorship of the proletariat under KPD leadership.[53] Ironically, Korsch and his left colleagues' enthusiastic embrace of Leninism and the Bolshevizing of the KPD was to result in the domination of the German movement by the Soviet Union and in the purging of the very left forces who spearheaded the Bolshevization process.

The need for a Leninist party and tactics was believed to be justified by the defeat of the coalition governments and the rise of a new fascist threat. Korsch had concluded in February, 1924, that "fascism" had triumphed over the November Revolution. He describes "fascism" as "the consciously planned counterrevolution of the bourgeoisie that in some lands today is carried along predominantly by lower middle-class groups, while in other lands, like ours, it is led by the upper bourgeoisie themselves and their paid agents . . . this counterrevolution in all its forms we call by the new word fascism, and what we have experienced in the last months was the progressive and consequent attempt to shift this counterrevolution into the saddle . . . and to stabilize it."[54] Korsch subscribed to the "social fascism" thesis that saw the Social Democrats as "nothing but a fraction of German fascism with socialist phraseology" and labeled the whole Social Democratic movement as a species of fascism.[55]

Korsch's acceptance of the "social fascist" thesis, which was to have such disastrous results, was motivated by extreme bitterness over Social Democratic opportunism since November, 1918, and the refusal of the Social Democrats to support any militant revolutionary action. Indeed, in the view of Korsch and others, Social Democratic opportunism and treachery were responsible, at least in part, for a whole string of working-class defeats, from the collapse of the workers' councils movement up to the recent refusal to support any militant action in the October, 1923, crisis which had resulted in the crushing of the workers' movement in central Germany and the outlawing of the Communist party (after a few months it was again declared legal).[56] In this heated atmosphere it was understandable that Korsch and others would label the Social Democrats as "social fascists." Korsch concluded: "The fateful failure of our politics in the year 1923 consisted entirely in the fact that although we theoretically recognize the identically 'fascistic' nature of Social Democracy and all other bourgeois 'democrats' with Hitler's fascism in virtue of its class content, we failed to draw from this knowledge correct consequences in our practical action with adequate decisiveness."[57] Korsch's agreement with the Comintern fascist theory and concept of social fascism is another sign of his orthodoxy and adherence to the dominant Communist policies and theories at the time.

Korsch saw the Dawes plan in 1924—which would regulate German reparation payments from World War I and would loan foreign capital (mostly American) to German industry—as a tactic to stabilize capitalism and the counterrevolution in Germany. He believed this plan signified increased suffering and exploitation for the German proletariat, who would have to submit to intensified rationalization of labor (speed-ups, technological unemployment, increased domination, etc.) and longer working hours.[58] He agreed with the KPD notion of a "revolutionary total perspective" that portrayed the present as a brief period of calm between "two waves of revolution."[59] The task at hand was thus to prepare for new working-class offensives.

Korsch was rewarded for his defense of Leninism and the Bolshevization of the Communist International with the editorship of the *Internationale*—the major German communist theoretical journal—and a position on the KPD central committee. Hermann Weber writes that in the months after the Frankfurt Party Day (April 7–10, 1924), Korsch was one of the leaders of the KPD and was in charge of ideological affairs: "The actual leaders of the KPD were: for politics Ruth Fisher and (from prison) Maslow, for organization Scholem directed, for foreign politics Rosenberg was responsible, and for the ideological line Korsch, the chief editor of the *Internationale* and Sommer, in charge of Agriprop, was responsible."[60] The period of 1924–27 was a fateful one for the communist movement in which the destinies of the German and Russian Communist parties were ever more closely linked. After the death of Lenin a brutal power struggle was going on in the Soviet Union, while in Germany the old antagonisms between the Communists and Social Democrats, and the left and the right, were intensifying and creating a confusing, complex situation.

Under these difficult conditions, Korsch and others had high hopes that the Communist International would be able to unite the demoralized revolutionary forces. In June and July of 1924, Korsch was a delegate to the Fifth World Congress of the Communist International in Moscow, which posed for itself the task of developing Leninism as a unitary ideological foundation for all parties in the International. Korsch shared the Comintern's aim of carrying out social revolution in Europe "in the spirit of Lenin." His contribution to the Congress, "Lenin and the Comintern," portrays Leninism as the "restored and fulfilled method of revolutionary Marxist science that is essentially the theoretical consciousness of the revolutionary action of the Proletariat class."[61] Korsch attacks the right-center ideologue Thalheimer (who was in charge of ideology under the previous Brandler KPD leadership and whom Korsch thus replaced as chief KPD ideologue) for reducing Marxism to a "purely historical empirical science and practice"—implicitly arguing against Thalheimer that Leninism can also be applied to Germany, that it is not bound to the specific conditions of the Soviet Union (as many German Marxists were arguing), but expresses real historical tendencies of proletarian revolution that also exist in Germany.[62] Korsch also defends the Leninist theory of the party and attacks Rosa Luxemburg for "onesidedness" in ascribing a painful excess of subjectivism to Leninism.[63] Korsch's Leninist orthodoxy here is thoroughgoing.

But the Korsch legend paints another picture. E. H. Carr in his influential history of the Russian revolution falsely claims that Korsch's article, "Lenin and the Comintern," "under the guise of an orthodox attack from the Left on Brandler and the Right, by implication denounced the whole united front policy and the current comintern line as a surrender of the Marxist dialectic of revolution to pragmatism and expediency."[64] According to Carr, the article is part of "the extension of the ultra-left campaign in the KPD against the policies of the Comintern and especially against the tactic of the United Front."[65] Carr's claims are bizarre, for there is no denunciation of the Comintern at all in the article, and in fact, as Carr's own account indicates,[66] the KPD and the Comintern itself sharply turned to the left at the Fifth World Congress and denounced the previous United Front policy—a position Korsch shared. Nor is there any evidence at all to categorize Korsch as part of the ultra-left at the time, as Carr and others are prone to do.[67] On the contrary, a careful reading of "Lenin and the Comintern" should show that far from denouncing the current Comintern line, Korsch is pledging his allegiance to Leninism and the Comintern.

In fact, after the World Congress, Korsch identified the Communist

International and the interests of the world's working classes, with the "proletarian state of Soviet Russia," just as he identified Leninism with the world proletarian struggles (i.e., as their theoretical consciousness) : "All measures and actions of Soviet Russia will be dictated by interests of the Communist movement for the liberation of the world proletariat. There is in Russia no dualism between state and proletarian class interests."[68] Moreover, throughout 1924, Korsch continually defended Leninist orthodoxy and attacked the ideological currents which were the main threat to the dominant line. He called for "erecting a protective wall against the revising flood of Communist revisionism," and attacked the "right" revisionism of Thalheimer, as well as the "left" deviations of Trotsky and Luxemburg.[69] In an essay, "Leninism and Trotskyism," Korsch wrote, "along with Luxemburgism, we must exterminate any Trotskyism in us."[70] Thus it is not correct, as Breines claims, that at the time of the Fifth World Congress Korsch "openly sought to articulate and give coherence to the idea of an oppositional theoretical current within the communist movement," and that "Korsch openly defined himself as the propagator of this dissident theoretical current."[71] For there is no evidence that Korsch attempted in his writings, speeches, or political activity to contrast an "oppositional" or "dissident theoretical current" to Leninism, nor had he yet declared himself in opposition to the policies of the Comintern or the KPD leadership.[72] From 1920 to 1925, Korsch consistently defended the Soviet Union as the "bulwark of the revolution," and defended the NEP, the doctrine of socialism in one country, and the identification of the destiny of the Soviet Union with the world revolution.[73] How, then, did the legend arise that already Korsch was in 1923–24 a left-oppositionalist who represented a heretical current at the Fifth World Congress of the Comintern?

First, it is clear in retrospect that *Marxism and Philosophy* and Korsch's theoretical writings present a dialectical version of Marxism that was to conflict in various ways with the developing Soviet orthodoxy, especially in areas of methodology, epistemology, and metaphysics, where the Korsch-Lukács positions contained a critique of the crude Soviet attempts to create an objectivistic "scientific socialism," metaphysical materialism, copy theory of knowledge, and correspondence theory of truth. It is on these grounds that Zinoviev carries out his infamous "critique" of Korsch at the Fifth Congress, which no doubt contributed much to the myth of Korsch as ultra-leftist and creator of an oppositionalist current.[74]

Zinoviev, who headed the Comintern, was allied with Stalin against Trotsky (although he would later change sides). He gave an address at the Congress on "The Struggle against the Ultralefts and Theoretical

Revisionism."[75] This speech represents an attempt by the Bolsheviks to exert ideological hegemony over the world communist movement through a critique of "revisionism" and "deviationism." Zinoviev's "critique" consists mainly of anti-intellectual denunciations of the "professors" (Korsch, Lukács, and others) and the application of derogatory labels like "idealist deviation" to Korsch and Lukács (there was supposed to be some kind of profound connection between "idealist deviations" and "ultra-leftism": Hegel would have smiled). What was happening under the cloak of a "philosophical dispute" was the beginning of the Bolsheviks' heavy-handed attempt to bully all sections of the International into submission to all Bolshevik theories and policies. Korsch and Lukács were two of the first major targets of this strategy which, in a certain sense, both were to submit to out of considerations of party discipline.

As the Congress went on, Zinoviev stepped up his bullying tactics. He offered Korsch, as editor of the *Internationale*, the "friendly advice" "to study Marxism and Leninism," and even went so far as to suggest that the KPD put its journal "in the hands of Marxists," rather than "those who still need to study Marxism."[76] The Bolsheviks were angered that Korsch had allowed an article by Boris (Roninger) to be published which dared to criticize Bukharin and the theory of the labor aristocracy. Bukharin himself took the issue up with Korsch who mildly replied that he had only brought the issue up for discussion. Bukharin curtly replied, "Comrades, we cannot put every piece of garbage up for discussion."[77]

Out of Korsch's confrontation with Bukharin and Zinoviev, no doubt, emerged the left-oppositionalist myth. The myth was fueled by (unsubstantiated) rumors that Korsch cried out from the floor "Soviet imperialism" during a speech at the Congress.[78] Fred Halliday contributes a story that "the Comintern Congress revealed Korsch's growing break with the Fisher-Maslow group. They later allied themselves with the Russian leadership while Korsch formed an opposition bloc with the Italian left faction led by Bordiga."[79] This is nonsense, for not only was Korsch supporting the Fisher-Maslow leadership at the time, he was part of the leadership. Although Korsch met Bordiga at the Congress there is no evidence that they thought of forming an international opposition bloc, nor did they actually do so later.[80] The facts are that Korsch actually sided with the Soviets and the KPD leadership on all major political issues at the time, and suppressed his theoretical differences with the newly emerging Bolshevik orthodoxy.

One might wonder from what theoretical position Korsch could support Leninism and the Bolshevization of the Communist International. Surely in 1924 he could perceive the detrimental features of the domination of the German Communist movement by the Soviet Union that he was later to attack. Hedda Korsch writes:

> He was growing increasingly concerned about developments in Russia and especially so after the death of Lenin. He had always had doubts, of course. But in Thuringia the KPD was strong and large, and the local comrades were very good people, willing to sacrifice personal comfort, money, time, jobs, for the class struggle. There were lots of meetings and commissions and all that. Then directives began to come more and more from Moscow, saying what was to be discussed at meetings and what resolutions were to be put to them. Whereas during the early 1920's, the rank-and-file felt that they themselves forged their actions, the international leadership now began to interfere and direct everything. But Karl still thought that the KPD was the only party that still tried to *fight* in any way. There was no question of the Social Democrats doing that. So he stayed in the party.[81]

If the negative effects of Bolshevization were so manifest, why did Korsch so assiduously toe the party line throughout 1924 and much of 1925?

The answer lies in the form of revolutionary historicism that underlies Korsch's theoretical position. We have seen that revolutionary theory for Korsch is an expression of revolutionary struggle. Leninism, Korsch believed, was the expression of revolutionary struggle in the age of imperialism and was embodied in the most revolutionary tendencies in the Soviet Union, Germany and elsewhere in the world. Since Leninism was the expression of the actuality of the revolution it was a real existent material force: revolutionary reality. Korsch's version of revolutionary historicism drove him to identify with and support those tendencies which represented real forces of revolution. It should be noted that this is far from being a left-oppositionalist position which puts theory above history and reality, and criticizes a situation because it fails to meet the demands of theory. Rather, theory is judged through its power in advancing the interests of the working class, in overcoming capitalism, and its ability to translate itself into socialist reality. Leninism, Korsch believed, had provided the correct theory and strategy that made possible the Russian Revolution and had become reality in the Soviet Union. This historicist position led Korsch to affirm Leninism as revolutionary theory and the Soviet Union—the embodiment of Leninism—as revolutionary reality. Moreover, Korsch's theory of Marxism as the expression of the historical forces of revolution should indicate that Korsch's Leninist period was no mere accident or tactical maneuver to advance himself in the party, but was a logical consequence of his theory of history, of Marxism, and of revolution in an era in which the current forces of revolution identified themselves as Leninist. The limits of both this theory and Leninism itself were soon forced upon Korsch by the ruthless Stalinization of the Soviet and German Communist movements.

Korsch in the Left Opposition

Both the German and Soviet Communist parties became engaged in bitter, internecine party struggles in 1925. The German party had refused coalitions with the Social Democrats and in the 1925 election ran their own candidate "Teddy" Thälmann.[82] Since no candidate had received the requisite majority there was to be a run-off election. The right chose the reactionary General Hindenberg as their candidate, and the Communists had to decide whether to join in a coalition with the Social Democrats to oppose the "monarchist danger" or to continue their rejection of united fronts and run their own candidate again. The party was bitterly divided on this issue and after acrimonious debates decided, with the Comintern's prodding, to support the Social Democrat candidate. But the Social Democrats had decided to support a center party candidate, and this was too much for the Communists, who decided to run Thälmann again.

In a close vote, Hindenberg won the election and the SPD accused the Communists of having helped Hindenberg gain power by their failure to support the left-center candidate.[83] The "left" leaders Fisher and Maslow supported by the Comintern now urged the KPD to enter a new united front under the slogan of the "monarchist danger."[84] Korsch was elected to the Reichstag in July 1924, and continued as editor of the *Internationale*. At this point, the Soviet Union intensified their Machiavellian machinations to control the KPD through purging independent, non-submissive members. Their tactic was to first support the "left" leadership of Fisher and Maslow, who were pushing the "new Line" (capitalist stabilization, monarchist danger, united front) that was outraging the ultra-left. They were then able to isolate and purge the extreme left, and when the process was underway they abandoned Maslow and Fisher who were included in the left purges![85]

Although Korsch did not join the first wave of left oppositionists who opposed the "new line," the Comintern leaders began attacking Korsch

and demanded his removal from the *Internationale*. Bela Kun, in charge
of the Agitprop division of the Comintern, wrote the KPD Central Committee a letter ordering them to tighten controls over the journal, part-
ticularly in regard to the "Russian question."[86] Korsch offered to resign
but his comrades unanimously urged him to stay on: evidence that Korsch
had not fallen out with the KPD leadership and that the attacks against
him were initiated by the Comintern. Evidently the Stalinists felt they
could deal more easily with table-pounding prolos like Thälmann than
with intelligent, honorable intellectuals like Korsch. Under continued attack from Kun and other Stalinist hatchetmen, Korsch finally resigned
with a parting shot at Kun, who, "from whatever grounds, accuses those
out of favor Party comrades as being pigs who are enemies of the Party
and who treats their works as crap."[87]

After being removed from the *Internationale* and the KPD Central
Committee, Korsch began developing a critique that would eventually
get him expelled from the party and push him into the forefront of the
left-opposition. In a subtle but forceful critique of the united front policy,
he wrote an article, "Karl Marx on Republic and Monarchy," which
argued that for Marx the natural ally of the proletariat is not necessarily
the "republican" strata of the bourgeoisie in the struggle against monarchy.[88] He cited Marx's point that the workers must learn that " 'the
slightest improvement of its situation remains a *utopia within* the bourgeois republic—a utopia that becomes a crime as soon as it wants to realize
itself'."[89] The real choice, Korsch suggested, was not between republic
and monarchy, but between the rule of the bourgeoisie or their overthrow
in creating the dictatorship of the proletariat, understood as a "red councils republic."[90] Hence for Korsch the real choice was between Lenin or
Hindenberg.

In a discussion group in Weimar in June, 1925, Korsch rejected the
thesis—pushed by the Comintern and their KPD allies—that there was
a distinctive difference between the purportedly feudal land-owning class
and industrial capitalist class in Germany, and that the proletariat should
side with the more progressive capitalists to destroy the last remnants of
feudalism. Korsch argued that there was no more feudalism in Germany
and that both capitalist classes carried out their quest for profit on the
basis of capitalist relations of production; thus, he maintained, the real
class struggle in Germany was between the proletariat and bourgeoisie.
Implicit in this analysis was the claim that the united front policy based
on the need to unite with the progressive bourgeoisie to fight the monarchist and feudalist elements was a surrender of the revolutionary per-

spective and was based on a false analysis of the situation in Germany. Buckmiller claims that at this conference Korsch for the first time can be characterized as "ultra-left."[91]

Before discussing the series of purges that was to eliminate Korsch from Communist politics and practically destroy the German Communist movement, let us pause a moment to pose the question of when Korsch first openly joined the left opposition. I have argued against the "Korsch myth" that he was a member of a left opposition from the moment he joined the Communist party in 1920 by examining his essays and speeches and newspaper articles which indicate he was an enthusiastic advocate of the union of the USPD with the KPD in 1920, totally supported the Soviet Union, and became a convinced Leninist who supported the Bolshevization of the KPD. I have attempted to show that there is no evidence that Korsch took a left oppositionalist position at the Fifth World Comintern Congress, nor is there evidence that he was developing an "oppositional theoretical current." None of his writings from 1920–1925 contain any critique of the Soviet Union and all adhere faithfully to Leninism. I have been able to find no evidence that Korsch *openly* opposed the political position or the leadership of the Soviet Union, Comintern, or KPD until September, 1925. Although he no doubt opposed the "new course" of the KPD ratified at the party Congress in July 1925 that urged a united front against the "monarchist danger," he did not join the left opposition at that time (represented by Scholem, Katz, Rosenberg, and others) and thus did not openly oppose the policy.[92] Hence Halliday is wrong to state that "In February 1925 he was dismissed from the editorship of *Die Internationale* and from then onwards was in declared opposition to the Party leadership."[93] And Bathrick's assertion that "Beginning in 1924, first as editor of the KPD's central organ *Die Internationale*, and finally as a member of various splinter groups outside the Party itself, Korsch waged an unending battle against Russian domination of the German Communist movement" is also unfounded.[94] The facts are that it was not until the publication of the so-called open letter of the Executive Committee of the Comintern to the KPD in late August, 1925, that Korsch openly joined the left opposition and waged his "unending battle" against Stalinists.

Hermann Weber describes the publication of the "open letter" as the third decisive turning point in the history of the KPD (after the union with the USPD in 1920 and the dissolution of the "right" Brandler leadership after the defeats in 1923).[95] The letter from the Soviet Union to their German "comrades" contained a detailed critique of the German left-leadership (Fisher, Maslow, etc.) and in effect demanded a new leadership and closer conformity to Russian policies. This letter hit the German movement like a bombshell and drove Korsch and others who had their doubts about openly attacking the Soviet leaders into resolute opposition. The open letter had the effect of shattering the German movement into various factions and thus contributed to the attempt of the Russian Communists to totally dominate the German party.

Korsch aggressively came out as a left oppositionalist for the first time at a party conference in Frankfurt on September 6, 1925, a few days after the publication of the open letter. He energetically attacked the line of the new KPD leadership (the Thälmann-Dengler group) that in the case of a conflict of interests between the Soviet Union and the Communist International, the revolutionary politics of the KPD must be dampened to accord with Soviet interests. Korsch reportedly described this policy as "red imperialism" and was promptly attacked by the Communist newspapers as a traitor "whose views coincide completely with the inflammatory articles of the Social Democratic and imperialist press."[96] Korsch denied that he was "anti-Bolshevik" and argued that his position was misrepresented; he even repeated his belief that the Soviet Union was the "bulwark of the revolution."[97] He continued, however, to be slandered in the vilest terms by the Stalinist hacks. The party newspaper *Die Rote Fahne* characterized him successively as "a victim of Social Democratic propaganda" (September 19, 1925); an enemy of the Soviet Union (September 22); a traitor who was part of an "anti-Bolshevik" bloc (September 23), and so on until Korsch was made a symbol of the enemy of communism and driven out of the party.

Korsch was one of the first victims of the new Stalinist smear and purge tactics that were to eliminate many of the most dedicated Marxists from the Russian and German revolutionary movement. In a remarkable display of power politics Stalin and his allies in the KPD were to eliminate all opposition and to splinter the Communist movement into a comico-tragic battleground of warring factions and sects.[98] In February, 1925, Stalin personally intervened in German affairs for the first time. He gave an interview to a German Communist, Herzog, and attacked Ruth Fisher, who was progressively losing the leadership position she had held since 1923–24. Stalin also sent a letter to her left comrade, Maslow, who was still in prison in Berlin, lecturing Comrade Maslow on party affairs.[99] Fisher and Maslow refused to submit to Stalin's heavy-handed power plays and the inner circle of Soviet leaders pressured the Germans in summer, 1925, to form a new "Leninist central committee" with representatives from all tendencies under the leadership of the "honorable proletarian Thälmann." They urged that proletarian workers and loyal party members be given the top leadership posts and that intellectuals, literati, and bohemians be excluded! At this time the inquisitions and purges that were to so horrendously stain the Communist cause began. Further, the Stalinist bag of dirty tricks was developing. Ruth Fisher was called to Moscow for "consultation" and "invited" to stay for ten months during the period Stalin wanted to install his favorites in the leadership of the KPD. Strange secret diplomacy was taking place between the Stalinist clique and German imperialists that would produce in 1925 the Soviet-German friendship treaty (and ultimately the Stalin-Hitler pact in 1939). Opponents or enemies of Stalin were sent to foreign embassies or to Siberia, and the secret police began to step up their activities; the Gulag archipelago was in business. The Stalinist apparatus of spies, police, and bureaucratic entrenchment was being developed, allowing generations of anti-Communists to gleefully identify communism with totalitarian dictatorship. The "Stalinization" of the German Communist party, parallel to the process in the Soviet Union, constituted a decisive change from a party organization that had been from the beginning relatively democratic, independent of the Soviet Union, open, and full of all tendencies from "left" to "right."[100] Now a "monolithic party of a new sort" was being constructed that became in effect a tool of the Stalinist leadership and the Soviet Union.[101]

Korsch was meanwhile becoming an nonentity in Communist circles. The party newspapers attacked him constantly and refused to print his articles. He was heckled by goon squads when he tried to speak out at Communist rallies, or was not allowed to participate in party discussions. Either by choice or interdiction he did not participate in the November 1, 1925, Party Congress that officially voted the Thälmann leadership in and the Fisher-Maslow out.[102] At about this time Korsch made contact with various left-oppositionalists and attended an ultra-left conference in Hanover in January, 1926. Weber reports: "At this conference there were distinctive differences of opinion; Scholem, Rosenberg, and their followers turned away from the sharp demands that were raised above all by Korsch and Schwartz who not only directed heavy attacks against the Soviet Union and the Comintern, but also called for unconditional work with Katz in order to preserve the unity of the ultra-left. Scholem and Rosenberg believed that such a position would lead to the split of the KPD and were therefore against it. After a sharp exchange of words, Scholem, Rosenberg, and their followers left the conference."[103] Korsch and his remaining friends formed a group called the "decisive left" (*die Entschiedene Linke*).

Korsch did not want to splinter the left opposition. Of the left opposition, he was one of the least sectarian and tried to continuously work for the unity of the left, first inside and then outside of the party. When Katz and two hundred supporters stormed the printing office of the Communist newspaper in Hanover after they refused to publish his views, and was subsequently kicked out of the party—the first ultra-leftist to be purged—Korsch tried to work with Katz and his newly formed Spartacusbund, although at the same time he signed a document with other leftists on the Katz question which affirmed the slogan: "No step against the Party! Unconditional recognition of party discipline. . . . All for the unity of the Party!"[104] Korsch even agreed to work with the Fisher-Maslow group against the wishes of Schwartz and others. To provide an organ for their views, Korsch and his fellow leftists began to publish a journal, *Kommunistische Politik*, in March, 1926, which was largely edited and financed by Korsch.[105] On April 2, 1926, the "decisive left" met to discuss oppositional strategy and the KPD central committee "concentrated their struggle against the Korsch-Schwartz group," directing their main artillery against Korsch.[106]

The left and the Stalinists struggled throughout Germany for control of local party organizations and there were even street battles between the followers of the Thälmann central committee and left-oppositionalists.[107] It is difficult to estimate how large the left opposition was. The Katz/ Spartacusbund oppositionalist Pfemfert estimated that "the KPD opposition represented about half of the Party."[108] Ruth Fisher said she had never received such enthusiastic response from party members than when she openly joined the opposition and started attacking the Stalinists.[109] Stalin numbered the German left opposition at around 12,000 in the summer of 1927 (about 10 percent of the KPD membership).[110] The German party had splintered at the time into about ten factions, and the left opposition was splintering itself into countless warring sects. Nonetheless, there were enough left oppositionalists to pose a serious threat to the hegemony of the Stalinists. Now at the center of the left opposition, Korsch was to develop the most penetrating critique of the "theories" that the Stalinists were using to legitimate their activities, and was to focus on the degeneration of the revolution in the Soviet Union under the Stalinists. The Bolsheviks in turn began to wage an all-out campaign against Professor Korsch, whom Zinoviev now described as a *"wild gewordene Kleinburger"* (a petty bourgeois gone mad).[111]

The platform of the Korsch-Schwartz group published in April, 1926, began by attacking the "relative stabilization of capitalism" thesis which the Stalinists used to justify their "right" united front policy. Korsch's group discerned tendencies toward destabilization and crisis which indicated to them that *"all objective elements for a concrete revolutionary politics"* are on hand.[112] They urged intensified struggle to gain *"revolutionary control of production"* and attacked the "parliamentary cretinism" of the KPD, urging the workers to struggle for the control of production "supported by revolutionary workers' councils."[113] Korsch and his colleagues were returning to the workers' councils concept that they had previously relegated to a secondary position in their commitment to the party and participation in party politics. Actually Korsch had never abandoned the workers' councils concept, which he was to defend as the authentic organ of socialism until the end of his life.

Although the platform designated the winning of the majority of the most advanced sections of the working class as their goal, Korsch's group also hoped to mobilize the millions of unemployed and other oppressed classes.[114] They took a broad internationalist perspective and called for the support and unity of "all exploited groups, the poor farmers in Russia, the oppressed people of India and Africa, all parts of the middle classes in Europe and America."[115] *Kommunistische Politik* devoted several articles to revolution in China and what is today called the Third World; Korsch was to consistently maintain a broad internationalist revolutionary perspective.[116] In August, 1926, Korsch and his friends were to call for a "new Zimmerwald" conference that would unite into an international left opposition movement all opponents of Stalinism under Lenin's motto, "Against the Stream." Korsch, in fact, continuously worked toward the unity of the left opposition and he must have been bitterly disappointed at the continual factionalism and splintering.

In short, the *Kommunistische Politik* group wanted to "restore" authentic Marxist theory and practice, both of which they believed were being perverted by the Soviet and German Stalinists. They argued that the KPD and Comintern were taking Social Democratic positions on the most important questions, and were engaged in the same reformist practice and falling prey to the same dislocation between theory and practice that had vitiated the Social Democrats. Moreover, the lack of "party democracy" and freedom of discussion were further destroying the very fiber of the communist movement. Above all, the submission of the KPD to the hegemony of the Soviet Union was destroying the German party by involving it in the bizarre interparty struggles going on in the Soviet Union. These criticisms were not received with equanimity by the Stalinists.

The Expulsion from the Party

In February, 1926, the Comintern set up a "German Commission" to study the "German question" and called a conference to answer Korsch and the left opposition's critique of the Soviet Union. Bukharin and Stalin spoke. Bukharin made Korsch his target. He claimed Korsch's thesis of a "State necessity" that sacrificed the interests of the world proletariat to the Soviet Union's interests was a "phantom of the brain" and "had nothing in common with communism."[117] He claimed that the alleged turn to the right was "absolutely slanderous and untrue." The ideas of the left opposition were, in left disguise, "a really half Social Democratic, half bourgeois ideology" and must therefore "be exterminated root and branch."[118] Stalin, in his first appearance before the Comintern, said he wanted to register his "complete solidarity" with the "excellent speech" of Comrade Bukharin and warned the comrades against the ideas of the "Speissbürgerlichen Philosophen Korsch" (the petty bourgeois philosopher).[119] Stalin defended the Central Committee of the KPD as a "truly Leninist committee" and said that the fact it was lacking in theoreticians was "no great unhappiness." Intellectuals who stir up trouble should be "thrown to the devil"! All "ultra-left sickness" must be rooted out and the party must be restored to (proletarian) health.[120] This was a typical Stalinist use of anti-intellectualism and invective to bully one's opponents into submission.

Korsch stepped up his attack on the Soviet Union and the process of Stalinization which he perceived was at the root of the degeneration of the Communist movement. He was invited to present his views at a conference in Berlin on April 16–17, 1926. He was literally fighting for his political life, as Thälmann had announced to his face in public that "The patience of the party is exhausted. We shall find ways and means to totally liquidate you."[121] In the remarkable speech, "The Way of the Comintern," which Korsch gave to a hostile audience under tense conditions, he began by saying that he was going to pose "the basic questions of revolution" and to avoid the pseudo-questions that had muddled previous debates. He wished to make clear his "oppositional position" that had been so badly distorted and slandered in the party press. He challenged his audience that they could have a "pogrom or discussion" and if they wanted a discussion they should focus on the issues he was raising.[122]

Korsch argued that the main issue was a decisive turn in the policy of the Comintern that required posing the "Russian question," which the Stalinists had attempted to veil over and suppress. The problem was a degeneration of the revolution in the Soviet Union itself. Every attempt had been made, Korsch claimed, to cover over the "struggle between two tendencies": "a peasant-oriented, opportunist tendency," supported by Stalin and Bukharin, and "a worker-oriented revolutionary counter-tendency," supported by the Leningrad workers' group and Zinoviev. The great danger was that "*within our Soviet brother party, opportunism has already gained the upper hand*".[123] Stalin's thesis of "socialism in one country" and his opportunist politics were condemned as a "falsification of true Leninist theory."[124] To combat this degeneration, Korsch agreed with Bordiga that " 'the European parties are the best guardians against the opportunist danger in Russia.' "[125] In Korsch's view, it was the duty of the KPD to discuss the "Russian question" which the Bolsheviks had ordered them to suppress.

Korsch argued that the roots of Soviet opportunism were a "degeneration of Leninist theory" that could be compared to the revisionism of Bernstein and Kautsky after the war: "One can best characterize the essence of this new phase of development of the Marxist-Leninist theory" of Stalin and Bukharin as " 'Bernsteinism' and 'Kautskyism' after the seizure of power."[126] In a devastating display of the similarity of Stalinism to Social Democratic theory and practice, Korsch read from an article in the leading German Communist newspaper that praised the Austrian Social Democrat Otto Bauer's recent work as "a great 'victory' for our Communist-Leninist standpoint"[127]—as if Bauer had converted to the Communist standpoint. Through a careful dissection of Bauer's article, Korsch showed the incorrigibly Social Democratic reformist nature of Bauer's position and unmasked the theoretical corruption of Communist "theoreticians" who could publish this and praise it as compatible with a genuine Marxist-Leninist point of view.[128] This degeneration of Communist theory expressed itself above all in a suppression of "The question of the *final goal* of Communism and the *revolutionary* way to this goal."[129] Korsch concluded, "All good Communists must in this period take the clear and decisive position: No Kautskyist glossing over of antitheses, but serious struggle aiming at the complete defeat and annihilation of the opportunist and reformist tendency that is currently advancing."[130]

The party leadership responded to this stinging critique with the demand that Korsch give up his seat in the Reichstag. Korsch refused, saying that he must first discuss the matter with his friends.[131] This was taken as a provocation and "open faction-building," and Korsch was thrown out of the meeting. The "resolute left" was holding a meeting the same day with other left oppositional groups and the Communists discussed expelling all the "ultra-lefts" from the party. The opposition-alists were labeled "anti-Bolsheviks" and Korsch's attempt to work to-gether with other leftists in the Comintern, such as the Norwegian, Hansen, and Bordiga, was condemned as particularly damnable. The Stalinists concluded: "It must be demanded that this plague of boils (*Pestbeule*) be cut out."[132]

At the end of April, 1926, the central committee of the KPD under-took a campaign to throw Korsch out of the party and to make him a symbol of the enemy of communism.[133] The party demanded again that Korsch give up his Reichstag seat and Korsch refused, responding, "I am convinced that the present leadership of the KPD is leading the party to the right and is following a line that is increasingly opportunistic and that is an uncommunist and unleninist politics. It is at the same time a suppression through a regime of ideological terror and police methods of all the remains of party democracy that were present up to now, to the degree that the struggle for the resurrection of a Communist politics within the party is almost no longer possible at all."[134] The German party leadership swiftly voted Korsch out in May when he refused to go along with the party in supporting the Soviet-German friendship treaty. The decision was confirmed by the Comintern on June 26, 1926. Korsch was now totally outside the party that he had worked for with such dedi-cation since 1920.

Korsch sharpened his attack against the Soviet Union and the Stalinist leadership. The Soviet Union was no longer a "proletarian dictatorship," but a "dictatorship against the proletariat, a dictatorship of Kulaks." The Comintern was termed a "czarist, bonapartist apparatus" of violence with "prussian-wilhelmish" features. The true anti-bolsheviks are the leaders of the Soviet Union, the Comintern, and the KPD who have betrayed true Leninist-Bolshevist principles and are thus traitors to the proletariat.[135] In a Reichstag speech against the German-Russian treaty, Korsch evoked Rosa Luxemberg's warning against the "most terrible and uncanny specter" imaginable: "a treaty of the Bolsheviks with the Germans," suggesting that the Soviet pact with German imperialism was a total sell-out of the revolutionary perspective and "paved the way for an August, 1914, for the Third International."[136] In a speech in the Reichstag on June 25, 1927, Korsch took up the plight of the persecuted workers' opposition in the Soviet Union and criticized Stalin's "red ter-ror": "With all principled affirmation of revolutionary red terror as the last, most extreme means of struggle of a threatened revolution against an immediate, present, dangerous attack of counterrevolution (which Rosa Luxemburg also approved of); nonetheless, every insightful worker-revolutionary must know how double-edged this terror-weapon is. In general the revolutionary class is always only the object of terror, although in exceptional cases utilizes terror when there remains no other way for the revolution. But the revolutionary worker's class has no reason whatsoever to sing the hymn of terror"[137] (as the Stalinists were doing). After condemning the red terror, Korsch argued that the Stalinist justification of red terror on the grounds that a "United Front from Chamberlin to Trotsky" existed which was threatening the existence of the Soviet Union was total "nonsense" (*Wahnsinn*).[138]

In a detailed and penetrating examination of "Ten Years of Class Struggle in the Soviet Union," Korsch turned his historical materialist method to the Soviet Union. The essay is a model of critical reflection and provides a sharp criticism of the degeneration of the revolution under Stalin. It is important to note that Korsch did not ever undialectically reject the Russian Revolution. Rather, his focus was on the class struggles that he saw going on in the Soviet Union from the beginning and which took, after Lenin's death, the form of a struggle between opportunistic, counterrevolutionary forces (represented by Stalin and his various allies) and genuine, proletarian revolutionary forces (represented at different times by the workers' opposition, Zinoviev, and Trotsky).[139] Like Marx in his analysis of class struggle in France, Korsch did not want to reduce political conflict to "personal power struggles between ambitious cliques of leaders."[140] Rather, he wanted to reveal the "*hidden material interests and social classes and class factions which represented and fought for these interests.*"[141] For Korsch, the "ten years of Soviet Russia" should be seen as "*a period of new and a new kind of class struggle.*"[142] From the beginning, the revolutionary proletarian forces had to struggle against those who wanted a "bourgeois agrarian revolution in Russia." From the beginning, the "dictatorship of the proletariat" had to exercise "state repression" against the previously ruling local bourgeoisie and an external defensive war against the capitalist powers, thus introducing "new forms of class struggle."[143] This process of defending the "Soviet fatherland" gave rise to a new contradiction that would fatefully plague the subsequent development of the Soviet Union and would have dire consequences for the entire international revolutionary movement: the contradiction between "revolutionary state necessity" and "proletarian class necessity."[144] This "objective contradiction" was to force/allow Lenin in the early 1920's to reject the demands of the workers' opposition and Trotsky to use the Red Army to crush workers' revolts. It then served to justify an increasingly centralized dictatorship of the party and diminution of the Soviets when the NEP replaced the previous "war communism." Then Stalin's version of the slogan "socialism in one conntry" was used to justify the suppression and purging of the revolutionary opposition and the construction of a counterrevolutionary state apparatus and party politics on both a national and international scale. Hence Korsch concluded that the revolutionary working class had suffered "an almost unbroken chain of defeats, including the Brest-Litovsk treaty, the 1920/1 suppression of the Leningrad workers opposition, the crushing of the Kronstadt uprising, the purging of the Trotskyists in 1923/4, the purging of the left opposition in 1925/6, and Stalin's recent victory over the Trotsky-Zinoviev left-oppositionalist bloc."[145] This meant that the counterrevolution had triumphed in the Soviet Union and had "sacrificed the proletarian revolution of Red October" through the erection of a "new capitalistic class state."[146] Or, to put it differently, the interests of the large farmers (the kulaks), the remnants of the bourgeoisie, and the Stalinist elements in the party-state apparatus had triumphed over the revolutionary working-class forces.

The triumph of the "bourgeois counterrevolution" in Russia was seen by Korsch as part of a world-wide resurrection of bourgeois power and the capitalist economy after its near collapse in World War I, from which had arisen a series of revolutionary struggles in Russia, Germany, Hungary, and other countries that took a bitter and intense form. Although at times the class struggles seemed to signal the triumph of socialist revolution on a world scale, the high tide of revolution (1917–1920) receded, and starting around 1921 the forces of counterrevolution began their world-wide offensive on the basis of a *changing of the economic situation itself and the power relationships conditioned by it.*"[147] With the restoration of capitalism in Europe and return to power of the bourgeoisie "*there was a wide-ranging transformation in the fundamental conditions under which all the international proletariat, as well as the Russian proletariat, had to fight their struggles in the newly beginning period.*"[148] Hence the defeat of the Russian proletariat was part of a series of defeats suffered by the proletariat on a world-wide scale. Further, the counterrevolution in Russia was part of an international counterrevolution which on the basis of a relatively stabilized capitalism had reinforced bourgeois domination.[149] The task was now to gather from defeat the remaining revolutionary forces "to win new powers for future struggles so as to transform the current defeat into a final victory."[150]

The Rejection of Leninism

Korsch's critique of the Soviet Union—up to this point—was carried out from a Leninist perspective. Stalinism was seen as a degeneration of Leninism, a perversion of Leninist revolutionary practice. As Buckmiller points out, "Korsch continued to deeply identify with the theory and practice of Lenin."[151] Korsch's call for a "new Zimmerwald" that would gather together all genuinely revolutionary forces to fight the degeneration taking place on the left was parallel to Lenin's Zimmerwald position in 1915–16 when he called for a restoration of genuine proletarian internationalism. Korsch, like Lenin, attempted to gather all left-oppositionalist forces. Unfortunately, Korsch's call for work with "all left groups within or outside the KPD, including the KAP," and his solidarity with Zinoviev and the left-opposition in the Soviet Union only served to splinter the left opposition in Germany which maintained more "purist," sectarian positions. In fact one of the left-oppositionalist groups split with Korsch's group because they claimed Korsch wanted to be a new Lenin![152]

Korsch's identification with Leninism at the time was not based on belief in the unshakable "truth" of the Leninist theory but rather arose from solidarity with the Leninist forces: those workers and groups who in the name of Leninism carried out actual revolutionary struggles. He saw a struggle taking place in Europe from about 1921–1928 between Leninist revolutionary forces and counterrevolutionary forces, and supported the revolutionary forces and thus Leninism. His critique of Stalinism as a counterrevolutionary opportunistic tendency was thus carried out from the standpoint of a Leninism rooted in the left-oppositionalist forces to Stalin in the Soviet Union and in the world Communist movement. It was only after the definite defeat of the left-revolutionary forces in the Soviet Union and Europe, who proclaimed themselves the true heirs of Leninism, that Korsch began to put Leninism itself in question. He concluded that Leninism had become an ideology utilized for counterrevolutionary purposes (by the Stalinists) and that therefore the time had come to "cut the umbilical cord to Leninism."

Korsch began the process of detaching himself from Leninism in a remarkable essay, "The Second Party," his most detailed analysis of the crisis in the Soviet Union and its import for the world revolutionary movement.[153] He begins by noting how the Fifteenth Party Day of the Communist party in the Soviet Union (December 2–19, 1927) had revealed an open split between Stalin and the left opposition (Trotsky, Zinoviev, the Sapronow group, etc.).[154] Korsch carefully examines the programs of the various Soviet opposition groups ("the second party") and indicates how their demands that the working class receive better working conditions, higher wages, more education and training, more meaningful work, and so forth might seem merely "reformist."[155] But in Korsch's view: "What appears in its abstract content as inadequate and 'reformist' demands of the oppositional 'workers' program loses immediately its seemingly reformist character as soon as one considers it just a little marxistically; that is, historically, concretely, and in the context of the real struggles of the Russian working class."[156] In the context of the struggle against Stalinism and the degeneration of Socialism in the Soviet Union, the demands of the left opposition are genuinely revolutionary because "the objective content of the demands which they raise must break through in the end the dominating party and state ideology."[157] Here for the first time since the early 1920's, Korsch juxtaposes revolutionary workers' struggles to a non-revolutionary state and party ideology, thus beginning to question the Leninist theory of the party and state. He argues that the opposition has *"the function of representing the real class interest of the Russian proletariat against the Soviet State ruled by the Communist party."*[158] But if this "second party" wants to solve the immense problems it faces, it must "break the umbilical cord through which its leaders—even the clearest and most consequent among them—have been chained up until this day to the 'Leninist' theory of the past."[159] Korsch is now—and not before now—the thoroughgoing oppositionalist of the Korsch legend. Leninism is now rejected as an ideology of the past, a chain and fetter on the working class movement, an umbilical cord that must be snapped to move forward into a new era of revolutionary struggle. Before breaking the cord, Korsch pays last homage to the old master, praising Lenin's "powerful historical achievement" and explaining that "all the Russian proletariat and with them the entire class conscious revolutionary vanguard of the international proletariat had to be Leninist in the past."[160] But the past is the past and Leninism has degenerated into a "Leninist ideology" full of "illusions" and "deceptive images" (*Trugbildern*). Thus, as Korsch put it in his 1930 reflections on Marxism and philosophy, "the Leninist theory is not theoretically capable of answering the *practical needs of the international class struggle in the present period.*"[161]

A bitter irony in the whole situation is that those who call themselves Leninists in the Soviet Union have forgotten, or suppressed, Lenin's two fundamental propositions on the situation in the Soviet Union: "1. the *theoretical proposition* that as a concrete task in Russia only the bourgeois revolution stands for the time being on the day's agenda; and 2. the *tactical principle* that the task of the Russian proletariat and its revolutionary party can only consist of carrying through the bourgeois revolution under these historical circumstances."[162] Korsch argues that both the Stalinists and the oppositionalists who stress the proletarian character of the October revolution are creating a "socialism legend."

Korsch now argued that Leninism was first used to hasten the development of capitalism and industrialization in Russia and to create the myth that the Soviet Union was socialist. Then after Lenin's death, Leninism degenerated further into a "legitimating tool" of the Stalinist leadership that functioned to occlude the real situation in the Soviet Union and to enslave the working class. This being the case, the demand to "restore the pure teaching of Lenin" (against Stalin's and Bukharin's falsification) "is completely useless and in its results is a reactionary effort."[163] For the " 'Leninist' ideology of the still existing 'revolutionary dictatorship of the proletariat' and the always 'stormily' progressing 'construction of socialism in Soviet Russia' has long become a legend, and at the same time has become a consciously utilized means of holding back the workers, not only in their conscious struggles for their independent class goals that have not been satisfied by the bourgeois transformation, but also in their struggle for their most immediate life-interests. For these reasons a break with this 'Leninist' ideology, which has developed at last into a fetter on the proletarian class struggle, is an immediate and pressing necessity."[164] Hence Korsch urges the Soviet opposition—and all other oppositionalists—to carry out "an *immediate and total break* with Leninism which—whatever its character in the past—has today in its content and function become a seemingly classless but in reality *bourgeois and anti-proletarian state ideology*."[165]

Korsch had now broken completely with Leninism. He was and would remain the great left-oppositionalist revered by the anti-Leninists. Korsch's break must have been difficult and painful and was performed in a moment of defeat and not raging glory. At the moment he was urging the left opposition to break with Leninism, the left opposition in the Soviet Union was defeated by Stalin and the German left opposition was hopelessly fragmented. Korsch sardonically recorded this fact with the cynical Stalinist announcement that "such a second party already is present in Russia but only in the prisons . . . in Siberia, in illegality, and in emigration."[166]

Korsch concluded "The Second Party" with the plea that the working class should no longer wage their struggles within the Communist party but should develop a truly communist politics outside the party: "Our task consists in destroying that dead 'communism' that lives on as a depressing and often idiotic specter in today's proletarian workers' movement; sending it to its death and carrying on with double energy today's *contemporary and real struggles of the working class* that are already beginning with perceptible new power."[167] Heroic and fine sounding words, but who was to carry on these new struggles, where were the new powers that were to carry out the struggles outside the communist party? "Here is Rhodes, leap here," Korsch concluded; "There is Marxism and Leninism and there is real *communist politics* under today's given conditions."[168] Tragically, Korsch could not really envisage a "second party" and real Communist politics in Germany outside of the KPD because of the disarray of the left opposition in Germany. The best he could do was to call upon "the Russian class-conscious proletariat and the entire class-conscious vanguard of the proletariat of the entire world to be summoned today anew to the old, powerful Marxist solution: 'PROLETARIAT OF THE WORLD UNITE.' "[169]

Korsch was standing at the end of a historical era looking back at the struggles and hopes of the previous ten years, looking for a new beginning. His tragedy was the tragedy of the European working-class movement whose string of defeats was so demoralizing after their hopeful advances in 1917–1921— a period which had seemed to put socialist revolution on the historical agenda. "The Second Party" was the last dying gasp of the German left opposition before the nightmare of fascism. The spectre of communism that had haunted Europe would be replaced by the reality of fascism. Those of the left opposition who did not die in Stalin's death camps would find refuge in Hitler's concentration camps or would be forced into exile.

Notes

An earlier version of this section appeared as "Korsch's Revolutionary Historicism" in *Telos* 26 (Winter 1975–1976). I wish to thank Paul Piccone for permission to reprint this material.

    1. Buckmiller, *Karl Korsch*, pp. 168ff.

    2. Ibid., pp. 171ff. and p. 376, where he lists Korsch's proposed courses.

    3. For two accounts of the Kapp putsch, see Albert S. Lindemann, *The "Red Years"* (Berkeley: University of California Press, 1974), and Werner T. Angress, *Stillborn Revolution* (Princeton: Princeton University Press, 1963).

    4. See the recent history of the USPD by Hartfried Krause, *USPD, Zur Geschichte der Unabhängigen Sozialdemokratische Partei Deutschlands* (Frankfurt: Suhrkamp, 1975).

5. In March, 1919, the USPD had around 300,000 members and grew to around 750,000 members by September. Krause, *USPD*, Supplement 3.

6. There is a report on Korsch's speech in *Neue Zeitung*, December 12, 1919; cited in Buckmiller, *Karl Korsch*, pp. 169–170.

7. Korsch citing Bebel in *Neue Zeitung*, March 3, 1920. Bebel made the speech at an SPD party congress in 1903.

8. Karl Korsch, "Was kann jeder Mann und jede Frau für die Befreiung des Proletariats tun?" in *Neue Zeitung*, May 1, 1920.

9. Krause, *USPD*, p. 147.

10. For an account of the 1920 USPD convention see Lindemann, *The "Red Years,"* pp. 249–256. The two standard German texts on the activities of the German Communist party are Ossip K. Flechtheim, *Die KPD in der Weimar Republik* (Frankfurt: Europaische Verlag, 1969), and Hermann Weber, *Die Wandlung des deutschen Kommunismus* (Frankfurt: Europaische Verlag, 1969). Fisher, *German Communism* offers a fascinating insider's account of the relation between the German and Soviet Communists, but her book is full of inaccuracies and Fisher very often self-servingly distorts her own role in the events which she so vividly re-creates. Fisher lists the twenty-one conditions on pp. 141–142.

11. See Gerlach's introduction to *Marxismus und Philosophie* (Frankfurt: Europaische Verlag, 1966), p. 18, n. 15. Gerlach first made Korsch's acquaintance in the late 1920's when Korsch was already an oppositionalist and sharp critic of the Communist parties, and no doubt Gerlach is reading Korsch's later position into an earlier period. Gerlach bases his claim on a reference to Korsch's 1941 essay "Revolution for What" in which Korsch analyzes the 1920's events from his later perspective but does not make the claim Gerlach is putting forth.

12. See the editor's comment in Karl Korsch, *Kommentare zur Deutschen 'Revolution'*, p. 45; Halliday, "Introduction," *Marxism and Philosophy*, p. 8; and Paul Breines' introduction to Karl Korsch, *Three Essays on Marxism* (New York: Monthly Review Press, 1972), p. 5. All these sources repeat and paraphrase Gerlach's claim.

13. Hedda Korsch, "Memories," p. 40.

14. Karl Korsch, *Neue Zeitung*, October 5, 1920.

15. Ibid., September 19, 1920.

16. Ibid., October 6, 1920.

17. Ibid.

18. See Buckmiller's discussion in *Karl Korsch*, pp. 180–181.

19. Karl Korsch, *Neue Zeitung*, October 6, 1920.

20. See "Quintessenz des Marxismus," "Kernpunkte der materialistischen Geschichtsauffassung," "15 Theses über wissenschaftlichen Sozialismus," etc. I discuss these essays in the introduction to section one, "Marxism and Socialization."

21. Karl Korsch, "Die Marxsche Dialektik," *Imprekorr*, March 10, 1923,

pp. 330–331; translated in this anthology as "The Marxist Dialectic," by Karl-Heinz Otto, and *Marxism and Philosophy*, pp. 47–48.

22. Karl Marx, cited by Korsch in *Marxism and Philosophy*, pp. 45–46; the quotation is the motto to Korsch's essay, "The Marxist Ideology in Russia," and is cited in many essays.

23. Karl Korsch, "15 Theses on Scientific Socialism," in *Politische Texte*, p. 51.

24. Korsch, *Marxism and Philosophy*, p. 36.

25. Ibid., p. 43.

26. Here I might note that by "historicism" I am not referring to the distorted notion operative in the work of Karl Popper, whose use varies considerably from the use of the concept in the continental tradition in the sense I am using it. See Maurice Mandelbaum's essay on "Historicism" in the *Encyclopaedia of Philosophy* (New York: MacMillan, 1967), 4:22–25, where he discusses various conceptions of historicism which he then defines: "Historicism is the belief that an adequate understanding of the nature of anything and an adequate assessment of its value are to be gained by considering it in terms of the place it occupied and the role it played within a process of development." Korsch, by the way, saw Popper's work as the "newest attack of Positivism against Marxism" which he found "very loathsome." See his letter to J. A. Dawson in this anthology.

27. Korsch, *Marxism and Philosophy*, p. 40.

28. Ibid., p. 41. A remarkably similar interpretation of Hegel is found in Herbert Marcuse's *Reason and Revolution* (Boston: Beacon Press, 1969), pp. 3ff. Marcuse favorably discusses *Marxism and Philosophy* in a 1931 article, "Das Problem der geschichtlichen Wirklichkeit: Wilhelm Dilthey," *Die Gesellschaft* 8 (1931): 350–367.

29. Korsch, *Marxism and Philosophy*, p. 45.

30. See, for example, Merleau-Ponty, *Adventures of the Dialectic* (Evanston: Northwestern University Press, 1973), and Iring Fetscher, "The Relationship of Marxism to Hegel," *Marx and Marxism* (New York: Seabury Press, 1971). Most of the new left in Europe and America has followed this interpretation.

31. Korsch, *Marxism and Philosophy*, p. 29.

32. Ibid., p. 52.

33. Ibid., pp. 67–68.

34. Ibid., p. 77.

35. Ibid., pp. 70–71.

36. See Antonio Carlo, "Lenin on the Party," *Telos* 17 (Fall 1973), for a discussion of the various phases of Lenin's work and the contradictory positions he often took in different political contexts. Korsch is unaware of, or glosses over, these contradictions and ambiguities in Lenin's theory and practice, hence his historicized version of Lenin is paradoxically ahistorical.

37. For a discussion of Lenin's *Materialism and Empirio-criticism* and an

all out attack on the scholasticized orthodoxy of Soviet Marxism grounded in this work, see Paul Piccone, "Towards an Understanding of Lenin's Philosophy," *Radical America* 4, no. 6 (September–October 1970), and "Phenomenological Marxism," *Telos* 9 (Fall 1971).

38. In his 1930 retrospective on *Marxism and Philosophy*, Korsch looks back on Zinoviev's attack on his book in the *"philosophical dispute"* of 1924, and records his amazement that his work was seen as an "idealist deviation" in its "repeated dialectical rejection of 'naive realism,' " and its critique of " 'so called common sense, the worst metaphysician,' and the normal 'positivist science' of the bourgeois society" (*Marxism and Philosophy*, p. 122). Korsch makes it perfectly clear that he did not intend his dialectical conception of the interaction of consciousness and reality as a critique of Leninism or Soviet Marxism, nor did he see himself as developing an oppositional theoretical current: "Because I then believed that this view was *self-evident* to any materialist dialectician or revolutionary Marxist, I assumed rather than spelt out this critique of a *primitive, pre-dialectical and even pre-transcendental conception of the relation between consciousness and being.* But *without realizing it* [emphasis added] I had hit on the very key to the 'philosophical' outlook which was then due to be dispensed from Moscow to the whole of the Western Communist world" (*Marxism and Philosophy*, pp. 122–123).

39. Buckmiller convincingly argues that Korsch lacks an adequate concept of mediation. See *Karl Korsch*, pp. 328ff.

40. Karl Korsch, "Eine Antikritik" and "Allerhand Marxkritiker," published in 1922 in the *Internationale* and reprinted in *Kommentare zur Deutschen 'Revolution.'*

41. The German journal *Kritische Justiz* has published Korsch's previously unpublished 1923 introductory lecture in the law faculty at Jena, "Jus belli ac pacis im Arbeitsrecht," accompanied by an introduction by Jürgen Seifert, discussing Korsch's contribution to the sciences of law; *Kritische Justiz* 2 (April–June 1972). A rather critical, even hostile, evaluation of Korsch's legal theory is found in Michael Wolff, "Karl Korsch und die Widersprüche des Sozialrechts," in Pozolli, *Uber Karl Korsch.* A sharp critique of Wolff and fine discussion of Korsch's legal theory is found in Buckmiller's *Karl Korsch*, pp. 264ff.

42. Karl Korsch, *Arbeitsrecht für Betriebsräte* (Frankfurt: Europaische Verlag, 1968).

43. Korsch, *Marxism and Philosophy*, p. 97.

44. Korsch, *Arbeitsrecht für Betreibsräte*, pp. 149–150.

45. Ibid.

46. Korsch, "Der 18 Brumaire des Hugo Stinnes" and "Die tote USPD und der lebendige Stinnes," in *Politische Texte.*

47. Korsch, *Politische Texte*, pp. 35 and 47.

48. Korsch, "Um die Arbeiterregierung," *Politische Texte.*

49. Fisher, *German Communism*, pp. 252–383, for a detailed account of

the unrest and chaos in Germany, and a description of the Byzantine machinations of the German and Russian communists to exploit the situation.

50. Flechtheim (*Die KPD*, pp. 182ff.) ironically comments that "the experiment of a socialist-communist government was only to shake the world for ten days," and suggests that their major accomplishment was the distribution of free carp to the unemployed.

51. The most detailed account of the complicated political maneuvering behind the scenes by the Weimar government in deciding how to deal with the revolutionary threat is found in Angress, *Stillborn Revolution*, pp. 426ff. See also, Weber, *Die Wandlung*, pp. 48ff. and the SED Autorenkollectiv, *Geschichte der deutschen Arbeiterbewegung* (Berlin: Dietz Verlag, 1967), 7:21ff.

52. Buckmiller, "Marxismus," pp. 55ff.

53. For an account of the rise to power of the left Fisher-Maslow leadership, see Fisher, *German Communism*, pp. 387–455, and Weber, *Die Wandlung*, pp. 53ff.

54. Stenographic report on the meeting of the Third Landstag in Thuringen, vol. 1 (Weimar: Thuringen Landstag, 1924); cited in Buckmiller, *Marxismus*, p. 56.

55. Cited in Buckmiller, *Marxismus*, pp. 56–57. The "social fascist" thesis was launched by Zinoviev who declared, "German Social Democracy is a fascistic Social Democracy." See Zinoviev's speech to the central committee of the Communist International, January, 1924; printed in *Imprekorr*, no. 37 (March 1924), pp. 426ff. Stalin chimed in that "Social Democracy is objectively the moderate version of fascism," and that the fascists and Social Democrats were "twin brothers" who "complemented each other." Stalin, *Werke* (Berlin: Dietz Verlag, 1952)6: 253. For a historical account of the "social fascist" concept, see Siegfried Bahne, "Sozialfaschismus in Deutschland," *International Review of Social History* 10, part 2 (1965): 211ff.

56. For a summary of a number of books which blame the defeat of the workers' councils movement and the November Revolution on Social Democratic opportunism, see Peterson, "Workers' Councils."

57. Karl Korsch, cited in Buckmiller, *Marxismus*, p. 57.

58. Karl Korsch, "Das Wortlaut des Dawes und McKenna Berichts" and "Die Durchfuhrung des Dawes-Gutachtens und den Kampf um den Achtstundestag," in *Kommentare zur Deutschen 'Revolution.'*

59. *Die Rote Fahne*, January 13, 1925.

60. Weber, *Die Wandlung*, pp. 74–75.

61. Karl Korsch, "Lenin und die Comintern," *Internationale* 10/11 (1924); translated in this anthology as "Lenin and the Comintern," by Roy Jameson.

62. Ibid.

63. Ibid.

64. E. H. Carr, *Socialism in One Country, 1924–6* (London: Penguin, 1971), 3(1):110.

65. Ibid.

66. Ibid., pp. 70ff, especially p. 74.

67. Ibid., pp. 78 and 110.

68. Karl Korsch, *Neue Zeitung*, August 11, 1924.

69. Korsch, "Lenin and the Comintern."

70. Karl Korsch, "Leninismus und Trotzkismus," *Neue Zeitung*, February 1925. See also Korsch's "Trotsky als Geschichtsschreiber" in *Neue Zeitung*, December 4–5, 1924. Korsch's changing attitude toward Rosa Luxemburg can be taken as a key to his evolving positions. Whereas in *Marxism and Philosophy* Luxemburg is along with Lenin one of the great restorers of genuine Marxism, she is now a "deviationist" whom he frequently attacks. As soon as he moves into the left opposition he again refers favorably to Luxemburg. Later he was to remark in a letter to Paul Mattick, "One's position towards Rosa always appears to me to still be the best proof-stone for revolutionaries," in *Jahrbuch Arbeiterbewegung* 2 (Frankfurt: Fisher 1974), p. 199.

71. Paul Breines, "Praxis and Its Theorists," *Telos* 11 (Spring 1972): 90.

72. Korsch's orthodoxy is crystal clear in his enthusiastic review of Lukács' celebration of Lenin and his rapturous praise of Stalin's book *Lenin and Leninism*. Both articles are reprinted in Karl Korsch, *Die materialistische Geschichtsauffassung und andere Schriften* (Frankfurt: Europaische Verlag, 1971). Korsch has nothing but kind words for Stalin and the Bolshevization process at this point: "Bolshevization is now practically and theoretically spreading itself below and is for the first time encompassing the inner structure of the Party's body down below to its individual cell. . . . The task is not only to formally appropriate and externally imitate and parrot Leninism but to *learn* it in a *special* sense: to truly understand the *organization, construction, method,* and *content* of the Leninist work and thus to concretely *carry through* Leninism: this task places on all European parties the highest demand not only from a practical-organizational view, but also from a *theoretical* one" (Korsch, *Die materialistische Geschichtsauffassung*, pp. 152–154). Korsch even repeats Stalin's view that "*Marxism is Leninism* as the 'theory of revolution' in the epoch of imperialism," and that we can dispense with studying the texts of Marx and learn Marxism in its "completed form" from Lenin (ibid., pp. 154–155).

73. See Korsch's articles in *Neue Zeitung*, April 2–4 1924; July 7, 1924; August 11, 1924; and December 5, 1924.

74. See Breines' account of Zinoviev's attack on Korsch, in "Praxis and its Theorists," pp. 82–92. Fisher offers some fascinating insights into Zinoviev, *German Communism*, p. 594, passim. For Carr's portrait, see *Socialism in One Country*, 1:152ff.

75. The full text of Zinoviev's speech appears in Georg Lukács, *Schriften zur Ideologie und Politik*, ed. Peter Ludz. (Neuwied and Berlin: Luchterhand, 1967), pp. 719–726.

76. Cited in Weber, *Die Wandlung*, p. 83.

77. Ibid.

78. The source for this story is a former Nazi diplomat, Gustav Hilger, *The Incompatible Allies* (New York: MacMillan, 1953), p. 108. Carr repeats the story, notes that the remark does not appear in the German edition of Hilger's book, and states, "but the fact is well attested." I have yet to discover any evidence for this story and suspect it is part of the Korsch legend.

79. Halliday, "Introduction," *Marxism and Philosophy*, p. 19.

80. Correspondence between Korsch and Bordiga after Korsch was expelled from the KPD indicates that there were insurmountable obstacles to forming an international opposition bloc. See Bordiga's letter to Korsch, and Christian Riechers' commentary in Pozolli, *Uber Karl Korsch*, pp. 243–265.

81. Hedda Korsch, "Memories," p. 42.

82. For portraits of Thälmann, who was to be the leading Communist politician in Germany during the Stalinist era, see Weber, *Die Wandlung*, pp. 186ff; Fisher, *German Communism*, pp. 423ff; and the SED Autorenkollectiv, *Geschichte der deutschen Arbeiterbewegung*, passim.

83. See Weber, *Die Wandlung*, pp. 101ff., and Fisher, *German Communism*, pp. 412ff., for an account of this period.

84. Zinoviev wrote the KPD a letter urging them to "openly recognize the stabilization of capitalism in Germany at the time" and the "monarchist danger"; printed in *Die Rote Fahne*, July 9, 1925.

85. See Fisher, *German Communism*, pp. 432ff. Fisher downplays her role in pushing the united front policy that was to so alienate the left of the party, implying it was Maslow's policy. Weber provides a correction, *Die Wandlung*, pp. 107ff.

86. Kun's letter attacking Korsch and the *Internationale*—a classic piece of Bolshevik stupidity—is reproduced in *Kommentare zur Deutschen 'Revolution,'* pp. 131–136. Kun criticizes issues 6–22 of the *Internationale*, which Korsch had edited. He found discussions of the Dawes Plan and the Fifth World Congress good but found 95 percent of the material blameworthy: "The *Internationale* shows no consequent revolutionary-Marxist (Leninist) line." For example, next to "a good article" of Maslow (that criticizes Trotsky) there is a "bad article that is grist to Trotsky's mill." Kun demands, "What is the opinion of the editorial staff?" "Further examples" of bad articles "are offered by the reviews of Comrade Lukács which *represent true paradigms of dead abstract critique that rests on purely verbal Marxism (Wortmarxismus)*." Kun is referring to Lukács' brilliant article, "The New Edition of Lassalle's Letters," and to "Bernstein's Triumph" (dismissed by Kun as "a purely formalistic critique of Kautsky"). Kun continues, "One cannot at the same time be for Stalin's book 'Lenin and Leninism' and on the other hand for such unmarxist things as Korsch's 'Quintessenz des Marxismus' and Lukács' work. *One must decide.*"

87. Karl Korsch, *Neue Zeitung*, March 21, 1925.

88. Karl Korsch, *Neue Zeitung*, April 27, 1925.

89. Karl Marx, "Class Struggle in France 1848–50," cited in ibid.

90. Karl Korsch, "Republik Hindenberg," *Neue Zeitung*, April 27, 1925.

91. Buckmiller, "Marxismus," p. 66.

92. Weber, *Die Wandlung*, pp. 112ff. Korsch either did not attend the conference or did not intervene.

93. Halliday, "Introduction," *Marxism and Philosophy*, p. 19.

94. David Bathrick, "Introduction to Korsch," *New German Critique* 3 (Fall 1974): 4.

95. See Weber's discussion of this masterpiece of Stalinist byzantinism, *Die Wandlung*, pp. 120–133. Fisher describes the power politics behind the document in the Soviet Union as a struggle between Stalin and Zinoviev, and claims she signed the document to support Zinoviev against Stalin, even though it contained her own political death warrant, *German Communism*, pp. 444ff.

96. *Die Rote Fahne*, no. 218, September 1925; reproduced in Karl Korsch, *Politische Texte*, pp. 70–71.

97. *Die Rote Fahne*, September 27, 1925.

98. See Weber, *Die Wandlung*, pp. 133ff; Fisher, *German Communism*, pp. 432ff; and Sigfried Bahne, "Zwischen 'Luxemburgismus' und 'Stalinismus': Die 'ultralinke' Opposition in der KPD," *Vierteljahresheft für Zeitgeschichte* 9 (1961): 359–383.

99. Fisher reproduces this letter in *German Communism*, p. 435.

100. The German historians Flechtheim and Weber stress this, as does Fisher. Angress in *Stillborn Revolution* sees the fall of party democracy in the KPD as a move from their Luxemburgian orientation to Leninism that took place in the early 1920's.

101. The SED celebrates this new party organization in *Geschichte der deutschen Arbeiterbewegung*, 8:88ff.

102. Weber, *Die Wandlung*, pp. 122ff.

103. Ibid., p. 150.

104. Printed in ibid., pp. 416–417. On the program of Katz's attempt to resurrect the Spartacus League, see Bahne, "Sozialfaschismus," pp. 366ff.

105. See Hedda Korsch, "Memories," p. 43.

106. Weber, *Die Wandlung*, p. 151.

107. Ibid., p. 152.

108. Bahne, "Sozialfaschismus," p. 363.

109. Fisher, *German Communism*, p. 453.

110. Stalin, cited in Bahne, "Sozialfaschismus," p. 363.

111. Cited in ibid., p. 363.

112. Karl Korsch, "Platform of the Left," in *Politische Texte*, p. 105.

113. Ibid., pp. 105ff.

114. Ibid., p. 107.

115. *Kommunistische Politik* 1(2):19.

116. See the article on China, "Die Chinesische Revolution," republished in *Politische Texte*, pp. 160ff. Hedda Korsch writes that "he also went deeply

into the problems of what today would be called the Third World. He studied the development of the various colonial countries because he thought that the liberation of the colonies was perhaps imminent and could change world politics completely" ("Memories," p. 43).

117. Bukharin, *Die Rote Fahne*, April 11, 1926; in Weber, *Die Wandlung*, p. 144.

118. Ibid.

119. Stalin, *Werke*, 8:102.

120. Ibid.

121. Thälmann, *Die Rote Fahne*, April 23, 1926; cited in Korsch, *Politische Texte*, p. 70.

122. Korsch, "The Way of the Comintern," in *Politische Texte*, pp. 73ff.

123. Ibid., pp. 74–75.

124. Ibid., p. 83.

125. Ibid., pp. 83–84.

126. Ibid., p. 86.

127. Ibid., pp. 87–88.

128. Ibid.

129. Ibid., p. 99.

130. Ibid., p. 102.

131. Weber, *Die Wandlung*, p. 151.

132. Ibid.

133. Ibid., pp. 152ff.

134. Korsch, cited in ibid., p. 153.

135. This analysis was developed in *Kommunistische Politik*, 2(2):18–19. Discussed in Bahne, "Sozialfaschismus," p. 375.

136. Korsch, in *Politische Texte*, pp. 119–120.

137. *Kommunistische Politik*, June 30, 1926.

138. Ibid.

139. Korsch, "Ten Years of Class Struggle in the Soviet Union," in *Politische Texte*, pp. 181ff.

140. Ibid., p. 182.

141. Ibid.

142. Ibid., p. 184.

143. Ibid., pp. 184–185.

144. Ibid., pp. 185–186.

145. Ibid., pp. 189–191.

146. Ibid., p. 191.

147. Ibid., p. 193.

148. Ibid.

149. In a series of essays in the 1930's, Korsch develops this theory of counterrevolution. See "Ten Years of Class Struggle in the Soviet Union," this anthology.

150. Korsch, ibid.

151. Buckmiller, "Marxismus," p. 71.
152. Bahne, "Sozialfaschismus," p. 380.
153. Korsch, "The Second Party," in *Politische Texte*, pp. 195ff.
154. Korsch had secret ties with the Sapronow Group who kept him informed of the activities of the left opposition in the Soviet Union. See Hedda Korsch, "Memories," p. 42.
155. Korsch, "The Second Party," pp. 197ff.
156. Ibid., p. 206.
157. Ibid.
158. Ibid., p. 207.
159. Ibid.
160. Ibid., p. 208.
161. Korsch, *Marxism and Philosophy*, p. 130.
162. Korsch, "The Second Party," pp. 209–210.
163. Ibid., p. 207.
164. Ibid., pp. 213–214.
165. Ibid., p. 214.
166. Ibid.
167. Ibid., p. 219.
168. Ibid.
169. Korsch, "Ten Years of Class Struggle in the Soviet Union."

3. The Crisis of Marxism

In 1928 the left opposition was hopelessly fragmented by sectarian splintering and had clearly failed to establish a living alternative to the Communist and Social Democratic parties. Korsch began working with independent leftist trade unions and gave lectures on economics, labor law, and Marxism. Since the parties had failed to materially advance the liberation of the working class, Korsch focused his energies on the activities of revolutionary unions and their struggles.[1] The results of over a decade of class struggle in Europe and the Soviet Union were, he bitterly concluded, an even greater enslavement of the workers—progress in domination.[2] Moreover, the Stalinization process in the Soviet Union and advent of fascism in Europe indicated the possibility of even greater suffering for the workers in the future. The failure of the focal working-class organizations forced Korsch to seek both new revolutionary possibilities, and the reasons for the shipwreck of the working-class advance which had seemed to put socialist revolution on the historical agenda. Korsch's tragedy was that he grasped the reasons for the failure of the working-class movement, anticipated the triumph of fascism and counterrevolution, but could envision no forces, groups, or strategies which could withstand the counterrevolutionary offensive. This state of affairs forced Korsch to put Marxism and his own theoretical position into radical question.

Let us reflect here a moment on the strange political-theoretical odyssey of Karl Korsch. He traversed the full spectrum of German left parties, moving from the SPD and Fabian socialism to the Independent Socialist Party (USPD) after the war, and then to the KPD in 1920. Further, Korsch was one of the first to be expelled from the KPD and the Communist International, and became one of the leading figures of the left opposition in 1926. Korsch—better than any Western Marxist—reflects the waves of revolution and counterrevolution that inundated Europe in the 1920's. Korsch's theorizing was rooted in the tumultuous class struggles of the Weimar republic, and he developed and modified his theory in relation to the ever-changing historical situation. The praxis philosopher Korsch was above all concerned to obtain a unity of theory and practice,[3] that is, to derive his theory from the requirements and possibilities of the historical situation, and then to translate the theory into action, to make theory a material force in revolutionary struggle. I have argued that Korsch's revolutionary historicism posited revolutionary theory as an expression of existing class struggles, and conceived of both ideology and revolutionary theory as realities that played an important part in social life and historical change. In this context one could see Korsch's own theoretical practice as embodying this dialectic that derives theory from the existing social reality and in turn aims at a unity of theory and practice.

Korsch's expulsion from the Communist party and the subsequent splintering of the left opposition into powerless small groups rendered problematical the unity of Korsch's theory with existing practice and put into question Korsch's theoretical position. Korsch seemed to think that authentic revolutionary theory had to be a reality, that is, embodied in an existing political movement. Mere theory that floats above the historical situation criticizing everything and changing nothing, projecting bountiful possibilities and realizing none of them, was for Korsch self-defeating negativism and idealist speculation. Korsch's hard-headed sense of the real and his fanatic attempt to ground his theory in existing practice is admirable and corrects some of the excesses of a hyper-critical negative dialectics whose negations posit no alternatives, as well as a utopian socialism whose alternatives hover above and outside of reality and the possible. But it seems clear that Korsch the political theorist of practice goes too far in rejecting the autonomy of theory and minimizing the anticipatory components of theory. For Korsch's theory fails to transcend the political vicissitudes of the moment and fails to create an autonomous theory rooted in a global conception of history, society, and human liberation. Moreover, the anticipatory/normative components of theory are sacrificed when theory is merely derived from existing practice. The early Korsch in fact brilliantly formulated the future-oriented quality of revolutionary Marxism in a passage we have already cited.[4] Korsch the Communist political activist, on the other hand, seemed to have neglected these anticipatory qualities that posited a better future based on a theory of liberation and socialism that could guide political practice, and from which standpoint one could judge whether one's practice was emancipatory and hence authentically revolutionary.

Further, the defeat of the revolutionary Communist forces meant for Korsch the shipwreck of his revolutionary historicism which identified Leninist theory with revolutionary reality. Reflections on Korsch's abortive Leninism should reveal the limits of his revolutionary historicism that grounds revolutionary theory in what one takes to be the actual revolutionary struggles. During periods of intense revolutionary struggle it appears that a theory such as Leninism, which is a historical actor and material force in the actual revolutionary struggles, represents the reality of revolution. In this context, it appears that the theory *is* an expression of the actual historical movement: the theoretical consciousness of the struggles themselves. But although there appears to be a unity/identity between revolutionary theory and practice in times of revolutionary struggle, what happens to the theory when a period of revolutionary upsurge grinds to a halt, or is defeated by a counterrevolutionary thrust? Moreover, if theory is merely the expression of revolutionary struggle, from what standpoint could one criticize Stalinism or fascism in a counterrevolutionary era when the forces of revolution are temporarily defeated and dormant? Further, Korsch's too hasty identification of Leninism and the Soviet Union with revolutionary reality—as the embodiment of revolutionary Marxism—raises the question: from what standpoint can one identify a struggle, a class, a situation, as revolutionary? Surely one's theory of revolution helps determine what really is revolutionary and what sort of practice one should thus defend or attack, participate in or struggle against. Korsch questioned the assumptions that Marxism or Leninism were intrinsically revolutionary and that whatever events coincide with the pattern of Marxian theory are in fact *the* revolution. Such an identification of Marxism-Leninism with revolution per se would imply that anything that does not fit in with the revolutionary scenario is not revolutionary. Korsch began to discern that the identification of Marxism-Leninism with revolutionary reality was a species of mysticism that found its temple (and delegitimation) in Stalin's trials and death camps.

Korsch's revolutionary historicism was bumping up against its own limits and forced him to put both Marxism and his own theory in question. The result of his reflections from the late 1920's through the 1940's led to, I believe, a modification of both his interpretation of Marxism and his own position vis-à-vis Marxism. The triumph of the counterrevolution in the Soviet Union and ascendency of fascism on a world-wide scale created a crisis of Marxism which Korsch was to analyze in detail.

Critique of Orthodox Marxism

Korsch began a new period of inquiry into the crisis of Marxism carried out in various discussion groups and lecture series in Berlin in the late 1920's. He published a critique of Social Democratic theory and practice as expressed in the recent work of Karl Kautsky in 1929.[5] Korsch showed how the purported differences between Bernstein's "revisionism" and

Kautsky's "orthodoxy" were nugatory.[6] Although Kautsky claimed his theory is "pure science," Korsch interpreted it as the "ideological expression of a determinate historical movement." More precisely, Kautskyism is the "ideology of German Social Democracy which in its latest phase presents the transition from a concealed to an open revisionism."[7] Korsch carries through a brilliant demonstration of Kautsky's falsification of Marx that at once suppressed the revolutionary content of Marxism and "cryptically veiled" Kautsky's own "hidden revisionist content."[8] Korsch shows how Kautsky's theory of history borrows much from the Marxian concept but at crucial points departs from and distorts the Marxian theory. Through an analysis of Kautsky's notions of "Dialectic and Development," "Nature and Society," "the State," "Class and Class Struggle," and the "Historical Significance of Kautskyism," Korsch argues that Kautsky completely suppresses the revolutionary components of Marxism by reifying Marx's historical materialism into an objectivistic set of categories and laws that passively reflects historical development, excluding activist, praxis-oriented, revolutionary features of Marxism. He shows further how Kautsky continually falls behind the level of Marxian theory to earlier bourgeois theories and ideas. Korsch concludes that Kautskyism has become a fetter on today's working class which limits its struggles to "the ideals and goals of the once revolutionary bourgeoisie" that sacrifices the revolutionary content of Marxism.[9]

In a 1930 addition to a new edition of *Marxism and Philosophy*, Korsch includes Lenin and Soviet Marxism in the current Marxist "orthodoxy" which in his view falsifies revolutionary Marxism. He marvels that Social Democratic and Communist critics both denounced *Marxism and Philosophy* on identical grounds.[10] Both maintained a dogmatic, scientistic-positivist conception of Marxism that suppressed its dialectical, historically specific, and critical components. Both maintained a *"materialist outlook that is colored by the natural sciences,"*[11] which in effect reflects the dominant bourgeois attitude of scientific positivism. Thus in Korsch's view, Lenin and his followers never abandoned the "spiritual legacy" of the Marxism of the Second International, "in spite of some things they said in the heat of battle."[12] The problem, Korsch believed, was that the Marxist orthodoxies really never adopted the whole of the Marxian theory. Rather, all they adopted were "some isolated economic, political and social theories, extracted from the general content of revolutionary Marxism."[13] This altered the meaning of Marxism and truncated and falsified its content.

The conclusions of Korsch's researches into the failure of Marxism to provide a satisfactory theory and practice of revolution are a major theme of his later work. "The Passing of Marxian Orthodoxy" provides a swan song to the hopes of an earlier epoch of revolutionary struggle. Korsch suggests that Bernstein's revisionism-reformism alone expressed the reality of the working-class movement which *was* engaged in reformist practice. In Korsch's view, the revolutionary rhetoric of the "orthodox" Marxists was a mere "ideological dissemblance" which had nothing to do with the practice and reality of the working class movement. Moreover, even the "left" Marxists Lenin and Luxemburg failed to penetrate to the core of the problem and focused on Bernstein's theory, whose power to seduce and mislead the workers they saw as the problem. Luxemburg, Korsch suggests, was guilty of an "ideological bedazzlement" in claiming that "Bernstein's theory was the first and at the same time the last attempt to give a theoretical base to opportunism" within a supposedly still revolutionary Social Democratic movement.[14] As it turns out, she was historically refuted in arguing against Bernstein (who claimed that the movement was everything and the final goal nothing) that the "final goal was everything," for it "revealed itself in subsequent actual history as in fact that *nothing* which Bernstein, the sober observer of reality, had already termed it."[15] Hence Luxemburg failed to see that the problem was not Bernstein's theory, but reformist practice which Bernstein merely —honestly and accurately—expressed.

Lenin too, Korsch argued, although "subjectively a deadly enemy of the 'renegade' Bernstein," tacitly and silently conceded Bernstein's main point about the reformism of the working-class movement by rooting the "revolutionary character" of the labor movement not in actual class struggles or the movement itself, but rather "only in the *leadership of this struggle by way of the revolutionary PARTY guided by a correct Marxist theory.*"[16] Korsch intensifies his critique of Lenin in "The History of the Marxist Ideology in Russia," where he suggests that Lenin transformed Marxism into "an ideological form assumed by the material struggle for putting across the capitalist development in a pre-capitalist country."[17] Ironically, Korsch is suggesting that Marxism played the same role in Russia as bourgeois ideology in Europe by serving to accelerate capitalist development. Whereas the populist Narodnik ideology stressed that capitalism was impossible in Russia, Lenin from the beginning represented the Marxist viewpoint that Russia must proceed through the stages of industrialization and capitalism to be able to ultimately construct a socialist society. Korsch shows how Marx, Engels, and Lenin all were willing to adopt their theory to the conditions in Russia and how from the beginning Marxism served as "an ideological cloak for a development which in its actual tendency is capitalistic." Hence, in

Korsch's view, Marxism in Russia was but a "revolutionary myth" which ideologically proclaimed that what was in fact capitalist development was revolutionary socialist development. Both Stalin and Trotsky—and official Soviet Marxists—followed the "new Marxist myth of the inherently socialist character of the Soviet State and of the thereby basically guaranteed possibility of a complete realization of socialist society in an isolated Soviet Russia."[18] Korsch sadly concludes, "This degeneration of the Marxian doctrine to a mere ideological justification of what in its actual tendency is a capitalist State and thus, inevitably, a State based on the suppression of the progressive revolutionary movement of the proletarian class, closes the first phase of the history of the Marxist ideology in Russia."[19]

Hence Korsch believed that both Soviet Marxism and Social Democratic revisionism had become ideologies that legitimated a reformist practice which in fact strengthened the capitalist system. Both were thus divorced from the reality of those genuinely revolutionary forces and struggles which sought the overthrow of capitalism and construction of socialism. Marxism had become an ideology vitiated by a split between theory and revolutionary practice, which both legitimated reformist practice and served as an instrument of domination (in particularly the Soviet Union). Whereas earlier Korsch had blamed the failure of the working-class movement on its neglect/suppression of the revolutionary core of Marxism and urged a restoration of revolutionary Marxism, he now began to assess the extent to which Marxism itself was responsible for the debacles of the working-class movement: "It is deceptive and even false to see the theoretical origins of the present crisis as resulting either from a perversion or an oversimplification of Marx's and Engels' revolutionary theory at the hands of their successors. It is equally misleading to juxtapose this degenerated, falsified Marxism to the 'pure theory' of Marx and Engels themselves. In the final analysis, today's crisis is the crisis of Marx's and Engels' theory as well."[20]

The crisis of Marxism, Korsch wrote, reveals itself both as a collapse of the dominant position Marxism held in the revolutionary movement, and in the transformation of Marxian theory and practice into a state orthodoxy and reformist practice. Marxism is a product of an earlier era of class struggle and "consequently lacks any real relation to contemporary class struggles emerging as a result of wholly new conditions."[21] Marx and Engels had carried out a full scale critique of "all aspects of the existing class society (economic base and superstructure) from the newly acquired perspective of the proletariat" and conceptualized both the *"real developmental laws* of the existing capitalist society and hence, at the same time, *the real conditions of revolutionary class actions.*"[22] But the current Marxist orthodoxy had "developed into a purely abstract and passive theory dealing with the objective course of social development as determined by external laws." Korsch was objecting to both a theoretical stagnation of Marx's theory which had failed to keep up with the vicissitudes of capitalist development, and to the reification of Marxism into a set of objectivistic laws that supposedly described the objective course of capitalist development (and crisis/collapse). These laws were formulated in a system of "scientific socialism" that allowed its adepts to predict the course of economic-political development. This scientization of Marxism fell prey, Korsch believed, to an "objectivistic fetishism" that reified economic laws into a deterministic system, and which excluded elements of class struggle and "the subjective action of the working class."

Korsch took up this theme in an essay "On Some Fundamental Presuppositions for a Materialistic Discussion of Crisis Theory." He criticized "objectivistic" theories of capitalist crisis which postulate the inevitable fall of capitalism, according to laws of "iron logic." Such a theory is based upon "insufficient deduction" and is therefore pseudo-scientific. Further it also is not the best sort of theory for producing revolutionary consciousness and action, since it induces fatalism and a passive waiting for the collapse. It can also contribute to mystifying the workers by their learned "theoreticians" who supposedly hold the key to historical development. Equally dubious from both a scientific and political point of view are those theories of capitalist stability maintained by Bernstein, Hilferding and the like, which claim that capitalism is now crisis-free and can overcome any temporary dislocations. This thesis flies in the face of a series of acute crises, Korsch believed, and reduces socialism to a moral demand or reformist practice. Hence the Marxist crisis theory resembles a "revolutionary myth" in Sorel's sense. No really scientific prediction can be made as to the avoidability or inevitability of capitalist crises. This does not mean, however, as Sorel seemed to believe, that revolutionary theory solely consists of myths that move the workers to action. "The materialist stance," Korsch wrote, "believes that certain, if only always very limited, prognostic statements sufficient for practical action can be made on the basis of always more exact and thorough empirical investigations of the present capitalist mode of production and its recognizable immanent tendencies of development. The materialist, therefore, investigates thoroughly the given situation of capitalist production including the contradictions found therein, among which are also the situation, the level of consciousness, the degree of organization, and the

readiness for struggle of the working class and all the various levels of
the working class in order to determine its action."[23]

Korsch appraised various Marxian theories by their consequences for
political action, as well as their general validity. From both a theoretical
and practical point of view, he dissected and put in radical question the
leading Marxian theories. He concluded that none of the current trends
in Marxism stood as an adequate theoretical expression for the continued
practical needs of the proletarian class struggle. In fact, in the past decades, he argued, "the most important living theory of proletarian class
struggle came from three different directions, each of which consciously
and unconsciously stood opposed to orthodox Marxist theory. These
three were: *unionist reformism, revolutionary syndicalism*, and *Leninist
Bolshevism*."[24] Each of these tendencies is rooted in living class struggles
and sought "to make the subjective action of the working class rather
than the objective development of capitalism the main focus of socialist
theory."[25] Korsch begins here his attempt to break the hegemony of
Marxism over revolutionary struggles and to assess alternative theories,
strategies, and movements which might aid the struggles of the working
class in their liberation from capitalism.

In the search for new revolutionary theories, possibilities, and open-
ings, Korsch applied a critical historical materialist method to analyze
the significance of the Paris commune, the Russian Soviets, the German
councils system, revolutionary syndicalism and anarchism, the workers'
collectives in Spain, and struggles in "the marginal areas of the international capitalist system,"[26] or what is today called the Third World. He
also called for a re-evaluation of the theories of the "utopian socialists
from Thomas More to the present day," and of such rivals of Marx as
Blanqui, and even his "sworn enemies" such as Proudhon and Bakunin.[27]
The assessment of the significance of alternative theories and practice
of revolution to Marxism would require putting elements of the Marxian
theory in radical question. The remainder of my essay will discuss: (1)
Korsch's critique of the Marxian theory of revolution; (2) his search
for new possibilities for revolution; (3) his analysis of new obstacles
to revolution in the emerging world-wide counterrevolution; and (4)
Korsch's appraisal of what is living and dead in Marxism.

Critique of the Marxian Theory of Revolution

Two articles on the Paris Commune, translated in this anthology, enabled
Korsch to assess the importance of the Paris Commune in the context of

an emerging critique of the Marxian theory of revolution. Korsch applied here his historical materialist method, and criticized the leading Marxists' lavish praise of the commune as the model of revolutionary practice and the "dictatorship of the proletariat," by interpreting the significance of the commune in the context of the history of class struggle in Europe. The Paris Commune for Korsch presented a task of "revolutionary self-criticism," and a demystification of the Marxian interpretation of it. Korsch showed that there is a contradiction in Marx's appraisal of the commune, where he at once esteemed it as the "finally discovered political form for the liberation of the proletariat," and then claimed that the commune is valuable because of its openness, its indeterminateness, and its potentialities for further development.[28] For Korsch, this contradiction disclosed a deeper contradiction at the heart of the Marxian political theory. For on one hand, Marx enthusiastically affirmed the commune—which was a decentralized people's government on the Proudhonian federalist model —and yet Marx himself was an admirer of centralized state power. This, according to Korsch, revealed a contradiction in Marx's attitude toward the state which at once is to be a "dictatorship of the proletariat," and is supposed to "wither away." In fact, Korsch believed that serious problems resulted from the Marxian failure to resolve the antinomy between a decentralized-federalist political model and the highly centralized dictatorship of the proletariat model.

Korsch himself was becoming increasingly critical of the Marxian political theory and theory of the state which were full, he believed, of unresolved problems. He was becoming increasingly distrustful of the Marxian notion of the centralized state and was becoming more sympathetic to decentralized/federalist concepts.[29] He thought the Marxian theory of the "two stages" from socialism to communism[30] provided a legitimation to indefinitely postpone the construction of the higher stage of socialism. He believed this problem was evident in the actual development of the Soviet Union where Stalin justified his counterrevolutionary politics by claiming that the Soviet Union was but in the first stage of transition, and that realizing the more radical demands of socialism must be postponed to the future.

Korsch also began to believe that the Marxian theory of revolution was tied to its own historical circumstances of development, and was infected with Blanquist-Jacobian features.[31] That is, Marx formulated his political theory in response to his study and experience of the French Revolution and class struggles in France. He remained highly impressed with the Jacobian dictatorship—a strong centralized state used as the instrument of revolution—and the Blanquist strategy of winning state power through the insurrection of a revolutionary elite. But the French revolution was after all a bourgeois revolution, Korsch reasoned in his relentless logic, and perhaps Marx's understanding of revolution was too closely connected to the historical development of the bourgeoisie, which might be inappropriate for today's working-class struggles under changed historical conditions.

As Korsch put it in "Theses on Hegel and Revolution," "The theory of proletarian revolution was not developed as such from its own foundation, but on the contrary arose from the bourgeois revolution and thus in every relation to content and method is still tainted with the birthmarks of Jacobinism, that is the bourgeois theory of revolution."[32] In Korsch's "Marx's Position on the European Revolution of 1848," he suggests that "Marx has remained dominated by the traditional conception" of revolution produced out of the French Revolution.[33] In this article, Korsch shows that the demands Marx put forth in his activities during the German Revolution of 1848–49 did not overstep those of the "democratic revolution" and concludes: "Marx rejects positing a future socialist utopia against the reality of the bourgeois revolution. But he continuously sought to force upon the new revolutionary movement of his time past actions which were hardly connected with the forms of its present conditions. He sought to lift the democratic revolution of his time to a higher level and failed to see that this 'higher level' in reality is but a historical level that was already once reached by the total revolutionary movement of a past epoch" [i.e., the bourgeois revolution].[34]

Further, Korsch argued in "Marxism and the Present Tasks of the Proletarian Class Struggle" that there is something odd about "the ideological character of this wholesale identification of an established doctrine with the revolutionary struggle of the working class."[35] That is, he found it peculiar that the doctrines of nineteenth-century bourgeois theorists such as Marx and Engels should be taken as the authentic expression and guide for contemporary proletarian class struggles and be expected to continue to lead the way in the future. Here Korsch broke with his earlier identification of Marxism and Leninism with the revolutionary movement. He now noted that "the identity of a bourgeois bred doctrine with all present and future truly revolutionary struggles of the proletarian class assumed the character of a veritable miracle."[36] He believed that the identification of Marxism with both the course of capitalist development and proletarian class struggles took on a quasi-mystical character and in effect denied both that capitalism might well develop (or collapse) in quite different ways than Marx envisioned. Further, the working class might well develop a quite different strategy and goals for their liberation. Hence Korsch rejected the "preestablished harmony between the Marxist doctrine and the actual proletarian movement itself" and urged looking at existing class struggles and the historical situation anew to discern possibilities for liberation and working class advancement.

Moreover Korsch discerned an exaggeration of the importance of politics and the state in both Marx and Lenin. The political thrust of much of Korsch's later work was to emphasize the importance of trade union struggles and the social and economic dimension for the liberation of the working class. He thought that a Marxian theory of revolution, which urged seizing state power and smashing the bourgeois state as the primary revolutionary task, exaggerated the fundamentality of the political dimension and underestimated the importance of economic and social struggles. The *"true secret* of the revolutionary commune," he argued, "lies precisely in its *social content"*—in the fact that the workers themselves took control of their everyday life in all its facets—and not in discovering some universally valid "political form."[37] Indeed, the political form of the commune, Korsch slyly and irreverently pointed out, is bourgeois to the core, and has its origins in the middle ages in early municipal political forms which the bourgeoisie developed, even before its centralized state, as a weapon against the former feudal ruling classes. The proletariat can learn important lessons from the Paris Commune and might be able to use some of its features in constructing a future society, Korsch believed, but it is a mistake to make a fetish of the commune and hold it up as the model for all revolutionary struggles now and forevermore. Korsch's conclusion to his study of the Paris commune contains an implicit critique of the Marxian concept of the "dictatorship of the proletariat," and instead urges as a Marxist concept of the state the earlier notion of a "free association": "The authentic end-goal of proletarian class struggle is not some 'more democratic,' 'more communal' or even 'more soviet-like' *state*, but the classless and stateless Communist *society* whose encompassing *form* is no longer political force but that '*association, in which the free development of each is the condition for the free development of all' (Communist Manifesto)."*[38]

New Forms of Revolutionary Struggle in Spain

Korsch's attempt to at once discern new possibilities and models of revolution, and to criticize a too narrow Marxian concept of revolution, was given decisive impetus by the Spanish Civil War, which was creating new forms of revolutionary struggle and new models of socioeconomic organization in the Spanish collectives.[39] Korsch hoped that Spain would provide possibilities for the development of a truly revolutionary movement that would be independent of the hegemony of the Soviet Union and Communist party and would thus avoid the pitfalls of Stalinism. In 1931 he visited Spain as a guest of the Spanish syndicalists, the CNT, in their congress at Madrid. He wrote a sober and realistic account of "The Spanish Revolution," published in September, 1931, as well as two later reports on Spain, "Economics and Politics in Revolutionary Spain" and "Collectivization in Spain"—the first two of which are collected in this volume. In an unpublished draft, "The Prehistory of the Spanish Revolution," Korsch showed how different waves of revolution and reaction in Spain in the last half-century paralleled European development. He pointed out that the "main tendency in the workers' movement in Spain was decisively *anti-statist, anarchist,* and *syndicalist.*"[40] The Social Democratic party in Spain, on the other hand, showed, even before its European counterparts, the reformist "state-preservative" position which would characterize European Social Democrats.[41]

In "The Spanish Revolution" Korsch carefully analyzed the situation that led the King to flee from Spain and opened the door to potential revolutionary change. He discussed the different leftist forces struggling for power and the tasks, problems, and obstacles they faced. He was especially sympathetic to the attempt of the revolutionary syndicalist CNT to throw off the yoke of oppression and "to build a truly free and autonomous workers' life."[42] He favorably discussed the detailed program set forth at the June, 1931, congress in Madrid which he visited, and he indicated the political and economic problems remaining to be solved. He also analyzed the dangers of counterrevolution posed by the old reactionary powers, which were in fact later to fuse together in a fascist crucible and overthrow the revolution.

In "Economics and Politics in Revolutionary Spain," written seven years later when Korsch was in exile in America, he summed up the achievements and lessons to be learned from experiences in Spain. Korsch was especially interested in the fact that the state power collapsed almost completely, enabling the workers to construct their own form of socioeconomic self-government in the Spanish collectives. The achievements of the Spanish collectives showed what the workers could do in every industry and realm of life to reorganize their activity when they had the power to control their own lives and working conditions. The collectivization of industry took place on a regional and local level in both small and large scale industries and revealed the power of the people to administer and govern their own life.

The failure to maintain the collectives against the counterrevolutionary powers resulted at least in part, Korsch believed, from the "traditional attitude of non-concernedness in all matters political and not strictly economic and social" of the Spanish syndicalists and anarchists.[43] Hence in Korsch's view the lesson to be learned from the ultimate failure of the revolution in Spain was "the *vital connection between the economic and political action in every phase of the proletarian class struggle.*"[44] Here it might be noted that Korsch never subscribed to the anarchist position on the unimportance of the state and political struggles. Although Korsch mistrusted Marxian over-emphases on the state and politics, he believed that the anarchists are just as one-sided in their neglect of the problem of the state and politics. Korsch himself urged a position that saw the vital importance of all economic, political and social struggles for liberation and the overthrow of capitalism.

Moreover, Korsch warned against judging the events in Spain (or anywhere else) from the standpoint of some ideal theory of revolution and then condemning a group or situation for failing to follow the model of the theory (as some Marxists were criticizing the Spanish for failing to follow the example of the Bolsheviks). Although one can, Korsch concluded, learn important lessons from revolutionary struggles of the past, one should be aware of the historical uniqueness of the specific conditions and not impose an abstract theory of revolution on conditions to which it may not be appropriate (this is a political consequence of Korsch's principle of historical specificity).[45] Korsch was concerned to break the hegemony of Marxism on revolutionary theory and to observe how specific revolutionary conditions produce a variety of forms of struggle and theory.

Korsch concretized his study of Spain further in an essay, "Collectivization in Spain," in which he discussed an anthology dealing with the details of the actual workers' struggles that let "*the Spanish revolutionaries speak for themselves*" so as to provide "the real content of the present struggles in revolutionary Spain."[46] The experiments with the collectivization of industry and agriculture provided, Korsch believed, "a new type of transition from capitalist to communist method of production that has been achieved, though incompletely, in an imposing variety of forms."[47] Korsch indicated some examples of the "new type of community production" and "new life of libertarian communism." The success achieved by the Spanish workers at reorganizing their life and work, despite incredible obstacles, testified to the initiative, endurance, and capacity for action in a working class unfettered by bourgeois domination. Especially praised is "the emerging of the anti-State attitude of the revolutionary Spanish proletariat, unhampered by self-created organizational or ideological obstacles."[48] The collectivization process was extended to not only capitalist firms and large farms, but also took place in municipal and state organizations, encompassing even barbershops and prostitution! This far-ranging process of socialization eloquently testifies "to the peculiar creative power of the revolution" that was attempting to transform all realms of everyday life.[49]

Franco and his fascist cohorts, supported by the minions of Hitler and Mussolini, were to end this inspiring experiment in libertarian self-management socialism, but the final defeat and liquidation did not, in Korsch's view, obliterate its importance as an example of working class struggle. Korsch was not in the least blind, however, to the menacing danger the working class faced from the monstrous expansion of fascism and counterrevolution on a world-wide scale. We recall that early in the 1920's Korsch focused on the fascist phenomenon in Germany and continued to analyze and struggle against the growth of fascism in the 1930's. The result is his theory of counterrevolution.

Korsch Analyzes the Counterrevolution

In 1931–32 as part of his educational work in Berlin, Korsch formulated "Theses Toward a Critique of the Fascist Concept of the State."[50] Fascism was not in his view primarily a regression to a pre-bourgeois type of state, but was rather a "modern state form" that was a negation of the liberal concept of the state. Although the fascists maintained "a completely irrational state mythology," they "carried out through the 'elite' a sober, illusion-free rational goal-directed state praxis." Korsch took the orthodox Marxian position that the fascist state arose from the foundation of monopoly capitalism, and exercised a monopoly of state power that represented the interests of monopoly capital, and that the fascist state took the explicit form of a class state exercised by the bourgeoisie. Hence, as opposed to Bolshevism, fascism attempted to preserve the previous relations of production and failed to "unleash new forces of production." Finally, the tendency of the fascist state was toward totalitarian control of the entirety of society and fascism threatened to spread throughout the capitalist world and to become an international counterrevolutionary menace.

Indeed this is exactly what happened. Hitler's national socialism triumphed in Germany and forced Korsch and other radicals to emigrate. Korsch went underground and attempted to organize resistance after the

Reichstag fire gave the Nazis an excuse to exterminate the left. Resistance was hopeless, however, and Korsch was forced to emigrate to England and later America.[51]

Korsch continued to analyze the fascist phenomenon and concluded after the triumph of fascism in Italy and Germany, after Franco's victory in Spain, and in light of the Stalinist crimes in the Soviet Union, that the counterrevolution had triumphed on a world-wide scale. The dimensions of the counterrevolution, the threat it posed to the working class, and possible actions to be taken against it were analyzed in "State and Counterrevolution," "The Fascist Counterrevolution," and "The Workers' Fight against Fascism"—all of which are published in this anthology. In "State and Counterrevolution," Korsch begins by exclaiming, "More than any preceding period of recent history and on a much vaster scale, our period is a time not of revolution but of counterrevolution."[52] The counterrevolution prevailed, he claimed, as a conscious attempt both to destroy an actual revolutionary process and to prevent a future one from taking place. The counterrevolution represented a decisive defeat for the working class, and the politics of European and Soviet leaders aimed at "the creation of conditions which will make impossible any independent movement of the European working class for a long time."[53]

Korsch analyzed the new role of the state in creating a "fascist state capitalism" that more consciously than ever before uses the state as an instrument of suppression. Further, "The imperialist war and its aftermath have greatly accelerated and intensified both the transformation of monopoly capitalism into state-monopoly capitalism and the monstrous oppression of the laboring masses by the state which becomes increasingly intertwined with the all-powerful capitalist combines."[54] In this context, Korsch believed that it is imperative to develop a theory of the counterrevolutionary role of the state and to discover ways to combat it:

> . . . the Russian and non-Russian workers today cannot confine themselves to experiencing the steadily advancing counterrevolution without making every effort to interpret its significance. By a careful examination of the past they must find out both the objective and the subjective causes for the victory of fascist state capitalism. They must closely watch its unfolding in order to discover the old and new forms of contradiction and antagonism appearing in that development. Finally they must find out a practical way to resist, as a class, the further encroachments of the counterrevolution and later to pass from an active resistance to an even more active counter-offensive in order to overthrow

>both the particular state capitalist form recently adopted and
>the general principle of exploitation inherent in all old and new
>forms of bourgeois society and its state power.[55]

The Soviet Union was included in Korsch's concept of the counter-revolution and he wished to call attention to the counterrevolutionary nature of the Soviet state. He indicated the need to analyze the process through which a "revolutionary dictatorship" has become "a counterrevolutionary state" and even "a powerful lever in the fascization of Europe."[56] The problem is rooted, he suggests, in an ambiguity in the political theory of Marxism and a failure to cut "the umbilical cord between Marxism and Jacobinism."[57] We noted the contradiction between the Marxian emphasis on a strong centralized state and a decentralized people's government, and between the "dictatorship of the proletariat" concept and the notion of "the withering away of the state." Marxism was too bound up, Korsch believed, with the Jacobian notion of a revolutionary dictatorship using a strong centralized state as an instrument of "permanent revolution." The problem is that the state can be used as a new instrument of domination that accrues ever more power and authority and refuses to "wither away." This happened in the Soviet Union through a "gradual degeneration" in which the state "abandoned more and more of its original proletarian features" and became "an instrument of the present day European counterrevolution."[58] Korsch never unambiguously offers a solution to the problem of the state but his analysis suggests a critique of the concept of the dictatorship of the proletariat and the over-emphasis of the role of the state in the revolutionary process in the Marxian theory.

Korsch criticizes those Marxists who applaud the triumph of fascism as preparing the way for the later advent of socialism, such as those in the KPD who advanced the slogan, "After Hitler, Us!" The problem, he suggests in "The Fascist Counterrevolution," is the lack of an adequate Marxian concept of counterrevolution. Korsch shows how Marx, Proudhon, Lassalle, and the Socialist Democrats all greeted various manifestations of counterrevolution as in some way creating conditions for a later victory of socialism. He argues that the disastrous position maintained by the Communists that fascism was but a step on the way to socialism is rooted in the Marxian failure to understand counterrevolution. Most Marxists, he claims, see counterrevolution as an "abnormal" interruption of a normally progressive development; hence they are caught up in nineteenth century bourgeois concepts of progress and an amelioristic evolutionary view of history. Moreover, the Marxists under attack fail to see how fascism is part of the evolutionary growth of capitalism itself. Korsch conceives fascism as an attempt to solve the tasks which the reformist parties and trade unions promised to achieve but were unable to carry out. After the "complete exhaustion and defeat of the revolutionary forces," fascism attempts to solve the labor problem, the problem of planning the economy, and the problem of capitalist crisis, in a counter-revolutionary manner that preserves the old relations of production. Korsch argues: "From this viewpoint all those comfortable illusions about a hidden revolutionary significance in the temporary victory of the counterrevolution, in which the earlier Marxists so frequently indulged, must be entirely abandoned."[59]

In view of the world-wide triumph of the counterrevolution and lack of any perceptible revolutionary alternative, Korsch was very pessimistic about the possibility of defeating fascism, or even beginning a decisive working class offensive.[60] He was especially skeptical of the strategy of gathering all the so-called democratic forces to defeat fascism: "Least of all can fascism be defeated by those people who, after a hundred years of shameless acquiescence in the total abandonment of their original ideals, now hasten to conjure up the infancy of the capitalist age with its belief in liberty, equality, fraternity, and free trade, while at the same time they surreptitiously and inefficiently try to imitate as far as possible fascism's abolition of the last remnants of those early capitalist ideas."[61] In an article, "The Workers' Fight against Fascism," he analysed the "crisis of democracy" and its tendency to either collapse in the face of a fascist offensive, or to be ready to adopt fascist methods in its own economy, society, and foreign politics. In "The Fight for Britain, the Fight for Democracy, and the War Aims of the Working Class," he doubted the sincerity of the desire of the British—who had appeased Hitler and for a century had been the bulwark of imperialism—to represent democracy and the interests of the working class.[62] Korsch rejected here the united front strategy pushed by both the Comintern and the Social Democrats. Instead, he urged the workers not to swallow whole the democratic slogans of the bourgeoisie but to attempt to advance their own class aims and demands, and to beware of tendencies toward fascization from within and without. This does not mean capitulation to fascism: "This criticism of the inept and sentimental methods of present-day anti-fascism does not imply by any means that the workers should do openly what the bourgeoisie does under the disguise of a so-called anti-fascist fight: acquiesce in the victory of fascism. The point is to fight fascism not by fascist means but on its own ground."[63] Fighting fascism on its own ground presumably means fighting for control of production, fighting for control of the state, and fighting against monopoly capital in all its forms. The old class contradictions have emerged more brutally than before, Korsch believes, and the workers' primary responsibility is to fight their major enemy, the capitalist ruling class:

> What, then, is the hope left for the anti-fascists who are op-
> posing the present European war and who will oppose the coming
> war of the hemispheres? The answer is that, just as life itself does
> not stop at the entrance of war, neither does the material work
> of modern industrial production. Fascists today quite correctly
> conceive the whole of their economy—that substitute for a genuine
> socialist economy—in terms of a "war economy" (*Wehrwirt-
> schaft*). Thus, it is the task of the workers and the soldiers to see
> to it that this job is no longer done within the restrictive rules
> imposed upon human labor in present-day capitalist, monopolist,
> and oppressive society. It has to be done in the manner prescribed
> by the particular instruments used; that is, in the manner prescribed
> by the productive forces available at the present stage of industrial
> development. In this manner both the productive and the destructive
> forces of present-day society—as every worker, every soldier knows
> —can be used only if they are used *against* their present monopo-
> listic rulers. Total mobilization of the productive forces presupposes
> total mobilization of that greatest productive force which is the
> revolutionary working class itself.[64]

Exactly what strategy Korsch had in mind here is unclear and in view of the powerful hegemony of fascism and monopoly capitalism, he despaired of any real possibility of eliminating them. In "The Workers' Fight against Fascism," he analyzed the "economic pythia" that workers in America faced in the highly concentrated and seemingly invulnerable power of corporate capitalism. Basing his analysis on Berle and Means' *The Modern Corporation and Private Property* and the 1939 Government Report "The Structure of the American Economy," Korsch outlined the incredible concentration of corporate capital and power in America. This state of affairs represents "the end of the market" and the development of a system of corporate and state capitalism where monopoly is the "general condition of present day economy."[65] He argued, "More than at any previous time the monopoly of political power reveals itself as the power to rule and control the social process of production. At the same time this means, under present conditions, the power to restrict production—both the production of industry in peace and the destructive production in time of war—and to regulate it in the interest of the monopolist class."[66]

In Korsch's view this new development of corporate capitalism is similar in many ways to fascism itself:

> There is very little difference between that economic "co-ordination" that is achieved, and sometimes not achieved, by the political decrees of victorious Nazism, Fascism, and Bolshevism, and this new "corporate community" that has been created by a slow but relentless process in this country through the system of "interlocking directorates," through the activities of the major financial institutions, through particular interest groups, through firms rendering legal, accounting, and similar services to the larger corporations, through "intercorporate stockholdings," and a number of other devices.[67]

and

> There is no essential difference between the way the *New York Times* and the Nazi press publish daily "all the news that's fit to print"—under existing conditions of privilege and coercion and hypocrisy. There is no difference in principle between the eighty-odd voices of capitalist mammoth corporations—which, over the American radio, recommend to legions of silent listeners the use of Ex-Lax, Camels, and neighborhood grocerys, along with music, war, baseball and domestic news, and dramatic sketches—and the one suave voice of Mr. Goebbels who recommends armaments, race-purity, and worship of the Fuehrer. He too is quite willing to let them have music along with it—plenty of music, sporting news, and all the unpolitical stuff they can take.[68]

Korsch's evaluation of the totalitarian domination by capital and the corporate state in advanced industrial society was amazingly similar in some respects to the analyses of the Frankfurt School.[69] These theories were developed in the 1930's and 1940's under the dual impact of the defeat of the working-class movement in the triumph of fascism, and exposure as emigrés to the new conditions of life in the emerging late-capitalist society in the United States. Horkheimer, Adorno, Marcuse, and Korsch were overwhelmed by fascism and the United States in quite similar ways. The experience of a European emigré whose hopes for socialist revolution were shattered on the twin reefs of fascism and corporate capitalism were clearly and interestingly expressed in a revealing letter to Paul Partos,[70] accompanied by a document "On American Science," written at the end of July, 1939. "America," Korsch wrote, "is truly different from Europe, certainly from the 'old' Europe in which we all lived, worked, and engaged in our struggles."[71] In Europe one had a relatively clear conception of the state and society, the possibilities for social change and how one could participate in the process. In Europe, "One stood within a movement with a well-known past that led from a familiar present to a sufficiently known future. One had a theory which one could relate to 'critically' at will, exactly because one stood so firmly in it." In America, however, "everything is too big, too wide, too incomprehensible, too dispersed to enable one to take a similar position." Moreover, "the isolated individual feels himself too small, too powerless, and too unknowing in view of the largeness, multiplicity, and changeability of the general existence and process." Both the individual and group found themselves in an "indeterminate" situation confronted with "unlimited possibilities": "an abstract infinity and freedom exists for everyone and for no one." Both the sciences and general conditions in America were subject to incredible change and the proliferation of novelty, making it impossible to get a firm grasp of things:

> The constant change of investigated facts, the uncovering of new
> regions, the discovery of new methods, and the instant classification
> of all countertendencies, the neutralization of all abnormality and
> illegality, the instrumentalization of business, politics, corruption,
> violence, criminality—all this is so much taken for granted that
> the eruption of novelty in science signifies neither conflict nor ten-
> sion but only the daily fulfilling of the moving principle—whereby
> fundamentally it doesn't matter much whether the new is truly new,
> since in the unceasing transition from what is now familiar to
> 'something new' the old (*Uralte*) and everyday (*Alltägliche*) will
> always be discovered again as New.[72]

Hence "change" (*Veränderung*) itself is the principle of American science.

In this situation of flux and seeming novelty a critical theory seems to have lost its purpose and foundation. Korsch has intimations here of Marcuse's "one-dimensionality" where all the classical contradictions of capitalism are stabilized in an unholy harmony. In the process of constant change, Korsch writes, "despite all fluctuation on the surface, there is no dangerous crisislike state, no conflict that isn't neutralized, no idea that is not at once ideologized and welcomed as a novelty by the dominant ideology."[73] All this simultaneous change and stability/sameness has "the appearance of true progress," but it is really just monopoly capitalism reproducing itself, creating a confusing garden of earthly delights for consumption to provide "Prosperity everlasting"—which means in effect higher profits and more efficient social control for the monopolists. "A science that is institutionalized along with an institutionalized Big Capital produces in one and the same way a new form of social demand. In this way monopoly capitalism reproduces here in its cornucopia once again the fortunate constellation from the early time of competitive capitalism: 'The sciences blossom, the arts prosper, it is a joy to live.' "[74] Marcuse's Happy Consciousness!

As for politics in America, Korsch could discover no point of insertion for his left-oppositionalist tendency. "One can only say and do here what is false, misunderstood, incomprehensible, if one does not wish to limit oneself to the Sisyphean task of struggling against the poisoning work of the C. P. [Communist party]."[75] Struggling against American reformist, bureaucratized, and corrupt unions, as against the Communist party, would only in any case serve the interests of the bourgeoisie against labor. (Horkheimer was later to take a similar political position.) The various political groups merely engage in a confused "tug of war" against each other, without the prospect of any decisive victory that will aid the working class. What could one do in this situation, Korsch wondered.[76] Yet, Korsch made a continuous effort to analyze the economic-political situation in America, contributed articles to the leading Marxist journals, gave lectures to workers and university people throughout his travels in the United States, and maintained close contact with Paul Mattick and the group of council communists—but had little hope of any possibility of real radical change or efficacious political activism. "What the relatively most active man of our tendency, Paul Mattick, does," Korsch wrote to Partos, "appears to me too isolated, too short term for me to get involved with it."[77]

For the last twenty years, Korsch noted, the "unresolved task of the revolutionary" was to seek a way that would be more than a mere "complement" to the Communist party. "The single historically real contribution here is that of the Spanish anarchists and you know better than anyone how short-lived and painful even this historically best contribution to the solution to the general task came out,"[78] Korsch wrote to Partos, whom he describes later to Brecht as "the last knight of the completed first revolutionary epoch of the European workers' movement who happily turned home from Valencia in the last hour."[79] The final result of twenty years of class struggle was, in Korsch's view, a string of defeats: "The entire past workers' movement in all its forms has really only prepared internal-capitalist progress, that is presently introduced in counter-revolutionary form through 'fascism' and on a world scale is executed and secured through all capitalist systems."[80] Thus, although Korsch continued to maintain that the working class had a "potentially revolutionary significance," he conceded that "phenomenally" it may well have a counterrevolutionary significance[81]—another position that Marcuse was later to defend. This state of affairs forced Korsch to put the Marxist theory of revolution in radical question and produced the positions he would later formulate in "Ten Theses on Marxism Today."

Korsch and Marxism

Korsch deeply pondered the tragic experiences of the working class movement in Europe, and continuously intended to write a study of social movements and social forces that would trace the itinerary of the revolutionary and counterrevolutionary movements from the French revolution to the present day. In a letter to Brecht, he wrote: "I am planning to re-specialize myself from 'Marxism' to sociology and to the 'Logic of the social sciences.' Two planned books: I) *Social Forces and Social Movements* should be divided into a very abstract first part, and an almost ideographical second part: dealing with revolution and counterrevolution. Working time: around two years (at least!); II) *Social Theories* should be a textbook for academic use that will eventually land me a job."[82] Korsch wished to appraise the various radical and bourgeois social theories in light of the historical development of those movements which either embodied them or repulsed them. He became increasingly interested in the process of history from the rise of capitalism to the present day and wrote a series of historical monographs and reflections upon history itself and those historians who interpreted it.[83]

But above all Korsch was obsessed with Marxism. What role had Marxism played in the defeat of the working-class movement? What validity did it have in the light of the triumph of fascism and the counter-revolution? Why had the Marxian socialist revolution failed to take place in the dominant capitalist countries? What in the Marxian theory was a hindrance to the further development of a revolutionary movement? What constructive role could Marxism still play in future revolutionary movements? Moreover, Korsch became increasingly concerned with the scientific-theoretical status of Marxism. How could Marxism stand up to the results of recent empirical and methodological research in the sciences? How could the Marxian methodology itself be strengthened and made more rigorous with the aid of recent developments in scientific theory? Finally, what was the relation between the scientific and the revolutionary-political aspects of the Marxian theory? Korsch was involved with these questions from the 1930's up until his debilitating fatal illness ended his theoretical labors in the 1950's.

In the 1930's Korsch became increasingly interested in the theoretical status of Marxism. In a series of essays and lectures, he tested the Marxian theory against the results of the philosophy of science developed by the Vienna Circle and Phillip Frank and Kurt Lewin, with whom he studied and worked.[84] Korsch never adequately mediated his interest in the political-revolutionary and theoretical-scientific components of the Marxian theory. In the 1920's, he maintained a mostly pragmatic attitude toward theory, and judged a theory solely by its ability to successfully guide practice, judging, for example, a theory like Leninism on its ability to carry through socialist revolution. But in the 1930's Korsch became more interested in the formal aspects of theory, and spent much time studying formal logic, the mathematical calculus, and the philosophy of science. He never swallowed whole, however, the dogmas of positivism, and maintained a critical attitude toward scientific empiricism, logical formalism, and the other pet theories of the Vienna Circle.[85] It is, in fact, my belief that Korsch studied philosophy of science and engaged in metatheoretical research primarily in the interest of strengthening the theoretical status of Marxism, which he felt had been neglected in the inept hands of the leading Social Democratic and Communist theoreticians.

Korsch at different times held two quite contradictory interpretations of the theoretical status of Marxism and points of view from which it could be evaluated. Many times he argued that Marxism requires no philosophical or scientific grounding because it is grounded in the working-class forces and class struggles in historical reality.[86] Moreover, he often cited his friend Brecht's dictum that "truth is concrete," that true theory is judged and evaluated according to its results in practice. But— to apply this criterion to testing Marxism—when the working class movement is defeated and its forces are exhausted or coopted, what foundation does Marxism then have and how can it be tested in practice? A possible solution, which Korsch seemed to consider but never committed himself to, would be to ground Marxism in the scientificity of its theory and evaluate it according to its truth as a description of social-economic-historical reality. Korsch in fact seemed to believe that Marxism was the true theory (in this sense) of history, society, and political economy, and that its truth did not solely rest in its embodiment in working-class forces and practice, but also in the scientific strength and cogency of the theory itself.[87] Although there is an unresolved tension in the later Korsch between the insufficiently mediated political-revolutionary and theoretical-scientific components of the Marxian theory, it would be a mistake to believe that Korsch fell into the snares of either a totally pragmatized theory that solely judges theory on its political use (Korsch criticized Lenin on these grounds),[88] or that he took a totally positivistic view of theory. In fact, Korsch continued to defend a version of *dialectical* Marxism and never fell into the dogmas of pragmatism or positivism.[89]

Indeed, a serious problem for Korsch, which he never adequately resolved, was the relation between dialectics and science. Korsch continuously reflected on Hegel and dialectics and how they were appropriated/transformed by Marx. Korsch tended to play down the conflicts between dialectics and science, finding much materialism and empiricism in Hegel, dialectics in science, and a successful synthesis in Marx.[90] In a letter to Paul Mattick giving a critique of his concept of Marxism and dialectics, Korsch argued that dialectics for Marx is not a magic wand, but "served him as a hand tool for seeking and finding his scientific results; he once learned this method and had no other (in a lesser degree this is still so for us today)."[91] Korsch opposed assigning too grand a role to the concept of synthesis in Marx's dialectic (as if, as Mattick wrote, the communist society was the grand synthesis of Marx's production), and concluded that he is "an opponent of *philosophical-absolute*" interpretations of dialectics because "thereby the strict empirical scientific knowledge of the current factual situation that lies before us, and above all *praxis* as 'human sensuous activity' is underplayed (*zu kurz kommt*)."[92]

Korsch was equally critical, however, of making a fetish of science. Of contemporary science, he wrote, "after the abolition of fetishism which adheres to science in the epoch of commodity production . . . science will truly be equivalent to accumulated human labor-growing forces of production."[93] Korsch suggested that science had fallen prey to fetishism, which could only be eliminated through "eliminating classes and class contradictions"—a "practical-historical task"—and then "science can be reconstructed with material production on a higher level, in so far as 'science' is abolished (*aufgehoben*)."[94] Korsch then indicated that he approved of the distinction between the natural sciences and the social sciences to the extent that it elucidated the class character of the propositions of the social sciences, but he also wished to stress that even the natural sciences have a class-interest: "the same class-character can be shown in an appropriate and rational way within the natural sciences."[95]

Further, Korsch argues against the Engels-Lenin emphasis on the primacy of the man-nature relation as fundamental—which demotes the relation between socialized human beings to a secondary position, and renders the social sciences secondary to the natural sciences. Korsch counters—and I believe he is on the right track here—"To me it appears that *nothing is primary here*; that *man-nature* and *man-man* are to be coordinated, that both are equiprimordial and fundamental, historically, logically, and practically. The 'new element added on with the appearance of the finished man—namely Society,' in Engels' citation—is to me clearly an expression of a bourgeois conception of history and theory of revolution."[96] Moreover, although Marxism "formally recognizes the *genetic* priority of nature," its "primary interest" is in historical-social development.[97] Korsch then chides Mattick for wanting uncritically to "allow the whole of science to stand as objective science (like the enchanted prince in the fairy tale!). This all hangs together with what I characterize above as the 'Engels-Lenin variant' of a tendency toward natural philosophy"; i.e., he is criticizing the tendency—championed by the positivists and positivistic Marxists—to take the natural sciences as the model of truth.[98]

Moreover, in his discussions of the theoretical status of Marxism, Korsch constantly emphasizes that the propositions of Marxism undercut the rigid positivist distinctions between fact and value, quantitative and qualitative propositions, description and critique. In a letter to Mattick, he reiterates a position he often took: "Marxism concerns itself with society primarily in dissolution. Thus crisis is 'normal' for Marxism"— which doesn't exclude, he warns, careful, empirical, quantitative analysis of the existing society.[99] Above all, Korsch endlessly claims, Marxism is a theory of revolutionary practice. Hence all of its propositions are geared toward critique and social change. Such a practically-oriented theory is subject to continuous change and modification: "*I wanted to say and have said* that it is a fallacy when one thinks that the militant character of revolutionary materialist theory (which is *obviously* to be preserved!) can be *protected* by *other* means against a weakening of its fiber than through the *complete readiness* to accept *all* theoretically *justified modification* . . . the sole means toward preserving the militant character consists in further developing science. . . . I do not believe that at any time true revolutionary interest can come in conflict with real progress in science. Thus, to the contrary, all true progress in science is welcome to revolutionary theory and practice."[100]

These issues raise the thorny question of the relationship between Marxian dialectics and science in Korsch's thought and the problem of Korsch and positivism. It is sometimes alleged that Korsch championed a positivistic version of Marxism and in his later work fell prey to the dogmas of positivism. Herbert Marcuse, for example, has written: "Brecht was strongly influenced by Korsch. Korsch's Marxism had a very strong positivistic content. And my friends in the Frankfurt school were against this positivistic content."[101] Italian critics have claimed that Korsch collapsed the Marxian distinction between the empirical level and method of research (Marx's *Forschungsweise*) and the conceptual level and method of presentation (Marx's *Darstellungsweise*).[102] It is claimed that Korsch collapsed/identified theory with the historical-empirical level, and thus deprived theory of (1) its autonomy; (2) its reflective-critical capacity; and (3) its anticipatory moment. Further, one could argue that Korsch operated with an instrumental concept of science and is not critical enough toward scientific methodology and practice.[103] Hence the argument that in the last analysis Korsch fell prey to positivism.

Although there is a case to be made for Korsch's kinship with some positivistic doctrines, one cannot simply label Korsch a positivist and end the matter without further discussion. I have tried to show that Korsch took a critical Marxist position on the sciences free from many of the positivist dogmas. Interestingly, in a letter to Partos, Korsch complained that Marx was not critical enough of the social sciences:

> As you know, in my orthodox period I always claimed that the revolutionary kernel of Marx's economic theory was in its "critique," i.e., the essential critical dissolution of bourgeois "political economy." . . .
> In my last lessons of winter 32–33 I have changed my viewpoint a little. I have shown how modest—if looked at very closely—is the critical contribution as opposed to *Capital*'s main economic content, how little developed were the critical points and how a real critique even of classical economy was traceable only in the first volume of *Capital*, edited by Marx himself, while the manuscripts worked on and edited by Engels and Kautsky (second and third volume of *Capital*; *Theories of Surplus Value*) show Marx only as a critic of vulgar economics and actually as a faithful disciple and follower of classical economics in the details of money, income, etc. . . .
> There was a connection between the bourgeois character of Marx's politics and the would-be continuation of the critical dissolution of bourgeois economics into a science directly social and therefore into a praxis directly revolutionary. . . . Marx certainly developed the *historical* critique of the economic categories well (and Sorel went too far when he challenged this) but he proclaimed the "over-

coming" of economics into a *directly social science* only in the abstract instead of actually bringing it about.[104]

This passage indicates that Korsch is criticizing Marx for being "too positivistic" and uncritical toward bourgeois science, and for not going far enough in the direction of creating a new revolutionary social science that breaks completely with previous bourgeois science. Korsch continually questioned the dogmas of orthodox Marxism and scientific positivism, and described his own theory as "a non-dogmatic approach to Marxism." Crucially, Korsch never surrendered the Marxian dialectic of theory and practice. It made no sense for him to discuss theory at all separated from social practice. In "A Non-Dogmatic Approach to Marxism," he wrote, "There is no use in discussing controversial points in any social theory (not even in that social theory which is commonly described as religion) unless such discussion is part of an existing social struggle . . . the result of any such materialist discussion must in all cases 'make a difference' in respect to the actual behavior not of an individual nor of a small group of people, but of a veritable collectivity, a social mass."[105] Against sterile, abstract discussions of Marxist dogmas, Korsch wrote, "it is here proposed to revindicate the critical, pragmatic, and activistic element which for all this has never been entirely eliminated from the social theory of Marx and which during the few short phases of its predominance has made that theory a most efficient weapon of the proletarian class struggle."[106] Korsch interestingly noted in a letter to Partos that he had earlier made "the theoretical and practical position of Marx toward *'politics'* the demarcation point of my division between what is living and dead in Marxism."[107] The crux of the matter is that Korsch is above all a revolutionary theorist and is primarily interested in theory, science, and philosophy to the extent that they can serve an emancipatory role in the process of social change.

Hence, although Korsch is in the last analysis often ambiguous as to where he stands vis-à-vis Marxism and positivism, dialectics and empirical science, one cannot simply label him a "positivist Marxist" (à la Marcuse or Adorno) without serious qualifications. Thus I reject those interpretations of Korsch which either dismiss him as a "positivist Marxist" or praise him for his purely "scientific Marxism."[108] On the other hand, I do not accept the interpretations of Korsch as a "Hegelian Marxist," for from the beginning, his appropriation of Hegel was highly critical and selective.[109] In some of his works, (for example, "Hegel and Revolution") and in some letters, there are sharp, often violent, attacks on Hegel.[110] The fact of the matter is that Korsch was neither a positivist Marxist or a Hegelian Marxist. Rather he had a dialectical version of Marxism that was at once critical of orthodox Marxism, Hegel, and positivist science, while appropriating aspects of these theories in his own project.

Korsch's major work of the 1930's, *Karl Marx*, is an attempt to mediate the contradictions between Marx and Hegel, dialectics and science, and the scientific and political-revolutionary components of the Marxian theory. However, I believe it is a mistake to take *Karl Marx* as Korsch's definitive work, or as his "masterpiece."[111] Moreover, I believe that Buckmiller is wrong in claiming, "Korsch's struggle with Marxism expresses itself especially in this book."[112] Rather, Korsch's critique of Marxism is better expressed in the series of essays collected in this anthology.[113] *Karl Marx*, in this sense, is non-representative of Korsch's later work, for it suppresses Korsch's radical critique of Marxism. *Karl Marx* is, and was intended to be, a popularization of Marxism that would exposit and defend the Marxist teaching for a wide audience.[114] As such, it is eminently successful and provides an excellent summary and overview of the Marxian teaching on "Society," "Political Economy," and "History."[115] But it is in no way as critical of Marxism as many of Korsch's essays from the period. The truth of the Marxian theory is assumed and defended throughout, as is its superiority to all bourgeois theories. Throughout *Karl Marx* there are laudatory passages like the following: "Marx's new socialist and proletarian science, which, in a changed historical situation, further developed the revolutionary theory of the classical founders of the doctrine of society, is the genuine social science of our time."[116] Or, Marxism "was far and away in advance of the other contemporary schools of social thought. It remains superior to all other social theories even now, in spite of the comparatively negligible progress which Marxists have in the meantime made in the formal development of the methods discovered by Marx and Engels. In a partly philosophical form, it has yet achieved a great number of important scientific results which hold good to this day."[117]

Hence, although the Korsch expert can sometimes read between the lines of *Karl Marx* "Korsch's struggle with Marxism," on the whole one finds a sympathetic and systematic defense of the Marxian theory. For example, in *Karl Marx*, Korsch does not question the Marxian theory of revolution, which he so penetratingly challenges in many of his other works. None of the critiques that I discuss in the introductory material are developed in *Karl Marx*, and Korsch generally cites the major Marxist texts as gospel. Even Lenin's essay, *Left-wing Communism—An Infantile Disease*," whose positions Korsch usually attacked, is favorably cited in *Karl Marx* (its non-critical insertion here drove Paul Mattick to a sharp critique).[118] It is true that Korsch generally develops a critical, dialectical version of Marxism in *Karl Marx* that is certainly superior to the Social Democratic and Communist orthodoxies, but there is no critique of Marxism of the sort that distinguishes the most challenging and stimulating work of the later Korsch.

On the other hand, not only *Karl Marx* but the overwhelming bulk of Korsch's later work refutes the judgment that Korsch abandoned Marxism.[119] Although Korsch radically questioned aspects of the Marxian political theory and theory of revolution, he never abandoned his commitment to the liberation of the working class and to the Marxian belief that the working class and its struggles are the motor and telos of our history and the vehicle of social change. Hence, Korsch never surrendered the Marxian position that the overthrow of capitalism and construction of socialism is the main task on the historical agenda. Korsch's friend and student, Heinz Langerhans, is on the right track when he claims that "the proletariat is the empirical foundation of Korsch's theory," and that "Korsch never discussed 'Marxism' through the omission of the authentic point-of-reference 'proletariat,' and to be sure proletariat as an active power."[120] For Korsch, in Langerhans' words, "the activity of the revolutionary proletariat as the empirical foundation of Marxism" remained the crucial pivot around which his own theory revolved. Korsch never abandoned a practical concern with the liberation of the working class, and continuously stressed the role of revolutionary practice in social change. As Langerhans notes, "this activistic component is the decisive characteristic of Korsch's theoretical efforts and his position within the communist movement right up until his death."[121]

To the end of his life, Korsch championed a "non-dogmatic Marxism," and the main source of his later despair was the belief that a defeated and enslaved working class could not realize the Marxian theory in a non-revolutionary era dominated by the counterrevolution. A new period of revolutionary struggles, however, would awaken interest in the Marxian theory and enable Marxism to arise again as a politically relevant historical force. This began happening in the so-called Third World with the national liberation movements, and Korsch welcomed these movements as providing a possible rebirth of revolutionary theory and new possibilities for revolutionary practice.[122] Indeed, Korsch had been keenly aware of this phenomenon since the 1920's and his group

Kommunistische Politik and later Mattick's group and journal published many articles on China and other revolutionary struggles in the Third World.[123]

In posing the question of whether Korsch abandoned Marxism it is significant to note that the project he was working on in the mid-1950's when he contracted sclerosis was a manuscript called "The Time of Abolitions," which attempted to take up a problematic that was central to the Marxist theory, but which had never been adequately developed. His wife Hedda writes: "He thought that as capitalist society had developed since Marx's time, Marxism too should have developed to understand it. His uncompleted text, the 'Manuscript of Abolitions,' is an attempt to develop a Marxist theory of historical development in terms of the future abolition of the divisions that constitute our society—such as the divisions between different classes, between town and country, between mental and physical labor."[124]

Korsch thought Marxism through to the end and lived through a period of history that put Marxism in radical question. Korsch himself never reached a final verdict on the present status and future fate of Marxism, and the movement of history has not yet put us in a position to write the final obituary or elegy to Marxism. It is our lot, as it was Korsch's, to live through a period of revolution and counterrevolution where the outcome is uncertain and the role of Marxism in this scenario is vital but problematical. Bertolt Brecht, who studied with Korsch, well understood the predicament of his former teacher. Walter Benjamin reports: "Yesterday after playing chess Brecht said: 'You know, when Korsch comes, we really ought to work out a new game with him. A game in which the moves do not always stay the same; where the function of each piece changes after it has stood in the same square for a while.' "[125] Korsch helps us to understand the changing moves of the game of revolution and counterrevolution in our time, but does not—no one does!—give us the rules, the strategy for winning, or the probable outcome.

Korsch in Exile

Korsch's years of exile in England, Denmark, and the United States are generally tragic and depressing. Forced to emigrate from Germany at Hitler's rise to power, Korsch went to England where he began work on *Karl Marx*. He found a generally cold reception there and was involved in the inevitable emigré politics and one sordid scandal.[126] He found moments of refuge and stimulating conditions for work in his visits with Brecht, who was living in Denmark. In travels throughout Europe before the outbreak of the second World War he attempted to maintain contact with leading left-oppositionalist figures and groups. But for the most part Korsch was cut off from contact with the revolutionary movement with which he had been so deeply involved.

In 1936 Korsch emigrated to America, where he was to remain for the rest of his life, outside of brief trips to Europe and Mexico. In America he was almost totally isolated from the revolutionary politics to which he had dedicated his life. He was never able to find satisfactory employment in America and was never able to carry through any of several major works which he outlined. He traveled widely, had contacts with many American intellectuals, European emigrés, and small working class groups, but was never able to find any adequate institutional arrangements or political involvement. He applied repeatedly for university appointments or financial support from American foundations, but was only able to receive infrequent visiting appointments, on the assistant professor level, at American universities (although he had been a full professor in Germany in the early 1920's). We have noted his general evaluation of America and the lack of a revolutionary movement with which he could get involved.

The main source of information on Korsch's exile period is his letters, which disclose his continuing interest in Marxist theory and practice. A letter to Paul Mattick, translated in this anthology, sheds light on the complex relation between Korsch and the Institute for Social Research.[127] Korsch, we recall, was the teacher and friend of Felix Weil who financed the Institute, and who purportedly wanted Korsch to head the Institute.[128] Korsch's students were active in the Institute while it was centered in Frankfurt, and Korsch frequently published in the Institute's journal. A growing strain evolved between Korsch and the Institute during the exile period, probably on account of Korsch's more orthodox— and political—version of Marxism. This tension is expressed in Korsch's pejorative evaluation of the Institute and its leading personalities in the letter to Mattick.[129] This tension explains why collaboration between Korsch and the Institute was unlikely to produce any positive results, and in fact Korsch seemed to have very little productive contact with the Institute thereafter.

Korsch did, however, remain in contact with Brecht, who provides an interesting picture of Korsch in America in his *Arbeitsjournal*: "Caught Korsch again who must leave the day after tomorrow. He has become heavier and speaks somewhat more in footnotes. He has really changed in personality (*typ*). He was always strong, was, however, rather thin, and had these deep blue eyes beneath the dark brown. He is now industrious, robust, the eyes are smaller, almost cunning. He lives from the $100 of the Institute and works on his essays. That is unchanged, he says he poeticizes (*dichtet*) his science, while I make my poems like a shoemaker makes shoes. At the moment, he is interested in Geopolitics."[130]

A remarkable letter from Korsch to Brecht fleshes out Korsch's 1940's perspectives.[131] Korsch's expulsion from the world revolutionary movement seems to have elevated him to an increasingly Olympian perspective. This drive to grasp the dynamics of the totality of world history, of the world-historical totality, is expressed in Korsch's report to Brecht on "The Present Situation and Perspectives." Korsch tells how he broke off his studies of the Phillipines and the struggles between the new colonialism and national liberation movements to grasp the dynamics of a "new era of regression on a world-wide scale." Korsch saw new tendencies of intellectual retrogression and new forms of imperialist barbarism that led him to a comparison with the decline of the Roman empire. Striking is his desire to grasp the dynamics of the whole process of history from the "century of Marx" (1848–1948) to the present day. Indicative of Korsch's historicism is his desire to grasp the interconnections between the theoretical dimensions of Marxism and its historical context, focusing on those "practical challenges" which led to a disintegration as well as a development of the Marxian theory. Korsch indicates to Brecht how the Cold War and the emerging spectre of "Yankee imperialism" has forced him to re-evaluate his position on the Soviet Union. He concludes with some cryptic remarks on the emerging "new world order."

It appears from Korsch's letters that his moods changed from deeply pessimistic and depressive to relatively cheerful.[132] He traveled around America a lot and continually sought contacts with political groups, maintaining a sharp interest in the political events of the day. In a 1948 letter to an Australian leftist journal, included in this anthology, he indicated his willingness to contribute articles and notes his plans to write a book that will "trace both the final results of the 'Marxist' era of the workers' movement to the original *theory and practice* of Marx: (1) before, during, and after 1848; (2) during the period of the Working Man's International Association in the 1860's."[133] He also indicated an interest in Bakunin and enclosed an article on the Paris commune which he says, "might interest people who have not freed themselves from the Marx-Lenin-Trotsky legend to the same extent as you or I might claim it for ourselves."[134]

The last document in the anthology is a letter to Erich Gerlach, with an additional note to Ruth Fisher. It shows both Korsch's attempt to make contact with the American working-class movement, and a desire to restore the "ideas of Marx."[135] Korsch, we see, never abandoned his interest in Marxism and was vitally concerned with the theory and practice of revolution right up until an attack of sclerosis ended his theoretical labors. Korsch spent his last years in McLean's Psychiatric Hospital and died in Belmont, Massachusetts, on October 21, 1961.

Korsch was in a sense ahead of his times. His version of critical Marxism that challenged Social Democratic and Communist orthodoxies and his search for new possibilities and forms of revolutionary change found an eager audience in the New Left throughout the world in the 1960's.[136] New Korsch translations and anthologies have recently appeared in every major European language, and there is a proliferating amount of literature discussing and appraising Korsch's work. Korsch-discussions in English-speaking countries have been hampered, however, by the inaccessibility of some of his most important texts which have not been translated, and/or lie buried in obscure, now defunct, journals. Moreover, there has been a general unfamiliarity with the Korschian opus as a whole and the historical circumstances within which his work was produced. The present introduction and anthology attempts to alleviate this condition, and to provide the necessary prerequisites for a critical Korsch reception in the English-speaking world, challenging us to discern "what is living and dead" in both Marxism and Korsch. My introduction has traced the complex development of Korsch's life and work, and has shown the need for a historical-theoretical reconstruction of the Korschian work, as well as the need for a critical reception that applies the same critical standards to Korsch that he applied to other thinkers, especially the Marxists. Korsch in an especially interesting way was connected with one of the most fateful political and intellectual dramas of our time, and his odyssey as a critical Marxist through the forlorn terrain of the working-class movement helps us to come to terms with a crucial segment of modern history. Korsch's adventures with Marxism have produced a body of work that continues to challenge and stimulate our own critical thinking and to this end the anthology is dedicated.

Notes

1. A series of articles on trade unions and wage-price controls were collected in a pamphlet, *Um die Tariffähigkeit* (Berlin: Prager, 1928).
2. Karl Korsch, *Um die Tariffähigkeit*, p. 5.

3. It is going too far, however, to claim that Korsch ever believed there was a mystical identity between his theory and existing political practice, as Adorno implies in making Korsch, along with Soviet Marxism (!), examples of "identity theory"; see T. W. Adorno, *Negative Dialektik* (Frankfurt: Suhrkamp, 1966), p. 144. The sentence equating Korsch and Diamat with Marxist identity theory was strangely omitted from the English translation of Adorno's book.

4. See above, "Korsch's Revolutionary Marxism," and "Fundamentals of Socialization."

5. Karl Korsch, *Die materialistische Geschichtsauffassung, "Eine Auseinandersetzung mit Karl Kautsky."* A fine discussion of Korsch's critique of Kautsky is found in Leonardo Ceppa, "Korsch's Marxism," *Telos* 26 (Winter 1975–1976): 88ff.

6. Actually, Rosa Luxemburg saw this as early as her *Social Reform or Revolution* in 1899. The same point was also developed by Lukács in "Bernstein's Revenge," in *Tactics and Ethics* (New York: Harper and Row, 1973).

7. Korsch, *Die materialistische Geschichtsauffassung*, pp. 4–5.

8. Ibid., p. 6.

9. Ibid., p. 130.

10. Korsch, *Marxism and Philosophy*, pp. 98–99. Korsch had alluded to the kinship of Lenin and Kautsky as representatives of the "Marxist center" in the *Anti-Kautsky*, p. 80.

11. Korsch, *Marxism and Philosophy*, p. 129.

12. Ibid., p. 109.

13. Ibid., p. 110.

14. Karl Korsch, "The Passing of Marxism Orthodoxy," *International Council Correspondence* 3, no. 11–2 (December 1937); also in this anthology.

15. Ibid.

16. Ibid.

17. Korsch, "The History of the Marxist Ideology in Russia," *Living Marxism* 4, no. 2 (March 1938): 44–50; also in this anthology.

18. Ibid.

19. Ibid.

20. Karl Korsch, "The Crisis of Marxism," unpublished manuscript, in this anthology.

21. Ibid.

22. Ibid.

23. Karl Korsch, "Uber einige grundsätzliche Voraussetzungen für eine materialistische Diskussion der Krisistheorie," *Proletarier* 1, no. 1 (February 1933): 20–25, translated in this anthology as "On Some Fundamental Presuppositions for a Materialist Discussion of Crisis Theory," by Karl-Heinz Otto and Andrew Giles-Peters.

24. Korsch, "The Crisis of Marxism."

25. Ibid.

26. Ibid.

27. Karl Korsch, "Ten Theses on Marxism Today," unpublished lecture, in this anthology.

28. See Karl Marx, *The Civil War in France*, in Robert Tucker, ed., *The Marx-Engels Reader* (New York: Norton, 1972), discussed by Korsch in "Revolutionäre Kommune," *Die Aktion* 19, nos. 5–8 (September 1929): 176–181, and *Die Aktion* 21, nos. 3–4 (July 1931): 60–64, translated in this anthology as "Revolutionary Commune" by Karl-Heinz Otto and Andrew Giles-Peters.

29. Karl Korsch, "Das Problem der Staatseinheit-Föderalismus in der Französischen Revolution," *Grünberg-Archiv* 15 (1930): 126–146. Here it should be noted that, although Korsch saw a certain sort of decentralization constituted by a workers' councils system as providing a corrective to an overly bureaucratized centralism, he never took the anarcho-syndicalist-federalist position, because he always believed that a complex socialist economy required state intervention and a central plan to regulate the production and distribution of goods.

30. See Marx's theory of the two stages in *Critique of the Gotha Program*, in Tucker, *Marx-Engels Reader*, which was favorably discussed by Korsch in a 1922 edition to which he wrote an introduction; compare his terse critique in "Ten Theses on Marxism Today."

31. See Lenin's *One Step Forward, Two Steps Back*, in *Selected Works* (New York: International Publishers, 1971), vol. 3, for an analysis of the Blanquian roots of Social Democracy; perhaps Korsch is applying this analysis to Marxism as a whole. Walter Benjamin compares Marx and Blanqui in the last part of his "Arcades" project; here it is interesting to note that Korsch and Benjamin were guests of Brecht at the same time in Denmark in 1935.

32. Karl Korsch, "Theses on Hegel and Revolution," in "A Non-Dogmatic Approach to Marxism," *Politics* 3 no. 5 (May 1946): 8–11, and in this anthology.

33. Karl Korsch, "Marx' Stellung in der europäischen Revolution von 1848," in *Politische Texte*, p. 374.

34. Ibid., p. 377.

35. Karl Korsch, "Marxism and the Present Tasks of the Proletarian Class Struggle," *Living Marxism* 4, no. 4 (August 1938): 115–119, and in this anthology.

36. Ibid.

37. Korsch, "Revolutionary Commune."

38. Ibid.

39. For more detailed information on the Spanish collectives, see Sam Dolgoff, ed., *The Anarchist Collectives* (New York: Free Life Press, 1974). For accounts of the Spanish Civil War, see Franz Borkenau, *The Spanish Cockpit* (London: Faber and Faber, 1962); Pierre Broue and Emile Temine, *Revolution and the War in Spain* (Cambridge: MIT Press, 1972); and, of

course, George Orwell, *Homage to Catalonia* (New York: Harcourt, Brace and World, 1953).

40. Karl Korsch, "The Pre-history of the Spanish Revolution," in *Politische Texte*, p. 243.

41. Ibid.

42. Karl Korsch, "Die Spanische Revolution," *Die Neue Rundschau* 42, no. 9 (September 1931): 284–302, translated in this anthology as "The Spanish Revolution" by Karl-Heinz Otto, Andrew Giles-Peters, and Heinz Peters.

43. Karl Korsch, "Economics and Politics in Revolutionary Spain," *Living Marxism* 4, no. 3 (May 1938): 76–82, and in this anthology.

44. Ibid.

45. For a discussion of Korsch's principle of historical specificity, see *Karl Marx*. I discuss the principle in the introduction to "Korsch and Marxism."

46. Karl Korsch, "Collectivization in Spain," *Living Marxism* 4, no. 6 (April 1939): 178–182.

47. Ibid.

48. Ibid.

49. Ibid.

50. Korsch, "Thesen zur Kritik des Faschistischen Staatsbegriffs," *Gegner* 7, no. 4–5 (March 1932): 20, translated in this anthology as "Theses Toward a Critique of the Fascist Concept of the State" by Karl-Heinz Otto and Andrew Giles-Peters.

51. See Hedda Korsch, "Memories," p. 44, for details of Korsch's attempt to organize anti-Nazi resistance in 1933.

52. Karl Korsch, "State and Counterrevolution," *Modern Quarterly* 11, no. 2 (Winter 1939): 60–67, also in this anthology.

53. Ibid.

54. Ibid.

55. Ibid.

56. Ibid.

57. Ibid.

58. Ibid.

59. Karl Korsch, "Fascist Counterrevolution," *Living Marxism* 5, no. 2 (Fall 1940): 29–37, also in this anthology.

60. Korsch's despair is evident in his letters to his more optimistic friend Paul Partos; see *Jahrbuch Arbeiterbewegung* 2, pp. 218–219, 222, and 225–226.

61. Korsch, "Fascist Counterrevolution."

62. Karl Korsch, "The Fight for Britain, the Fight for Democracy, and the War Aims of the Working Class," in *Living Marxism* 5, no. 4 (Spring 1941): 1–6.

63. Korsch, "Fascist Counterrevolution."

64. Ibid.

65. Karl Korsch, "The Workers Fight against Fascism," *Living Marxism* 5, no. 3 (Winter 1941): 36–49, also in this anthology.

66. Korsch, "Fascist Counterrevolution."

67. Korsch, "Workers Fight against Fascism."

68. Korsch, "Fascist Counterrevolution."

69. For a discussion of Korsch's relationship with the Frankfurt School members and their Institute for Social Research, see "Korsch's Revolutionary Marxism," and the letter to Paul Mattick in this anthology.

70. Karl Korsch, "On American Science," from a letter to Paul Partos, end of July, 1939, in *Jahrbuch Arbeiterbewegung* 2, pp. 227ff. Paul Partos (1911–1964) was Hungarian by birth and studied with Korsch in Berlin in the 1920's; he seems to have been one of Korsch's closest and most intelligent students. Partos emigrated to Paris in 1933 and participated in many anti-fascist groups. He fought in the Spanish Civil War and emigrated to England in 1939.

71. Korsch, "On American Science," p. 227.

72. Ibid., p. 229.

73. Ibid.

74. Ibid.

75. Korsch to Partos, July 26–29, 1939, in *Jahrbuch Arbeiterbewegung* 2, p. 225.

76. Ibid.

77. Ibid., p. 226.

78. Ibid.

79. Korsch to Brecht, July 31, 1939, in *Jahrbuch Arbeiterbewegung* 2, p. 233.

80. Korsch to Partos, July 26–29, 1939, p. 226.

81. Ibid., p. 227.

82. Korsch to Brecht, July 31, 1939, p. 233.

83. See Korsch's later essays, "War and Revolution," "The World Historians," "Notes on History," and "A Historical View of Geopolitics."

84. See Korsch's essays, "The Law of Casualty and Its Limits" and "Mathematical Constructs in Psychology and Sociology," and his 1930 lecture, "Albert Einstein." These themes are discussed in Gian Rusconi's "Dialectik in pragmatischer Anwendung," in Pozolli, *Uber Karl Korsch*.

85. See Korsch's letters to Partos for critiques for positivist doctrines, in *Jahrbuch Arbeiterbewegung* 2, pp. 219, 223–224, and 230–232.

86. Karl Korsch, *Karl Marx* (London: Chapman and Hall, 1938).

87. Ibid.

88. Korsch, *Marxism and Philosophy*, pp. 126ff.

89. See my discussion in the introduction to "Korsch and Marxism" for an elaboration of this theme.

90. Karl Korsch, "Der Empirismus in der Hegelschen Philosophie" (1931 lecture, discussed in Rusconi, "Dialectik"); "The Marxist Philosophy and the

Sciences" (a review of Haldane's book in *Living Marxism* 5, no. 1 [Spring 1940]: 59–61) ; and *Karl Marx.*

91. Korsch to Paul Mattick, May 10, 1935, in *Jahrbuch Arbeiterbewegung 2*, p. 138. Paul Mattick was a member of the extreme left party, the KAPD, in Germany during the early 1920's, and emigrated to the United States in 1926. He worked in Chicago with offshoots of the IWW, and in the 1930's organized an international Communist group that published their views in *International Councils Correspondence* (later *Living Marxism* and *New Essays*) to which Korsch was a frequent contributor. Later Mattick published *Marx and Keynes* and many books and articles. See Mattick's essay "The Marxism of Karl Korsch" in *Survey* (London), no. 53 (1964), pp. 86–87.

92. Korsch to Mattick, May 10, 1935, p. 139.

93. Ibid., p. 137.

94. Ibid., p. 137. In a letter to Paul Partos, December 16–17, 1935, in *Jahrbuch Arbeiterbewegung 2*, pp. 169–170, Korsch argues that "fetishism" is a more useful concept than "reification" and explains his preference: "You still always use the Lukácsian concept of 'reification.' Now to be sure Marx in fact occasionally speaks of a 'thinglike disguise' and a 'thingification' (*Versachlichung*) of the social character of production. But the expression 'fetishism' is infinitely better for materialist and sociological conception and description of this form of thought. With Lukács, who extends the use of this concept without measure, it is at bottom a matter of a protest of a 'philosophy of life' against the cold, rigid, fixed factual and material world. . . . 'Fetish' is in its very form a sociological category. Further, it expresses what is really taking place in reality: the transference of human social powers to things, of the production of currently living labor to accumulated dead labor of the past as capital." Actually, Korsch's definition of fetishism here is compatible with Lukács' notion of reification. See George Lukács, "Reification and the Consciousness of the Proletariat," in his *History and Class Consciousness* (London: Merlin Press, 1971).

95. Korsch to Mattick, May 10, 1935, pp. 142–143.

96. Ibid., p. 142.

97. Ibid., p. 149.

98. Ibid., p. 143.

99. Ibid., p. 150. See further, Korsch, "Why I am a Marxist," p. 69.

100. Korsch to Mattick, December 12, 1938, in *Jahrbuch Arbeiterbewegung 2*, pp. 195–196.

101. Herbert Marcuse, radio broadcast in West Germany, Saarländischen Rundfunks, from October 8, 1973, "Brecht im Exil." Further, see T. W. Adorno, *Vorlesung zur Einleitung in die Soziologie* (Frankfurt: Junius-Drucke, 1973), p. 37.

102. The distinction is made by Marx in the introduction to *Capital*. See the articles by Leonardo Ceppa, "Korsch's Marxism," and Furio Cerutti,

"Hegel, Lukács, and Korsch," both in *Telos* 26 (Winter 1975–1976), for criticisms of Korsch's failure to develop this distinction.

103. Here one might compare Korsch's position toward science with that of Horkheimer and Adorno in *Dialectic of Enlightenment* (New York: Seabury, 1972), Horkheimer in *Eclipse of Reason* (New York: Seabury, 1973), and Marcuse in *One-Dimensional Man* (Boston: Beacon, 1964).

104. Korsch to Partos, June 12, 1939, in *Jahrbuch Arbeiterbewegung 2*, pp. 160–162. This is an extremely interesting letter full of illuminating insights.

105. Korsch, "A Non-dogmatic Approach to Marxism."

106. Ibid.

107. Korsch to Partos, June 12, 1939, p. 161.

108. "Positivism" was always a perjorative term for Korsch which he, like the Frankfurt school, juxtaposed as the polar opposite to dialectical Marxism. See his letter to J. A. Dawson (in this anthology), where he negatively refers to Popper's "positivism." For a discussion of those advocates of "scientific Marxism" who take Korsch as an ally, see Giacomo Marramao, "Korsch in Italy," *Telos* 26 (Winter 1975–1976).

109. See his critiques of Hegel in *Marxism and Philosophy* and *Karl Marx*. I might note that Korsch's critique/appropriation of Hegel is remarkably complicated and would require a long study to adequately sort out and fully develop. Especially interesting in this regard is his unpublished lecture "Der Empirismus in der Hegelschen Philosophie" and the essay "The Old Hegelian Dialectic and the New Materialist Science," *International Council Correspondence* 3, nos. 9–10 (October 1932): 16–21.

110. See Korsch's letter to Paul Mattick, March 27, 1939, *Jahrbuch Arbeiterbewegung 2*, p. 210, where he writes about Hegel: "It is really a shame that the nonsense, overcome by the bourgeoisie, of a genuinely 'German' mystic from a hundred years ago, who at best mirrored the experience of the great *bourgeois* revolutions from 1789 to 1830 in a *distorted form*, is still today hindering again the activity of the workers and their thoughts."

111. Ceppa, "Korsch's Marxism," p. 107.

112. Buckmiller, "Marxismus," p. 82.

113. I develop this point in the introduction to "The Crisis of Marxism."

114. See Korsch's letters to Mattick (May 10, 1935, and August 29, 1935) and Partos (January 19, 1939) where he makes this point, pp. 135, 153, and 202. Here I might note that the German edition of *Karl Marx*, ed. Gotz Langkau (Frankfurt: Europaische Verlag, 1967), contains material from the original German manuscript that was not published in the English edition.

115. A Review of *Karl Marx* in the *Sociological Review* in 1939 referred to the book as "the Marx study most solidly close to the actual teachings of Marx . . . and invaluable help in finding out about Marx, the real Marx as distinct from the figment his disciples made of his doctrine"; cited approvingly

by Erich Gerlach in "Karl Korsch's Undogmatic Marxism," *International Socialism* (London), no. 19 (1964), no. 22.

116. Korsch, *Karl Marx*, p. 23.

117. Ibid., p. 231.

118. In a letter responding to Mattick (May 10, 1935), Korsch concedes, "With Lenin, it would be in fact better *never* to cite his 'infantile disease' essay without some kind of fundamental critical reservation. It was in fact in its content, function, and intention a basically counterrevolutionary work" (p. 193).

119. The orthodox Communist position on Korsch from the 1920's to the present day is that Korsch is a renegade who is anti-Marxist to the core. For an example of the stupidity of this point of view, see Richard Albrecht, "Die gegenwärtige Korsch-Renaissance in der BRD und Westberlin," *Sozialistische Politik* 5, no. 22 (February 1973): 49ff. Ceppa in "Korsch's Marxism," p. 118, concludes (wrongly) that "few doubts remain as to Korsch's total rejection of the Marxian perspective." I hope here to demonstrate the groundlessness of this position.

120. "Revolution und Konterrevolution: Eine Diskussion mit Heinz Langerhans," in Pozolli, *Uber Karl Korsch*, p. 273.

121. Ibid.

122. See my discussion of Korsch and the third world in the Introduction to "Models of Revolutionary Struggle."

123. See "Die Chinesische Revolution," in *Politische Texte*.

124. Hedda Korsch, "Memories," p. 45.

125. Walter Benjamin, *Understanding Brecht* (London: New Left Books, 1973).

126. A woman, Doris Fabian, who was involved with Korsch, committed suicide and Korsch was accused of being responsible. See his disclaimer in a letter to a "comrade Balabanow," August 1, 1935, where he defends himself. *Jahrbuch Arbeiterbewegung* 2, pp. 154–157.

127. Karl Korsch, "Letter to Paul Mattick," November 20, 1938, translated in this anthology.

128. See "Korsch's Revolutionary Marxism."

129. One might compare Brecht's equally negative opinion of "the gentlemen from the Institute," expressed throughout his *Arbeitsjournal* (Berlin: Suhrkamp, 1973).

130. Brecht, *Arbeitsjournal*, p. 280.

131. Karl Korsch, "Letter to Brecht," April 18, 1947, *Alternative* 105, no. 18 (December 1975): 253–257, translated in this anthology by Mark Ritter.

132. The sources here are Korsch's letters in *Jahrbuch Arbeiterbewegung* 2, pp. 175–235, passim.

133. Karl Korsch, "Letter to J. A. Dawson," May 3, 1948, in this anthology.

134. Ibid.

135. Karl Korsch, "Letter to Erich Gerlach," December 16, 1956, translated in this anthology.

136. For a discussion of the Korsch reception in Europe, see Buckmiller, "Marxismus," and Nick Xenos, "Introduction to Korsch," *Telos* 26 (Winter 1975–1976). Giacomo Marramao discusses the Korsch reception in Italy in *Telos* 26, and Paul Piccone discusses "Korsch in Spain" in *New German Critique* 6 (Winter 1975).

Political Writings of Karl Korsch

4. Marxism and Socialization

Introduction

Korsch's first important essays attempt to grasp the essential features, first, of socialization and, then, of revolutionary Marxism. Korsch's essay "What Is Socialization" is described by his friend and later editor Erich Gerlach as "the first and most important of Korsch's writings on workers' councils."[1] It was written in January, 1919, and was published in March as a brochure by a left-wing Hannover publisher.[2] Korsch argues in clear and terse prose, divided into concise, topical sections that in order to realize the radical goals of socialist theory not only the nationalization of the means of production but a total reorganization of society is necessary. His position contains a radical critique of the dominant views of socialization maintained by the leading Social Democratic "theoreticians" of the Second International. His primary target is Bernstein's idea of attempting gradually to socialize the existing capitalist society through "social politics." Bernstein advocated public control and regulation (but not ownership) of industry through laws and political measures. He maintained that "more socialization can be inserted in a good factory law than in the nationalization of a hundred or so businesses and enterprises."[3] Envisaged was a gradual transition from private property to public property and increasingly public control of the economy. This process would proceed gradually step-by-step (*Schrittweise*: a favorite word of Bernstein's) and would proceed by legal means.[4] Bernstein argued that the disarray of the German economy after World War I necessitated that socialization proceed slowly and cautiously: "Before the War, Germany was, taken as a whole, a rich land. Today, after the War, it is a poor land, compelled to the sort of economic policy that poor countries carry out. That is also a reason why we must proceed with socialization carefully."[5]

Against Bernstein's notion of evolutionary socialism, Korsch urges a concept of revolutionary socialism. "*Social politics*," he argues "can never change into a true socialization without a radical break and change in direction."[6] Moreover, Korsch firmly maintains that there can be no socialization of the means of production without "the *complete* elimination of the private property owner from the social process of production."[7] Korsch is criticizing here the central political concept of the Second International for whom "socialization" became the key to their program and practice. He noted that the term "socialization" was first used by Eugen Dühring in his 1875 "Cursus der Philosophie."[8] The term found its way into the Erfurt Program and became a central concept of Bernstein, Kautsky, the Fabians, the Austrian Marxists, and others. Korsch believed that their conceptions of socialization were but a series of "half-measures" which failed to provide a truly socialized society with new relations of production. He argued that such Social Democratic conceptions as a more equitable distribution of property or power, the breaking up of monopolies and large estates, Kautsky's idea that land should be nationalized and the plants existing on it should be leased from the state, profit sharing and workers' participation within the framework of the existing system—all these pet projects of the Second International were but "partial payments at best" that were often "directly opposed to the true interests of the working class moving toward emancipation."[9]

Not only did Korsch urge against Social Democratic thinkers the complete elimination of the capitalist private property owner from the financial exploitation and control of the economy and social-political life, but he also argued that genuine socialization involved new social relations of production. For Korsch, the construction of socialism required that the public rather than private enterprise would profit from and control the socioeconomic life of a country. This meant for Korsch both that public property must replace private property (the complete elimination of the capitalist from the production process) and that new social relations among producers, and between workers and society as a whole, must be created to ensure the liberation of labor, the abolition of domination and hierarchy, and the development of a truly socialized economy and public.

Korsch wrote in 1919–1920 a series of articles in which he attempted to provide a synthesis of current competing concepts of socialization whose deficiencies and one-sidedness would be overcome. More precisely, he wished to develop a concept of socialization which would mediate/synthesize those concepts that equated socialization with nationalization (and understood socialization as a technical-political task administered from above), and those syndicalist concepts which understood socialization in mainly economic terms as the autonomous self-activity of the workers freed from bureaucracy, hierarchy, exploitation, and alienated labor. "Syndicalism," Korsch believed, "contains the important insight that the crux of the revolutionary struggle for socialization does not lie in the state-political domain but in the economic realm: that monopoly of trade, nationalization of production, communal socialism and the other 'political means' are not themselves alone adequate to 'improve the

lot of the worker, to elevate its spirit, and to increase its joy in work.'
Further, the syndicalists see that successful socialization will first come
into being in a sense adequate to the working and productive class, when
the workers have become fully authorized participants in production on
the way to direct socialization."[10] The syndicalists grasped, Korsch believed, that no purely political means would bring about the "liberation
of the working class from capitalist exploitation."[11] But one must avoid,
he warned, "regressing into anarchist foolishness" and anti-authoritarian-
ism.[12] Socialism requires the full development of the productive forces
and this means full scale industrialization and the use of "mechanical
heavy industry." Factories, machines, and heavy industry require, as
Lenin saw, a certain amount of organization, authority, and "the continuing subordination of the workers under the unitary will of the direction."[13] But a process of "industrial democracy" will ensure that the old
hierarchy and domination of capitalism are not reintroduced in the
socialist relations of production: "who carries out this function and for
how long is decided by the workers' democracy of the socialist society, in
business assemblies which have a place in the factory and in the system
of industrial workers' councils, structured from the bottom up; it is decided with complete freedom and with the right to change the decisions
which have been made at any time."[14]

In a relentlessly dialectical fashion, Korsch attempted to mediate the
contradictions between nationalization and syndicalist concepts, between
the universal interests of the general public and particular interests of different units of production, between objective-technical-economic interests
in efficiency and productivity and subjective-humanistic interests in the
liberation of labor, and between intellectual and physical labor. The workers' council system was the key to a successful synthesis, Korsch believed,
which would at once make possible (1) more efficient economic production and (2) the liberation of labor. With this concept Korsch could
answer the charges both that socialism would lead to inefficiency, lower
productivity, and waste, or that it would lead to bureaucratic or state
domination and thus a decrease in freedom. Korsch argued that if one
took the positive contribution from nationalization projects and syndicalism and rejected their deficiencies then one could create a democratic
socialism that could achieve both an efficient reorganization of the economy and the liberation of labor.

While writing his essays on socialization, Korsch began more inten-
sively studying Marxism. "What is Socialization?" shows but a perfunc-
tory grasp of the Marxist critique of political economy and contains few
actual references to Marxist texts and concepts. In "Fundamentals of So-

cialization" Korsch's turn to Marxism is visible. Indeed, he specifically defines himself as an "inheritor of Marx and Engels," clearly identifying himself for the first time as a Marxist.[15] Evident in this essay is Korsch's activistic concept of Marxism where the primary emphasis is on the unity of theory and revolutionary practice: "The contradiction between the further developing forces of production and the traditional relations of production, together with their superstructure, creates only the material pre-conditions for the solution of a *'task'* which is to be recognized as solvable and is solved solely through revolutionary practice. The new scientific world-view first fulfills itself in this unification of theory and practice. In it Marx's fiery soul has smelted together the act-shy (*Tatfremde*) knowledge of the old sciences of society and the knowledge-shy (*Erkenntnisfremden*) will to act (*Tatwillen*) of utopianism into the *identity of objectifying knowledge and activity.*"[16]

Korsch's practical socialism here takes the form of a theory of socialist revolution. He poses himself the problem of explaining the fact "that a large number of still valuable remarks are to be found in the works of Marx and Engels which are concerned with the transformation of socialism into practical reality, and therefore with socialization, but yet the entire later Marxian literature contributed nothing essential to the advancement of these practical problems until right up into the war years."[17] What is needed, Korsch believes, is both a clear vision of socialism (the goal) and "concepts of action" (the means) that will make possible the realization of socialism.

Korsch wrote in the early 1920's a series of studies which attempted to restore the revolutionary core of the Marxist teaching so as to bring back to life the revolutionary force of Marxism which had been surpressed by Social Democratic orthodoxy. The context of Korsch's feverish study/appropriation of Marxism was his enthusiasm for the construction of socialism in the Soviet Union and Leninism, coupled with his work in the German Communist party, in which he daily confronted the vicissitudes of an explosive period of class struggle in Germany. His first thorough study of Marxism found characteristic expression in an essay "Quintessenz des Marxismus," which was an attempt to clearly define the basic ideas of Marxism.[18] It contained a series of questions and answers (modeled on Engels' "Principles of Communism"), and focused on the "economic teaching of Marxism." Korsch saw Marxism as a theory of class struggle which contained "a) the teaching of the goals of communism and the means to reach these goals; b) the scientific insight into the necessity of these goals and means."[19] The necessity of Marxism resulted from the increasingly intense struggles in the last hundred years between the working class and the bourgeoisie, fueled by the fundamental contradiction between capital and labor. At present, "for the realization of communism only the complete carrying out of the organization of the proletariat as a class capable of social and political action is still lacking."[20]

Marxism for Korsch was thus a theory of class struggle and revolution that provided an analysis of the contradictions of capitalism and the theory and strategy of socialist revolution. The task of the proletariat was to gain economic and ideological maturity through participation in class struggle and the study and realization of Marxism. Korsch's own project unfolded in this framework in the coming years.

Korsch developed his appropriation of the Marxian theory in a series of studies that prepared the basis for *Marxism and Philosophy*,[21] and in a series of essays that combatted bourgeois attacks on and distortions of Marxism and what Korsch considered misleading interpretations within the working class movement itself.[22] In the series of essays that attempted to clearly present the essence of Marxism, Korsch repeatedly argued that the materialist dialectic is the basis of Marxism. Two of these essays, "The Marxist Dialectic" and "On Materialist Dialectic," are included in this anthology. Here one might stress the importance of the Hegelian-Marxist dialectical method in overcoming Korsch's earlier, somewhat positivistic, somewhat idealistic-moralistic, theoretical position that shaped his university writings, his English Fabian essays, and his first essay on practical socialism.

In "The Marxist Dialectic," Korsch argues that the *content* of the Marxian theory is the ideas and viewpoint of the proletariat produced in their class struggles, while the *form* of the theory is the dialectical method, which is "intrinsically critical and revolutionary." Korsch distinguishes between the bourgeois form of dialectic maintained by Hegel and its materialist form held by Marx. Hegel sees the dialectic coming to a standstill in the idea of the bourgeois state which reconciles all oppositions in a harmonious synthesis. Marx, on the other hand, posits the material reality of the suffering proletariat as a real opposition to bourgeois society and the state, thus creating an explosive contradiction within the heart of bourgeois society. The materialist dialectician wants to eliminate this contradiction through revolutionary activity and thus is in opposition to the bourgeois state, society, and ideology. A revolutionary materialist dialectic posits overcoming the contradictions of capitalist society (capital-labor, wealth-poverty, etc.) through class struggle aiming at a classless socialist society which will resolve all present contradictions. "The materialist dialectic therefore forms the necessary methodological foundation for 'scientific socialism' as the 'theoretical expression' of the proletarian class's historical struggle for liberation."[23]

In "On Materialist Dialectic," Korsch more explicitly stresses the importance of Hegel for understanding the dialectical method.[24] He polemicizes against those positivist Marxists like Bukharin who wish to surrender the dialectical method for "the empirical methods" of the natural and social sciences, which are after all the bourgeois method of research. But Korsch also polemicizes against theoreticians such as Thalheimer, a KPD ideologue, who suggests that one must take over Hegel's dialectic, "not only in regard to the method, but also in regard to the content." Here Korsch strongly disagrees, arguing that Hegel's categories, and his attempt to systematize all the categories of thought, are but an inventory of bourgeois thought, which must give way to new concepts, relations, and contents in a materialist dialectic. Further, the subject-matter of materialist dialectic is not merely a set of abstract categories but is the concrete totality of the society and evolving historical matrix, in which all ideas, consciousness, and philosophy are produced. Whereas bourgeois philosophy and economics merely reflect the existing ideology and economy of the bourgeois society, materialist dialectic represents a negation of this ideology and society which seeks to explode the contradictions of bourgeois thought and society through revolutionary practice aiming at a new social order and way of thought. Thus it is false to merely characterize Marx's dialectic as a "turning upside down" of Hegel's dialectic, for materialist dialectic is the concrete negation of bourgeois society and thought rooted in the struggles of the working class for emancipation. Unlike Hegel's philosophy, no complete system of thought is possible for materialist dialectic which is still evolving in the theory and practice of the working class movement.

"The Marxian Dialectic" and "On Materialist Dialectic" should be read in the framework of *Marxism and Philosophy*, and what I call Korsch's revolutionary historicism which sees philosophy as an expression of existing social reality and revolutionary theory as a moment of a revolutionary movement.[25]

Notes

1. Erich Gerlach, editor's introduction to Karl Korsch, *Schriften zur Sozialisierung* (Frankfurt: Europaische Verlag, 1969), p. 6.
2. Karl Korsch, "What Is Socialization?" *New Germany* (Fall 1975): 60–

81, translated by Frankie Denton and Douglas Kellner. Here I might note that the term "socialization" for Korsch refers to the active, conscious activity of constructing a socialist society, socializing the forces and relations of production. This process of socialist socialization should be distinguished from the process of socialization in bourgeois society that has become an increasingly central concern of social scientists who discuss role behavior, political socialization, and the socializing effects of the family, peer groups, the mass media, etc. Korsch's emphasis is on the social relations of production and process of socializing society, rather than on the socialization of the individual into prefabricated roles, behavior, attitudes, etc. which are discussed by social scientists in their theories of socialization and criticized by Marxists and others in their critiques of false consciousness, alienation, reification, etc. Whereas "socialization" in bourgeois society serves the function of stabilizing the current capitalist system of production, and induces the individual to conform to the system, "socialist socialization," in Korsch's sense of the term, advocates democratic control of the means of production by the workers who decide on their use and are to engage in human self-activity. An interesting discussion of the concept of socialization used by Korsch is found in Felix Weil's study *Sozialisierung*, published in Berlin in 1921 in a series edited by Korsch, and reissued by Underground Press (Berlin, 1968). Weil notes the confusion surrounding the term *Sozialisierung* and then in a study heavily influenced by Korsch attempts to clarify the concept in terms of the task of constructing a genuinely socialist and thus socialized society.

3. Bernstein's short essay "Was ist Sozialisierung" is published as an appendix to Korsch's "What Is Socialization?" in Korsch, *Schriften zur Sozialisierung*, p. 44.

4. Bernstein, "Sozialisierung," pp. 44–45.

5. Ibid., p. 43.

6. Korsch, "What Is Socialization?"

7. Ibid.

8. Korsch, "Fundamentals of Socialization," translated in this anthology by Roy Jameson and Douglas Kellner.

9. Korsch, "What Is Socialization?"

10. Karl Korsch, "Das sozialistische und das syndikalistische Sozialisierungsprogramm," in *Schriften zur Sozialisierung*, p. 55.

11. Ibid., p. 56.

12. Ibid., p. 27.

13. Ibid.

14. Ibid., p. 58.

15. Korsch, "Fundamentals of Socialization."

16. Ibid.

17. Ibid.

18. Karl Korsch, "Quintessenz des Marxismus" (Berlin-Leipzig: Franks, 1922).

19. Ibid., p. 5.

20. Ibid., p. 22.

21. Karl Korsch, "Quintessenz des Marxismus," "Kernpunkte der Material-istischen Geschichtsauffassung," "Die Marxsche Dialektik," and "Uber Materialistische Dialektik." The latter three essays are collected in the German edition of *Marxismus und Philosophie* (Frankfurt: Europaische Verlag, 1966).

22. Karl Korsch, "Eine Antikritik," "Allerhand Marxkritiker," and "Die im Wandel der Zeiten unveränderliche bürgerliche Marxkritik." The first two of these essays are collected in *Kommentare zur deutschen 'Revolution.'*

23. Karl Korsch, "Die Marxsche Dialektik," *Imprekorr*, March 10, 1923; translated in this anthology as "The Marxist Dialectic," by Karl-Heinz Otto.

24. Karl Korsch, "Uber materialistische Dialektik," *Internationale*, June 2, 1924; translated in this anthology as "On Materialist Dialectic," by Karl-Heinz Otto.

25. See my discussion of "Korsch's Revolutionary Historicism."

Fundamentals of Socialization

The word "socialization" was incorporated into common usage after the November Revolution. It appears earlier sporadically. As far as I have been able to determine, it was first used in 1875 by the insipid "universal" philosopher Eugene Dühring, who attained historical importance through Friedrich Engels who tore him to shreds.[1] But the *particular* meaning in which it has seized the consciousness of the masses is present neither in Dühring nor is it to be encountered in the writings of the non-revolutionary period. For Dühring "socializations" are (1) ideologically grounded world improvements. Where others speak of socialization the word indicates either (2) the historical process of development of an automatically self-constituting "socialization" observed purely theoretically, or else something which lies much further from the current revolutionary concept of socialization: namely, (3) the merely social-reform type of progressive development of the modern state, in the sense of those social-political ideals which are maintained and labeled "socialism" by Edward Bernstein and his followers.

The *conception of socialization* which flourishes today in the minds of those revolutionary elements which are class-organized stands in radical opposition to all of these three notions (utopian world improvement, theoretical observation of history, social political reforms). For these people, the concept of socialization first and above all means something essentially revolutionary—that is, if we care to grasp the idea in its formal universality and not yet in its individual substantial determinations. *Socialization is the social revolution*—it is the socialistic concept in flesh and reality developed through practical human-sensuous activity.

Part of the conceptual structure of the Marxist world-view which had been misperceived and misunderstood, even by those who call themselves Marxist, has recently come into its own and resulted in the passing over of socialism from science into socialism as action, as revolution, as "practical-critical activity," as "revolutionary praxis." Those who up until now have seen Marx and Engels' conception of historical materialism as a particular *theory* of historical knowledge which demands no *practice* must today (finally!) comprehend that they have yet to grasp the essentials of "scientific socialism" in the specific sense laid down by Marx and Engels. In opposition to the materialistic knowledge of nature, for Marx the "material" knowledge of societal development from the very beginning never consisted merely in a purely theoretical comprehension of an entity under the form of an object or of an institution, but rather always simultaneously consisted in subjective, human-sensuous, practicocritical, and therefore "revolutionary" practice.[2] Of course the organization of revolutionary elements as a class presupposes the "mature existence of all the forces of production which can generally be engendered in the womb of the old society." And the epoch of social revolution commences only when the stage is reached at which "the already acquired forces of production and the current societal institutions *can* no longer co-exist." But when this point has come, this stage has been reached, then of all the forces of production which break the chains of the old societal order, "the strongest force of production is the revolutionary class itself." When their time has come, the external conditions of the established order change themselves not from themselves, but rather solely through human practice. The contradiction between the further developing forces of production and the traditional relations of production, together with their superstructure, creates only the material pre-conditions for the solution of a "*task*" which is to be recognized as solvable and is solved solely through revolutionary praxis. The new scientific world view first fulfills itself in this unification of theory and practice. In it Marx's fiery soul has smelted together the act-shy (*Tatfremde*) knowledge of the old sciences of society and the knowledge-shy (*Erkenntnisfremden*) will to act (*Tatwillen*) of the old utopianism into the *identity of objectifying knowledge and activity*. Thus, and only thus, can it be understood that precisely the most genuine Marxists, the "most scientific" socialists were also those most strongly gripped by the practice-concept (*Tatidee*) of socialization in that historical moment when, destroyed by its own antagonisms, the structure of the old capitalistic order collapsed in turmoil. Only from this standpoint is it understandable why the word "socialization"—for those immature times too unscientific and utopian—totally lost its ideological overtones in the revolutionary epoch. Moreover, only so is it understandable why that version which sees the "social revolution" as an *historical development* effected by non-human forces and carried out by quasi-natural laws appears as an ideology far separated from reality in that moment in which socialization can only be grasped and understood and effected as a practical task.

Having once recognized from the correctly understood standpoint of a theory of historical "materialism" (through the eyes of scientific socialism as a theoretical expression of the proletariat) that in a particular epoch of societal development and decisive transformation from a theoretical to a practico-critical "revolutionary" activity is unavoidably necessary, socialistic theory and prophecy "must show in practice (praxis) the truth, that is, the reality and power, the this-worldliness of its thought"—Marx. But the following still remains to be investigated: To what extent and in which manner has the scientific socialism of our time done justice to this, its final and most important task? We ask: To what extent has the socialistic theory of those "classes which are called to action," having first "brought them to the consciousness of the conditions and the nature of their own actions" (Engels), also managed to opportunely thrust into their hands the practical way to the completion of this action—that is, the "*forms*" in which "*socialism*" can become praxis and reality?

In raising this question we—we who are putting forth the claim of being the inheritors of Marx and Engels—must feel great shame in our hearts. Those few who are truly revolutionary in their thought, who feel the coming necessity of action as a living reality, those who have stood up for the German proletariat after the departure of Marx and Engels, must expend their best forces in the battle against the growing number of those who still mouth the memorized slogans of a radical idiom but who themselves no longer carry in their hearts a full belief and a genuine revolutionary readiness to act. These same people conducted inquisitions against those who no longer desired to pay homage to such lip service to mere slogans in the non-revolutionary interim of the time. Thus we have to explain the fact that a large number of still valuable remarks are to be found in the works of Marx and Engels which are concerned with the transformation of socialism into practical reality, and therefore with socialization, but yet the entire later Marxian literature contributed nothing essential to the advancement of these practical problems until right up into the war years.

Instead, throughout this entire period of increasingly noticeable stagnation, which grew out of unperceived beginnings, and which appears to us today as the epoch of the Second International, the majority of spokesmen of revolutionary socialism sought to guarantee the "scientific" character of the Marxian doctrine by rejecting from the beginning every attempted clarification of the following question as a relapse into pre-Marxian ideology and utopianism: How, on the basis of each economic and social-psychological stage of development, can the socialistic demand "socialization of the means of production" be practically realized? Consider, for example, the following sentences from Kautsky's *Comments on the Fundamental Components of the Erfurt Program:* "Social democracy can make *positive proposals* only for today's society, not for the coming one. Proposals which surpass it can only reckon with contrived *presuppositions* instead of *facts,* and are therefore fantasies, dreams which even in the best cases remain ineffectual. If their author is talented and active enough to influence the intellects, then this effect can consist solely in error and waste of energy."

These sentences of Kautsky's are self-evident; viewed in and for themselves they are thoroughly correct and no one who has breathed into himself the essence of Marx's spirit would expect any light from such "proposals" alone. But in the past year of revolution something entirely different from such arbitrarily fabricated proposals and projects towards the quick and complete solution of the social question was just given to us again in abundant fulness. Namely, the concepts of realization (*Verwirklichungsgedanken*) which arise out of a full knowledge of the economic and psychological totality (*Gesamtlage*) and its perceivable tendencies of development. Through these concepts the science anticipates the individual emerging social reality. Through their conscious anticipation of the future these concepts also posit one of the realities through which the creative transformation from the old to the new forms of social and individual being alone can be accomplished. Scientific knowledge can of course take this particular form only in the creative fantasy of a *revolutionary* who has already previously carried out the transformation from the old to the new in his thought. And from the fact that Kautsky and all of these who stand close to him do not possess such creative, faithful revolutionary fantasy we can explain their all too long denial of practical future-oriented thoughts. From this lack of revolutionary fantasy we may also explain the ghostliness of the programs of action and the plans for socialization—pale and genuinely sufficient for no one, least of all satisfactory to the striving masses—which these people still developed at various times before and after the November Revolution, despite their doubt as to the usefulness of such action.

But by and large one can say in summary that, right up into the war and revolutionary times, the socialistic thought of the preceding epoch rejected every investigation into the forms of socialistic construction. Moreover, and in ever increasing degree, the essentially unrevolutionary view was set forth "as if the transformation (from capitalistic to socialistic society) had to automatically execute itself, since the bed of the socialistic society had been so perfectly prepared by the development of capitalism that one needed only to modify the relations of ownership, while the economic organization could be utilized for the new purposes without modification."[3] The few who saw this condition of increasing passivity as dangerous and fatal stood mostly outside of the actual socialistic movement, and their views were therefore not able to become fruitful for socialism.[4]

Thus it is by no means to be traced back to purely external coincidences that in the enormously fateful months after November, 1918, as the political power organizations of the bourgeoisie collapsed and nothing external stood in the way of the transition from capitalism to socialism, that great hour had nonetheless to slip by unseized because the *social-psychological* presuppositions for its utilization were greatly lacking: A decisive *belief* in the immediate capacity for realization of the socialistic economic system which could have carried the masses onward was nowhere to be found, nor was there a clear knowledge of the nature of the first steps to be carried out. Of course, also contributing to the problem was the total confusion which developed in the proletarian ranks: the proletariat had been wholly torn out of the normal life conditions of the industrial wage earners by the long war and thus in the decisive moment could not at all be reorganized as a revolutionary class. Next to such basically external factors, and seen from today's revolutionary standpoint, the practically incomprehensible backwardness of socialistic *theory* with regard to all problems of practical realization contributed decisively to the fact that the "cry for socialization"—proclaimed loud and massively enough two or three times in the course of the year and taken in the camps of the bourgeois classes and their troops with fear and trembling—actually brought forth no practical results. On the contrary, the year 1919 went into history as the year in which the German middle class constituted itself politically and economically as the ruling class after the last remains of pre-bourgeois government forms and after the liberation from the chains of the war economy. Landmarks of this development were the eleventh of August, 1919, when the new German Constitution went into effect, and the eighteenth of August, 1919, when Wissel's ideas on "Planned Economy" were finally abandoned and the return to a free economy was also proclaimed in the "Weimar Decrees" for the sphere of export trade.[5]

This short review of the history of the concept of socialization in Germany from the birth of scientific socialism up to the beginning of the new revolutionary epoch—whose realization we hope for—should irrefutably demonstrate the following: In order for the social revolution to move forward at the present point in time, the further conscious development and clarification of *concepts of action* toward the final realization of socialism attains an importance that increases daily, passing beyond a summons to action that was at first only formal, to substantively fulfilling the slogan "socialization." Next to this in importance remain the goals of the proletarian mass movement that are superficially directed toward the present (higher wages, better living conditions, increased rights within the capitalistic social organization) which are to be accomplished through the organization of hand- and head-working proletariat as a revolutionary class. On the other hand, from the Marxian standpoint, it is just as clear that this substantive fulfillment of the concept of socialization cannot be attained through pure thought and the ideological will of talented "social technicians." Rather for this purpose that combination of theoretic-historical and practico-critical and practice-forming/ thought-informed activity is required whose example—not reached again, even up to the present day—Marx gave us in all his works. If we approach the question of *The Forms of Socialization* with this attitude, then, temporarily ignoring less important details, we can distinguish three complexes of economic-historical realities out of which we can distill the outlines of such forms in historico-critical practico-scientific "Marxian" observation.

Moreover we can also establish that, within the extensive literature on socialization which has appeared since the November Revolution or in part even since the war, each of these three reality-complexes has found its own particular expression in the literature. These three main directions taken by the concept of socialization are to be successively discussed in detail in later essays so that in the emergent synthesis a total picture can be depicted of the transformation of the ruling economic order striven for by revolutionary socialism and communism—one more or less corresponding to today's states of consciousness and reality. For the present it shall suffice to point out in a wholly general manner the three large

groups of economic-historical realities and the resulting plans of socialization. It is unavoidable that in such a generalized grouping the individually
indicated projects will be presented as somewhat more one-sided than they
actually are. The originators of these plans have also brought into view
in varying degree the remaining realities which are open equally for all,
besides the one reality-complex to which they owe their decisive stimulation. Each of them has already conceived of his truth as the synthesis of
various individual truths. But of course what is important here is obviously not the assessment of the merits of individuals, but rather solely
the subject itself. We choose this manner of presentation and grouping,
although it may not be adequate to the intentions of the originators of
the different models of socialization, precisely because of our interest in
this subject and the most complete and distinct depiction possible.

The German war economy constitutes the first group of economic-
historical realities out of which some of the most important publications
of the literature on socialization have received decisive stimulation. The
most important literary outcomes of these realities comprise the plans of
socialization of Otto Neurath (Schumann and Kranold)[6] on the one
hand, and the Wissel-Mollendorf Plan for Planned Economy[7] on the
other. Although no socialist or communist can see even a partial fulfillment of his exertions in any of the forms of *state* economic management
or economic regulation of the sort which up until now have materialized
in peace and in war; although Engels so pertinently fought and ironized[8]
the identification of socialization and nationalization; and although it is
especially necessary today to stress again and again that state socialism is
not socialism, just as the previous state capitalism is also not at all state
socialism—in spite of all this, it remains undeniably true that the *central
government organization*, superordinate to all the existing economic
units, and which the followers of the concept of nationalization for the
most part have solely in view when they speak of the "state," is indispensable for every genuine socialistic demand and public economy.[9]

And next to its military task, in the last war the German state had also
above all a purely economic task in fulfilling economic demands. In a
situation requiring the most extreme utilization of all available forces of
production the German state had to secure—besides the increasing war
needs in a state of increasingly felt lack of raw materials and labor
power—the bare necessities of life of a large number of people so that
only thousands and not millions of its productive active citizens would
perish because of hunger, exhaustion and the concomitant diseases. And
one must recognize that the wartime state—supported by an immense
increase in gold certificates and a financial politics that piled up loan after

loan in a capitalistically "unhealthy" way (which even England attempted to avoid if possible!)—sought to disregard in truly marvelous ways the standpoint of a private enterprise economy *profitability* and hence passed beyond the central standpoint of how every private capitalistic economy is guided. Exactly as in a natural-economy *administrative economics* (that is not calculated and decided by a money-economics) for the duration of the war the consideration of social production possibilities and social consumer needs—and not profit as in a private economy—was the standpoint which was supposed to decide on the Whether and How of the social production of goods: as a completely socialized and thoroughly socialist economy would be ultimately represented. Thus it would be as unmarxist as possible if the practical socialist wanted to carelessly pass by this gigantic experiment of a centralized economic regulation in seeking the forms in which the transition from a capitalist profit-economy to a social demand-economy would be carried out. It is obvious that in no way could there be a simple imitation of the bureaucratic measures and institutions of a war economy that is burdened with all the lacks of makeshift expedients; rather it is from the knowledge of its failures, mistakes, and half-measures, which occurred everywhere, that one can learn the most.

This consideration itself leads us to the second of today's three main groups of pre-socialistic forms of economic organization. Briefly stated, this group consists in the most recent development of the modern forms of *private capitalistic economy*.

The view that capitalism not only negatively prepares the way for socialism in inducing its own collapse through the continued development and sharpening of its inner antagonisms, but also positively in already developing within its own womb the forms of a transpersonal social economic organization which is no longer overseeable and regulable for the individual economic subjects, belongs so much to the ABC's of Marxian theory that it need not be further taken up here. It might only be briefly mentioned which important publications of the present literature of socialization appear to me to have issued forth out of these realms of experience. This includes all the varied plans for socialization which, in exact antithesis to all state socialistic and centralist tendencies of whatever form, thrust to the foreground the idea of *economic self-government of autonomous associations*. Above all, this includes Rathenau, who in his most recent writing has advocated with increasing decisiveness the conception of an "autonomous economy."[10] Here belong also a whole line of other plans of socialization composed by various authors[11] which we shall investigate later—above all the socialization program of the Austrian Social Democrats written by Otto Bauer, which is very important for the entire post-revolutionary socialization movement.[12] The most important application of this "principle of guilds" (*Gildenprinzips*) in a single economic area is represented by the Coal Report of the official German socialization commission.[13] A private-capital economic self-government was realized in practice by Ernst Abbe in 1889 in the socialized Zeisswerk in Jena, which was carried out in a manner exemplary for those times (its constitution is of course no longer adequate for today's requirements, just as the normal economic self-administrative body is no more common in the large association of industrial trusts than in the single autonomous business).[14]

The third and most important group of realities, out of which the general concept of socialization can obtain a more specific content and a more solid form, is to be met in those organizations which are already today constituted purely out of the proletariat, and which the German and especially the victorious Russian proletariat also created (and is today still further building) in the pre-revolutionary class struggle and revolutionary final struggle: This is to say, in the workers' professional groups (*Arbeiterfachverbanden*) and especially in the revolutionary council organizations (*Räteorganizationen*). It is a deplorable lack of the otherwise so excellent and instructive study of Heimann's—which unites a great number of impulses towards socialization into a shrewd synthesis—that its author in no way grasped the importance of the councils for the construction of a truly socialistic economy. According to Heimann, "The introduction of factory councils has conceptually nothing to do with socialization." Socialism needs factory councils, not because socialism is socialistic, but rather because it is also democratic, because it requires the participation of all its people (*Volksgenosse*) and wants the best of everyone. But for Heimann the people are to participate solely "in all questions of working conditions," though, to be sure, they are also allowed to take "a peek into the business procedures." But above and beyond this there is "no room" . . . for them in Heimann's projected economic organization.

Let us recall that in the Soviet Union there is already a *united working together of the higher and lower councils* which in wide application has been successfully carried through and has reached a balanced equilibrium that is completely satisfactory between the most far reaching *autonomy* and simultaneous strict articulation of all single economic bodies in a *planned total administration*.[15] Thus it is difficult to comprehend how the socialist Heimann can believe that a socialization in the sense of socialism—which is the total replacement of the capital economy (based on unfree work) through a "planned-societal regulation of production according to *the needs of the totality as well as those of each individual*"

(Engels)—can be achieved today except through the workers councils. If, however, one looks more closely, one discovers by no means only one but rather simultaneously two reasons for this strange position: First, Heimann lacks the Marxian concept of socialization as identity of the historical process of development and revolutionary human activity. Just as for other organization technicians, for Heimann socialization is in the last analysis nothing more than "a rational system of organizing measures." . . . Secondly, he also fails to overcome the mechanistic bourgeois ideology of the state: In place of a *power organization* that violently forces together into an artificial unity the multifarious social and individual interests that are variously divided, Heimann postulates that, in the socialist community, the state will "wither away" and that an infinitely more open system will hold things together in a stateless "society." Hence for Heimann "the state" is still identical with "the totality in which all special interests truly come to equilibrium." But on the basis of this conception he can naturally attain no understanding of the enduring conflict which can in no way be entirely eliminated by a state-produced "equilibrium," for in even a fully socialized community there must still exist a conflict between the particular *interests of the individual* producers and the universal *interests of the general consumers* which are grouped together in productive units in united working groups.[16] But how for Heimann could such conflict be possible since as totality "the state" holds the producing groups together with all other producing groups as consumers into a unified democratic total organization?

I conclude that only after overcoming this last remnant of the formal-democratic *state ideology* can the necessity of the workers councils for the construction of a classless and stateless socialistic *society* be understood in its innermost essence.

Translated by Roy Jameson and Douglas Kellner

Notes

1. Compare E. Dühring, *Cursus der Philosophie* (Leipzig, 1875), sec. 7: *Sozialisierung aller Gesamttätigkeiten*, and Fr. Engels' article, *Herrn Dührings Umwalzung der Wissenschaft* (written 1877–1878). The word "socialization" is to be met in the non-foreign literature of the English Fabian Society, somewhat later in a work by the Belgian Vandervelder which has been translated into German by von Südekum.
2. One should consider here and in the following Marx's eleven *Theses on*

Feuerbach of 1845, which first formulated the theory of revolutionary will in pregnant brevity, and which was then further developed in "The Poverty of Philosophy" (*Elend der Philosophie*) shortly thereafter.

3. Compare Eduard Heimann: *Die Sozialisierung*, in the *Archiv für Sozialwissenschaft und Sozialpolitik* vol. 45, book 3, p. 528.

4. Numerous years ago this author already pointed to the dangers for the realization of socialism developing out of these concerns in his essay *The Socialistic Formula for the Organization of Public Economy* which appeared in the bourgeois monthly *Die Tat*. Proceeding from the fact that under one and the same formula—negatively determined, i.e., totally undetermined in a positive manner and saying nothing—of the "socialization of the means of production," so many such different lines as "state socialists, syndicalists, cooperative associations (*Genossenschaftler*) and various others" could be found together, he continued, that "this contentlessness of the socialistic formula for the organization of the public economy (*Volkswirtschaft*) was innocuous (and still is) so long as the practical efficacy of socialism in fighting and removing existent abuses remains limited. This contentlessness will, however, become harmful once the moment has come in which socialism somehow and somewhere approaches the government and demands the execution of the socialistic organization of the public economy. If this moment were to arise today (1912), socialism would be found unprepared; socialism must recognize that it has not yet formed the adequate formula of construction for the organization of the public economy."

5. Cf. my article in no. 4 of the *Sozialist*, January 24, 1920.

6. Neurath's main writings: 1. *Durch die Kriegswirtschaft zur Naturwirtschaft*, 2. *Wesen und Weg der Sozialisierung*, 3. *Die Sozialisierung Sachsens*, 4. *Können wir heute sozialisieren?* (with Schumann)—All were published in 1919: 1. and 2. by Callwey, Munich; 3. and 4. in Chemnitz and Leipzig—Also, 5. *Vollsozialisierung* (Jena, 1920).

7. See particularly F. Wissel: "Praktische Wirtschaftspolitik," published by Verlag "Gesellschaft und Erziehung," in Berlin 1919 (with all official material).

8. "Otherwise the royal sea-trade, porcelain manufacture and even the company tailor in the military would be socialistic institutions" (Engels, from *Anti-Dühring*, p. 299).

9. Heimann stresses this appropriately in his previously mentioned study on socialization, particularly pp. 544 and 587.

10. In his writings: *Von kommenden Dingen* (1917), *Die Neue Wirtschaft* (1918), *Der Neue Staat* (1919), *Die autonome Wirtschaft* (1919). Remarkably enough, this entire direction within the struggle for socialization has a precursor out of the older times little touched by the modern capitalistic development in the bourgeois national economist, Schäffle. Schäffle not only employs the notion of economic self-government in his great major work "*Bau und Leben des sozialen Korpers*" (The construction and life of the social

body) and in his well-known short essay "Quintessenz des Sozialismus" (Quintessence of socialism) (1875), but he also published a special treatise on "Die Trennung von Staat und Volkswirtschaft" in the journal *Zeitschrift für die gesamte Staatswissenschaften,* vol. 45 (which he edited) in 1889 on the occasion of the great Coal Strike. Although no one investigating the problem of socialization should neglect this extremely clear sighted and basic exposition, everyone has passed over it until now.

11. Those socialization plans well known up to the beginning of 1919 are critically discussed in my essay: "What Is Socialization?" published at the beginning of 1919 in Hanover, presently available through the publisher "Gesellschaft und Erziehung," in Berlin. In its positive part the essay develops a detailed plan of socialization, which in opposition to the socialistic centralism and syndicalistic federalism is designated *socialization* in the form of *"industrial autonomy."*

12. Partially published in the appendix to my just mentioned work on socialization, complete in Wilbrandt: "Socialism" (Jena, 1919) pp. 191 ff.

13. Published by R. V. Decker, Berlin, 1919.

14. For information on the organization of the Jena Zeiss Factory see especially Korsch, loc. cit., p. 28, Wilbrandt loc. cit. pp. 153ff, and E. Zschimmer: "The Socialization of the Optical Industries of Germany," published by the Jenaer Volksbuchhandlung in 1919.

15. A more detailed presentation of this Russian development is found in the report over "The Administration of production through the workers in Soviet Russia" (published in 1919 by the "Kommunistische Rätekorrespondenz"; reprinted in no. 48 of the Vienna "Rote Fahne" and in many German newspapers).

16. For further information on this conflict—which as a central problem of the entire question of socialization is to be more closely laid out in the future—compare for the present my work on socialization, "What Is Socialization?"

The Marxist Dialectic

The immense significance of Marx's theoretical achievement for the practice of proletarian class struggle is that he concisely fused together for the first time the total content of those new viewpoints transgressing bourgeois horizons, and that he also formally conceptualized them into a solid unity, into the living totality of a scientific system. These new ideas arose by necessity in the consciousness of the proletarian class from its social conditions. Karl Marx did not create the proletarian class movement (as some bourgeois devil-worshippers imagine in all seriousness). Nor did he create proletarian class consciousness. Rather, he created the theoretical-scientific expression adequate to the new content of consciousness of the proletarian class, and thereby at the same time elevated this proletarian class consciousness to a higher level of its being.

The transformation of the "natural" class viewpoint of the proletariat into theoretical concepts and propositions, and the powerful synthesis of all these theoretical propositions into the system of "scientific socialism," is not to be regarded as a mere passive "reflex" of the real historical movement of the proletariat. On the contrary, this transformation forms an essential component of the real historical process. The historical movement of the proletariat could neither become "independent" nor "unified" without the development of an independent and unified proletarian class consciousness. Just as the politically and economically mature, nationally and internationally organized proletarian class movement distinguishes itself from the, at first, dispersed and unorganized stirrings and spasms of the proletariat, so too "scientific socialism" distinguishes itself as the "organized class consciousness" of the proletariat from those dispersed and formless feelings and views in which proletarian class consciousness finds its first immature expression. Therefore, from a practical point of view, the theoretical evolution of socialism towards a science, as expressed by Karl Marx in the *Communist Manifesto* and in *Capital*, appears as a quite necessary element within that great historical developmental process in which the proletarian class movement gradually moved away from the bourgeois revolutionary movement of the "third estate" and constituted itself as an independent and unified class. Only by taking the form of a strict "science" could this complex of proletarian class views, contained in "modern socialism," radically purify itself from the bourgeois views with which from its origin it was inextricably connected. And only by becoming a "science" could socialism actually fulfill the task which Karl Marx and Frederick Engels had set for it: to be the "theoretical expression" of revolutionary proletarian class action which is to ascertain the historical conditions and nature of this revolutionary proletarian class action, thereby "bringing that class which is called to action, and is today suppressed, to a consciousness of the conditions and nature of its own action."

While in the foregoing exposition we have characterized the practical meaning of the *scientific form* of modern or Marxian socialism, we have at the same time also described the meaning of the *dialectical method* which Karl Marx applied. For as certainly as the content of scientific socialism was in existence as an unformed viewpoint (proletarian class viewpoint) before its scientific formulation, just as certainly is the scientific form in which this content lies before us in the works of Marx and Engels. Thus "scientific socialism" properly so-called is quite essentially the product of the application of that mode of thought which Marx and Engels designated as their "dialectical method." And it is not the case, as some contemporary "Marxists" might like to imagine, that by virtue of historical accident those scientific propositions which Karl Marx produced by the application of his "dialectical method" could today be separated at will from that method and simply reproduced. Nor is it the case that this method is out of date because of the progress of the sciences. Nor is its replacement by another method today not only possible but rather even necessary! Whoever speaks in these terms has not comprehended the most important aspects of the Marxist dialectic. How could one otherwise come to the thought that today—as at a time of increased class struggle in all spheres of social, thus also so-called intellectual, life —that method could be abandoned "which is intrinsically critical and revolutionary." Karl Marx and Frederick Engels simultaneously opposed the new method of proletarian science to the "metaphysical mode of thought" ("that specific weakness of thought of the last century") and to all earlier forms of "dialectic" (in particular the idealistic dialectic of Fichte-Schelling-Hegel).

Only those who completely overlook that Marx's "proletarian dialectic" differs essentially from every other (metaphysical *and* dialectical) mode of thought, and represents that specific mode of thought in which alone the new content of the proletarian class views formed in the proletarian class struggle can find a theoretical-scientific expression corresponding to its true being; only those could get the idea that this dialectical mode of thought, as it represents "only the form" of scientific socialism, consequently would also be "something peripheral and indifferent to the matter," so much so that the same material content of thought could be as well or even better expressed in another form. It is something quite similar when certain contemporary "Marxists" put forward the notion that the proletariat could wage its practical struggle against the bourgeois economic, social and political order in other "forms" than the barbaric uncivilized form of revolutionary class struggle. Or when the same people fool themselves and others by saying that the proletariat could achieve its positive task, the realization of Communist society, by means other than the dictatorship of the proletariat, for example, by means of the bourgeois state and bourgeois democracy. Karl Marx, who already in an early work had written the proposition, "Form has no value if it is not the form of its content," himself thought about these things quite differently. Later Marx always emphasized anew that the real understanding of historico-social development (i.e., consciously revolutionary understanding that is at the same time positive and negative)—this understanding, which constituted the specific essence of "scientific" socialism, can only be brought about by the conscious application of the dialectical method. Of course, this new, or "proletarian," dialectic on which the scientific form of Marxism is founded differs in the extreme, not only from the ordinary, narrow-minded metaphysical way of thinking. For, it is also "quite different" in its fundamental position from the bourgeois dialectic which found its most comprehensive form in the German philosopher Hegel, and in a definite sense it is even its "direct opposite." It is impracticable and superfluous at this point to enter more deeply into the manifold consequences of these differences and contrasts.

It is sufficient for our purposes that these differences and contrasts that we have pointed out lead us back without exception to Marx's "proletarian" dialectic as just that form in which the revolutionary class movement of the proletariat finds its appropriate theoretical expression. If one has understood this, or has just the faintest notion of the connection, one can comprehend immediately a whole series of phenomena otherwise difficult to grasp. One understands why the bourgeoisie of today has so completely forgotten the times when it had to fight as the "third estate" a tough and heroically ever-increasing class struggle against the feudal economic order and its political-ideological superstructure (aristocracy and church), and when its spokesman, the Abbe Sieyes, hurled against the ruling social order the quite "dialectical" outburst: "What is the third estate? Everything. What is it in the existing order? Nothing. What does it demand? To be something." Since the feudal state has fallen and the bourgeois class has become not only something in the bourgeois state, but everything, there are only two positions in question on the problem of dialectics for the bourgeoisie today. Either the dialectic is a standpoint today completely out-of-date, only historically respectable as a kind of lofty madness of philosophical thought transcending its natural barriers, to which a realistic man and good burgher ought under no circumstances be a party. Or the dialectical movement must even today, and for all the future, make a halt at that absolute end point at which the last revolutionary philosopher of the bourgeois class, the philosopher Hegel, once made it come to halt. It must in its concepts not cross those borders which bourgeois society likewise cannot cross without negating itself. Its last word, the great all-embracing synthesis, in which all opposites are dissolved, or can be dissolved, is the state. Opposite this bourgeois state, which in its complete development exemplifies the complete fulfillment of all bourgeois interests and is therefore also the final goal of the bourgeois class struggle, there is consequently no other dialectical antithesis to bourgeois consciousness, no irreconcilable opposite. Whoever may yet oppose this absolute fulfillment of the bourgeois idea in practice and theory departs from the hallowed circle of the bourgeois world; he puts himself outside bourgeois law, outside bourgeois freedom and bourgeois peace, and therefore also outside of all bourgeois philosophy and science. One understands why as far as concerns this bourgeois standpoint, which ordains contemporary bourgeois society as the sole thinkable and possible form of social life for humanity, the "idealist dialectic" of Hegel, which finds its ideal conclusion in the idea of the bourgeois state, must be the only possible and thinkable form of dialectic. Yet likewise, and understandably so, this "idealist dialectic" of the bourgeoisie is no longer of value to that other class within contemporary bourgeois society which is driven directly to rebellion against this whole bourgeois world and its bourgeois state by "absolutely compelling need which can no longer be denied or disguised—the practical expression of necessity." In its whole material conditions of life, in its whole material being, this class already truly expresses the formal antithesis, the absolute opposition to this bourgeois society and its bourgeois state. For this class, created within bourgeois society through the inner mechanism of development of private property itself, "through an independent and unconscious development by the very nature of the matter proceeded against its will"—for this class, the revolutionary aim and actions are "obviously and irrevocably indicated by its own conditions of life as well as by the whole organization of contemporary bourgeois society." The value of a new revolutionary dialectic that is no longer bourgeois-idealist, but is rather proletarian-materialist follows therefore with equal necessity from this social life-situation. Because the "idealist dialectic" of the bourgeoisie transcends the material opposites of "wealth" and "poverty" existing in bourgeois society only "in the idea," namely in the idea of a pure, democratic, bourgeois state, these "ideally" transcended oppositions continue to exist unresolved in "material" social reality where they even continually increase in extent and severity. In contrast thereto stands the essence of the new "materialist dialectic" of the proletariat which really abolishes the material opposition between bourgeois wealth ("capital") and proletarian misery through the supersession of this bourgeois class society and its bourgeois class state by the material reality of the classless Communist society. The materialist dialectic therefore forms the necessary methodological foundation for "scientific socialism" as the "theoretical expression" of the proletarian class's historical struggle for liberation.

Translated by Karl-Heinz Otto

On Materialist Dialectic

Vladimir Ilich Lenin declared two years ago in his article "Under the Banner of Marxism," published in issue no. 21 of the journal *Communist International*, that one of the two great tasks which communism must deal with in the field of ideology is "to organize a systematic study of Hegel's dialectic from a materialist standpoint; that is to say, the dialectic which Marx so successfully employed in a concrete manner not only in *Capital* but also in his historical and political works." Lenin then did not share the great anxiety that someone just might "via the idealist philosophy of neo-Hegelianism" smuggle "ideological byways" into Marxist-communist theory—an anxiety which is commonly voiced today by many of our leading comrades as soon as anyone at any time tries to undertake a practical attempt to engage himself in this program of Lenin's. A few examples might prove this contention: when a year ago, for the first time in 80 years, the Meiner Publishing Company published an edition of the larger Hegelian *Logic*, a formal warning appeared in the *Red Flag*, May 20, 1923, of the danger this new Hegel would pose to all those who, in studying Hegel's dialectic, "lacked a critical knowledge of the whole history of philosophy and moreover an accurate familiarity with the main results and methods of the natural sciences since Hegel's time." Eight days later, in the *Red Flag* of May 27, 1923, another representative of the faction then practically and theoretically dominant in the KPD formally condemned Georg Lukács for his attempt, by way of a collection of essays, to "provide the beginning or even just the occasion for a genuinely profitable discussion of dialectical method." The scientific journal of the German party, the *Internationale*, completely ignored the whole book by Lukács for reasons of simplicity. Bela Kun, in his essay on "The Propagation of Leninism" in the latest issue (no. 33) of the *Communist International*, not only draws attention to deviations already current but moreover observes that "some Communist publicists, as yet without a political name, could deviate in the near future into revisionist bylaws, departing from orthodox Marxism." (!)

After these examples, of which there are many, one might suggest that the detailed demand—which Lenin raised earlier and lastly in the essay of 1922—that in our work of Communist enlightenment we must organize a systematic study from a materialist standpoint, not only of the dialectical method of Marx and Engels but also of "Hegel's dialectic," did not meet with very much understanding in the leading theoretical circles of the Comintern, and still less among the theoreticians of the German Communist party. When we look for the causes of this phenomenon we must make distinctions. To one faction (typified by Bukharin's book *The Theory of Historical Materialism*) the whole of "philosophy" has fundamentally already reached a point that in reality it was to reach only in the second phase of Communist society after the full victory of the proletarian revolution, viz. the transcended standpoint of an unenlightened past. These comrades believe that the question of "scientific" method is solved once and for all in the empirical methods of the natural sciences and the corresponding positive-historical method of the social sciences. Little do they realize that just this method, which was the war-cry under which the burgher class undertook its struggle for power from the beginning, is also today still the *specific bourgeois* method of scientific research, which, it is true, is sometimes theoretically renounced by the representatives of modern bourgeois science in the present period of the decline of bourgeois society, but which in practice will be clung to.

To the other faction this matter is more complicated. Here people see a "danger" in a however "materialistically" turned occupation with Hegel's dialectical method for the reason that they know only too well this danger from their own experience, and indeed secretly become its victims as often as they are exposed to it. This perhaps somewhat bold-sounding assertion will not only be illustrated but proven outright by the example of a little article, "On the Matter of Dialectic," by A. Thalheimer, published in *International* 6, no. 9 (May 1923), and at the same time also in the information sheets of the Communist Academy in Moscow. In this article, Comrade Thalheimer links up with Franz Mëhring's thesis—which I share and hold tenable—that from the Marxist dialectical-materialist standpoint it is no longer practical and factually not even possible to deal with this "materialist dialectical" method separated from a concrete "matter." Comrade Thalheimer declares that although Mëhring's rejection of an abstract treatment of the dialectical method represents as such a correct nucleus, it nevertheless "oversteps its goal." To work out a dialectic is "an urgent necessity," inter alia, because "in the most progressive parts of the world proletariat the need arises to create a comprehensive and orderly world-view (!), something that lies beyond the practical demands of the struggle and the building of socialism," and this, furthermore, contains within itself "the demand for a dialectic." Comrade Thalheimer then goes on that in composing such a dialectic one ought to critically link up with Hegel "not only in relation to the method, but also to the matter." The genial progressiveness of Hegel is his demand that "the inner, all-embracing systematic connection of all categories of thinking be revealed." This task would apply equally to the materialist dialectic. Hegel's method need only be turned over; by which a materialist dialectic would emerge that would determine not reality by thought but rather thought by reality.

We believe that in all their brevity these words of Comrade Thalheimer prove conclusively that he is altogether incapable of imagining the dialectical method in any other way than an Hegelian-idealist one. Nevertheless far be it from us to say that Comrade Thalheimer is an idealist dialectician. We have stated elsewhere (*Lenin and the Comintern*) that Comrade Thalheimer avows an apparently materialistic-dialectical method in a later essay which is in reality not dialectical at all but is pure positivism. We can here supplement this statement by saying that as far as Comrade Thalheimer is a dialectician he is an idealist dialectician and conceives the dialectical method in no other than its Hegelian-idealist form. And the proof thereof we wish to arrive at *positively* by stating what in our conception constitutes the essence of materialist dialectic, that is, *Hegel's dialectic applied materialistically by Marx and Lenin*. In doing so, we connect with the results of our earlier published investigations on the relation of Marxism and Philosophy.

It is high time to dispense with the superficial notion that the transition from the idealist dialectic of Hegel to the materialist dialectic of Marx would be such a simple matter as to be achieved by a mere "overturning," a mere "turning upside down," of a method remaining otherwise unaltered. There are certainly some generally known passages in Marx where he himself characterized in this abstract way the difference of his method from Hegel's as a mere contrast. However, whoever does not determine the meaning of Marx's method from these quotations, but instead delves into Marx's theoretical practice, will soon easily see that this "transition" in method, like all transitions, represents not a mere abstract rotation, but rather has a rich concrete content.

At the same time as classical economics developed the *theory of value* in the "mystified" and abstract unhistorical form of Ricardo, classical German philosophy also made the attempt, in a likewise mystical and abstract manner, to break through the barriers of bourgeois philosophy. Like Ricardo's theory of value, the "*dialectical method*" developed at the same time in the revolutionary epoch of bourgeois society, and already shows in its consequences the way beyond bourgeois society (just as the practical revolutionary movement of the bourgeoisie also partly aimed beyond bourgeois society before and until the proletarian revolution movement was to confront it "independently"). But all these perceptions brought forward by bourgeois economics and bourgeois philosophy had yet to remain in the last instance "pure" perceptions, their concepts the "reconstituted being," their theories nothing but passive "reflections" of this being, real "ideologies" in the narrow and more precise sense of this Marxian expression. Bourgeois economics and bourgeois philosophy could well recognize the "contradictions," the "antinomies" of the bourgeois economy and bourgeois thought, and could even illuminate them with the greatest of clarity, yet in the end the contradictions prevailed. It is only the new science of the proletarian class which can break this ban, a science that unlike bourgeois science is no longer just "pure" theoretical science, but is *revolutionary practice* at the same time. The political economy of Karl Marx and the materialist dialectic of the proletarian class lead in their practical application to a dissolution of these contradictions in the reality of social life, and thereby at the same time in the reality of thought which is a real component of this social reality. It is thus we must understand Karl Marx when he credits proletarian class consciousness and his materialist-dialectical method with a power that the method of bourgeois philosophy never possessed, not even in its last, richest and highest Hegelian development. Just for the proletariat, just for it and only for it, will it be possible, through the development of its class consciousness become *practical* in tendency, to overcome that fetter of a still remaining "immediacy" or "abstraction" which for all purely perceiving behavior, for Hegel's idealist dialectic as well, clearly remains standing in the final analysis in insuperable "contradictions." It is here, and not in a merely abstract "inversion" or "turning upside down," that lies the revolutionary further development of the idealist dialectic, of classical bourgeois philosophy, into that materialist dialectic which has been theoretically conceptualized by Karl Marx as the method of a new science and practice of the proletarian class, and has been applied in theory and practice alike by Lenin.

When we look at the "transition" from Hegel's bourgeois dialectic to the proletarian dialectic of Marx-Lenin from this historical viewpoint, we immediately grasp the complete absurdity of the notion that an independent "system" of materialist dialectic is possible. Only an idealist dialectician could undertake an attempt to free the totality of forms of thought (determinations of thought, categories)—which are in part consciously applied in our practice, science, and philosophy, and in part move through our minds instinctively and unconsciously—from the material which is the subject of our intuiting, imagining and yearning, and in which they are otherwise shrouded, and then to examine it as a separate material in itself. The last and greatest of the idealist dialecticians, the burgher Hegel, had already partly seen through the "untruth" of this standpoint and had "introduced content into logical reflection" (see his preface to the second Lasson edition of the *Logic*, p. 16). But this abstract method is completely absurd for the materialist dialectician. Apart from its respective concrete historical content a real "materialist" dialectic can state nothing at all about the determinations of thought and the relations between them. Only from the standpoint of the idealist and thus bourgeois dialectic is it possible to fulfill Thalheimer's demand according to which dialectics would have to map out the connection of the determinations of thought as an "inner, all-round, systematic connection of all the categories of thought." Rather, from the standpoint of the materialist dialectic, that sentence which Karl Marx once voiced in relation to "economic categories" is to be applied to the connection of categories or determinations of thought in general: they stand to one another not in a connection "in the idea" (for which "washed out notion" Marx thrashed Proudhon!), not in an "inner systematic connection," but even their apparently purely logical and systematic sequence is "determined through the relations which they have to one another in modern bourgeois society." With the alteration of historical reality and practice the determinations of thought and all their connections also alter. To overlook their historical context and to wish to bring the determination of thought and their abstract relations into a system means the surrender of the revolutionary proletarian materialist dialectic in favor of a mode of thought which is only "materialistically" inverted in theory, but which in practical reality remains the old, unchanged, "idealist" dialectic of bourgeois philosophy. The "materialist dialectic" of the proletarian class cannot be taught as a practical "science" with its own particular abstract "material," nor by so-called examples. It can only be applied *concretely* in the practice of the proletarian revolution and in a theory which is an immanent real component of this revolutionary practice.

Translated by Karl-Heinz Otto

5. Lenin and the Soviet Union

Introduction

During his political activities with the German Communist party in the 1920's, the Soviet Union and Leninism became a major thematic focus for Korsch. His positions on Lenin and the Soviet Union are highly contradictory, reflecting the ambivalence of a complex, changing historical situation. Roughly, Korsch's position can be grouped into three phases, the first being a period of zealous Leninism marked by a whole-hearted adherence to Leninism and the Soviet Union. This position is evident in "Lenin and the Comintern," a speech that Korsch delivered at the Comintern World Congress in 1924 and then published in the Communist journal the *Internationale*, of which he was editor.[1] Korsch unstintingly defends Leninism as the basis for a truly revolutionary politics and believes that Leninism could solve a whole series of political and theoretical tasks. Thus it was the duty of the entire Comintern "to take on the inheritance of Lenin, both *theoretically and ideologically* to preserve, to enliven, and to further develop in the current situation the 'spirit' of Lenin in its theory and practice as historical reality."[2]

Korsch proposed the task of replacing "the dead Lenin in his theoretical-ideological function through a large powerful collective of living Leninists."[3] This project of appropriating/developing Leninism was described as "a wholly colossal task that has never before in world history been set before a party in this form."[4] As an index of Korsch's total adherence to Leninism, note his polemic against the German KPD theoretician Thalheimer, who wanted to historicize Leninism to a theory of proletarian revolution in the Soviet Union, whereas Korsch felt that Leninism and the model of the Soviet state bore general validity for the world revolutionary movement. Korsch concludes with the call for "protective walls against the rising flood of Communist revisionism," and advocates a total commitment to Leninism as a method, theory, and strategy of proletarian revolution. The context of Korsch's thoroughgoing Leninism was the collapse of the united front strategy in Germany in 1923 after the violent suppression of the workers' governments in Saxony and Thuringen and the subsequent outlawing of the Communist party.[5] This experience signified to Korsch the need for a turn to the more successful Leninist theory and strategy of revolution to revitalize the found-ering German movement. With this end in view, Korsch became a devoted Leninist for the next several years, until new historical events forced the honest and committed revolutionary Korsch to put his Lenin-ism in radical question, and finally to break off with Leninism.

Korsch's second phase in his relation to Lenin and the Soviet Union involves the development of a sharp critique of, first, the Soviet Union and then Leninism itself. The context of this turn is Korsch's expulsion from the German Communist party and his move into the forefront of the left opposition.[6] Korsch noted a contradiction between revolutionary Leninist theory and the increasingly counterrevolutionary practice of the Stalinists in the Soviet Union and the KPD. The standpoint of Korsch's emerging critique of Stalinism and the Soviet Union was his identification with those left-oppositionalist forces in the Soviet Union and the German movement who Korsch believed were genuinely Leninist and revolution-ary (at the time "Leninist" and "revolutionary" were synonymous for Korsch). He feared the triumph of opportunist-reformist forces em-bodied in Stalin and his allies, which would lead to a degeneration of Leninism and counterrevolutionary regression. This position is expressly worked out in the essay, "Ten Years of Class Struggle in the Soviet Union."[7] Korsch saw a contradiction developing between "Russian state necessity" and "proletarian revolutionary necessity," that found its theo-retical formulation in Stalin's doctrine of "socialism in one country." This signified the subordination of the world revolutionary movement to the interests of the Soviet Union and thus the collapse of autonomous proletarian internationalism (earlier, we recall, Korsch saw no contradic-tion between the interests of the Soviet Union and the world revolutionary movement).[8] With the defeat of the left opposition forces, Leninism was no longer a revolutionary reality but had become an ideology used to justify the counterrevolutionary politics of the Soviet Union, the Comin-tern, and the KPD. Hence, Korsch now felt that it was time to criticize Leninism itself. Here one should note that during the beginning of Korsch's left opposition period he was paradoxically still a true-believer Leninist who criticized Stalinism as a degeneration of Leninism. But with the splintering and defeat of the left opposition, there were no longer any revolutionary Leninist forces with which one could identify—hence the acute need to break with Leninism.

Korsch first formulates his break with Leninism in "The Second Party," where he argues that it is now time to "cut the umbilical cord" to Leninism, which had become an "ideology," full of "illusions" and "deceptive images."[9] In an essay "The Marxist Ideology in Russia," first published in Germany in 1932 and published in an expanded version in America in 1938, Korsch argued that Marxism-Leninism was used as an ideology to legitimate capitalist development in Russia, and to create the myth that the Soviet system was really "socialistic."[10] From the beginning, Lenin had argued for the necessity of passing through capitalist development and heavy industrialization, and he used his unparalleled influence to restore features of capitalism which were veiled by a socialist ideology. Worse, after Lenin's death, Leninism degenerated into "an ideological justification of what in its actual tendency is a capitalist state, and thus inevitably a state based on the suppression of the progressive revolutionary movement of the proletarian class."[11] In this situation, it would be a useless and reactionary effort "to restore the pure teaching of Lenin"; for since Leninism had become a fetter on the progressive revolutionary movement, it is time for *an immediate and total break* with Leninism."[12]

The third period of Korsch's relation to Lenin and the Soviet Union is his most ambiguous and contradictory one. Although Korsch continued to believe that the left-oppositional critique of Leninism and the Soviet Union was correct,[13] he felt that criticizing Leninism and the Soviet Union was a futile and worthless task that really only served reactionary capitalist-bourgeois interests. The reason behind this position was his belief that there were really no revolutionary forces anywhere which could be opposed to the Soviet Union and the Leninists, hence the critique didn't really advance the interests of the working class. The crux of the matter is that *"One cannot protest against a reality simply in the name of an abstract principle."*[14] This striking formulation found in the middle of an unpublished paper, "Position on Russia and the Communist Party," (1935) expresses Korsch's reluctant decision not to continue polemics against the Soviet Union, for the Soviet Union was the only "reality" that represented the interests of the working class. There are contradictions in this position, for Korsch continued to label the Soviet Union a counter-revolutionary power throughout the 1930's,[15] and sided with the anarcho-syndicalists against the Stalinists during their brief moment of glory in the Spanish Revolution. But he never really developed his critique of Stalinism or the Soviet Union in his later writings. In an interesting letter to his pro-Soviet friend Bertolt Brecht in 1947, Korsch revealed a surprising softening of his critique of the Soviet Union, reflecting his belief that in the Cold War, the Soviet Union was the only counterforce against Yankee imperialism. In the context of the Cold War, Korsch seemed to believe that one had to choose between the two superpowers and ruefully concluded: "In all respects Russian imperialism is better for the world than Yankee imperialism and there is hardly a third chance."[16] But in fact

Stalinism and the Soviet Union were a great trauma and burden for a generation of socialist radicals, and Korsch painfully mirrors this phenomenon in his changing and contradictory attempts to characterize and relate to Leninism and the Soviet Union.

Notes

1. Karl Korsch, "Lenin und die Komintern," in *Internationale*, June 2, 1924; translated in this anthology as "Lenin and the Comintern," by Roy Jameson.
2. Korsch, "Lenin and the Comintern."
3. Ibid.
4. Ibid.
5. See my "Korsch and Communism."
6. "Korsch and Communism."
7. Karl Korsch, "10 Jahre Klassenkämpfe in Sowjetrussland," *Kommunistische Politik* 2, nos. 17/18 (October 1927). Reprinted in *Politische Texte*.
8. "Korsch and Communism."
9. Karl Korsch, "Die Zweite Partei," in *Kommunistische Politik*, December 28, 1927; reprinted in *Politische Texte*.
10. Karl Korsch, "Zur Geschichte der marxistischen Ideologie in Russland," in *Gegner*, February 5, 1932; expanded English version, "The Marxist Ideology in Russia," in *Living Marxism* no. 2 (March 1938).
11. Korsch, "The Marxist Ideology in Russia."
12. Karl Korsch, "Die Zweite Partei."
13. The critique of Leninism and the Soviet Union was developed by groups of international council Communists in Europe and the group around Paul Mattick in the United States.
14. Karl Korsch, "Position on Russia and the Communist Party," unpublished manuscript, 1935; translated in this anthology by Douglas Kellner, Korsch amplifies this theme in a letter to Paul Partos where he tells how around 1928 he modified his intransigent left-oppositional position because, "I came to see that one could not carry out a struggle against the whole world and the whole age with nothing behind oneself except nothing, and thus with the prospects of nothing as nothing; not because I was in itself against carrying out hopeless struggles—for, yes, I have already consciously done that earlier—but because I thought that there is no value in doing something only in thought, that even the worst reality would be better than merely standing in thought" (letter to Partos, in *Jahrbuch Arbeiterbewegung* 2, p. 171).
15. Korsch most strikingly takes this position in "State and Counterrevolution."
16. Korsch to Brecht, April 18, 1947.

Lenin and the Comintern

I

The first item on the agenda of the Fifth World Congress of the Communist International reads: "Lenin and the Comintern. On the Basic Principles and Propaganda of Leninism." This indicates not only a commitment by the Congress to the spirit of Leninism and a widely perceivable declaration of the will of the participants to solve all questions which stand before them in the spirit of true Leninism. This does not merely indicate that particular problems which have entered into the focal point of the struggle in the last year of the Communist International in Central and Western Europe, and which appear later on in the agenda, should be taken care of from the beginning before the analysis of the economic situation which fills out its second item. Certainly the most important task of the present developmental period of the Communist International, among all of the tasks of the Central and West European and American Communists, consists in the task assigned us by Lenin: "conquering the majority of the most important strata of the working classes." Moreover, this task which is not yet resolved can only be truly solved in the spirit of Leninism; that is, concretely in the spirit of those "consequences" which Lenin derived in a most impressive manner at the end of his classic writing on Radicalism—the infantile sickness of communism—out of the history of the Russian Bolsheviks and out of the experiences of the European parties. "The main task of contemporary communism in Western Europe and America" lies today, in the year 1924, just as Lenin expressed it four years ago, after three years of the so-called united front tactics, now even more obviously than then, in "finding, feeling, and realizing the concrete plan of the not yet entirely revolutionary measures and methods which will *lead the masses to a real, decisive, last great revolutionary struggle.*" But the solution of this *practical* main task of the Leninists is relevant to an entire row of items on the agenda, and no single one in particular, and only in this sense does it also serve all other tasks with this first item, which speaks of the "Fundamentals and Propaganda of Leninism." It comes down to the following: Today the entire Comintern, after the shattering event of the death of its great founder and leader, V. I. Lenin, can now first show, and must, that it is able and willing to take on the inheritance of Lenin, both *theoretically and ideologically*, to preserve, to enliven, and to further develop in the present situation the "spirit" of Lenin in its theory and praxis as historical reality, as *Leninism*. Thus, in this manner the Comintern must replace the dead Lenin in his theoretical ideological function through a large powerful collective of living Leninists.[1]

In setting "Lenin and the Comintern" on the agenda of the Fifth World Congress, the executive committee has declared before the entire world that towards the fulfillment of this great task—a wholly colossal task that has never before in world history been set before a party in this form—not only the natural main inheritors of Lenin, the Russian Bolshevik party, but all the other sections of our great Communist party, the Communist International, should theoretically and practically work together. And the Congress itself will have to take the first important steps down this path; its task will be, clearly and completely and in detail, to formulate the slogans of the "Propaganda of Leninism" (which in the agenda are only indeterminately indicated) in a manner valid for the entire Comintern; to point each section of the International to the particularly important individual tasks according to their situation and their state of development, and to determine the larger guiding principles by which the solution of all these tasks is to be carried out.

But the importance of the first item on the agenda of the Fifth World Congress extends much further. One should make clear to oneself that with the closer determination of the manifold partial tasks out of which the "Propaganda of Leninism" is composed, the Congress will have taken a position with regard to the question of "Leninism" only according to the, if we may express it so, technical side. Obviously, this technical side of the question also has an inordinately large importance: The "Propaganda of Leninism" constitutes an important part of the great Communist total task of the "Organization of the Revolution." And, of course the fulfillment of precisely this propagandistic task shows itself to be in those sections of the Communist International which have not yet won state power (that is, therefore, in all European and American sections already under legal, but probably at first under illegal conditions) inordinately more difficult than in the proletarian Soviet Union. In those lands it will therefore, for the most part, have to take on entirely different forms—exactly conforming to the particular situation of each land—which by all means need a more precise explication and determination through the highest organ of the Communist International, the world Congress. But these more or less technical questions comprise in no way the kernel of the matter.

In reality the *method of the Bolshevik theory* as such is placed on the agenda by the inclusion of the question, "Lenin and the Comintern. On

the Fundamentals and the Propaganda of Leninism." Through the clarification of the "Basic Principles of Leninism," and the development of a
system of Leninistic propaganda based on these principles in all sections
of the Communist International, the entire Comintern should be smelted
ideologically into one firm unity on the common basis of the *revolutionary
Marxian method in that form in which the theoretician of Bolshevism,
Lenin, "restored" it and opposed it to the falsification and confusions of
the so-called Marxists of the united Second International.* The third item
of the agenda, the *Program* of the Communist International, as well as
the *method* of our revolutionary Bolshevist theory, is placed before
debate in the question of "Leninism."

II

Will the Fifth World Congress be able to solve this immensely important, but at the same time immensely difficult task? Will it be able to
formulate the *methodological fundamentals of Leninism* so sharply and
correctly that a methodical and systematic Leninistic propaganda can be
constructed on this basis? Will the process of ideological unification
within the Communist International have progressed enough to allow all
sections and groups of the Comintern to unite in a commitment to one
theoretical method which in its essential features is identical for all?

Here immense difficulties arise which nearly exclude a radical solution
of the task. On the one hand, we cannot yet at all speak of a unitary commitment in the various sections of the Communist International, and
particularly in the German Communist party, to "Leninism" as "the"
sole valid method of Marxian theory. On the other hand, in relation to
the question, in what the essence of "Leninism" as a method consists,
(even among those who count themselves as Leninist), there exist presently several views which depart from one another in essential features.
A large number of leading and other Marxian theoreticians who belong
to the organization of the Communist International and are prepared in
their practical politics to act "according to Lenin," soundly reject in
theory the principle of the method of Lenin as "the" restored method of
"scientific Marxism." They recognize the Leninist method as one method
of orientation, sufficient for the practical-political purposes of the proletarian class struggle in the present period (that is, in a period which in
international scope and in European and American national scope, does
not yet represent *the period of the seizure of political power!*)—but do
not recognize it as the most concrete and truest method of materialistic
dialectics, as the restored method of revolutionary Marxism. For them the

valid method is either the method of the founder of the German Communist party, Rosa Luxemburg, or they declare the Leninist as well as the Luxemburgian method to be one-sided, and want to recognize only the method applied by Karl Marx in his scientific period of maturity as the true Marxian method. It is not possible in this short essay to even begin a thorough debate with these absolute opponents of the Leninist method (as one, or "the" method of scientific Marxism). This task shall be taken up in the following issues of this journal in the collective work of as large a circle of Communist theoreticians as possible. For the present we suffice ourselves with the observation that the political praxis of Bolshevism and the restored form of revolutionary Marxian theory (by Lenin) builds such an undivisible cohesive whole that we are not able to see how, for example, one can bring it about to take, in regard to the role of the Communist party for the proletarian revolution, as "practical politician," the Communist standpoint on the resolution of the Second World Congress, and simultaneously as "scientific Marxist" to comprehend the relationship between the economic development and the proletarian class struggle in the specific Luxumburgian form of the dialectical materialist method. It seems to us that solely from the standpoint of the wholly "materialistic" materialism of Marx, "restored" by Lenin and advanced one step further, which also comprehends *human sensuous activity* and *praxis* as such in its *objectifying reality*, can the Bolshevist version of the "role of the party" be recognized. On the other hand, from the standpoint of the Luxemburgian dialectic, which on its practical side is not nearly so "materialistic" a dialectic as the Leninist one, there is always a painful remnant of "subjectivism," as regards the Leninist account of the role of the party. But be this as it may, so much seems clear: a resolution on the "Basic principles of Leninism," and a system of "Leninist Propaganda," which could be collectively agreed upon at the Fifth World Congress by Luxemburgian and Leninistic Marxists (to this must be added, thirdly, those Marxists who recognize neither the Luxemburgian further development nor the Leninistic restoration of the Marxian method as genuine and complete Marxism) would unavoidably remain just as unsatisfactory as a Communist program overwhelmingly agreed upon by these same theoreticians for the entire Communist International. The complete clarification of the relation between the Luxemburgian and the Leninistic methods of Marxian theory comprises the indispensable presuppositions for the determination of the "Basic Principles and Propaganda of Leninism."

Irrespective of the conflict between the Luxemburgians and the Leninists, there exists no general agreement today on the question of the essence of Leninism as a theoretical method; or stronger, this agreement exists today even less than previously. And it is also entirely understandable that, at a time when as the consequence of an acute crisis the most important questions of Bolshevik praxis have become the object of a bitter factional controversy, the question of the theoretical method of Leninism has also to be pulled into the maelstrom of the struggle, for the methodological consciousness of a Marxian-Communist party does not stand outside of, or in any sense above, the praxis of the party, but rather builds an important constituent of this revolutionary praxis itself. We should therefore not wonder that we find again in the presently undertaken attempts at a determination of the methods of Leninist dialectics—undertaken by various sides—all the factions which today also practically oppose one another in the struggle over tactics and other practical-political questions inside the Comintern. Particularly interesting in this regard is an essay by the comrade *Thalheimer*, "On the Application of the Materialistic Dialectic by Lenin in Some Questions of the Proletarian Revolution," which appeared in volumes 1/2 of the new Communist journal *Arbeiterliteratur*.

III

Comrade *Thalheimer* wants to explicate the Leninist method, which according to him is nothing but the same *Marxist method of materialist dialectics* which Lenin applied with the same boldness and with the same foresight and exactness as Marx himself. He shall do this by the development of three particular questions: the question of proletarian dictatorship; the agrarian question, and the question of the nationalist and imperialist wars. The section on the question of the dictatorship ends with the statement that Lenin characterized the Soviet form of the state not as "the finally discovered political form" of the dictatorship of the working class, but rather only as "a new type" of state in which the possibility of deviating "species, varieties, forms" of this type is contained. The section on the agrarian question explains that Lenin, by his treatment of this question, has given "a particularly instructive and exact application of the materialist-dialectical method." (This application consists, according to Thalheimer's portrayal, in the fact that Lenin, in order to save the kernel of the matter of the proletarian revolution—that is, the transfer of the political power to the proletariat—allowed to let fall all "rigid" demands of the previous Bolshevist agrarian program and trust that in the course of "life" everything else would find itself "by itself" "as the result of the power of example, as the result of practical considerations.") In the third and last section Comrade Thalheimer characterizes Lenin's treatment of the national question as "a true model of *concrete* dialectical analysis." For Lenin, on the one hand, critically destroyed the falsifications of social patriotism, and on the other hand also stressed that under certain conditions even in Europe during the World War the transformation of the imperialist war into a nationalist war would be to be sure, "not probable" but was certainly nonetheless "theoretically not impossible."

It lies far from us to want to stand back even by one hair's breadth from the admiration with which Comrade Thalheimer appraises Lenin's solution to these three important and difficult questions. We must, however, very seriously raise this question: To what extent has Lenin in his treatment of these questions *as portrayed by Comrade Thalheimer* given such "particularly" instructive and exact model examples of the application of the materialist method of Marxism? In what, for example, consists the particularly instructive and exact use of the materialist dialectical method in the Leninist approach to the agrarian question? *Karl Marx* also, as is known, recognized the capability of the revolutionary class, as soon as they had raised themselves, "to find *immediately* in their own situation the content and the material of their revolutionary activity: to strike down enemies, to seize measures given by the need of war, to carry forward the consequences of their own deeds. They set no theoretical undertakings above their own tasks" (*Class Struggles in France*, Dietzsche edition, p. 31). The theoreticians and practitioners of the Russian Revolution could trust in the middle of the struggle to the immanent, unconscious and natural dialectic with the same right which permeates in "life" and in the revolutionary class struggle as a part of this life "from itself." But does he apply the dialectical method here, precisely where he (to speak with Marx) "denies theoretical undertakings"? Does he apply the dialectic thereby in a "particularly instructive" and "particularly exact" form?

We suggest, rather, that to the contrary, precisely the position is reached where the highly developed materialist dialectic, which according to its conception of the historical process of the proletarian revolution should be fully comprehended, reaches its limit, where the concrete historical process in its material living reality, to be sure, proceeds dialectically but at a certain point in the course of its process cannot be grasped by the dialectician. It belongs to the requirements of an exact theory of the Marxian method not to ignore the existence of this limit; but it is already too much when one wants precisely to see in this the actual *kernel* of the "materialist dialectics" of Marx and Lenin. Similarly, although in another way, Comrade Thalheimer constructs his two other chosen examples of Lenin's application of the Marxian method in a way which certainly belong to a true materialism, and in no sense *to any* metaphysical methodology, but nonetheless, for heaven's sake, does not make up the *innermost essence* of this dialectical materialist method, the main feature and the kernel of materialism, of Marxism and Leninism generally. And to this distortion of the essence of the Marxist-Leninist method, which he accomplishes concretely in his three examples, he further adds, in the introduction and in scattered remarks in his essay, an equally contorted general theory of the essence of this method. He exaggerates the Marxian basic principle that the truth is always concrete into the caricature that the *results* of materialist dialectical thought in Lenin as well as Marx could not at all, never, and in no form *generally* be valid beyond the momentary realm of experience out of which it is derived and for which it is determined—as if Marx (e.g., in his letter to Michailowski) and Lenin (e.g., in the introduction to "Radicalism," which has the subtitle: "In what form can one speak of the international importance of the Russian Revolution?") had not very exactly *distinguished* between those results of *their* materialist dialectical research which have such general importance and those which do not. What then is a "materialistic-dialectical" method worth which gives us nothing more than that which in some sense reaches out beyond the already known present experience? Or further, as Thalheimer expresses it, brings forth nothing more than *historical* results, on the one side theoretical reflections (!), analysis of a particular time, on the other only guidelines for the struggle of the proletariat, "likewise in a particular time"?

In reality this new method, created by Comrade Thalheimer and transformed out of the Marxist-Leninist materialist dialectic, has nothing more to do with the materialist dialectics. In his efforts to grasp the materialist methodology of Marx and Lenin totally "materially," as a method of a pure historical science of experience and practice, Comrade Thalheimer has already overstepped the limits of that which one can call materialist dialectics, and has achieved a completely undialectical historicism, positivism, and practicism. While Rosa Luxemburg, as we have indicated above, in her version of human praxis has not wholly become materialistic, and in this one respect has remained a Hegelian dialectician, Comrade Thalheimer, on the contrary, has driven out with the remains of the Hegelian dialectic at the same time everything dialectical in the methodology of Marxian science; the materialist dialectical method of Marx, which essentially is the concrete comprehension of the proletarian revolution as historical process and as a historical action of the proletarian class, transforms itself in Thalheimer into a merely passive, ideological "reflection" of solitary historical factualities diverse in time and place.

This theoretical falsification of the essence of the Marxist-Leninist dialectical method leads practically to a devaluation of all the results won by Marx, Engels, Lenin, and others through these methods. And it is fairly easy to see where this tendency towards the devaluation of the results of the Marxist-Leninist research method has come from and where it leads. Let us take the example, repeated a hundred times by Thalheimer, that the Soviet state is characterized by Lenin only as a type with possible varieties and species. One can devalue the results of the Marxist-Leninist methodology so much only when one, whether consciously or unconsciously, wants to *disengage oneself from these results*. The conception of the Soviet state as only one type of proletarian dictatorship, with a multiplicity of possible forms, makes it possible for the theoretician of "Leninism" to disengage himself from the "rigid" form of the council dictatorship (which is, according to Lenin, capable of further development, but is even so, "the" beginning of "the" socialistic forms of democracy!) and reach the various possible "species, varieties" and degenerations of this "type," for example, the Saxony "workers' government." And likewise with all other "results" of the Marxist and Leninist theory. If they all are purely "historical creations," bound to their particular historical presuppositions, applicable only to the relation of a particular time and land, then it is self-evident that under new relations, against new experiences, and changed political needs all of these previous "results" of Marxism would lose their validity and could and must be replaced by new knowledge and guidelines, in which these new situations now "are reflected" for the "Leninist" application of the materialist dialectic. In transforming the revolutionary dialectical materialism of Marx and Lenin into a no longer dialectical and therefore also no longer revolutionary (and the converse: no longer revolutionary and thus also no longer dialectical), *purely historical, empirical science and practice*, Comrade Thalheimer posits under the seductive clothing of "Leninism" actually a *method* which by tendency is *opportunistic* and *reformistic* in place of the revolutionary method of Marxism.

IV

We have treated Thalheimer's conception of the Leninist method with such detail not only because Comrade Thalheimer has been named as the second speaker on the "question of the program" at the Fifth World

Congress, and thus for that reason will be heard at the Congress with particular attention on the question of the essence of Leninism as methodology. More importantly, it was crucial to show by a typical example, in detail and clearly, that the attempt of a determination of the "Basic Principles of Leninism," and particularly a fixing of the essence of the Leninist method at the Fifth World Congress is bound up not only with great present difficulties, but beyond this also with certain *dangers* which are all the greater in so far as they remain very much unrecognized and unwatched precisely in this seemingly purely theoretical region, far removed from the practical struggle of the factions. Recently there have been attempts to smuggle in under the revered, revolutionary flag of "Leninism," various revisionistic, reformistic, opportunistic and liquidating contraband in the *praxis and the theory* of revolutionary communism. And in its innermost foundation the theory of Leninist method which Thalheimer has now formulated signifies only a false theory of a false political praxis. Just as the opportunist and reformist united front tactic is related to the revolutionary method of agitation and mass mobilization applied in Germany since the Leipzig Party Congress, so does the "Leninist" method of Thalheimer and his close comrades relate to the genuine method of revolutionary Leninism, that is to the dialectical method of revolutionary Marxism completed and restored by Lenin. The Fifth World Congress, in the explication of the fundamentals of this position, will have to erect particular *protective walls against the rising flood of Communist revisionism in the questions of the program* and in the question of the *Basic Principles of Leninism*, just as with all other, immediately practical questions of Communist politics. By the fullfillment of this *negative* function it can powerfully counteract the threatening collapse of the completed method of revolutionary Marxist science restored by Lenin, which in its essence is nothing other than the theoretical consciousness of the revolutionary actions of the proletarian class. For a *positive* fixation of the essence of Leninism as *method*, the present moment in the development of the Comintern is just as little appropriate as for the fixation of a final Communist *program*, valid for an entire epoch of Communist politics.

Translated by Roy Jameson

Note

1. More on this can be found in the last section of Zinoviev's essay, "V. I. Lenin—Genius, Teacher, Leader, and Human," nos. 31/32 of KI, and in a special essay by Bela Kun, "The Propaganda of Leninism," in no. 33.

The Marxist Ideology in Russia

> Communism, for us, is not a state of things to be established nor an
> ideal to which reality must adapt itself; we call communism the
> actual movement which transforms existing conditions.—Marx

We have to deal here with an especially pointed example of the striking
discrepancy which in one form or another is noticeable in all phases of
the historical development of Marxism. It may be characterized as the
contradiction between the Marxian ideology on the one hand, and the
actual historical movement which, at a given time, is concealed beneath
that ideological disguise.

It is now almost a century since a special censor, dispatched from Berlin to supplant the local authorities of Cologne in the difficult task of
garroting the "ultra-democratic" paper edited by the 24 year old Karl
Marx, reported to the Prussian government that the *Rheinische Zeitung*
might now safely be permitted to continue as the "spiritus rector of the
whole undertaking, Dr. Marx," had definitely retired from his job and
there was no possibility of a successor capable of keeping up the "odious
dignity" hitherto achieved by the paper or of "prosecuting its policy with
energy." That advice, however, was not followed by the Prussian authorities who in this matter were directed, as has now become known, by the
Russian Tsar Nicholas I whose vice-chancellor, Count de Nesselrode, had
just then threatened the Prussian ambassador in Moscow to lay before
His Imperial Majesty's eyes "the infamous attack which the *Rheinische
Zeitung*, published at Cologne, had recently made on the Russian cabinet." That happened in Prussia, 1843.

Three decades later, the censorship authorities of tsarist Russia herself
permitted the publication in Russia of Marx's work—the first version of
Capital ever to appear in another than the German language. The decision was based on this precious argument: "Although the political convictions of the author are entirely socialist and although the whole book
is of a definitely socialist character, the manner of its presentation is
certainly not such as to make the book open to all, and in addition it is
written in a strictly mathematically scientific style so that the committee
declares the book to be immune from prosecution."

The tsarist regime which was so eager to suppress even the slightest
offence committed in any European country against the Russian supremacy, and so utterly careless as to the dangers implied in Marx's scientific

exposure of the capitalistic world as a whole, was in fact never touched by the fierce attacks directed by Marx in all his later career against the "immense and unresisted encroachments of that barbarous power whose head is at St. Petersburg and whose hands are in every cabinet of Europe." Yet it was to succumb to just that apparently altogether remote menace which had invisibly lurked in the Trojan horse inadvertently admitted into the precincts of the Holy Empire. It was finally thrown over by the masses of the Russian workers whose vanguard had learned its revolutionary lesson from that "mathematically scientific" work of a lonely thinker, *Das Kapital*.

Unlike Western Europe—where the Marxist theory arose in a period when the bourgeois revolution was already approaching its close and Marxism expressed a real and actualized tendency to pass beyond the goals of the bourgeois revolutionary movement, the tendency of the *proletarian class*—Marxism in Russia was from the beginning nothing more than an ideological form assumed by the material struggle for putting across the capitalist development in a pre-capitalist country. For this purpose Marxism was taken up greedily as the last word of Europe by the entire progressive intelligensia. Bourgeois society fully developed in Western Europe was here just in its birth pangs. Yet on this new soil the bourgeois principle could not make use, once again, of those historical outworn illusions and self-deceptions with which it had concealed from itself the restricted bourgeois content of its developmental struggles in its first heroic phase in the West, and had kept its passions to the level of great historical events. For penetration into the East, it needed a new ideological costume. And it was just the Marxist doctrine taken over from the West which seemed to be most able to render the growing bourgeois development in Russia that important historical service. Marxism was far superior, in this respect, to the native Russian creed of the revolutionary Narodniki (populists). While the latter started from the belief that capitalism as existing in the "unholy" countries of the West was impossible in Russia, Marxism, by reason of its own historical origin, presupposed a fully accomplished capitalistic civilization as a necessary historical stage in the process of the ultimate realization of a truly socialistic society.

Yet in order to render the rising bourgeois society in Russia such ideological mid-wife service, the Marxist doctrine required a few modifications even in its purely theoretical contents. This is the basic reason for the considerable theoretical concessions, otherwise hard to explain, which Marx and Engels in the 70's and 80's made to the set of ideas, essentially quite irreconcilable with their theory, that up to then had been held by the Russian populists. The final and most comprehensive form of those concessions is contained in the well-known oracular statement of the *Foreword* to the Russian translation of the *Communist Manifesto* (1882):

> The object of the Communist Manifesto was to proclaim an in-evitably impending dissolution of present-day bourgeois property. In Russia, however, we find by the side of the capitalist order which is developing with feverish haste and by the side of bourgeois landed property which is as yet in the process of formation, the larger half of the land owned by the peasants in common.
>
> Thus arises the question. Can the Russian peasant community in which the primitive common ownership of the soil subsists, although in a stage of already far advanced disintegration, be immediately transformed into a higher and communistic form of landed property, or must it previously go through the same process of dissociation which is represented in the historical development of the West?
>
> The only possible answer to this question at the present time is the following:—If the Russian Revolution becomes the signal for a workers' revolution in the West so that the two supplement each other, then the present-day Russian system of common ownership can serve as a starting-point of a communistic development.

In these sentences, and in numerous similar utterances occurring in their correspondence, in the letters to the Russian populist writer Nikolai-on, in the letter to Vera Sassulitch, and in Marx's reply to a fatalistic interpretation of his theory of necessary historical stages by the Russian critic, Michaelovski, there is already anticipated in a way the whole of the later development of Russian Marxism and thus also the ever widening gap between its ideology and the actual historical content of the movement. It is true that Marx and Engels qualified their acknowl-edgement of the intrinsic socialist possibilities of existing pre-capitalistic conditions in Russia by the cautious proviso that it was only together with a workers' revolution in the West that the Russian Revolution might skip the capitalist stage and pass from the prevailing semi-patriarchal and feudal conditions directly to socialist conditions. (The same proviso was later repeated by Lenin.) It is also true that this condition was not fulfilled (neither then nor after October, 1917) and that, on the contrary, the Russian peasant community to which Marx as late as 1882 attributed such a powerful future role, was shortly afterwards completely wiped out of existence. Yet it cannot be denied that even such apparently anti-Marxian slogans as the recent Stalinist "theory" of building up socialism in one country, misusing Marxism as an ideological cloak for a development which in its actual tendency is capitalistic, can appeal not only to the precedent set by the orthodox Marxist Lenin, but even to Marx and Engels themselves. They, too, had been quite prepared, under certain historical conditions, to remold their critico-materialistic "Marxist" theory into a mere ideological adornment of a revolutionary movement which claimed to be socialistic in its ultimate tendency, but which in its actual process was inevitably subject to all sorts of bourgeois limitations. There is only this difference, and a remarkable difference indeed, that Marx, Engels and Lenin did so in order to promote a future revolutionary movement while Stalin definitely applied the "Marxist" ideology for the defence of a non-socialistic status quo, and as a weapon against every tendency of revolutionary realization.

And so began—actually during the life-time and with the conscious and active collaboration of Marx and Engels—that particular historical *change of function* through which Marxism, adopted as a ready-made doctrine by the Russian revolutionists, was in the further development transformed from a theoretical tool of a proletarian socialist revolution into a mere ideological disguise of a bourgeois-capitalist development. As we have seen, that change of function implied from the very outset a certain transformation of the doctrine itself which in this case was achieved through a mutual interpenetration and fusion of the traditional populist creed and the newly adopted Marxist ideological elements. Though that transformation of the Marxist theory was at first admitted by Marx and Engels (as they imagined) as a transitory step only, to be retraced by the imminent "workers' revolution in the West," it soon turned out to have been in fact the first step toward the permanent transformation of their revolutionary Marxist theory into a mere revolutionary myth which could at the utmost work as an inspiration for the first stages of a beginning revolution but in its final outcome was bound to act as a brake upon the real revolutionary development rather than as its furtherance.

It is a spectacle worth noting, the way this historical process of ideological adaptation of the Marxist doctrine has been worked out during the following decades by the different schools of the Russian revolutionaries themselves. It may be safely said that in those violent debates on the perspective of the capitalist *development* in Russia which were waged in the closely restricted circles of the Russian Marxists at home and in emigration from the 90's to the outbreak of the war and to the overthrow of the tsarist government in 1917, and which have found their most important theoretical expression in the principal economic work of Lenin,

The Development of Capitalism in Russia (1899), the true content of
the original Marxian theory as a theoretical form of an independent
proletarian and strictly socialist movement was, in fact, no longer represented by either side. This is certainly true with regard to the so-called
legal Marxists who in their "scientific" exposition of the objective aspect
of the Marxist doctrine boasted of a particularly unadulterated "purity,"
but abundantly made up for that doctrinal righteousness by utterly aban-
doning all practical consequences of the Marxist principles which might
possibly pass beyond the restricted bourgeois goals. Nor was the whole
of the revolutionary Marxian theory represented by other currents which
during that period sought to combine in one form or another a recognition of the transitory necessity of capitalist development in Russia with
an anticipated ultimate struggle against the future conditions of society
which were to be created by that very development. Here belongs the
above-mentioned learned populist writer Nikolai-on, the Russian translator of *Das Kapital*, who in the early 90's, under the direct influence of
the Marxian doctrine, made the transition from the orthodox populist
belief in the absolute *impossibility of capitalism in Russia* to the Marxistically revised populist theory of the *impossibility of a normal and
organic development of capitalism in Russia*. Here belongs too, the lusty
materialistic opponent of populist "idealism," the orthodox Marxist
Lenin, and his followers who, in the later period, after their break with
the Western-minded "Mensheviks" claimed to be in their theory as well
as in their practice the only true inheritors of the entire revolutionary
contents of Marx's theory as revived and restituted in the doctrine of
Bolshevist Marxism.

When from our present vantage point reached by historical experience
we look back at the heated theoretical disputes of that earlier phase there
seems to be a quite obvious relationship between the populist theory of
the "impossibility of a normal and organic development of capitalism
in Russia" (as represented by the Marxian Narodnik Nikolai-on and
combated at the time by the Marxists of all shades, the "legal" as well as
the "revolutionary," the Mensheviks and Bolsheviks) on one side, and
the two mutually opposed theories which in a recent phase of the development of Russian Marxism faced each other in the form of a ruling
"Stalinism" and an oppositional *"Trotskyism."* Paradoxically enough,
both the prevailing "national-socialist" theory of Stalin as to the possibility of building up socialism in one country, and the apparently diametri-
cally opposed "internationalist" thesis, set up by Trotsky, of the inevitability of a "permanent" revolution—that is, of a revolution passing
beyond the bourgeois revolutionary goals simultaneously on the Russian

and on the European (or the world-wide) scale—rest on the common ideological basis of a neo-Narodnik belief in the absence or impossibility of a "normal and organic" development of capitalism in Russia.

Both Trotsky and Stalin base their versions of the Marxist ideology on the authority of Lenin. Indeed, even the most orthodox of the orthodox Marxists who had fought a bitter struggle both against the Narodnikism of Nikolai-on and against the Parvus-Trotskyist theory of the "permanent revolution" before October, 1917, and who, in the same way, had most consistently opposed after October the then prevailing tendency to glorify the meager achievements of the later so-called war-communism of 1918–20, concluded that life-long fight for critico-revolutionary realism by upholding at a decisive moment the neo-populist concept of a home-made Russian socialism against the actually prevailing conditions. Within a few weeks those who had opposed the socialistic idealization of the first years and who at the first announcement of the NEP of 1921 had still quite soberly declared this "new economic policy of a worker's and peasant's state" to be a necessary step backward from the further-going attempts of war-communism, discovered the socialistic nature of state capitalism and a cooperatively tinged yet essentially bourgeois economy. Thus, it was not the Leninist epigone Stalin but the orthodox Marxist Lenin who, at that historical turning-point of the revolutionary development when the hitherto undecided practical tendencies of the Russian Revolution were "seriously and for a long time" directed to the restoration of a non-socialistic economy, at the same time added what he then deemed to be an indispensable ideological supplement to that final restriction of its practical aims. It was the orthodox Marxist Lenin who in opposition to all his earlier declarations first set up the new Marxist myth of the inherently socialist character of the Soviet state and of the thereby basically guaranteed possibility of a complete realization of socialist society in an isolated Soviet Russia.

This degeneration of the Marxian doctrine to a mere ideological justification of what in its actual tendency is a capitalist state and thus, inevitably, a state based on the suppression of the progressive revolutionary movement of the proletarian class, closes the first phase of the history of the Marxist ideology in Russia. This is at the same time the only phase during which the development of Marxism in Russia seems to show an independent character. Yet it should be pointed out that from a more comprehensive viewpoint, in spite of appearances and of many real differences caused by the specific conditions prevailing at different times in different countries, the historical development of *Russian Marxism* (inclusive of its last Leninist and Stalinist stages) is essentially the same as that of so-called *Western (or Social Democratic) Marxism* of which it really was and still is an integrating, though at present outwardly detached, component. Just as *Russia* never was the unique and holy country as dreamed by the Panslavists, and *bolshevism* never was that crude and backward form of a pseudo-Marxist theory corresponding to the primitive conditions of the tsarist regime as it was represented by the would-be refined Marxists of England, France, and Germany, so the *bourgeois degeneration of Marxism in Russia today* is in no way essentially different from the outcome of the series of ideological transformations which, during the war and post-war periods and, even more visibly, after the ultimate annihilation of all former Marxist strongholds by the unopposed advent of fascism and nazism, befell the various currents of so-called Western Marxism. Just as the "national socialism" of Herr Hitler and the "corporative state" of Mussolini vie with the "Marxism" of Stalin in an attempt to invade, by the use of a pseudo-socialist ideology, the very brains and souls of their workers as well as their physical and social existence, so does the "democratic" regime of a people's front government presided by the "Marxist" Leon Blum or, for that matter, by Mr. Chautemps himself, differ from the present-day Soviet state not in substance, but only by a less efficient exploitation of the Marxist ideology. Less than at any previous time does Marxism today serve as a theoretical weapon in an independent struggle of the proletariat, for the proletariat, and by the proletariat. All so-called "Marxist" parties, both theoretically and in their actual practice, appear deeply engaged in contributing, as minor partners of the leading bourgeois protagonists, their modest share to the solution of the problem which the American "Marxist," L. R. Boudin, quite recently called "the greatest problem in Marxism—our relation to the internal struggles of capitalist society."

Position on Russia and the Communist Party

In the time after Lenin's death and after the current "stabilization" of capital domination on a world-wide scale, and the year's long "prosperity" in some countries, especially the USA, many people have newly come to "communism" or "Soviet Russia" who cannot at all understand the critique of today's Russia and the Communist party which we developed in the first decade of the Revolution 1917–1927. These people, whom I have for a long time designated in conversations as the "second wave of conscripts of Leninism," have themselves never been united with the revolution of the Russian workers as a direct component of a world revolutionary movement in which they themselves participated. Rather, they are aroused by the "new Russia" and its leading Bolshevik party, with its "five year plans," with its cultural progressiveness in pedagogical fields, law, art, and film, which have arisen from the Russian Revolution in its consequently forced national limitation to the Russian *state*, and which still has continuing vitality as a powerful revolutionary movement. They see that in Russia another group has risen to power, influence, and effectiveness than in the old European and American world, and to be sure another group with which the new Communists, or "friends of the new Russia" to whom I am referring, can more easily identify with than with the previous type of leader in their own land, or the new fascist type of leader who is advancing toward this position in some lands (and who belongs to the historical group of a still older human type). The new friends of communism have in a sense the same relation to the new Russian state that Hegel once represented in regard to the new Prussian state: "We are today so advanced that we can only hold as valid Ideas and that which has arisen from Reason. More closely seen, the Prussian State corresponds to Reason."

The application of the Hegelian principle "what is real is rational" to today's Russian state, and the Communist parties which are related to it and supported by it in other lands, holds not only for that universally freedom loving and progressive layer from which in a time of a rising revolutionary movement the struggling proletariat received reinforcement, support, and the widening of its front, but to a certain extent holds also for the workers themselves. *One cannot protest against a reality simply in the name of an abstract principle.* There is today nowhere in the world any longer an organization of revolutionary-inclined workers, or even a "direction" which really embodies in itself revolution as a spiritual ideal, which one can oppose as the *truly revolutionary movement* to the "degenerated" Russian Communist party, which "puts the national state interest above the international proletarian class interest." If the belief in "the construction of socialism in Soviet Russia" is only a metaphysical consolation, a myth, or a revolutionary faith-in-the-beyond (*Jenseits-Gläubigkeit*) for the workers of countries outside of Russia who are attracted by communism, this faith-in-the-beyond no longer today confronts a revolutionary here-and-now (*Diesseitigkeit*) in any intelligible form. The Russian Revolution from February and October, 1917, and in the following years, was, considered purely as a movement, the proletarian movement that most involved the masses in the entire previous history. It destroyed the tsarist state and demolished the old capitalist ruling class. In all other lands the workers were either defeated or in cruel ways were robbed of all previously won positions, through sharpened pressure from outside and through increasing decay from within. Everywhere the workers are threatened in the present economic crisis, into which in some countries already a sharpening of exploitation and oppression has entered, and the destruction of all remains of an independent proletarian class movement and even a class consciousness through fascism. Everything that the workers are told about the state-capitalist continuation, restoration and sharpening of already developed forms of capitalist oppression and exploitation in Russia, comes either from the mouths of their old well-known enemies, capitalists, fascists, and social democrats, or it unavoidably remains extremely vague, abstract, incomprehensible, and unsympathetic. All these critiques do not contain and cannot at this time contain any sort of call to action for revolutionary workers. For all these reasons it is unavoidable that up until the rise of a new, independent class movement of the international proletariat, even the working class itself and precisely its most revolutionary components can look at today's Soviet Russia as the *real* and thence revolutionary-*rational* implementation of the posited goals that are today still not implemented in their own countries.

London, March 30, 1935

Translated by Douglas Kellner

Note

Korsch accompanies this unpublished document with the note: "only as an enclosure in private letters to friends; please do not duplicate." First published in *Jahrbuch der Arbeiterbewegung 2* (Frankfurt, 1974), pp. 146–148.

6. The Crisis of Marxism

Introduction

After the left opposition was hopelessly splintered, Korsch began a new period of inquiry into the crisis of Marxism with various discussion groups and lecture series in Berlin in the late 1920's. From November, 1928, to February, 1929, Korsch gave a lecture series on "scientific socialism," and throughout 1931 he participated in a work group on dialectical materialism that met in the home of Bertolt Brecht. In 1932 he participated in a "study circle of critical Marxism" concerned with the theme, "what is living and dead in Marxism."[1] Many of the ideas in these lectures and discussion groups were formulated into theses and short essays such as "The Crisis of Marxism" and the material later published in English as part of "A Non-dogmatic Approach to Marxism" (i.e., "Theses on Hegel and Revolution," "On an Activistic Form of Materialism and on the Class and Partisan Character of Science").

The seven theses of "The Crisis of Marxism" contain a pithy summary of Korsch's emerging critique of Marxism. They were formulated perhaps as early as 1927, were developed and discussed in seminars and lectures, but were never published by Korsch himself.[2] Korsch was continuously applying the historical materialist method to Marxism itself. Whereas in *Marxism and Philosophy*, he saw Marxism entering a new revolutionary phase that promised a renewal of Marxist theory and practice, now, after the clear failure of the German revolution, Korsch was not so optimistic as to the possibility of restoring Marxism to an efficacious revolutionary force in the working-class movement. There was no longer any movement that really embodied revolutionary Marxism, Korsch concluded, and Marxism's actual function was to legitimize reformist practice with revolutionary rhetoric, hence creating a rupture between theory and practice. Korsch now began to ponder whether there was even any sense in trying to restore Marxist theory which, after all, was the product of the nineteenth century. At this point, although Korsch saw Marxism as *"the classical expression of the new revolutionary consciousness of the proletarian class fighting for its liberation,"*[3] he wasn't really clear as to what role Marxism could or should play in the class struggles of the future. This profound ambiguity toward Marxism was to haunt Korsch for the rest of his life.

Korsch's analysis of the crisis of Marxism took the form of both a critique of Marxist orthodoxy (the "Marxist center") and a critical confrontation with the Marxian theory itself. In "The Passing of Marxist Orthodoxy," first published in Germany in 1932 and republished in English in 1937,[4] Korsch questioned the relevance of the theories of "Bernstein-Kautsky-Luxemburg-Lenin" for today's class struggles. Marxian orthodoxy, Korsch complained, both in the German Social Democratic movement and in the Bolshevik movement, was used as a theoretical veil that covered the non-revolutionary political practice of the working-class parties and governments, and thus served as an instrument of legitimation for working-class movements that were no longer revolutionary. The veil of revolutionary Marxist rhetoric created a "socialism legend" that concealed the fact that the actual practice was non-socialist and merely served to dupe the workers into submitting to the party, union, or state. Rather than serving as a force for the liberation of the working class, Marxism had degenerated into an instrument of its domination. The title, "The Passing of Marxian Orthodoxy," indicates that an era has passed, and Korsch holds out no vision of a new era in this sober and bleak retrospective on the failure of Marxian orthodoxy to achieve the liberation of the working class.

In "On Some Fundamental Presuppositions for a Materialist Discussion of Crisis Theory," Korsch submitted the current versions of the Marxist capitalist crisis theories to a withering critique. This article appeared in the ultra-left Dutch council Communist journal *Der Proletarier* in 1933 and is translated in this anthology for the first time.[5] Korsch saw an exaggeration of the role of the crisis theory in Marxist discussions of revolution, which he believed has a detrimental effect on political practice. The problem is that the leading Marxist crisis theorists either postulate an "iron law" of capitalist collapse for a system in its "death crisis" (Kautsky and the Marxist center), or postulated capitalist stabilization that precludes intense crises (Bernstein and the "revisionists"). In any case, Korsch believed that the leading crisis theories were but "a merely passive reflection of previous stages of economic development," and did not represent, and did not contribute to developing, "revolutionary class consciousness" and the "capacity for action." Moreover, the theories often ideologically reflect a political position rather than denoting real tendencies of capitalist development. For instance, Bernstein refused to surrender this theory of capitalist stabilization despite intense crises in

1900, 1907, World War I, and 1920–1921. Korsch concluded that the crisis theory played more of the role of a myth that legitimated a certain kind of political practice than a scientific prognosis of capitalist development. He did believe that the economic system of capitalism was crisis-ridden and would generate constant working-class struggles, but he did not think that one could predict in advance the actual crisis, and called instead for "exact and thorough investigation of the present capitalist mode of production and its recognizable immanent tendencies of development," emphasizing the readiness for struggle and possibilities for action of the working class. Korsch thus wants to focus the Marxist theory on the struggles of the working class, rather than on the objective economic situation.

In "Marxism and the Present Task of the Proletarian Class Struggle," Korsch sums up his thoughts on the crisis of Marxism, and offers his most hitherto blistering critique of the Marxian theory itself. It is significant that this article, published in 1938, the same year as Korsch's book *Karl Marx*, appeared in the journal *Living Marxism* under a pseudonym, l.h.[6] It is interesting here that all of Korsch's critique of Marxism which is not expressed in *Karl Marx* is found in a highly condensed, suggestive, and subtle form in this essay. As such, it is an important summary of Korsch's critique of Marxism. It should be noted, however, that Korsch identifies with the "critical and materialistic principle of Marx" against the "quasi-religious attitude" of those Marxists who identify Marxism both with the objective course of capitalist development and the struggles of the working class. Korsch is highly skeptical here about the possibility of "restoring Marxism" which in its current form is characterized as a "dead revolutionary ideology," a "ghost," a "mythology." It is not clear whether these negative characterizations adhere merely to bankrupt Marxian orthodoxy or to Marxism itself. For after a highly negative critique of Marxism the article ends by claiming that "the whole criticism raised above concerns *only the ideological endeavors* of the last 50 years to 'preserve' or to 'restore,' for immediate application, a thoroughly mythicized 'revolutionary Marxist doctrine.' Nothing in this article is directed against the scientific results reached by Marx and Engels and a few of their followers on various fields of social research which, in many ways, hold good to this day. Above all, nothing in this article is directed against what may be called, in a very comprehensive sense, *the Marxist, that is, the independent revolutionary movement of the international working class.*"[7] Korsch concludes that "There seems to be good reason, in the search for what is living or may be recalled to life in the present deathly standstill of the revolutionary workers' movement, to 'return' to that practical and not merely ideological broadmindedness by which *the first Marxist (at the same time Proudhonist, Blanquist, Bakunist, trade-unionist, etc.) International Working Men's Association* welcomed into its ranks all workers who subscribed to the principle of an independent proletarian class struggle. As enunciated in the first of its rules, drawn up by Marx, *'the emancipation of the working classes must be conquered by the working classes themselves.'* "[8]

Hence, we see that the overall effect of Korsch's analysis of the crisis of Marxism discloses a profound ambiguity toward Marxism, rooted in the ambiguity of a situation in which it was not clear whether the existing Social Democratic and Communist movements were advancing or containing the liberation of the working class. Nor was it clear whether Marxism was playing an emancipatory or mystificatory role in this historical process. Korsch's succeeding theoretical labors would be above all concerned with further exploring the crisis of Marxism and seeking its resolution.

Notes

1. *Alternative* 105, no. 18 (December 1975), published the announcement and program of the lecture series held in the Karl Marx Schule where Korsch and his wife taught; see also Hedda Korsch, "Memories," pp. 43–44.

2. Karl Korsch, "Krise des Marxismus," unpublished manuscript. In a letter to Paul Partos, April 26, 1935, in *Jahrbuch Arbeiterbewegung 2*, Korsch refers to "his theses on the crisis of Marxism, 1927"; translated by Otto Koester as "The Crisis of Marxism" in this anthology.

3. Korsch, "Crisis of Marxism."

4. Karl Korsch, "Ausgang der Marx-Orthodoxie," in *Gegner 6*, nos. 4–5 (March 1932); published in English in *International Council Correspondence* 3, nos. 11–12 (December 1937). In this anthology as "The Passing of Marxian Orthodoxy."

5. Karl Korsch, "Uber einige grundsätzliche Voraussetzungen für eine materialistische Diskussion der Krisentheorie," *Proletarier 1*, no. 1 (February 1933), translated in this anthology as "Some Fundamental Presuppositions for a Materialist Discussion of Crisis Theory," by Karl-Heinz Otto and Andrew Giles-Peters.

6. Karl Korsch, "Marxism and the Present Task of the Proletarian Class Struggle," *Living Marxism* 4, no. 4 (August 1938).

7. Ibid.

8. Ibid.

The Crisis of Marxism

1

Marxism today is in the midst of an historical and theoretical crisis. It is not simply a crisis within the *Marxist movement*, but a crisis of *Marxism itself*.

This crisis reveals itself externally in the complete collapse of the dominant position—partially illusory, but also partially real—that Marxism held during the pre-World War I era in the European working-class movement. It reveals itself *internally* in the transformation of Marxist theory and practice, a transformation which is most immediately apparent in Marxists' altered position vis-à-vis their own national state as well as with respect to the bourgeois system of national states as a whole. It is deceptive and even false to see the theoretical origins of the present crisis as resulting either from a perversion or an oversimplification of Marx's and Engels' revolutionary theory at the hands of their successors. It is equally misleading to juxtapose this degenerated, falsified Marxism to the "pure theory" of Marx and Engels themselves. In the final analysis, today's crisis is the crisis of Marx's and Engels' theory as well. The ideological and doctrinaire separation of "pure theory" from the real historical movement, as well as the further development of theory, is itself an expression of the present crisis.

2

The form of Marxism which is currently entering a critical stage was a product of the second half of the nineteenth century. It was created from elements of a theory which was itself formulated under earlier historical conditions, conditions that differed fundamentally from those of the late nineteenth century. These elements were actively incorporated into the working-class movement at a time when European capitalism was not yet fully developed. And here is the genesis for the separation of theory from practice inherent in the entire history of Marxism. From its very beginning, this theory is never the "general expression of existing class struggles." Rather, it is the composite result of the class struggles of a previous historical era, and it consequently lacks any real relation to contemporary class struggles emerging as a result of wholly new conditions.

In the course of historical development, this separation of theory from practice has widened rather than narrowed.

The three contemporary forms of Marxism—"revisionism," "orthodoxy," and the periodic efforts to "restore" original revolutionary Marxism in its pure form—are all based upon this separation. In the final analysis, it is also the source of the present crisis.

3

After 1850 the *altered historical conditions of the new capitalist epoch and of the working-class movement* itself prevented the further development of a living Marxist theory within the unfolding praxis of the workers' movement.

By the year 1850 the first great cycle in the historical development of capitalism had come to a close. During this cycle and on the basis of its *limited capacity* at that time, capitalism had completed all stages of its development to the point where the class-conscious sector of the proletariat was in a position to place social revolution on the historical agenda. Thus, on the limited economic basis of that period, the *class movement of the proletariat* had reached a *relatively high level* of development. This development found practical expression in the revolutionary struggles of that period, and theoretical expression in the early formulations of the so-called utopian socialists concerning the content of proletarian class consciousness and the goals of the proletarian revolution.

It was during this time and in the later development of their theories, which resulted from the experiences of this period, that Marx and Engels arrived at their *twofold theoretical achievement.* On the one hand, they criticized all aspects of the existing class society (economic basis and superstructure) from the newly acquired perspective of the proletariat. In so doing, they appropriated unaltered the *content* of this new proletarian class consciousness directly from the reality of existing class struggles and as it was formulated theoretically by the utopian socialists. Simultaneously, however, they criticized the practice of the proletarian movement as well as the theories of the utopian socialists. Drawing upon the highest achievements of bourgeois science, they were able to conceptualize for the proletarian class *the real developmental laws* of the existing capitalist society and hence, at the same time, *the real conditions for revolutionary class actions.*

After 1850 and on an *expanded basis* (geographical, technological, organizational), capitalism began a *new historical cycle* of its development. Under these altered conditions, it was no longer possible for the proletariat to *draw directly* upon Marxist theory in its original form, a theory which had assumed its revolutionary character under the conditions of a past historical epoch. During the 1870's—a *period of crisis and depression* which was particularly conducive to the development of class consciousness—the working class was able to adopt this theory in a formal way. Yet even then it was unable to appropriate completely its revolutionary content—either practically or theoretically.

4

The Marxist theory appropriated by the European workers' movement in the second half of the nineteenth century had partially altered its original revolutionary character during the reception process itself.

The *materialist view of history* grew out of a revolutionary period prior to 1850 as an integral part of the *subjective action* of a revolutionary class, which continually criticizes in theory and overthrows in practice the false illusions and transient appearances of all existing social relationships. In the succeeding period, it developed into a purely abstract and passive theory dealing with the *objective course* of social development as determined by external laws.

Marxist economy was originally formulated as a radical *critique* of bourgeois political economy, a critique which was to have found both theoretical and practical culmination in a real revolution. This original schema was later changed by Marx and altered even more by Engels. Today the apologists for as well as the critics of Marxism view *Marxist economics* as little more than a *scientific system* in which all economic phenomena of bourgeois society are deduced theoretically from an uncritical, axiomatic concept of "value." Marx's revolutionary critique of political economy aimed at the theoretical and practical sublation (*Aufhebung*) of *fetishism*. But fetishism has become the idol of Marxist scientific economists and a thorn in the side of bourgeois and reformist critics of Marxism.

5

Having been absorbed by the modern working class as mere ideology, Marxist science completely ceased developing as a living theory after the death of Marx, Engels and the first generation of their direct disciples. During this period the leading representatives of revolutionary principles in the Marxist parties were forced to fight a defensive battle against the increasingly dominant trend towards reformist theory and practice. At the same time, they opposed any attempts to revitalize the theoretical expression of proletarian class struggle. Confronted with the threat of bourgeois falsifications of traditional Marxist theory, they tended to view their own stagnation as the lesser of two evils. (See Rosa Luxemburg's article "Stillstand und Fortschritt im Marxismus" ["Stagnation and Progress within Marxism"].) At this time the most important impetus for further developing a living theory of proletarian class struggle came from three different directions, each of which consciously *and* unconsciously stood opposed to orthodox Marxist theory. These three were: *unionist reformism, revolutionary syndicalism* and *Leninist Bolshevism.* Despite vast differences, all three shared one common tendency. In one way or another, each attempted to make the subjective action of the working class rather than the objective development of capitalism the main focus of socialist theory. In this regard, all three appear as progressive tendencies within the development of working-class movement and simultaneously as the forerunners of that proletarian class theory and practice which was to develop on a new historical basis.

6

From this overview of the historical origins and determinants of the current Marxist crisis, several conclusions emerge which point to ways for overcoming it.

None of the current trends in Marxism stands as an adequate theoretical expression for the continued needs of the proletarian class struggle— a struggle which, despite occasional defeat, remains revolutionary in its means and its goals. Certainly so-called orthodox Marxism provides the least adequate solution. Of all the contemporary forms of Marxism, this is the most damaging to the progressive development of the proletarian class. After having long since stagnated into ideology, "orthodox Marxism" collapsed as such (Kautsky) in its final phase. Today it is nothing but a hindrance blocking the development of the theory and practice of the proletarian class struggle.

The two other trends which are continuations of pre-World War I Marxism are a different matter. From the perspective of the revolutionary proletariat, neither the *reformist state socialism* of the Social Democratic parties nor *Communist anti-imperialism* can be written off simply as reactionary movements. The relationship of today's proletariat to the Social Democratic parties and the Communist party is virtually identical to the relationship of the proletarian classes as a whole to the theory and practice of the radical, progressive bourgeois party at that time in history when the European bourgeois class was still relatively progressive.

It is an irrevocable fact of history that during and immediately after World War I, the once revolutionary and anti-statist ideology of Social Democratic Marxism as it existed in the most powerful *core nations of international capitalism*—the so-called imperialist nations—was transformed into reformist state socialism. This is analogous to the transformation of revolutionary, anti-statist Christianity into the official religion of the Roman state during the Middle Ages.

On the other hand, there are the struggles taking place in the *marginal areas of the international capitalist system*, where capitalism has not yet developed locally. The repressed and exploited classes of these areas appear to be developing theories in their current struggles which are continuous with so-called communism. These theories cannot take up and continue old Marxism for two reasons: first, the older theory is based on the triumph of capitalism over pre-capitalist socioeconomic formations and the advantageous relationship of this stage of history to the proletarian class struggle; and secondly, old Marxism proceeds from the immediate, positive relationship of the bourgeois to the proletarian revolution. In these marginal areas the relationship of the struggles of the proletarian class to those of the indigenous and foreign bourgeoisie is different—not fundamentally, but in its immediate form. These movements cannot seek connections with reformism, since it is inseparably tied to the expansionist and colonialist policies of the core nations of the world capitalist system today. However, they will find in Leninist Bolshevism and communism a form of Marxist ideology which is strongly anti-imperialist. It could be used as a transitional ideology for their own anti-imperialist class sttruggle. Such a process would again be analogous to the spread of Christianity among the barbarians outside the territories of the Roman Empire.

7

Marxism as an historical phenomenon is a thing of the past. It grew out of the revolutionary class struggles of the first half of the nineteenth century, only to be maintained and re-shaped in the second half of the nineteenth century as the revolutionary ideology of a working class which had not yet regained its revolutionary force. Yet in a more fundamental historical sense, the theory of proletarian revolution, which will develop anew in the next period of history, will be an historical continuation of Marxism. In their revolutionary theory, Karl Marx and Friedrich Engels gave the first great summarization of proletarian ideas, in the first revolutionary period of the proletarian class struggle. This theory remains for all time *the classical expression of the new revolutionary consciousness of the proletarian class fighting for its own liberation.*

Translated by Otto Koester

The Passing of Marxian Orthodoxy
Bernstein—Kautsky—Luxemburg—Lenin

Nothing reveals in such glaring colors the enormous contrasts which have existed in the last thirty years between the *being* and *consciousness*, between the *ideology* and the *actuality* of the proletarian movement as does the final issue of that great dispute whose first passage at arms has come down in the annals of party history under the name of the *"Bernstein Debate."* Having to do with both the theory and the practice of the socialist movement, it erupted publicly for the first time in the German and international Social Democracy, now a generation ago, shortly after the death of Friedrich Engels. When at that time Edward Bernstein, who was already able to look back upon important achievements in the field of Marxism, expressed for the first time from his exile in London his "heretical" opinions (drawn mainly from study of the English labor movement) regarding the *real relation between theory and practice in the German and all-European socialist movement of the time*, his views and designs were for the moment and still for a long while thereafter, both among friends and foes, uniformly misinterpreted and misunderstood.

In the entire bourgeois press and specialized literature his work *"Die Voraussetzungen des Sozialismus und die Aufgaben der Sozialdemokratie"*[1] was greeted with hymns of joy and showered with paeans of praise. The leader of the then just founded National Socialist party—the social-imperialist ideologist Friedrich Naumann—declared in his sheet, without circumlocution: "Bernstein is our farthest advanced post in the camp of the Social Democracy." And in broad circles of the liberal bourgeoisie there existed at the time the confident hope that this first fundamental "revisionist" of Marxism in the Marxist camp would formally also separate himself from the socialist movement and desert to the bourgeois reform movement.

These hopes of the bourgeoisie found their counterpart in a strong sentiment from the camp of the Social Democratic party and trade union movement of the time. However much the leaders of this movement were privately clear on the point that Bernstein's "revision" of the Marxist program of the Social Democracy was nothing more than the public blurting out of the development *which had long since been accomplished in practice* and through which the Social Democratic movement *had been transformed from a revolutionary class struggle movement into a political and social reform movement,* still they took good care not to give utterance to this inner knowledge toward the outside. Bernstein having ended his book with his advice to the party that it "might venture to appear that it is: a democratically socialist reform party," he was confidentially tapped on the shoulder (in a private letter published later) by that sly old demagog of the party executive committee, Ignaz Auer, with the friendly warning: "My dear Eddy, that is something which one does, but does not say." In their public utterances, all the practical and theoretical spokesmen of the German and of the international Social Democracy, the Bebels and Kautskys, Victor Adlers and Plekhanovs, and by whatever name they are called, were opposed to the insolent blabber of the carefully guarded secret. At the party congress in Hanover in 1899, in a four-day debate opened by Bebel with a six-hour report, Bernstein was subjected to a regular trial. He barely managed to avoid formal exclusion from the party. For many years thereafter, Bernstein was the butt of attack before the members and the voters, in the press and party meetings, at the great official party and trade union congresses; notwithstanding the fact that Bernstein's revisionism had already been victorious in the trade unions and finally was no longer to be resisted in the party either, the *anti-capitalist revolutionary "class-struggle party"* continued to be played without hesitation, literally to the very last moment—that is, until just before the closing of the social peace pact of 1914, followed by the pact of partnership between capital and labor in 1918.

For this double-faced attitude toward the first serious attempt at a *theoretical formulation of the actual ends and means of the bourgeois labor policy which they actually practiced,* the practical and theoretical representatives of the policy pursued by the Social Democratic party executive and the affiliated trade-union apparatus had their good reasons. Just as today the representatives of the Communist party apparatus in Russia and in all national sections of the Communist International, in order to veil the actual character of their policy, need the pious legend of the ever-advancing *"construction of socialism in the Soviet Union"* and of the "revolutionary" character (guaranteed if only by that very fact) of the whole policy and tactic, at any particular time, of all Communist party leadership in all countries, so at that time the crafty demagogs in the Social Democratic party executive and at the head of the trade-union apparatus needed, for the concealment of their actual tendencies, the pious legend that the movement which they were conducting was obliged, to be sure, for the present time, to restrict itself to merely tinkering at the bourgeois state and the capitalist economic order by way of all sorts of reforms, but that *"in the final goal"* it was on the way to the social revolution, to the overthrow of the bourgeoisie and the abolition of the capitalist economic and social order.

But it was not only the demagogs of the Social Democratic party executive and their "theoretical" advocates who, through the pseudo-struggle which they waged at that time against Bernstein's revisionism, lent aid to the danger of an advancing reformist and bourgeois degeneration of the socialist movement. Rather in the same direction with them there worked for a considerable time, unconsciously and against their will, also such radical revolutionary theoreticians as Rosa Luxemburg in Germany and Lenin in Russia, who according to their subjective design conducted a serious and uncompromising struggle against the tendency expressed by Bernstein. When at the present time, on the basis of the new experiences of the last three decades, we look back on those earlier directional struggles within the German and all-European labor movement, it is somewhat tragic to see how deeply even Luxemburg and Lenin were stuck in the illusion that "Bernsteinism" represented only a deviation from the basically revolutionary character of the then Social Democratic movement, and with what objectively inadequate formulas they too sought to conduct the struggle against the bourgeois degeneration of the socialist party and trade union policy.

Rosa Luxemburg closed her polemic against Bernstein, published in the year 1900 under the title *"Sozialreform oder Revolution?"*[2] with the catastrophically false prophecy that *"Bernstein's theory was the first, and at the same time the last attempt to give a theoretic base to opportunism."* She was of the opinion that opportunism, in Bernstein's book in theory, and in Schippel's position on the question of militarism in practice, *"had gone so far that nothing more remained for it to do."* And although Bernstein had emphatically stated that he "almost completely accepted the present *practice* of the Social Democracy" and at the same time had devastatingly laid bare the entire practical insignificance of the then usual revolutionary phase of the "final goal" with his open acknowledgement: *"The final goal, of whatsoever nature, is nothing to me; the movement everything,"* still Rosa Luxemburg, in a remarkable *ideological bedazzle-*

ment, did not direct her critical counterattack against the Social Democratic *practice* but against Bernstein's theory, which was nothing more
than a truthful expression of the actual character of that practice. The
feature by which the Social Democratic movement was distinguished
from the bourgeois reform policy, she saw not in practice but expressed
in the *"final goal"* added on to this practice merely as ideology and very
often only as a phrase. She declared passionately that *"the final goal of
socialism constitutes the only decisive factor distinguishing the Social
Democratic movement from bourgeois democracy and from bourgeois
radicalism*, the only factor transforming the entire labor movement from
a vain effort to repair the capitalist order into a class struggle against this
order, for the suppression of this order." This general "final goal" which
according to the words of Rosa Luxemburg should be *everything*, and by
which the Social Democratic movement of that time was distinguished
from the bourgeois reform politics, revealed itself in subsequent actual
history as in fact that *nothing* which Bernstein, the sober observer of
reality, had already termed it.

For all those people whose eyes have not yet been opened by all the
facts of the last fifteen years, a convincing confirmation of this historical
state of affairs is furnished by the express declarations on the matter
which have come from the main participants themselves on the occasion
of the various "Marxian" anniversary celebrations of recent times. Among
these belongs, for example, that memorable banquet which was arranged
in 1924 by the exemplars of Social Democratic Marxism, who were
assembled in London for the sixtieth anniversary celebration of the first
"International Working Men's Association" in honor of the *seventieth
birthday of Kautsky*. Here the historical "dispute" between Kautsky's
"revolutionary orthodox Marxism" and Bernstein's "revisionist" reformism found its harmonious close in those "words of friendship" (reported
by "Vorwaerts") spoken by the seventy-five-year old Bernstein in honor
of the seventy-year old Kautsky and in the symbolical embracing cere-
mony by which the words were followed: "When Bernstein had ended,
and the two old men whose names have long since become honorable
to a younger, the third generation, embraced each other and remained
for several seconds clasped together—who on that occasion could avoid
being moved, who could wish to avoid it?" And in the year 1930, the
seventy-five-year old Kautsky writes in exactly the same sense in the
Social Democratic "Kampf" of Vienna, in honor of the eightieth birthday of Bernstein: "In party-political matters we have been since 1880
Siamese twins. Even such persons can quarrel occasionally. We have
attended to that now and then quite extensively. But even at such times

it was impossible to speak of the one without thinking also of the other."

Subsequent testimonials of Bernstein and Kautsky illuminate quite clearly the tragic misunderstanding with which in the pre-war period those German left-radicals who, under the slogan *"revolutionary final goal against reformist daily practice,"* sought to conduct the struggle against the practical and in the last analysis also theoretical bourgeoisification of the Social Democratic labor movement, in reality merely supported and promoted this historical process of development carried out by Bernstein and Kautsky in their respective roles. With due allowances, the same may be said, however, of still *another slogan* by means of which in the same period the Russian Marxist Lenin, in his own country and on an international scale, sought to draw the dividing line between the bourgeois and the "revolutionary" labor policy. Just as Rosa Luxemburg in her subjective consciousness was the sharpest adversary of Bernsteinism, and in the first edition of "Reform or Revolution?" in the year 1900 still expressly demanded Bernstein's exclusion from the Social Democratic party, so also was Lenin subjectively a deadly enemy of the "renegade" Bernstein, and of all the heretical deviations committed by him, in his "herostratically celebrated" book, from the pure and undefiled doctrine of the "revolutionary" Marxist program. But exactly like Luxemburg and the German left-radical Social Democrats, so also the Bolshevist Social Democrat Lenin made use, for this struggle against Social Democratic revisionism, of a wholly *ideological platform*, in that he sought the guarantee for the "revolutionary" character of the labor movement, not in its actual economic and social class content, but expressly only in the *leadership of this struggle by way of the revolutionary PARTY guided by a correct Marxist theory.*

Notes

1. Translated by Edith C. Harvey under the title "Evolutionary Socialism: A Criticism and Affirmation" and published in London (1909) by the Independent Labor Party.

2. "Reform or Revolution?" Three Arrows Press, 21 E. 17th Street, New York. 25 cents.

Some Fundamental Presuppositions for a Materialist Discussion of Crisis Theory

I

A great shortcoming of the form in which the discussion of crises took place hitherto, especially in the circles of the left and far-left wings of the workers' movement, was to be found in their search for a "revolution-ary" crisis theory per se, just as in the middle ages one searched for the philosopher's stone. Historical examples, however, can demonstrate quite easily that possession of such a supposedly highly revolutionary crisis theory says little about the actual level of class consciousness and revolu-tionary preparedness for action of a group or individual believing in the theory.

Thus it is well known that for thirty years, from 1891 to 1921, the Social Democratic party of Germany had in the crisis section of the *Erfurt program* an especially revolutionary crisis theory which even today can hardly be improved on in respect of radical clarity. The Erfurt program was not satisfied with tracing crises back to the "planlessness" or so-called anarchy of the present capitalist mode of production—as its first draft which was criticized by Engels still had done and as is likewise today the case with the 1925 *Heidelberg program* accepted by the SPD. Neither was it satisfied with lamenting the "ruin of broad sections of the people" or the aggravation of the "torment" of the unemployed proletariat caused by these crises. Rather it explained the crises as a phenomenon "founded on the nature of the capitalist mode of production" which cannot be "overcome" through some "planned economy" reforms of the capitalist mode of production but can only be superseded through the revolutionary cancellation (*Aufhebung*) of this whole mode of production. The Erfurt program recorded as the most significant effect of crises the fact that it is the crisis which "further widens the chasm between the proprietors and the propertyless workers." It asserted moreover with distinct clarity—despite the "revisionist" tendencies already emerging then—that the crises thus described "*will ever widen in extent and destructiveness*, will raise general insecurity to a normal condition of society and furnish the proof that the forces of production *have outgrown* contemporary society and that private ownership of the means of production *has become* no longer compatible with their efficient application and full development."

This contradiction between theory and practice becomes still more drastic when we cast our eyes towards some well-known individual crisis theorists of pre-war Social Democracy. There is the subsequent arch-reformist *Heinrich Cunow* who in 1898 in the *Neue Zeit* founded the first explicit collapse and catastrophe theory. It was none other than *Karl Kautsky* who in July, 1906, in the preface to the fifth edition of Engels' *Utopian and Scientific Socialism* announced the directly imminent "death crisis" of the capitalist system which "this time has no chance ever again to be softened by a new era of prosperity on a capitalist basis!" In the controversy over crisis and collapse theory arising since 1913 from *Rosa Luxemburg's* book on *The Accumulation of Capital* we find from the beginning reformists and revolutionaries on *both* sides (among the followers *inter alia Paul Lensch*, among the opponents *Lenin* and *Pannekoek*), and even the two most important present day epigones of Luxemburgian theory, *Fritz Sternberg* and *Henryk Grossman*, can hardly be described as especially determined and efficacious representatives of a practical revolutionary politics.

In the immediate postwar period the apparently unavoidable and already commencing collapse of the capitalist system on a world scale awoke unfounded illusions among a wide section of revolutionaries. At this time, the *then* "left Communist" theoretician *Bukharin* had already collated fantasies for a new scientific theory of this supposed capitalist destruction of the world in his notorious *Economics of the transition period.* But the revolutionary practitioner *Lenin* coined the *revolutionary* phrase—later to be repeated by his followers *ad infinitum under quite different conditions*, but during the conditions *prevailing* then *revolutionary* in its effect—that "there is no such thing as a situation with no way out for capitalism."

II

The various crisis theories that have hitherto emerged in the worker's movement are in reality much less of an indication of the revolutionary class consciousness and capability for action achieved by their originators and followers than a *passive and belated reflection* of the *objective reality* of the ongoing crisislike total condition of the capitalist mode of production or even of only a temporary economic crisis. One could from this viewpoint represent the whole historical development of socialist crisis theories from *Fourier* and *Sismondi* to the various subsequent temporal phases of Marx-Engels and the later Marxists (and the crisis theories of the Marx epigones up to Sternberg and Grossman, Lederer and Naphtali), right into their ultimate theoretical details, as merely a passive reflection of the respective previous objective economic development.

From the same viewpoint one could also, beyond the framework of crisis theories, represent all the important struggles over direction which have arisen within the socialist movement during the last fifty years as *mere consequences and reflexes* of the immediately preceding *conjuncture* within the capitalist crisis cycle.

A lot of noise has been made about the question as to whether the old Engels in the introduction to Marx's essay on class struggles in France had surrendered a part of the revolutionary political basic propositions of original Marxism. One can better pose this question with regard to certain remarks of Engels in the preface to the German edition of the *Poverty of Philosophy* (1884) (p. xviii) and in a footnote (no. 8) to the third volume of *Capital* (1894, II, p. 27). Here there is talk about a recently quite changed character in the *cycles* of modern industry and about the removal or strong decline of "most of the old crisis-points and circumstances for crisis formation." It is quite possible that these remarks of Engels constituted the first ideological reference point of that theory, seemingly only represented by *Bernstein's* revisionism at the turn of the century, but today already quite openly represented by all Social Democratic doctrinal experts, which saw the task of the socialist workers' movement no longer as that of exploiting the crisis for increased struggle for the revolutionary overcoming of the capitalist mode of production, but rather as that of weakening down and "subduing" such crisis within the framework of capitalist mode of production. Of course Friedrich Engels was far removed from such conclusions; the replacement of the previous crisis-cycles by a "new form of equilibrium" forecast on the basis of the conditions of the previous two decades he termed, on the contrary, a transition to "*chronic stagnation as the normal condition of modern industry.*" He thereby not only became the direct originator of crisis theory of the 1891 Erfurt program discussed above, but also became the real father of the notion of the so-called death crisis which, as pictured already at the Erfurt congress by Wilhelm Liebknecht, and later by Cunow, Kautsky and many others, was to drive contemporary society with an "iron logic" into a "catastrophe, into its own unavoidable doom."

Things developed differently when the stagnation already declared "chronic" by Engels turned in the mid-nineties into a new immense upswing of the capitalist mode of production. *Edward Bernstein* then and later said publicly that it was these new economic facts which at this time brought about his fundamental attack on all revolutionary elements of hitherto existing Social Democratic politics and caused him, in particular with regard to crisis theory, to categorically state that due to the latest development of the capitalist system *"general business crises after the fashion of earlier ones are now to be regarded as unlikely, at least for a long time."*

From Bernstein's remarks, and the theoretical and practical consequences already deduced thereupon by its originator, a straight line leads to the official Social Democrat crisis theory as represented for and by Hilferding and Lederer, Tarnow and Naphtali. I term this fundamental stance of today's Social Democrat crisis theory as the *subjective* stance in contrast to both of the other two fundamental stances to the crisis problem still to be discussed. The Social Democratic theory states that in modern "organized capitalism," whether actual or "tendential," necessary and unavoidable crises will not occur any more. The first "scientific" argumentation or proof for this thesis, at first only set up by Bernstein as a factual assertion, is contained in the familiar theory of Hilferding's *"Finance Capital."* It forecasts the overcoming of capitalist crises by a capitalist "general cartel" to be created by and with the acceptance and support of the working class, which will carry through the planned regulating of bourgeois production, based on capital and wage labour. After the war (1927) Hilferding declared once more expressly that he always had "rejected every economic theory of collapse." The fall of the capitalist system *"would not emanate from the intrinsic laws of this system"* but would have to be "the conscious *deed* of the working class."

This "theory" of Hilferding is until this day the basis of not only the Social Democrats—but also that of the Bolshevist-Soviet theoreticians and plan-engineers and others advancing subjective and voluntaristic crisis theories and theories for overcoming such crises. One must not think however, that these theories, modulations of which echoed still some years ago through a whole forest of Social Democrat journals and books, have for their originators and followers been "proven false" by the facts of the existing capitalist reality. Experience has shown that, for instance, Edward Bernstein still adhered to his thesis of crisis-overcoming designed in 1899, when in the following year, 1900, the economist crisis broke out, and a further crisis followed seven years thereafter; and again when seven years later the already then noticeable new crisis was only deferred by the world war only to reoccur once again in 1920–1921 on a world scale, after the first liquidation of the war and its direct results. The Hilferdings and Lederers, Tarnows and Naphtalis will react quite like that, yesterday, today and tomorrow. It is just the characteristic of this kind of crisis theory that they always *ideologically reflect* the just *past* phase of the real movement of capitalist economies and place it vis-à-vis the changed present reality as a fixed rigid "theory." Of course there are a host of other excuses, like the explanation of the current world economic crisis as result of wars, as result of reparation and war debts and other "extra-economic" causes. The practical consequences of all of these crisis theories based on this *subjective* fundamental stance is the *complete destruction of all objective bases of the proletarian class movement.* The Goerlitz Program of Social Democracy of 1921 has coined already the classical phrase for this position by declaring the class struggle for the liberation of the proletariat as a mere "moral demand."

But even the other fundamental stance to the crisis questions that is almost directly opposed to the one we just investigated—which in the perfection of the almost *classical form* of the accumulation theory of *Rosa Luxemburg* has found expression unrivaled by any of the numerous predecessors and successors—can not be recognized as a truly materialist, and, as regards its practical efficiency, revolutionary position on the crisis question. The significance of the theory, as espoused by its followers, lies in Rosa Luxemburg's position of "holding fast to the fundamental thought of *'Capital,'* of an absolute *economic limit* for the continued development of the capitalist mode of production, in conscious contrast to and protest against the attempts of distortion by the New-harmony theoreticians" (Grossman). The stance based on this theory could appropriately be described as an *absolute* one. I should like to characterize it in contrast to the already discussed "subjective" and the still to be discussed "materialist" stance, as an objective or "objectivist" fundamental stance. It is of no consequence here, from which assumed objective system of laws of the capitalist mechanism of production the objectively guaranteed economic necessity of its imminent collapse is derived in detail. On the other hand, nothing will change the "objectivism" of these theories, not even their followers' assurance that they are not at all recommending to the proletariat "a fatalist awaiting of the automatic collapse," but "only" (!) are of the opinion that the revolutionary action of the proletariat "achieves the conditions for successfully defeating the resistances of the dominating class only through the objective tremors of the existing system" (Grossman). *Such a theory of an objectively given economic tendency of development whose ultimate goal can be grasped* in advance employs pictorial notions rather than unequivocally determined scientific concepts. Furthermore, it is founded inevitably on insufficient induction and appears to me as not suitable for bringing forward that full earnestness of self-disciplined activity of the proletarian class struggling for its own goals, which is as much necessary for the class war of the workers as it is for every other ordinary war.

In contrast to the two fundamental stances so far illustrated, it appears to me that a third fundamental stance to the crisis question is possible and just this one alone deserves the designation of a truly Marxian *materialist* stance. This position explains the whole question of the objective necessity or avoidability of capitalist crises as a *senseless question in this general form* (within the framework of a practical theory of the revolution of the proletariat). It agrees with the revolutionary critic of Marx *Georges Sorel* who will not consider Marx's general tendency of capitalism to catastrophe generated by the insurrection of the working class—colored in a strong idealist-philosophical "dialectical" manner of speech—as a valid scientific prognosis, but merely as a "myth" whose whole significance is limited to determine the *current* action of the working class. The materialist stance is, however, not in accord with Sorel when he quite generally wants to *limit* the function of any future social theory of revolution to form such a myth. The materialist stance rather believes that certain, if only always limited, prognostic statements sufficient for practical action can be made on the basis of always more exact and thorough empirical investigation of the present capitalist mode of production and its recognizable immanent tendencies of development. The materialist therefore investigates thoroughly the given situation of capitalist production including the contradictions found therein, among which are also the situation, the level of consciousness, the organization, and the readiness for struggle of the working class and all the various levels of the working class in order to determine its action. The most important basic traits of this *theoretical and practical materialist fundamental stance* have been classically formulated, in general form, without being specially related to the crisis problem, in the polemic of the year 1894 where the young *Lenin* attacked the subjectivism of the popular revolutionary *Michailowski* together with the objectivism of the then-leading Marxist theoretician *Struve* and confronted both with his own activist-materialist standpoint: "When proving the necessity of a given number of facts, the objectivist always runs the risk of assuming the standpoint of an apologist of these facts; the materialist reveals the class contradictions and thereby establishes his standpoint."

Translated by Karl-Heinz Otto and Andrew Giles-Peters

Marxism and the Present Task of the Proletarian Class Struggle

> Let the dead bury their dead. The proletarian revolution must at last arrive at its own content.—Marx

Of Karl Marx may be said what Geoffroy St. Hilaire said of Darwin, that it was his fate and his glory to have had only forerunners before him and only disciples after him. Of course, there stood at his side a congenial life-long friend and collaborator, Friedrich Engels. There were in the next generation the theoretical standard-bearers of the "revisionist" and the "orthodox" wings of the German Marxist party, Bernstein and Kautsky and, besides these pseudo-savants, such real scholars of Marxism as Antonio Labriola the Italian, Georges Sorel in France, and the Russian philosopher Plekhanov. There came at a later stage an apparently full restoration of the long forgotten revolutionary elements of the Marxian thought by Rosa Luxemburg in Germany and by Lenin in Russia.

During the same period Marxism was embraced by millions of workers throughout the world as a guide for their practical action. There was an imposing succession of organizations, from the secret *Communist League* of 1848 and the *Working Men's International Association* of 1864 to the rise of powerful Social Democratic parties on a national scale in all important European countries and to an ultimate coordination of their scanty international activities in the so-called *Second International* of the pre-war period which after its collapse found its eventual resurrection in the shape of a militant *Communist party* on a world-wide scale.

Yet there was, during all this time, no corresponding internal growth of the Marxian theory itself beyond those powerful ideas which had been contained within the first scheme of the new revolutionary science as devised by Marx.

Very few Marxists up to the end of the nineteenth century did so much as find anything wrong with this state of affairs. Even when the first attacks of the so-called revolutionists brought about what a radical bourgeois socialist, the later first president of the Czechoslovak republic, Th. G. Mazaryk, then called a philosophical and scientific "crisis of Marxism," the Marxists regarded the condition existing within their own camp as a mere struggle between an "orthodox" Marxist faith and a deplorable "heresy." The ideological character of this wholesale identification of an established doctrine with the revolutionary struggle of the working class is further enhanced by the fact that the leading representatives of the Marxian orthodoxy of the time, including Kautsky in Germany and Lenin in Russia, persistently denied the very possibility that a true revolutionary consciousness could ever originate with the workers themselves. The revolutionary political aims, according to them, had to be introduced into the economic class struggle of the workers *"from without,"* i.e., by the theoretical endeavors of radical bourgeois thinkers "equipped with all the culture of the age," such as Lassalle, Marx, and Engels. Thus, the identity of a bourgeois-bred doctrine with all present and future truly revolutionary struggles of the proletarian class assumed the character of a veritable miracle. Even those most radical Marxists who came nearest to the recognition of a spontaneous development of the proletarian class struggle beyond the restricted aim pursued by the leading bureaucracies of the existing Social Democratic parties and trade unions, never dreamt of denying this pre-established harmony between the Marxist doctrine and the actual proletarian movement. As Rosa Luxemburg said in 1903, and the Bolshevik Rjazanov repeated in 1928, "every new and higher stage of the proletarian class struggle can borrow from the inexhaustible arsenal of the Marxist theory ever-new weapons as needed by that new stage of the emancipatory fight of the working class."

It is beyond the scope of this article to discuss the more general aspects of this peculiar theory of the Marxists concerning the origin and development of their own revolutionary doctrine, a theory which in the last analysis amounts to a denial of the possibility of an independent proletarian class culture. We refer to it in our present context only as one of the many contradictions to be swallowed by those who in striking contrast to the critical and materialistic principle of Marx dealt with "Marxism" as an essentially completed, and now unchangeable, doctrine.

A further difficulty of this quasi-religious attitude towards Marxism arises from the fact that the Marxian theory was never adopted as a whole by any socialist group or party. "Orthodox" Marxism was at no time more than a formal attitude by which the leading group of the German Social Democratic party in the pre-war period concealed from themselves the ever-continuing deterioration of their own formerly revolutionary practice. It was only this difference of procedure which separated that distinguished "orthodox" form from an openly revisionistic form of adapting the traditional Marxist doctrine to the new "needs" of the workers' movement arising from the changed conditions of the new historical period.

When amidst the storm and stress of the revolutionary struggle of 1917, in view of a "clearly maturing international proletarian revolution," Lenin set himself the task to restate *the Marxian theory of the state and the tasks of the proletariat in the revolution,* he no longer contented himself with a mere ideological defense of an assumedly existing orthodox interpretation of the true Marxist theory. He started from the premise that revolutionary Marxism had been totally destroyed and abandoned both by the opportunist minority and by the outspoken social-chauvinist majority of all "Marxist" parties and trade unions of the late Second International. He openly announced that *Marxism was dead* and proclaimed an integral *"restoration" of revolutionary Marxism.*

There is no doubt that "revolutionary Marxism," as restored by Lenin, has led the proletarian class to its first historical victory. This fact must be emphasized not only against the pseudo-Marxist detractors of the "barbarous" *communism* of the Bolsheviks—as against the "refined" and "cultured" *socialism* of the West. It must be emphasized also against the present beneficiaries of the revolutionary victory of the Russian workers, who have gradually passed from the revolutionary Marxism of the early years to a no longer communist but merely "socialist" and democratic creed called *Stalinism.* In the same way, on an international scale, a mere "anti-fascist" coalition of the united fronts, people's fronts, and national fronts was gradually substituted for the revolutionary class struggle waged by the proletariat against the whole economic and political regime of the bourgeoisie in the "democratic" as well as in the fascist, the "pro-Russian" as well as the anti-Russian, states.

In the face of these later developments of Lenin's work, it is no longer possible to stick to the idea that the restored old revolutionary principles of Marxism, which during the war and the immediate post-war period had been advocated by Lenin and Trotsky, resulted in a genuine revival of the revolutionary proletarian movement which in the past had been associated with the name of Marx. For a limited period it seemed, indeed, that the true spirit of revolutionary Marxism had gone east. The striking contradictions soon appearing within the policy of the ruling revolutionary party in Soviet Russia, both on the economic and on the political fields, were considered as a mere outcome of the sad fact that the "international proletarian revolution" firmly expected by Lenin and Trotsky did not mature. Yet in the light of later facts there is no doubt that ultimately, Soviet Marxism as a revolutionary proletarian theory and practice has shared the fate of that "orthodox" Marxism of the West from which it had sprung and from which it had split only under the extraordinary conditions of the war and the ensuing revolutionary outbreak in Russia. When finally in 1933, by the unopposed victory of the counterrevolutionary *"national socialism,"* in the traditional center of revolutionary *international socialism,* it became manifest that "Marxism did not deliver the goods," that judgment applied to the Eastern Communist as well as to the Western Social Democratic church of the Marxist faith, and the separate factions were at last united in a common defeat.

In order to make intelligible the true significance and the far reaching further implications of this most important lesson of the recent history of Marxism, we must trace back the duplex character of the *"revolutionary dictatorship of the proletarian class"* which has become widely conspicuous by recent events both within present-day Stalinist Russia and on an international scale, to an original duplicity appearing in the different aspects of Marx's own achievements *as a proletarian theorist* and *as a political leader* in the revolutionary movement of his time. On the one hand, as early as 1843, he was in close contact with the most advanced manifestations of French socialism and communism. With Engels he founded the *Deutsche Arbeiterbildungsverein* in Brussels in 1847 and set about to found an international organization of proletarian correspondence committees. Soon afterwards, they both joined the first international organization of the militant proletariat, the *Bund der Kommunisten*, at whose request they wrote the famous "Manifesto" proclaiming the proletariat as "the only revolutionary class."

On the other hand, Marx as an editor of the *Neue Rheinische Zeitung* during the actual revolutionary outbreak of 1848 expressed mainly the most radical demands of the bourgeois democracy. He strove to maintain a united front between the bourgeois revolutionary movement in Germany and the more advanced forms in which a struggle for direct socialist aims was at that time already waged in the more developed industrial countries of the West. He wrote his most brilliant and powerful article in defense of the Paris proletariat after its crushing defeat in June, 1848. But he did not bring forward in his paper the specific claims of the German proletariat until a few weeks before its final suppression by the victorious counterrevolution of 1849. Even then, he stated the workers' case in a somewhat abstract manner by reproducing in the columns of the *Neue Rheinische Zeitung* the economic lectures dealing with *Wage-Labor and Capital* which he had given two years before in the *Arbeiterbildungsverein* at Brussels. Similarly, by his contributions in the 1850's and 60's to Horace Greeley's *New York Tribune*, to the *New American Cyclopaedia* edited by George Ripley and Charles Dana, to Chartist publications in England, and to German and Austrian newspapers, Marx revealed himself chiefly as a spokesman of the radical democratic policies which, he hoped, would ultimately lead to a war of the democratic West against reactionary tsarist Russia.

An explanation of this apparent dualism is to be found in the *Jaco-*

binic pattern of the revolutionary doctrine which Marx and Engels had adopted before the February Revolution of 1848 and to which they remained faithful, on the whole, even after the outcome of that revolution had finally wrecked their former enthusiastic hopes. Although they realized the necessity of adjusting tactics to changed historical conditions, their own theory of revolution, even in its latest and most advanced materialistic form, kept the peculiar character of the transitory period during which the proletarian class was still bound to proceed towards its own social emancipation by passing through the intermediate stage of a preponderantly political revolution.

It is true that the revolutionary political effects of the economic warfare of the trade unions and of the other forms of championing immediate and specific labor interests became increasingly important for Marx during his later years, as attested by his leading role in the organization and direction of the International Working Men's Association in the 60's and by his contributions to the programs and tactics of the various national parties in the 70's. But it is also true, and is clearly shown by the internecine battles waged within the International by the Marxists against the followers of Proudhon and Bakunin, that Marx and Engels never really abandoned their earlier views on the decisive importance of politics as the only conscious and fully developed form of revolutionary class action. There is only a difference of languages between the cautious enrollment of "political action" as a subordinate means to the ultimate goal of the "economic emancipation of the working class" as contained in the Rules of the IWMA of 1864, and the open proclamation, in the *Communist Manifesto* of 1848, that "every class struggle is a political struggle" and that the "organization of the proletarians into a class" presupposes their "organization into a political party." Thus, Marx, from the first to the last, defined his concept of class in ultimately political terms and, in fact though not in words, subordinated the multiple activities exerted by the masses in their daily class struggle to the activities exerted on their behalf by their political leaders.

This appears even more distinctly in those rare and extraordinary situations in which Marx and Engels during their later years again were called to deal with actual attempts at a European revolution. Witness Marx's reaction to the revolutionary *Commune* of the Paris workers in 1871. Witness further Marx's and Engels' apparently inconsistent positive attitude toward the entirely idealistic attempts of the revolutionary *Narodnaja Volja* to enforce by terroristic action the outbreak of "a political and thus also a social revolution" under the backward conditions prevailing in the 70's and 80's in tsarist Russia. As shown in detail in an

earlier article (*Living Marxism*, March 1938), Marx and Engels were
not only prepared to regard the approaching revolutionary outbreak in
Russia as a signal for a general European revolution of the Jacobin type
in which (as Engels told Vera Sassulitch in 1883) "if the year 1789
once comes, the year 1793 will follow." They actually hailed the Russian
and all-European revolution as a workers' revolution and the starting
point of a Communistic development.

There is then no point in the objection raised by the Mensheviks and
other schools of the traditional Western type of Marxist orthodoxy that
the *Marxism of Lenin* was in fact only the return to an earlier form of
the *Marxism of Marx* which later had been replaced by a *more mature
and more materialistic form*. It is quite true that the very similarity between the historical situation arising in Russia in the beginning of the
twentieth century and the conditions prevailing in Germany, Austria,
and elsewhere at the eve of the European revolution of 1848 explains the
otherwise unexplainable fact that the latest phase of the revolutionary
movement of our time could have been represented at all under the paradoxical form of an ideological return to the past. Nevertheless, as shown
above, revolutionary Marxism as "restored" by Lenin did conform, in its
purely theoretical contents, much more with the true spirit of all historical phases of the Marxian doctrine than that social democratic Marxism
of the preceding period which after all, in spite of its loudly professed
"orthodoxy," had never been more than a mutilated and travestied form
of the Marxian theory, vulgarizing its real contents, and blunting its
revolutionary edge. It is for this very reason that Lenin's experiment in
the "restoration" of revolutionary Marxism confirmed most convincingly
the utter futility of any attempt to draw the theory of the revolutionary
action of the working class not from its own contents but from any
"myth." It has shown, above all, the ideological perversity of the idea
to supplant the existing deficiencies of the present action by an imaginary
return to a mythicized past. While such awakening of a dead revolutionary ideology may possibly help for a certain time, as the Russian revolution has shown, to conceal from the makers of the revolutionary "October" the historical limitations of their heroic efforts, it is bound to result
ultimately not in finding once more the spirit of that earlier revolutionary
movement but only in making its ghost walk again. It has resulted, in our
time, in a new and "revolutionary Marxist" form of the suppression and
exploitation of the proletarian class in Soviet Russia, and in an equally
new and "revolutionary Marxist" form of crushing genuine revolutionary movements in Spain and all over the world.

All this shows clearly that Marxism today could only be "restored" in its original form by its transformation into a mere ideology serving an altogether different purpose and, indeed, a whole scale of changing political purposes. It serves at this very moment as an ideological screen for the debunking of the hitherto predominant role of the ruling party itself and for the further enhancement of the quasi-fascist personal leadership of Stalin and of his all-adaptable agencies. At the same time, on the international scene, the so-called anti-fascist policy of the "Marxist" Comintern has come to play in the present struggles between the various alliances of capitalist powers exactly the same role as its opposite, the "anti-communist" and "anti-Marxist" international policy of the regimes of Hitler, Mussolini, and the Japanese warlords.

It should be understood that the whole criticism raised above concerns *only the ideological endeavors* of the last fifty years to "preserve" or to "restore," for immediate application, a thoroughly mythicized "revolutionary Marxist doctrine." Nothing in this article is directed against the scientific results reached by Marx and Engels and a few of their followers on various fields of social research which in many ways hold good to this day. Above all, nothing in this article is directed against what may be called, in a very comprehensive sense, *the Marxist, that is, the independent revolutionary movement of the international working class.* There seems to be good reason, in the search for what is living or may be recalled to life in the present deathly standstill of the revolutionary workers' movement, to "return" to that practical and not merely ideological broadmindedness by which *the first Marxist (at the same time Proudhonist, Blanquist, Bakunist, trade-unionist, etc.) International Working Men's Association* welcomed into its ranks all workers who subscribed to the principle of an independent proletarian class struggle. As enunciated in the first of its rules, drawn up by Marx, *"the emancipation of the working classes must be conquered by the working classes themselves."*

7. Models of Revolutionary Practice

Introduction

Throughout Korsch's life he was concerned with developing models of revolutionary practice and socialism. In one of his first essays, published in 1912, "The Socialist Formula for the Organization of the People's Economy," Korsch was already searching for a model of socialism. Seven years later, after the German November Revolution, he was to develop such a model in his essays on socialism and the workers' councils.[1] The early Korsch, we recall, defended the workers' councils or soviets as the authentic organs of socialism. In his Leninist phase, Korsch temporarily accepted the Leninist theses on the party and state as the crucial instruments of revolutionary practice, but even in this period as a Leninist militant in the German Communist party, he put strong emphasis on working-class self-activity and the workers' councils. With the collapse of Korsch's Leninism he was forced to search for new revolutionary forces and new possibilities for and models of revolutionary change. In his left-opposition period in the late 1920's, he harshly criticized the politics of the Communist party and Soviet state, and supported the struggles of revolutionary trade unions.

Korsch never spun out abstract theories that were not rooted in historical realities. Hence, his rethinking of the Marxist theory of revolution moved through the stages of a historical inquiry into the models of revolution in the Paris Commune, the Russian soviets, and the German workers' councils. With the outbreak of the revolution in Spain in 1931, Korsch carefully studied the struggles of the Spanish working class and the Spanish collectives. Finally, Korsch became increasingly interested in the national liberation movements in the non-European countries as new possibilities for socialist revolution. He never posited an ahistorical model of revolution, but always reflected on existing revolutionary movements to discern what features of their struggles and achievements could serve as models for further revolutionary practice.

In his two articles on the Paris Commune, Korsch engages in serious reflection on the nature of revolutionary politics. The first article was published in the leftist journal *Die Aktion* in 1929, and the second article was published in the same journal in 1931 in response to discussions and criticisms of his earlier piece.[2] Korsch wanted to argue that it was not the *political form* of the Paris Commune that made it so important as a model of revolutionary practice, as much as its *social and economic content*; that is, what was exemplary about the Paris Commune is that the people themselves struggled for control over their own lives and attempted to create new forms of government and social life. Indeed, it was not even clear, Korsch points out, what the "political form" of the lamentably short reign of the Paris Commune was. Marx stressed the open-endedness and potentiality for development as the distinctive features of the Commune, and Korsch concurs, suggesting that it should be seen as a tragically brief, but heroic experiment in self-government and radical social change.

Korsch's political strategy in his study of the Paris Commune was parallel to Marx's strategy in his great essay on the Civil War in France. For, as Korsch points out, "*Marx not only wanted to annex the Marxism of the Commune but also at the same time the Commune to Marxism.*" Similarly to Marx's essay, Korsch's study was a "fractional polemical treatise" concerned to stress the primacy of the social and economic struggles against those who would subordinate all struggles to political power and the state, and would thus urge the party as the focal point of the organization of the working class. Korsch assigns this focal role to the trade unions at the end of the first essay, and urges that the primary focus of revolutionary struggle should be the social and economic struggles for the liberation of the working class. At the end of his second essay on the "Revolutionary Commune," Korsch polemicizes against those who would exaggerate the role of the state in the construction of socialism by arguing that "The essential *final goal* of proletarian class struggle is not any one *state*, however 'democratic,' 'communal,' or even 'councillike,' but is rather the classless and stateless Communist *society*, whose comprehensive *form* is not any longer some kind of political power but is '*that association in which the free development of every person is the condition for the free development of all*' ('*Communist Manifesto*')."[3]

Korsch's search for new models of revolutionary practice is embodied in his essays on the Spanish revolution. After visiting Spain in 1931, Korsch wrote an article for the journal *Neue Rundschau* on the events in Spain.[4] This essay shows Korsch's careful attention to historical detail and his hardheaded political realism. He provides an account of the historical background of the Spanish revolution and an analysis of the current problems and tasks. Since there was no indigenous Communist party in Spain, Korsch hoped that the developments in Spain would provide the possibility for new forms of revolutionary struggle that would be independent from the Soviet Union and Stalinism, and would serve to significantly advance the struggle for liberation of the Spanish people. Korsch saw the struggles between federalism and centralism, between the republic and the Catholic church, and between radical reform of agriculture and those who would contain the transformation, as the emerging central issues of the Spanish revolution.

While in exile, Korsch continued to pay careful attention to the events in Spain which he deemed of utmost importance for the future of a genuinely revolutionary movement free from the hegemony of the Soviet Union. His friend and student Paul Partos, as well as other of his former comrades, participated in the Spanish Civil War and kept Korsch up-to-date as to its vicissitudes. During his exile in America, Korsch wrote two articles on Spain, "Economics and Politics in Revolutionary Spain," and "Collectivization in Spain."[5] He intended them for the Frankfurt Institute's *Zeitschrift für Sozialforschung*, but ended up publishing them in *Living Marxism* after the *Zeitschrift*'s editors "politically castrated" them and "distorted their form."[6] Korsch attached great importance to his essays on Spain, writing to his friend Paul Mattick that they could have a bombshell effect.[7]

Korsch believed that the events in Spain were especially instructive because they showed the connection between political and economic struggles. The failures of the anarcho-syndicalists to see this connection and to fuse political and economic forms of struggle were fatal errors in Korsch's view.[8] Korsch was attempting to develop a balanced, dialectical theory of revolution that would fuse political and economic forms of struggle into one unitary movement. He polemicized against both Marxian theories that exaggerated the role of the state, party, and vanguard in revolutionary struggle, and the anarcho-syndicalist tendencies who exaggerated economic and trade union struggle, while neglecting problems of politics and the state. Korsch himself fell into these extremes at different stages of his political development, but in the 1930's he sought a dialectical fusion of the political and economic struggles as the heart of revolution. In an essay "On the Trade Union Question" he writes, "The fusion of both forms of struggle into the completely developed, unitary, economic, political, and revolutionary proletarian class struggle seeking to annihilate the economic and political bourgeois organization of power and to erect in its place the state and the economic power of the revolutionary working class (the revolutionary class dictatorship of the proletariat) will finally reach the goal sought by the isolated 'economic' and 'political' partial struggles of the preceding period (which, in their external manifestations, appeared to pursue other goals) : *the constitution of the proletariat as a class.*"[9]

In an essay "On the New Program of the 'American Workers Party,' " Korsch again argues for a fusion of economic and political struggles to overcome the onesidedness of Leninist or Social Democratic theories of the primacy of the political, or economistic syndicalism: "a genuine combination of the economic and political struggle and of all other forms of activity of the working class into the single whole of a directly revolutionary struggle is the necessary goal of all proletarian revolutionists."[10] Marx, he points out, "called every class struggle a 'political struggle' " and "in exactly the same sense called politics a 'concentrated economics.' "[11] It is above all in the workers' councils, Korsch adds, that the political and economic components are best fused, hence it is suggested that the councils are the focus of revolutionary struggle.

Korsch's interest in councils communism was revived by the class struggles in Spain, where workers' collectives sprang up as spontaneous organs of working class self-organization. Indeed Korsch believed that the other great lesson of Spain was its testimony to the creative powers of the people in creating their forms of struggle and self-management. In an article, "Collectivization in Spain," Korsch described the attempt of the Spanish people to create a "new, free type of communal production attempted here for the first time on a larger scale."[12] He reviewed a French anthology of reports on the Spanish collectivization of industry and agriculture, and stressed their importance as models of revolutionary struggle which attest "to the peculiar creative power of the revolution."

In a sense, with the unfolding of the Spanish revolution Korsch returned to the councils as the crux of socialist revolution. In a letter written in November, 1941, Bertolt Brecht suggests to Korsch, "I would be extremely interested in a historical investigation of the relationship between the councils and the parties. The specific reasons for the failure of the councils, the historical grounds, would interest me immensely. . . . Outside of yourself, I know no one who could investigate this."[13] Unfortunately, Korsch never completed an oft-projected history of the councils and other forms of revolutionary struggle since the French revolution, but the topic was continually on his mind and constituted the heart of his political theory.

A brief note on Korsch and the Third World. Korsch was interested in social change in the non-European world since his student days. In one of his first articles, published in 1909, he wrote on "Japanese labor relations," and in 1922 Korsch wrote an unpublished manuscript "India's

Awakening."[14] In the 1920's his journal *Kommunistische Politik* published articles on China, and Korsch stretched out an unpublished manuscript "China in Transition" and wanted to edit an anthology of the writings of Mao-Tse Tung.[15] He later drafted notes "On the Russian Revolution and the Emancipation of Asia and Africa," and wrote an article "Independence Comes to the Philippines," where he explicitly stresses the importance of national liberation movements for international socialist revolution.[16] Hence Korsch was thoroughly open to all forms of revolutionary struggle and continually searched for and appraised new models of revolution.

Notes

1. See my discussion, in "Korsch's Road to Marxian Socialism," pp. 6ff.
2. Karl Korsch, "Revolutionäre Kommune I," *Die Aktion* 19, no. 5–8 (September 1929); and "Revolutionäre Kommune, II," *Die Aktion*, 21, nos. 3–4 (July 1931). Translated in this anthology as "Revolutionary Commune," by Karl-Heinz Otto and Andrew Giles-Peters.
3. Korsch, "Revolutionary Commune."
4. Karl Korsch, "Die spanische Revolution," *Die Neue Rundschau* 42, no. 9 (September 1931). Translated in this anthology as "The Spanish Revolution," by Karl-Heinz Otto, Andrew Giles-Peters, and Heinz Schutte.
5. Karl Korsch, "Economics and Politics in Revolutionary Spain," *Living Marxism* 4, no. 3 (May 1938) published in this anthology; and "Collectivization in Spain," *Living Marxism* 4, no. 6 (April 1939).
6. See the Letter to Paul Mattick translated in this anthology and a following letter to Mattick (October 30, 1938) in *Jahrbuch Arbeiterbewegung 2*, pp. 186–187.
7. Korsch to Mattick, October 30, 1938, p. 186.
8. Korsch, "Economics and Politics in Revolutionary Spain."
9. Karl Korsch, "The Restoration of Marxism in the So-called Trade Union Question," cited in Oskar Negt, "Constitution in Korsch," *Telos* 26 (Winter 1975–1976): 133.
10. Karl Korsch, "On the New Program of the 'American Workers Party,'" in *International Council Correspondence*, no. 4 (January 1935), p. 24.
11. Ibid.
12. Korsch, "Collectivization in Spain."
13. Bertolt Brecht, letter to Karl Korsch, cited in Gerlach's introduction to *Schriften zur Sozialisierung*, p. 5.
14. Karl Korsch, "Japanische Arbeitsverhältnisse," *Jenaer Hochschulzeitung*, January 20, 1909; and "Indiens Erwachen," unpublished manuscript, 1922.

15. Karl Korsch, "China in Transition," unpublished manuscript.

16. Karl Korsch, "Independence Comes to the Philippines"; although there is a printed manuscript extant from 1946, it is not clear where or if this was ever published. A slightly shortened German translation was published in *Alternative* 41 (April 1965) : 85–88.

Revolutionary Commune

I

What should every class-conscious worker know about the revolutionary commune in the present historical epoch which has on its agenda the revolutionary self-liberation of the working class from the capitalist yoke? And what is known about it today by even the politically enlightened and therefore self-conscious segment of the proletariat?

There are a few *historical facts*, together with a few appropriate remarks by *Marx, Engels,* and *Lenin,* which now after half a century of Social Democratic propaganda prior to the Great War and after the powerful new experiences of the last fifteen years, have already become part and parcel of proletarian consciousness. However, this piece of world history is today mostly dealt with as little in the schools of the "democratic" (Weimar) republic as it was earlier in the schools of the Kaiser's imperial monarchy. I am referring to the history and significance of the glorious Paris Commune, which hoisted the red flag of proletarian revolution on March 18, 1871, and kept it flying for seventy-two days in fierce battles against an onslaught of a well-armed hostile world. This is the revolutionary commune of the Paris workers in 1871 of which *Karl Marx said in his address to the General Council of the International Workers Association May 30, 1871, on the civil war in France,* that its "true secret" lay in the fact that *it was essentially a government of the working classes,* "the result of the struggle by the producing class against the propertied class, the finally discovered political form under which the economic liberation of labor could develop." And it was in this sense that twenty years later, when on the occasion of the founding of the *Second International* and the creation of *proletarian May Day celebrations* as the first form of direct international mass action, the propertied classes once again were overcome with holy terror whenever the alarming words "dictatorship of the proletariat" were sounded. Friedrich Engels flung the proud sentences into the faces of the startled philistines: "Well then, gentlemen, would you like to know what this dictatorship looks like? *Look at the Paris Commune. That was the dictatorship of the proletariat."* And then again, more than two decades later, the greatest revolutionary politician of our time, Lenin, analyzed in exact detail the experiences of the Paris Commune and the struggle against the opportunist decline and confusion in regard to the theories of Marx and Engels in the main part of his most important political work *State and Revolution.* And when a few weeks later the Russian Revolution of 1917, which had begun in February as a national and bourgeois revolution, broke through its national and bourgeois barriers and expanded and deepened into the first *proletarian world revolution,* the masses of West European workers (and the progressive sections of the working class of the whole world), together with Lenin and Trotsky, welcomed this new form of government of the *revolutionary "council system"* as the direct continuation of the *"revolutionary commune"* created half a century earlier by the Paris workers.

So far, so good. As unclear as the ideas may have been that bound together the revolutionary workers under the formula "all power to the councils," following that revolutionary period of storm and stress which spread far and wide over Europe after the economic and political upheavals of the four war years; however deep already then the rift may have been between these ideas and that reality which in the new Russia had come to the fore under the name of "Socialist Councils Republic"— nonetheless, in that period *the call for councils was a positive form of development of a revolutionary proletarian class will surging toward realization.* Only morose philistines could bewail the vagueness of the councils concept at that time, like every incompletely realized idea, and only lifeless pedants could attempt to alleviate this defect by artifically contrived "systems" like the infamous "little boxes-system" of *Däumig* and *Richard Müller.* Wherever in those days the proletariat established its revolutionary class-dictatorship, as happened in *Hungary* and *Bavaria* temporarily in 1919, it named and formed its *"government of the working class"*—which was *a result of the struggle by the producing class against the propertied class* and whose *determined purpose was to accomplish the "economic liberation of labor"*—as a *revolutionary council government.* And if in those days the proletariat had been victorious in any one of the bigger industrial countries, perhaps in *Germany* during the big commercial strikes of spring, 1919, or in the counteraction of the Kapp putsch in 1920, or in the course of the so-called Cunow strike during the Ruhr-occupation and the inflation year of 1923, or in *Italy* at the time of the occupation of factories in October, 1920—then it would have established its power in the form of a *Council Republic* and it would have united together with the already existing "Federation of Russian Socialist Soviet Republics" within a *world-federation of revolutionary council republics*.

Under today's conditions, however, the *council concept* has quite another significance, as does the existence of a so-called socialist and *"revolutionary" council government*. Now after the overcoming of the world economic crisis of 1921 and the related defeat of the German, Polish, and Italian workers—and the following chain of further proletarian defeats including the British general strike and miners' strike of 1926—*European capitalism has commenced a new cycle of its dictatorship on the backs of the defeated working class*. Under these changed objective conditions we, the revolutionary proletarian class-fighters of the whole world, cannot any more hold subjectively onto our old belief, quite unchanged and unexamined, in the revolutionary significance of the council concept and the revolutionary character of *council government* as a direct development of that *political form of the proletarian dictatorship* "discovered" half a century ago by the Paris communardes.

It would be superficial and false, when looking at the flagrant *contradictions* existing today between the name and the real condition of the Russian *"Union of Socialist Soviet Republics,"* to satisfy ourselves with the statement that the men in power in present-day Russia "betrayed" that *original "revolutionary" council principle*, just as in Germany *Scheidemann, Müller*, and *Leipart* have "betrayed" their "revolutionary" *socialist principles of the days before the war*. Both claims are true without doubt. The Scheidemanns, Müllers, and Leiparts were traitors to their socialist principles. And in Russia the "dictatorship" exercised today from the highest pinnacle of an extremely exclusive government-party apparatus by means of a million-headed bureaucracy over the proletariat and the whole of Soviet Russia—that only in name is still reminiscent of the "Communist" and "Bolshevik" party—has as little in common with the revolutionary council concept of 1917 and 1918 as the Fascist party dictatorship of the former revolutionary Social Democrat *Mussolini* in Italy. However, so little is explained in both cases in regard to "betrayal" *that rather the fact of betrayal itself requires explanation*.

The real task that the contradictory development from the once revolutionary slogan "All Power to the Councils" to the now capitalist-fascist regime in the so-called socialist soviet-state has put on the agenda for us class-conscious revolutionary proletarians is rather a task of *revolutionary self-critique*. We must recognize that not only does that *revolutionary dialectic* apply to the ideas and institutions of the feudal and bourgeois past, but likewise to all thoughts and organizational forms which the working class itself has already brought forward during the hitherto prevailing stages of its historical struggle for liberation. It is this dialectic which causes the *good deed* of yesterday to become the *misery* of today— as *Goethe* said in his *Faust*—or as it is more clearly and definitely expressed by *Karl Marx*: every historical form turns at a certain point of its development from a *developing form* of revolutionary forces of production, revolutionary action, and developing consciousness into the *shackles* of that developing form. And as this dialectical *antithesis* of revolutionary development applies to all other historical ideas and formations, it equally applies also to those *philosophical* and *organizational results of a certain historical phase of revolutionary class struggle*, which is exemplified by the Paris communards of almost 60 years ago in the "finally discovered" political form of government of the working class in the shape of a *revolutionary commune*. The same is applicable to the following new historical phase of struggle in the revolutionary movement of the Russian workers and peasants, and the international working class, which brought forth the new form of the *"revolutionary councils power."*

Instead of bewailing the "betrayal" of the council concept and the "degeneration" of the council power we must gather by illusion-free, sober, and historically objective observation the beginning, middle, and end of this whole development within a *total historical panorama* and we must pose this *critical question*: What is—after this total historical experience—*the real historical and class-oriented significance of this new political form of government*, which brought about in the first place the *revolutionary Commune of 1871*, although its development was forcefully interrupted after 72 days' duration, and then the *Russian Revolution of 1917* in concrete, more final, shape?

It is all the more necessary to once again basically orient ourselves concerning the historical and class-oriented character of the *revolutionary commune* and its further development, the *revolutionary councils system*, for even the barest of historical critique shows how completely unfounded the widely spread conception is today among revolutionaries who theoretically reject and want to "destroy" in practice the *parliament*, conceived as a bourgeois institution with regard to its origin and purpose, and yet at the same time see the so-called *council system*, and also its predecessor the *"revolutionary commune,"* as the essential form of proletarian government which stands with its whole essence in irreconcilable opposition to the essence of the bourgeois state. In reality it is the "commune," in its almost thousand years of historical development, which represents an *older,* bourgeois form of government than parliament. The commune forms from the beginnings in the eleventh century up to that highest culmination which the revolutionary movement of the bourgeoisie found in the French Revolution of 1789/93 the almost *pure class-oriented manifestation of that struggle which in this whole historical epoch the then revolutionary bourgeois class has waged in various forms for the revolutionary change of the whole hitherto existing feudal order of society and the founding of the new bourgeois social order.*

When Marx—as we saw in the previously quoted sentence of his "Civil War in France"—celebrated the *revolutionary Commune of the Paris workers of 1871* as the *"finally discovered political form under which the economic liberation of labor could be consummated,"* he was aware at the same time that the "commune" could only take on this *new character*—its traditional form having been passed on over hundreds of years of bourgeois struggle for freedom—if *it radically changed its entire previous nature.* He expressly concerns himself with the misinterpretations of those who at that time wanted to regard this *"new commune which shatters the modern state power"* as a "revival of the medieval communes which preceded that state power and thence formed their foundation." And he was far removed from expecting any wondrous effects for the proletarian class struggle from the political *form* of the communal constitution per se—detached from the definite proletarian class-oriented *content,* with which the Paris workers, according to his concept, had for one historical moment filled this political form, achieved through struggle and put into the service of their economic self-liberation. To him the decisive reason enabling the Paris workers to make the traditional form of the "commune" the instrument of a purpose which was so completely opposed to their original historically determined goal lies, rather, on the contrary, in its being *relatively undeveloped and indeterminate.* In the *fully formed bourgeois state,* as it developed in its classical shape especially in France (i.e., in the *centralized modern representative-state*), the supreme power of the state is, according to the well known words of the *"Communist Manifesto,"* nothing more than *"an executive committee which administers the common affairs of the bourgeois class as a whole"*; thus its bourgeois class character is readily apparent. However, in those underdeveloped early historical forms of bourgeois state constitutions, that also include the medieval "free commune," this bourgeois class character, which essentially adheres to every state, comes to light in a quite different form. As opposed to the later ever more clearly appearing and ever more purely developed character of the bourgeois state power as a "supreme public power for the suppression of the working class, a machine of class rule" (Marx), we see that in this earlier phase of development the originally determined goal of the bourgeois class organization still prevails as an organ of the revolutionary struggle of liberation of the suppressed bourgeois class against the medieval feudal rule. However little this struggle of the medieval bourgeoisie has in common with the proletarian struggle for emancipation of the present historical epoch it yet remains as a *historical class struggle*. And those instruments created then by the bourgeoisie for the requirements of their revolutionary struggle contain to a certain extent—but only to a certain extent—certain formal connecting links with the formation of today's revolutionary struggle of emancipation which is being continued by the *proletarian class* on another basis, under other conditions, and for other purposes.

Karl Marx had already at an earlier date pointed out the special significance which these earlier experiences and achievements of the bourgeois class struggle—which found their most important expression in the various phases of development of the *revolutionary bourgeois commune of the middle ages*—had in regard to the forming of modern proletarian class consciousness and class struggle; in fact, he pointed this out very much earlier than the great historical event of the Paris Commune insurrection of 1871 permitted him to praise this new revolutionary commune of the Parisian workers as the finally discovered political form of economic liberation of labor. He had demonstrated the *historical analogy* existing between the *political development of the bourgeoisie* as the suppressed class struggling for liberation within the medieval feudal state and the *development of the proletariat in modern capitalist society*. It is from this perspective that he was able to win his main theoretical support for his special dialectical revolutionary *theory on the significance of trade unions and the trade union struggle*—a theory which until this day is still not completely and correctly understood by many Marxists from both the left and right wing. And he arrived at it by comparing the modern *coalitions* of workers with the communes of the medieval bourgeoisie, stressing the historical fact that *the bourgeois class likewise began their struggle against the feudal social order by forming coalitions*. Already in the *polemical treatise against Proudhon* we find in regard to this point the following illustration, classical to this day:

> In the bourgeoisie we have two phases to distinguish: that in which it constituted itself as a class under the regime of feudalism and absolute monarchy, and that in which, already constituted as a class, it overthrew feudalism and monarchy to make society into a bourgeois society. The first of these phases was the longer and neces-

sitated the greater efforts. This too began by partial combinations against the feudal lords.

Much research has been carried out to trace the different historical phases that the bourgeoisie has passed through, from the commune up to its constitution as a class.

But when it is a question of making a precise study of strikes, combinations and other forms in which the proletarians carry out before our eyes their organization as a class, some are seized with real fear and others display a *transcendental* disdain. (Marx, *The Poverty of Philosophy*, chapter 2, #5)

What is theoretically articulated here, by the young Marx in the 1840's, who only recently crossed over to proletarian socialism, and what he repeats in a similar form a few years later in the *Communist Manifesto* by illustrating the diverse phases of development of the bourgeoisie and the proletariat, he also articulates once again 20 years later in the well known *resolution of the Geneva Congress of the International Association of Workers with regard to trade unions*. He argues that the trade unions have already during their hitherto prevailing development become *"the focal points of organization of the working class . . . just as the medieval municipalities and villages had become focal points for the bourgeoisie."* This is so although the trade unions are not aware of their focal significance beyond the immediate daily tasks of defending the wages and working hours of the workers against the continuous excessive demands of capital. Hence in the future the trade unions *must act consciously as such focal points of the organization of the whole working class.*

II

If one wants to understand Marx's later position regarding the *revolutionary commune of the Parisian workers* in its real significance, one must take his original concept on the historical relationship between the organizational forms of the modern proletarian and the earlier bourgeois class struggle as a starting point. The commune arose from the struggle of the producing class against the exploiting class and broke up in a revolutionary act the prevailing bourgeois state machinery. When Marx celebrates this new commune as the finally discovered form for the liberation of labor, it was not at all his desire—as some of his followers later claimed and still do so to this day—to designate or brand a *definite form of political organization*, whether it is called a *revolutionary commune* or a *revolutionary council system*, as a singularly appropriate and potential form of the revolutionary proletarian class dictatorship. In the immediately preceding sentence, he expressly points to "the multifariousness of interpretations which supported the commune and the multiplicity of interests expressed in the commune," and he explained the already established character of this new form of government as a *"political form thoroughly capable of development."* It is just this *unlimited capability of development* of new forms of political power, created by the Paris communardes in the fire of battle, which distinguished it from the "classic development of bourgeois government," the centralized state power of the modern parliamentary republic. Marx's essential presupposition is that in the energetic pursuit of the real interests of the working class this form can in the end even be used as that lever which will overthrow the economic bases forming the existence of classes, class rule, and the state. The *revolutionary communal constitution* thus becomes under certain historical conditions the political form of *a process of development,* or to put it more clearly, of a *revolutionary action* where the basic essential goal is no longer to *preserve any one form of state rule,* or even *to create a newer "higher state-type,"* but rather to create at last the material conditions for the "withering away of every state altogether." *"Without this last condition, the communal constitution was an impossibility and an illusion,"* Marx says in this context with all desired distinctness.

Nonetheless, there remains still an unbalanced *contradiction* between on one hand Marx's characterization of the Paris Commune as the finally discovered *"political form"* for accomplishing the economic and social self-liberation of the working class and, on the other hand, his emphasis at the same time that the suitability of the commune for this purpose rests mainly on its *formlessness*; that is, on its indeterminateness and openness to multiple interpretations. It appears there is only one point at which Marx's position is perfectly clear and to which he professed at this time under the influence of certain political theories he had in the meantime come up against and which were incorporated in this original political concept—and not least under the practical impression of the enormous experience of the Paris Commune itself. While in the *Communist Manifesto* of 1847–48 and likewise in the *Inaugural Address to the International Workers' Association* in 1864, he still had only spoken of the necessity *"for the proletariat to conquer political power,"* now the experiences of the Paris Commune provided him with the proof that "the working class can not simply appropriate the ready-made state machinery and put it into motion for its own purposes, but *it must smash the existing bourgeois state machinery in a revolutionary way."* This sentence has since been regarded as an essential main proposition and core of the whole political theory of Marxism, especially since *in 1917 Lenin at once theoretically restored the unadulterated Marxian theory of the state in his work "State and Revolution" and practically realized it through carrying through the October Revolution as its executor.*

But obviously nothing *positive* is at all yet said about the *formal character* of the new revolutionary supreme state power of the proletariat with the merely *negative determination* that the state power cannot simply "appropriate the state machinery" of the previous bourgeois state "for the working class and set it in motion for their own purposes." So we must ask: for which reasons does the "Commune" in its particular, determinate form represent the finally discovered political form of government for the working class, as *Marx* puts it in his *Civil War*, and as *Engels* characterizes it once more at great length in his introduction to the third edition of the *Civil War* twenty years later? Whatever gave Marx and Engels, those fiery admirers of the *centralized system of revolutionary bourgeois dictatorship realized by the great French Revolution*, the idea to regard precisely the "*Commune*" as the "political form" of the *revolutionary dictatorship of the proletariat*, when it appeared to be the complete opposite to that system?

In fact, if we analyze more exactly the political program and goals to be attained as proposed by the two founders of scientific socialism, *Marx and Engels*, not only in the time *before the Paris Commune insurrection*, but also *afterwards*, the assertion cannot be maintained that the form of proletarian dictatorship realized by the Paris Commune of 1871 would in any particular sense be in unison with those political theories. Indeed, Marx's great opponent in the First International, *Michael Bakunin*, had on this point the historical truth on his side when he sarcastically commented on Marx's having annexed the Paris Commune retrospectively: "The impact of the Communist insurrection was so powerful that even the Marxists, who had all their ideas thrown to the wind by it, were forced to doff their hats to it. They did more than that: *in contradiction to all logic and their innermost feelings, they adopted the program of the Commune and its aim as their own.* It was a comic, but enforced travesty. They had to do it, otherwise they would have been rejected and abandoned by all—so mighty was the passion which this revolution had brought about in the whole world." (Cf. *Brupbacher*: Marx and Bakunin, pp. 114–115.)

The revolutionary ideas of the Paris communardes of 1871 are partly derived from the federalistic program of *Bakunin* and *Proudhon*, partly from the circle of ideas of the revolutionary Jacobins surviving in *Blanquism*, and only to a very small degree in *Marxism*. Twenty years later,

Friedrich *Engels* claimed that the *Blanquists* who formed the majority of the Paris Commune had been forced by the sheer weight of the facts to proclaim instead of their own program of a "strict dictatorial centralization of all power in the hands of the new revolutionary government" the exact opposite, namely the *free federation of all French communes with the Paris Commune.* On this issue the same contradiction arises between *Marx* and *Engels*' political theory upheld so far and their now prevailing unconditional acknowledgment of the commune as the "finally discovered political form" of the government of the working class. It is erroneous when *Lenin* in his 1917 work "State and Revolution" describes the evolution of the Marxian theory of state, as if Marx had in the transition period up to 1852 already concertized the abstract formulation of the political task of the revolutionary proletariat (as proposed in his "Communist Manifesto" of 1847–48) to the effect that the victorious proletariat must *"destroy"* and *"smash"* the existing bourgeois supreme state power. Against this thesis of Lenin speaks *Marx and Engels*' own testimony, who both declared repeatedly that just the *experience of the Paris Commune of 1871* provided for the first time the effective *proof* that "*the working class cannot simply appropriate the ready made state machinery and set it in motion for its own purposes.*" It was *Lenin* himself who provided the logical gap appearing in his presentation of the development of revolutionary Marxist state theory at this point by *simply jumping over a time-span of 20 years* in his otherwise so historically correct and philologically exact reproduction of Marx and Engels' remarks on the state. He proceeds from the *18th Brumaire of Louis Bonaparte* (1852) straight on to the *Civil War in France* (1871) and in so doing overlooks among other things the fact that Marx summarized the whole "political program" of the working class in this one lapidary sentence of his *Inaugural Address of the First Internationale: "It is therefore the great task of the working class now to seize political power."*

Yet even in the *time after 1871*, when Marx, on account of the experience of the Paris Commune, advocated in a far more certain and unequivocal way that ever before the indispensible necessity of crushing the bourgeois state machinery and building the proletarian class dictatorship, he was far removed from propagating a *form of government modelled on the revolutionary Paris Commune* as the *political form* of proletarian dictatorship. Just for that one historical moment—in which he unconditionally and without reservations came forward on behalf of the heroic fighters and victims of the commune vis-à-vis the triumphant reaction— did he, or so it appears, uphold this standpoint—and I am referring to the *Address to the General Council of the International Workers' Asso-*

ciation on the "Civil War in France," written in blood and fire on behalf of this first international organization of the revolutionary proletariat. For the sake of the revolutionary *essence* of the Paris Commune, he repressed the critique which from his standpoint he should have exercised on the special *form* of its historical manifestation. If beyond that he even went a step further and celebrated the political form of the revolutionary communal-constitution directly as the "finally discovered form" of the proletarian dictatorship, then the explanation does not lie any more merely with his natural *solidarity* with the revolutionary workers of Paris, but also in a special *subsidiary purpose.* Having written the Address to the General Council of the I.W.A. directly after the glorious battle and defeat of the Paris communardes, *Marx* not only wanted *to annex the Marxism of the Commune but also at the same time the Commune to Marxism.* It is in this sense that one must understand this remarkable document, if one wishes to correctly grasp its meaning and range of significance not only as a classic historical document looked at as a hero's epic or as a death lament. Rather beyond all that, it should be seen as a *fractional polemical treatise of Marx against his most intimate opponents in the bitter struggles which had already broken out and would soon thereafter lead to the collapse of the First International.* This fractional subsidiary purpose hindered Marx from appraising in a historically correct and complete way that interconnecting revolutionary movement of the French proletariat which began with the *insurrections of the Commune in Lyon and Marseilles in 1870* and had its climax in the *Paris Commune insurrection of 1871.* It also forced him to explain the *revolutionary communal constitution,* welcomed as the "finally discovered political form" of proletarian class dictatorship, as a *centralist* government as well—although this was in contrast to its actual essential being.

Already Karl Marx and Friedrich Engels themselves, and more so Lenin, deny the charge that the Paris Commune had an essentially federalist character. If Marx cannot help but explain in his short account of the sketch of the *All-French Communal Constitution* produced by the Paris Commune the unambiguous federalist aspects of this constitution, then in so doing he still emphasizes purposively the fact (naturally not denied by such federalists as *Proudhon* and *Bakunin*) that *"the unity of the nation was not to be broken but on the contrary was to be organized"* through this communal constitution. He underlines *"the few but important functions"* which are *still remaining to be dealt with by a "central government"* within this communal constitution. He remarks that according to the plan of the Commune these functions *"were not—as some intentionally falsified—to be abolished, but were to be transferred to communal (and strictly responsible) civil servants."* On this basis, *Lenin* later declared that *"not a trace of federalism is to be found"* in Marx's writings on the example of the Commune. "Marx is a centralist and in his explanations cited here there is no deviation from centralism" ("State and Revolution"). Quite correctly so, but Lenin omits to mention at this point that Marx's exposition of the Paris Commune is also everything else but a historically correct characterization of the revolutionary commune constitution aspired to by the Paris communardes and realized in the first beginnings.

In order to deflect from the federative and anti-centralist character of the Paris Commune as much as possible, *Marx* and *Engels*, and likewise *Lenin*, have emphasized above all else the negative aspect, that it represents as such the *destruction of the prevailing bourgeois state power*. On this point there is no quarrel among revolutionaries. Marx, Engels, and Lenin have justly emphasized that the decisive foundation for the proletarian revolutionary character of the form of political supreme power as stated by the Commune is to be sought in its *societal being* as a realization of proletarian class dictatorship. They pointed out to their "federalist" adversaries with great severity *that the decentralized, federative state form as such is quite as bourgeois as the centralist form of government of the modern bourgeois state.* They nevertheless committed the same error which they so strongly opposed in their opponents, not by concentrating on the "federalist" character of the communal constitution, but rather by emphasizing too much the other *formal differences which distinguished the Paris Commune from parliamentarism and other surpassed forms of the bourgeois state constitution* (for example, on the *replacement of the standing army through the militia, on the unification of executive and legislative power*, and on the *responsibility and right of dismissal of "communal" functionaries*). They thereby created a considerable confusion of concepts out of which emerged not only harmful effects with regard to the *position of Marxists vis-à-vis the Paris commune*, but also likewise for the *later positing of the revolutionary Marxist direction vis-à-vis the new historical phenomenon of the revolutionary council system.*

As incorrect as it may be to see with Proudhon and Bakunin an overcoming of the bourgeois state in the "federative" form, it is just as incorrect when today some Marxist followers of the revolutionary commune on the revolutionary council system believe on the basis of such misunderstood explanations by Marx, Engels, and Lenin that a parliamentary representative with a short-term, binding mandate revocable at any time, or a government functionary employed by private treaty for ordinary "wages," would be a less bourgeois arrangement than an elected parliamentarian. It is completely erroneous when they believe that there are any "communal" or "council-like" forms of constitution whose introduction may cause the state governed by the revolutionary proletarian party in the end to relinquish completely that character of an instrument of class suppression which adheres to every state. The whole theory of the final "withering away of the state in Communist society," taken over by Marx and Engels out of the tradition of utopian socialism and further developed on the basis of practical experiences of the proletarian class struggle in their time, loses its revolutionary meaning when one declares with *Lenin* that there is a state where the minority does not suppress anymore the majority, but rather "the majority of the people themselves suppress their own suppressors"; and *such a state of proletarian dictatorship then in its capacity as "fulfiller" of true or proletarian democracy "is already a withering away of the state"* ("State and Revolution").

It is high time again to posit with full clarity the two *basic theories* of the real revolutionary proletarian theory which by *temporary adapting* to practical requirements of such certain phases of struggle as the *Paris Commune insurrection* of 1871 and the *Russian October Revolution of 1917* in the end ran into danger of being abrogated. The essential *final goal* of proletarian class struggle is not any one *state*, however "democratic," "communal," or even "council-like," but is rather the classless and stateless Communist *society* whose comprehensive *form* is not any longer some kind of political power but is *"that association in which the free development of every person is the condition for the free development of all"* ("Communist Manifesto").

Irrespective of whether the proletarian class can "conquer" more or less unchanged the surpassed state apparatus following the illusion of the Marxist reformists, or whether it can only really appropriate it according to revolutionary Marxist theory by radically "*smashing*" its surpassed form and *"replacing" it through a new voluntary created form— until then*, in either case this *state* will *differ from the bourgeois state* in the period of revolutionary transformation of capitalist into Communist society only *through its class nature and its social function, but not through its political form. "The true secret" of the revolutionary commune, the revolutionary council system, and every other historical manifestation of government of the working class* exists in this social content and not in any one artificially devised *political form* or in such special institutions as may once have been realized under some particular historical circumstances.

Translated by Andrew Giles-Peters and Karl-Heinz Otto

The Spanish Revolution

I

The last foreign minister of the fallen Spanish monarchy, Count Romanones, reports that the overpowering victory of the republican parties
(who in the municipal elections of April 12, 1931, obtained the overwhelming majority of votes in almost all—47 out of 51!—provincial
capitals) and the fall of the Bourbon monarchy which resulted in a few
hours "was a surprise for all." And Leon Rollin, correspondent of "New
Europe," who is familiar with the most intimate secrets of the Spanish
opposition, has explicitly confirmed it. It was a surprise for the king, who
had wanted these elections "sincerismis" (most sincerely) (and had at
the same time providently transferred the greatest part of his fortune
across the border); it was a surprise for the European press which still a
few weeks ago had celebrated the last Spanish autocrat during his short
visit to Paris and London as the "first politician of Spain." And it was
a surprise also for the victorious oppositionalists themselves who had
only counted on victory in the big cities and already had prepared for
new revolutionary action.

Instead of this, in one blow the whole old order collapsed without any
attempt at resistance. The hitherto most reliable pillars of the monarchy,
the army and the church, abandoned the king almost immediately and
put themselves at the disposal of the persecuted emigrés, the sentenced
traitors of yesterday who formed the revolutionary government of today.
They offered the new government the same traditional loyalty and fidelity
with which already in 1808, after the abdication of Ferdinand VII enforced by a Napoleon, a deputation of the grandees of Spain addressed
the new King Joseph put on the throne by Napoleon: "Sire, the grandees
of Spain have at all times been famous for their loyalty to their sovereign,
and your majesty will also find in them the same fidelity and devotion."
The infamous chief of the monarchist Civil Guard, General Sanjurjo,
did the same. This general, who had changed over to the republic from
the monarchy immediately after its fall and was received with open arms
by the new republican powerholders, is the same person who later at the
time of the Cortes elections suppressed, in the name of the republican-
conservative Interior Minister Maura, the alleged conspiracy of the popular revolutionary hero Ramon Franco, and a month after that the real
general strike and insurrection of the urban and rural workers in Seville

and Andalusia. General Sanjurjo used such brutal measures that the conservative English "Daily Mail" congratulated the revolutionary Spanish government for its strength of character proven on this occasion.

But all of this was still in the future in the beautiful spring days of April. This revolution of April, 1931, was later gloriously characterized by its leaders and eyewitnesses as more a fiesta than a fight. This was indeed for the Spain of today the "beautiful revolution," following the description by Karl Marx of the French Revolution of 1848, which was followed even in the same year by the social catastrophe of the June defeat of the Paris proletariat and on December 2, 1851, by the coup d'état of the third Napoleon. In Marx's well-known characterization, written in the middle of the previous century for revolutionary France, it was "the beautiful revolution, the revolution of universal sympathy, because the conflicts which erupted in the revolution against the monarch were underdeveloped and slumbered side by side, because the social war, which formed its background, had only developed in a lofty existence, the existence of the phrase, of words."[1]

Indeed it is striking how little, in these first months between the municipal elections of April and the meeting of the constituent assembly (Cortes) in July, the newly formed provisional government, so aptly designated by the "Economist" as "republican-conservative and moderate socialist," was concerned with the social and class demands of the proletariat which required acute, practical immediate fulfillment. There is a striking difference between the two last European revolutions, which were unleashed in Russia in 1917 through the crisis of the world war, and in Spain through the new "peaceful" world economic crisis which has overtaken the world since the autumn of 1929. This difference is partly explained by the basically changed general European situation of today compared with the one of 1917–1920. It depends, on the other hand, on the thoroughly peculiar character of the Spanish workers' movement, which is not new but has already developed for the past sixty years.

First of all, there was never and does not exist in Spain until this day practically any Communist party. Neither are there signs that such a party might emerge in the near future. There was a time when the agricultural workers, vegetating in indescribable poverty in Andalusia and Estremadura, and the permanently overworked peasants of Galicia and Asturias, gaining from their tiny parcels of land a miserable support and the hated rent ("fuero") for an unknown landowner, listened attentively when they heard about the dividing up of the agricultural soil in the Soviet Union. But all this today is long gone. What appears today under the name of "communism" in the revolutionary movement in Spain is, as the Cortes elections of June 28 should have proven even to the foreign doubters, still only the shadow of a shadow. There are but three weak Communist sects, which are fighting more amongst themselves, and with the real revolutionary organizations of the Spanish proletariat, than with the bourgeois class enemy. Of these, one follows the orders of Stalin, the second those of Trotsky, while the third group alone, the Catalonian Federalist Communists led by the Spaniard Maurin, can be looked upon as a relatively home-grown product of the Spanish labor movement. None of these three directions exerts an effective practical influence within the Spanish labor movement. None of them is represented in the Cortes even by one single deputy.

However, the two branches of the workers' movement to be found in Spain which are also strong social forces have not in these first months dimmed the happy spring morning of the young Spanish revolution through an all too radical mounting of their particular class demands. It is not surprising that one of these two directions, the Social Democratic reformist party and union movement, has refused to raise these radical demands in the light of its whole statesmenlike and state-maintaining tradition, formed already during the pre-war period. But it must appear strange and surprising, to the highest degree for the other direction, the syndicalist revolutionary movement, not to have raised radical demands, in the light of the whole historical character of this movement. "If one looks at the workers' movement south of the Pyrenees only from the viewpoint of threats it contains to social peace, then the danger does not appear to come so much from socialism as from anarchism; of course less under the ideological form which it still had a few years ago, and in the platonic theories to which some survivors of the International may still commit themselves, and not even in the individual deeds of a number of fanatics, but rather from the new point of view of revolutionary syndicalism through which it can reorganize itself."

This historical prognosis, which was put forward by the bourgeois social politician Angel Marvaud in 1910, has been confirmed by the real development to a surprising degree. Today, after twenty years of further development of Spanish social democracy, which from its beginning represented a tendency of state preservation, and after the success accelerated by the war of the same state maintaining tendency in all other European social democratic parties also, the Spanish social democratic party stands, in spite of its extremely small number of members, with its 130 mandates as the strongest party in the constituent national assembly (Cortes). With its three ministers it is directly participating in the new bourgeois-republican governmental power, and even within this governing coalition, it is only still formally on the left wing, while in actual fact, however, it is much more on the right. It stands to the right of the radical bourgeois-revolutionary tendency which is represented in the present cabinet by the foreign minister Lerroux. And it stands far to the right of the federalist republican parties in Catalonia, Andalusia, and Galicia, in particular to the right of the popular-federalist party of the Catalonian state president Macia, who still to this day opposes in his area all demagogical instructions of the Madrid guardians of order with a stiff-necked and successful resistance.

The most glaring illustration of this character of today's Spanish governing socialists is provided by the fact that its leader, Largo Caballero, the present republican labor minister and at the same time chairman of the Social Democratic National Trade Union (UGT), possesses the dubious fame that he had already under the dictatorship of Primo de Rivera participated in the government as a state councillor. At a time when the whole radical bourgeoisie, the petty bourgeoisie, and the revolutionary part of the working class fought with all means the unconstitutional regime of the dictatorship, and even the liberal and conservative ex-minister from the pre-dictatorship period boycotted the dictator and all his undertakings, there was a Spanish party loyal to the government, and that was the Spanish Social Democrats. They supported even the so-called joint committees (a kind of arbitration committee) which had been introduced by the dictator in imitation of Mussolini's labor-charter, and used the thus created indirect governmental organization for the coerced formation of a factual monopoly benefitting these hitherto relatively weak trade unions in their fight to eliminate the syndicalist trade unions prohibited and prosecuted by the dictatorship.

The fall of the dictatorship and the monarchy did likewise change this condition very little and not at all to the advantage of the revolutionary section of workers. The "joint-committees" of the dictator are still retained by the republic unchanged today, as are the direct measures of repression which the present "revolutionary" government applies to striking syndicalist workers through the Sanjurjos and Pistoleros[2] they inherited from the dictatorship. But they serve much less the general purpose of a "defense of the state" than the much more palpable task of strengthening the reformist trade unions of the republican minister of labor Largo Caballero, who is also a reformist trade union secretary, through the renewed suppression of the syndicalist trade unions of the National Federation of Labor (CNT).[3]

The aversion of the present Spanish social democratic party to energetically pursue any revolutionary proletarian class demands goes so far that the party considered their victory in the Cortes elections as being most inopportune. In accordance with a secret plan of the coalition parties, the Social Democrats were meant to be the opposition in the constituting National Assembly—now this role will perhaps be taken on by the right wing after some time. The socialists would have rather not been further participants in a bourgeois coalition government for a considerable period since by nature the freshly turned-over revolutionary ground calls for a new positioning of societal forces at great speed. Now, however, after their surprisingly large electoral victory, they had to be satisfied with announcing their categorical rejection of participating in a bourgeois government while simultaneously directing the three socialist ministers to remain on their posts until the final promulgation of the new constitution. In fact they can count themselves lucky in not having gained the absolute majority in the elections, for the discrepency between their socialist talk and bourgeois deeds would have been much more embarassing. And the pressure of the masses to part company with the bourgeois politicians and follow the course of the social revolution of the proletarian class would have assailed them with much greater force.

The tactics employed by the other line of the Spanish workers' movement were far more noteworthy than this "moderate" bearing of the Social Democrats during the initial developmental phase of the Spanish revolution now already coming, or so it seems, to an end. Anyone who in these weeks spent some time among the revolutionary workers of Spain and observed not only their theoretical programmes, but more so their practical activities and actual stance toward the new situation brought about by the April revolution, could not help considering the following impressions: perhaps there was a newly founded consciousness of power, or as I would rather suppose, the newly won freedom of movement was naively seen as a new era that would continue undisturbed after so many years of oppression. In any case, this whole great mass of workers, after sixty years of revolutionary propaganda and direct action, and a recent eight-year period of immensely accelerated powerful oppression from which they arose to a new life, was, nonetheless, still fanatically bound to their old revolutionary goals even today. Although they were still independent, active, and prepared for any sacrifice, at this one historical moment they never thought to wage from the beginning the "open warfare" against this new republican state that they theoretically declared against every form of state, with their traditional vigor or with still increased severity at the end. The bourgeois republic corresponded in no way to their programmatical demands; it only provided the momentary release from an immense pressure and compliance with some small but humanly practical and important wishes such as the freeing of their prisoners, a pause for breath in the never-ending persecution and a partial recognition of their organizations. Thus the revolutionary workers did not immediately oppose the new republic in a hostile manner, but were first and foremost concerned with consolidating their revolutionary mass organization, the syndicalist CNT, which had, after almost complete destruction, in less than two months gained a strength of 600,000 members and was still rapidly increasing its members, as well as looking after all other possible centers, so as to fashion a really free and autonomous worker's life in accord with their concept. When in mid-June they gathered in Madrid 432 delegates from all parts of Spain, representing industrial and rural workers, for their first national congress, they affirmed their traditional principles and expressly stated that this congress of the CNT "regards and will relate to the constituting Cortes as it would to every oppressing power." At the same time, however, they put forward a plan of minimum demands which they directed to this same Cortes, concerning those areas of social life they considered at this time as most important, namely: education and the school system ("as long as the state exists, one has to demand that the evil of analphabetism be eliminated!"), the freedom of the individual, freedom of speech and the press, the right of coalition and strike, the elimination of unemployment in city and country, and the breaking of the narrow bourgeois property concepts where they hinder the fulfillment of these productive demands.

One notices at first sight that among these demands there is not one which could not have been managed by a radical bourgeois and democratic revolution that was true to its own principles. In fact, there was not one demand that has not been recognized even by the liberal monarchists of the pre-revolutionary regime as theoretically justifiable. But nevertheless, at this hour not a single one of these demands has been fulfilled in revolutionary Spain, nor is their fulfillment being seriously considered. The provisional government, aghast at a definite and immediate break with the old powers, already during its first hour was concerned to again fetter, in concert with these old powers, as quickly as possible, this freedom-movement of the revolutionary forces created unavoidably in the movement of violent overthrow. It took advantage of the strike of telephone workers, beginning on July 6th in Barcelona as, at first, a mere trade union matter, later followed by strikes of solidarity in the remaining parts of the country, to provoke the uprising in Seville and the whole of Andalusia. It then put down this movement with brutal force and on July 24, 1931, ultimately prohibited by decree the syndicalist organizations in all of Spain, and thereby put the syndicalist movement "outside the law." With this complete return to the methods of the old militarist-reactionary system of suppression, the provisional government of the new Spanish state has, as it wished and intended, prevented the on-going tendencies of a proletariat dissatisfied with the bourgeois revolution. Thereby and at the same time, it also impeded immensely the progress toward those immediate tasks recognized by itself, and which are regarded today, by the overwhelming majority of all classes of the Spanish people, as not postponable.

2

The immediate tasks of the present bourgeois revolution in Spain are above all the following: (1) creation of a new form of state which will at once maintain a large uniform economic area commensurate with the development of modern production and will satisfy the stormy and relentless demand of Catalonians, Galicians, and Basques for autonomous government of their own affairs in the fields of education, culture, public works, transport, law and police. (2) The immediate and complete separation of church and state, church and school, together with a return (without compensation) of those mobile and immobile goods of the people that are today possessed by the church: several thousand monasteries, and other institutions of the dead hand. Finally (3) the chief and central task—on the solution to which in all great revolutions of the last centuries the whole development, victory or defeat of the revolutionary principle decisively depended, from the great French Revolution of 1789 to the great Russian Revolution of 1917—the core task is and was in all cases the implementation of the agrarian revolution. The unsuccessful solution to this task already caused the last Spanish revolution of 1868 to fail and the Spanish republic of 1873 likewise to expire.

Of all the questions, as they stand today and fill the agenda of the Spanish revolution, the relatively easiest one to answer is that of so-called federalism. When viewed superficially from outside, it appears as a catastrophic danger to the new republican statehood when the Madrid central government (where there are also some followers of federalist Catalonia in the parliament!) now permits the constituting Cortes not only to submit a unitarian, but an extremely centralist constitutional concept, and when at the same time the Catalonian "State-President" Macia arranged in his area a formal plebescite which determined with an overwhelming majority, almost unanimous, a quite different concept of the constitution for the united Catalonian provinces, namely the so-called Catalonian Statute. But already the British "Economist" points to, and rightfully so, the extraordinary watering down of privileges which had actually been demanded in this statute "for the independent Catalonian State within the Spanish Republic," and which would not even measure up to what in the unwritten constitution of the British Empire is called "dominion status." And another prosaic Englishman calls what is presently formed under the name of "Generalidad de Catalunya" (as a cross between a state and a mere utilitarian association of provinces), in a highly disrespectful manner, "a kind of glorified county-council."

Be that as it may, one sees that the former extreme separatist Macia and his followers have already dampened their original demands for independence to a high degree. The stick lies with the dog. It is not accidental that the Catalonian state leaves to the central Spanish state authorities such matters as foreign relations, declarations of war, and post, as well as "indirect taxes and custom's duty." The Catalonian bourgeoisie is well aware that just because Catalonia is industrially the most developed region of Spain, it will also in the future be dependent on the total Spanish market for the sale of their products which today are secured by high tariffs. Already several decades ago the well-known revolutionary ideologist Miguel de Unamuno accused the Catalonian bourgeoisie in a similar situation, that during their negotiations for Catalonian autonomy, "they had exchanged their soul for a custom tariff."[4]

On the other hand, through this intelligent moderation of the Catalonian demands, the Madrid central government is put in a position where it can hardly refuse its agreement to this quite acceptable proposal. When it hitherto has done so, when Madrid and Barcelona today oppose each other apparently on this question like two enemy camps, then it is in this case not merely a formal political controversy of principles. The concern here is not just a more general contrast between a backward servile and bureaucratic and courtly atmosphere of Madrid and the quite different atmosphere of Catalonia, which is not only industrially, but also socially much further developed (where incidentally the working class takes up a quite different position in public life than anywhere else in Spain since here it follows indivisibly the revolutionary syndicalist and anarchist line). The prohibition of syndicalist organizations decreed by the Madrid central government for the whole of Spain is in Catalonia to this day officially and actually being ignored.

Far more critical for the continuation of the Spanish revolution than the controversy between centralism and federalism is the unavoidable struggle between the old republican state and the real reactionary main force of the old monarchist Spain, the Catholic church. It is not as if the church were opposing the new republican state power with any kind of open enmity; quite to the contrary, the Catholic church (which has been until the fall of the dictator Primo de Rivera a loyal follower of the dictatorial regime and until the overthrow of Alphonse XIII, a true ally of the monarchy) put herself firmly behind the new republican state right from the day of the collapse of the monarchy. She did not even withdraw her fullest confidence from a government that had condoned the storming of monasteries in May, a government in which two loyal sons of the Catholic church served in the most important functions (the minister-president Alcala Zamora and the minister of the interior Miguel Maura). And when the reactionary Archbishop of Toledo, the infamous Cardinal Segura, had to flee Spanish soil due to a careless statement, it was the Bishop of Taranza who immediately referred Spanish Catholics by means of a pastoral letter to the young German republic, where Catholicism bloomed as peacefully as had never been the case under the Kaisers.

Yet just in this prudent conforming by the church to its defeat, suffered with the fall of the Catholic monarchist state order, there lies one of the greatest dangers for the future development of the Spanish revolution. Both as a national Spanish and international European power, the Catholic church very soon after the critical twelfth of April has begun a masterly battle of retreat, which at the same time already bore the seeds for a new attack. The Catholic party was the first and the only one of those old parties defeated in the April 12 elections who gathered together their followers and a large section of former monarchists (as well as their leading newspaper "El Debater" and their parliamentary group "Accion National") for the elections to the constituting Cortes on June 28. At the same time, it organized immediately on an international scale all leading Catholic newspapers of Europe in a unified defensive campaign against the alarming secularization of the new republican affairs of state in Catholic Spain: the "Vie Intellectuelle" of the French Dominicans, the "Correspondent" of the Catholic school "Montalembert," the "Etudes" of the Jesuits, the "Vita e Pensiero" edited by scholars of the Milan Catholic University and the German "Hochland." The tendency represented today by all these modern Catholic newspapers is best expressed by "Vie Intellectuelle" which clearly and succinctly characterized on May 10 the emerging new situation: "It is said that the church has lost the battle. It is said too rashly. At worst she has lost a battle not of her own making, but rather that of her ally, the monarchy. Now there will be a battle to be fought, and this time in her own domain—and that is the battle of democracia cristiana." One must compare this with the declaration given by the present minister-president, Alcala Zamora, during the first days following the setting up of the new republic: "It is imperative that we have the cooperation of the elements of order, of capitalism, and the clergy, because without them the republic would be ephemeral and ultimately doomed, since her failure would infinitely protract the possibility of stabilizing this regime." Thus one can build up a sufficiently clear picture of one of the possible ways in which the republic can develop and will develop, when the radical break with the reactionary power, so far strenuously being avoided by the present republican powers, is not in the course of events violently enforced and accomplished by new and stronger societal forces.

The only form in which one can expect the unleashing of such new societal forces in today's condition of the Spanish revolution—which, however, is already clearly indicated by the recent revolutionary upheavals in Andalusia—is the confrontation with the agrarian question pending now by historical necessity—and it probably will take this form. One would have to write a separate essay if one were to sketch merely an approximate picture of the most miserable and suppressed position of the Spanish rural workers and the so-called independent small holders, whose hopeless misery indeed equals that of the landless workers. Or, of the monstrous contrast between the giant estates of the large property owners and the slavish life of the farm workers ("braceros"), spiced still with regularly occurring periods of endless unemployment, of their ever and again flaring and desperate revolts being crushed bloodily time and time again, of the waste and retarded growth of the agricultural production capacity thus conditioned. All parties representing the public consciousness of Spain have unanimously recognized these unbearable conditions for a very long time. But all well-meaning projects of reform have repeatedly come to nothing against the thousand secret and open obstructions which were bound to arise in a country where the king, the officer-corps, the church and the leaders of the pseudo-parliamentary government parties of the ever-changing restoration period 1876–1923 were all rooted to their whole being, with all their power and privileges and emoluments in huge land estates. All these forces, and their willing instruments, ruled society officially and unofficially: the ordinary countryside and the little and middle-sized towns were exploited by brutal profiteering for personal interest and the infamous "kaziks" who prepared the ground for election on behalf of the governing men in Madrid. All agrarian conditions in Spain have thus been resting for five hundred years now in one and the same disconsolate immutability, which in recent times has become all the more pressing and inflammatory due to the manifold scientific and experiental evidence for the technical possibilities and economic productivity of a radical reform. Apart from this we must recognize the fact that a progressive industrial development has only taken place in a few provinces in the east and northeast, and that agricultural production in Spain therefore determines the whole economic and social life of the nation to a far different degree than in the industrially developed countries. The agrarian problem therefore is of immense significance to the fate of the present Spanish revolution. At the same time one could guess the fatal and ultimately insoluble problems a revolutionary government is confronted with when it meekly avoids any interference with dusty medieval privileges instead of solving this great problem with fortitude and disregard. And one can see, as the present "provisional government" has, that the first minute and insufficient projects toward social reform can only be won during and after an already progressing agrarian revolt which this government suppressed by bloody repression.

We cannot any better characterize the circumstances into which the provisional government of the Spanish republic is already today visibly deeper and deeper enmeshed than by recapitulating the description given by an open enemy of this government, who is at the same time one of Spain's largest landowners, Count Romanones, who wrote in the article in the "Revue des Deux Mondes" which we have already mentioned:

> In the last instance it will not be the big cities which will force their guidelines on this new political order but rather the country. People in the country are less interested in the political regime than in the question of distribution of the land. And it is among the day workers in the fields where we find the greatest threat of the present hour.
>
> The rural agitation, particularly in the Andalusian provinces, must not be neglected when one knows how to apprehend the lessons of history. What happened in the provinces between 1870–92, with "the Black Hand," a kind of Mafia of Camorra organization in the south of Spain, with the rising of rural workers in Jerez, with the convulsions of Cordoba, Espejo, Montilla, etc.; all these events will repeat themselves now with greater destructive force. The mentality of the Spanish rural populace is the same today as it was sixty years ago; the economic conditions of their life have not changed for the better and the means for containing them are weaker than yesterday. This rural populace is less isolated than half a century ago. It is in contact with its brothers in the cities, and is in some places organized in societies with most extreme convictions, and is far more inclined towards violent and tumultuous action than in 1873. Neither does this require any goading from Moscow; their souls have already

experienced frightful storms before the winds of Russia blew over them; not only can the Soviet propaganda induce them to an uprising but it is rather their own tendency, developed through the social conditions under which they have lived for centuries.

As far as these well chosen words, fitting for more than one purpose, of Count Romanones are only a characterization of the present actually pertaining situation, we need not add anything. If, however, the unspoken purpose of his description is to frighten the hesitant and undecisive statesmen of the republic with these terrifying difficulties in fulfilling their task, then one must say that such a task as the radical solution to the agrarian problem in present-day Spain cannot be conjured away by little diplomatic tricks and playful magic—the more so when the task is clearly situated in the whole objective situation and is regarded with urgency by the overwhelming majority of all the people's classes. Whether those men who were called to the leadership of the first phase of the Spanish revolution through the election of April 12 and June 28 wish to further or hinder it, the starting point and content of the second phase of this revolution will nevertheless be the struggle over the agrarian revolution.

Translated by Karl-Heinz Otto, Andrew Giles-Peters,
and Heinz Schutte

Notes

1. Karl Marx, *Class Struggles in France 1848–1850.*
2. Former general and police chief under the dictatorship of Primo de Rivera who were used by the government to suppress the workers during the Spanish Republic. Sanjurjo later became a military chief under Franco.—D.K.
3. The Confederacion National del Trabajo (CNT) was founded in Barcelona in 1910 and had 500,000 members in 1931 and would grow to one million members by 1936. The union was heavily influenced by anarchist-syndicalist ideas of refusing to participate in bourgeois institutions. Korsch was very sympathetic to their program and practice.—D.K.
4. Korsch is referring to the Spanish religious writer Miguel de Unamuno who wrote *The Tragic Sense of Life* and was for a while a sharp opponent of dictatorship and a champion of the Spanish Republic, before his later political capitulation to fascism.—D.K.

Economics and Politics in
Revolutionary Spain

In order to work out a realistic approach to the constructive work of the
revolutionary proletariat in Catalonia and other parts of Spain, we must
not confront its achievements either with some abstract ideal or with
results attained under entirely different historical conditions. There is no
doubt that the actual outcome of "collectivization," even in those industries of Barcelona and the smaller towns and villages of Catalonia where
it can be studied at its best, lags far behind the ideal constructions of the
orthodox socialist and communist theories, and even more so behind the
lofty dreams of generations of revolutionary syndicalist and anarchist
workers in Spain since the days of Bakunin.

As to historical analogies, the achievements of the Spanish revolution
during the period which began with the rapid counter-action of the revolutionary workers against the invasion of Franco and his fascist, National-
Socialist, and bourgeois-democratic supporters, and which now rapidly
approaches its final phase, should not be compared with anything which
happened in Russia after October, 1917, nor with the phase of the so-
called war communism 1918–20, nor with the ensuing phase of the NEP.
During the whole process of revolutionary movement beginning with
the overthrow of the monarchy in 1931, there has not been one single
moment when the workers, or any party or organization speaking in the
name of the revolutionary vanguard of the workers, have been in possession of the political power. This is true, not only on a national, but
also on a regional scale; it applies even to the conditions prevailing in the
syndicalist stronghold of Catalonia during the first months after July,
1936, when the power of the government had become temporarily invis-
ible, and yet the new and still undefined authority exercised by the
syndicates did not assume a distinct political character. Still the situation
arising from these conditions is not adequately described as that of a
"dual power." It represented rather a temporary eclipse of all state power
resulting from the split between its (economic) substance which had
shifted to the workers and its (political) shell, from the various internal
conflicts between the forces of Franco and the forces of the "Loyalists,"
Madrid and Barcelona, and, finally, from the decisive fact that the main
function of the bureaucratic and military machinery of any capitalistic
state, the suppression of the workers, could not operate in any event
against workers in arms.

There is no use arguing (as many people have done) that during the many phases of the revolutionary development of the last seven years there has evolved more than once—in October, 1934, and, again, in July, 1936, and in May, 1937—an "objective situation" in which the united revolutionary workers of Spain might have seized the power of the state but did not do so either on account of theoretical scruples or by reason of an internal weakness of their revolutionary attitude. This may be true in regard to the July-Days of 1936 when the syndicalist and anarchist workers and militias of Barcelona had stormed the arms depots of the government and further equipped themselves with the weapons seized from the defeated fascist revolt, just as it may be true in regard to the July-Days of 1917, when the revolutionary workers and soldiers in Petrograd demonstrated under the Bolshevik slogans "*all power to the Soviets*" *and* "*down with the capitalist ministers,*" and when during the night from the seventeenth to the eighteenth a reluctant Central Committee of the Bolshevik party was finally compelled to reverse its earlier refusal to participate in a "premature" revolutionary attempt and unanimously to call upon the soldiers and the people to take arms and join what they still described as a "peaceful demonstration."

As against those people who today, twenty years after the event, extol the revolutionary consistency of the Bolshevik leadership of 1917, to the detriment of the "chaotic irresolution" displayed by the dissensions and waverings of the Spanish syndicalists and anarchists of 1936–38, it is quite appropriate here to recall the fact that in those black days of July, 1917, three months before the victory of the Red October in Soviet Russia, Lenin and his Bolshevik party also were unable to prevent or to turn into victory a situation which was described at the time in the following manner by the late S. B. Krassin who had been a Bolshevik and was later to accept high office in the Soviet government, but at this time was the manager of an industrialist establishment: "The so-called masses, principally soldiers and a number of hooligans, loafed aimlessly about the streets for two days, firing at each other, often out of sheer fright, running away at the slightest alarm or fresh rumor, and without the slightest idea of what it was all about."[1]

Even a considerable time later when the process of glorification of victorious Bolshevism had already set in, but a mild "self-criticism" was still possible among the higher ranks of the ruling party, the Bolshevist people's commissar, Lunacharsky, recalled the situation of July, 1917, by the following words: "We are bound to admit that the party knew no way out of the difficulty. It was compelled to demand of the Mensheviks and Socialist-Revolutionists, through a demonstration, something they were organically unable to decide upon, and, meeting with the refusal the party had expected, it did not know how to proceed further; it left the demonstrators around the Taurida Palace without a plan and gave the opposition time to organize its forces, while ours were breaking up, and consequently we went down to a temporary defeat with eyes quite open."

Nor were the immediate consequences of what may be called here, in answer to the oft-repeated indictment of the lack of revolutionary leadership manifested by the Spanish syndicalist, a *"failure" of the revolutionary Bolshevik party to seize the political power in an objectively revolutionary situation,* any better for the Russian Bolsheviks of 1917 than they have been in 1934 and '36 and '37 for the Spanish syndicalists and anarchists. On the eighteenth of July, 1917, the mischievous accusation was raised against Lenin that all his actions since his arrival in Russia, and particularly the armed demonstrations of the preceding two days, were secretly directed by the German General Staff. The Bolshevik headquarters were raided. Their newspaper offices were closed. Kamenev and Trotsky and numerous other Bolshevik leaders were arrested. Lenin and Sinovjev went into hiding, and Lenin was still in hiding when, almost two months later, he warned his comrades against jeopardizing their revolutionary independence by an unreserved support of the people's front government of Kerensky against the counter-revolutionary rebellion of the commander-in-chief of the Russian Armies, General Kornilov.

Thus, it cannot be said in fairness that the Spanish workers and their revolutionary syndicalist and anarchist leadership neglected to seize the political power on a national or even on a regional Catalonian scale under conditions when this would have been done by a really revolutionary party such as the Russian Bolsheviks. It makes no sense to accept the tactics of the Russian Bolsheviks in July, 1917, as a "cautious and realistic revolutionary policy" and denounce the same policy as a "lack of revolutionary foresight and decision" when it is repeated, under exactly analogous conditions, by the syndicalists in Spain. One might then as well subscribe to the paradoxical statement made by Pascal two-hundred years ago that "what is true on this side of the Pyrenees is a lie on the other."

This is not to say that the revolutionary actions of the Catalonian workers have not been fettered by their traditional attitude of non-concernedness in all matters political and not strictly economic and social. Even their most radical steps in the field of economic reconstruction, taken at a time when they appeared and held themselves to be unrestricted masters of the situation, were suffering from a certain lack of that single-mindedness and consistency of purpose by which the economic and political measures of the Bolshevik dictatorship in Russia both infuriated and terribly frightened their enemies at home and in every bourgeois country all over the world. There is, in the bourgeois reports on conditions in revolutionary Spain, very little of the uneasiness with which foreign spectators looked at the assumed "atrocities" of the Bolshevik Revolution in Russia at the time of the "sanitary cordon." (Even the formerly revolutionary Marxist, Karl Kautsky, in those days repeated and, as I think, seriously believed in the news that the Bolshevik dictatorship in Russia had crowned their expropriatory measures by a "socialization of the wives of the bourgeoisie.") There is, as compared with those exuberances, even a touch of humor and a certain jovial reliance on what the reporter calls the persisting "individualism" of the Spanish people, in the story of the Spanish "collectivizations" given by a special correspondent of the (London) *Times* at the hour of the arrival of the Negrin government at Barcelona:

> The arrival of the central government brought new life to Barcelona. The huge city was beginning to droop under the burden of collectivization. Happiness cannot be collectivized in Spain, where the individual persists in remaining his own master. An hotel proprietor who could not endure to be a waiter in his own establishment is a waiter elsewhere. Of a well known Catalan actor it is told that, wearying of playing the principal part on the scene and a humble one on the payroll, he proposed exchange with a scene shifter, saying: "We earn the same, let me pull the ropes while you go and pull the faces." It has become quite a joke, though a poor one, among audiences at cinemas to point out professors of the Conservatoire playing second fiddle in the band.

Even the more elaborate and much more hostile report given one month later by the Barcelona correspondent of the *New York Times* was supplemented by some quite attractive pictures which illustrated the life and work in "Collectivized Shops in Spain," and which were made even more attractive to the state-worshipping and bond-speculating readers of the *Times* by the cheerful remark that "Because loyalists prefer state control to workers' control and wish to protect foreign interests in Spain, collectivization—as in the clothing plants pictured here—is being limited." In the same vein "Spain's Strong Man" (the now-debunked defence minister of the loyalist government, Indalecio Prieto) was shown in a photograph and described to the petty bourgeois readers of the *Evening Standard* of March 7, 1938, as a "comfortably fat newspaper owner, with a chin or two to spare" and with a "fondness for eels as his only gastronomic luxury," a man by the way whose "worth" is "even recognized by General Franco" and who is personally well acquainted with "the financier of Franco's movement," the illustrious Juan March.

The very fact that the CNT and FAI themselves were finally compelled to reverse their traditional policy of non-interference in politics under the pressure of increasingly bitter experiences, demonstrated for all but some hopelessly sectarian and illusionary groups of foreign anarchists (who even now refuse to besmirch their anti-political purity by whole-hearted support of the desperate strife of their Spanish comrades!), *the vital connection between the economic and political action in every phase and, most of all, in the immediately revolutionary phase of the proletarian class struggle.*

This, then, is the first and foremost lesson of that concluding phase of the whole revolutionary history of post-war Europe which is the Spanish revolution. It becomes even more important and particularly impressive if we consider the wide difference of the character of the Spanish working-class movements from all other types of proletarian class struggles in Europe and the USA as established by well-nigh three quarters of a century.

The validity of this lesson is not weakened by the relatively moderate contents of the political demands raised by the CNT at the present juncture. There is no doubt that the proposal of a "new constitutional period which would sympathize with popular aspirations within the socialist republic, which would be democratical and federal" does not demand anything which the people's front government could not, in principle, decide upon without a revolutionary change of its hitherto professed bourgeois policy. Nor could the proposed creation of a "National Economic Council on a political and trade unionist base, with an equal representation of both the Social Democratic UGT and the syndicalist CNT," transform the hitherto bourgeois-reformist bias of the government into a revolutionary-proletarian tendency. But here again appears a close analogy between the tactics followed by the syndicalists in present-day Spain and the attitude observed by the Russian Bolshevik party up to and even after the collapse of the Kornilov rebellion. If this analogy is true, if we can show that even a revolutionary party so predominantly political and politically experienced as the party which made the Russian October did not rise to its ultimate perfection before the advent of an altogether different historical situation, how then could we expect such super-human and supra-historical excellence from a hitherto unpolitically-minded and politically almost inexperienced group of proletarian revolutionaries under the undeveloped conditions of present-day Spain, where the counterrevolutionary rebellion of the Iberian Kornilov has not collapsed but has spread victoriously over the whole country and is now attacking the very heart of industrial Spain, the last stronghold of the anti-fascist and anti-capitalist forces, the proletarian province of Barcelona?

There is indeed from the standpoint of a sober historical research ample proof that the revolutionary Bolshevik leadership of 1917 was in no way exempt from those human waverings and want of foresight which are inherent in any revolutionary action. Even after the victorious conclusion of that masterpiece of political strategy which the Bolsheviks, led and inspired by Lenin, performed in the days of the Kornilov-affair in August and September, 1917, when, in accordance with Lenin's most subtle instruction, they endeavored "to fight against Kornilov, even *as Kerensky's troops do,*" but did not support Kerensky but, "*on the contrary* exposed his weakness," Lenin still acted on the assumption that the Provisional Government had become so manifestly weak after the defeat of Kornilov, that it offered an opportunity for a peaceful development of the revolution on the basis of the replacement of Kerensky by a government of socialist-revolutionists and Mensheviks responsible to the Soviets. In such a government the Bolsheviks would not participate, but they would "*refrain from immediately advancing the demand for the passing of power to the proletariat and the poorest peasants, and from revolutionary methods of struggle for the realization of this demand.*" Of course, in suggesting this line of action in his famous article "*On Compromises*" in September, 1917, Lenin did not boast of such flawless revolutionary righteousness as does for instance Stalin in present-day Russia or those state-denying anarchists in present-day ultra-capitalist Holland. Yet this small piece of real history shows how little the minor followers of Lenin are entitled to criticize the deficiencies of the syndicalist achievements in revolutionary Catalonia, let alone the well-known ambiguity of the "help" given to the revolutionary workers of Spain during the first and later stages of their strife by the Communists and the Russian state both in Spain and in the Non-Intervention Committee.[2]

There is thus a deep shadow thrown on the constructive work resulting from the heroic efforts and sacrifices of the revolutionary workers in all parts of Spain where the syndicalist and anarchist slogan of "collectivization" prevailed over the Social Democratic and Communist slogans of "*nationalization*" and "*state interference.*" All this constructive work was done, as it were, preliminarily only. Its further advance and its very existence depended upon the progress of the revolutionary movement and, first of all, upon a decisive defeat of the counterrevolutionary attack of Franco and his powerful fascist and semi-fascist allies. Even at this late stage, when the defeat of the highly advertised now loyalist army has already so strongly manifested the intrinsic weakness of the Negrin government that the above-mentioned chief representative of the fascist and capitalist forces within the people's front government, Indalecio Prieto, had to be kicked out ingloriously, and a "reconstruction" of the government in a "leftist" direction became inevitable, a last hour victory of the revolutionary proletarian forces rallied in Barcelona—either with or without a rehearsal of the insurrection of the communards in besieged Paris 1871—would immensely enhance the immediate historical and practical importance of the great experiment in a genuine proletarian collectivization of industry, which was initiated and carried through by the workers and their unions during the last two years.

Short of such a favorable turn, the story of the Catalonian *collectivization* which is told in the most impartial and impressive manner in a small book, published by the CNT-FAI and hitherto not translated into English,[3] and on which we propose to base our analysis and criticism of the Spanish experiences in the next issue, cannot claim any greater merit than what we know from Marx, Engels, Lissagarays, and other writers about the economic experiments of the revolutionary Commune of the Paris workers in 1871. They are a part of the historical past just as are today the attempts of the revolutionary Italian workers in 1920, which were later annihilated by the hordes of Mussolini subsidized by the frightened Italian landowners and capitalists, and as are the equally frustrated attempts made several times between 1918 and 1923 by the vanguards of the German and Hungarian workers. In the same way the more comprehensive and certainly much more illustrious temporary achievements attained by the revolutionary Russian workers in the period of a really Communistic experimentation of 1918–20 did not retain any practical importance for the later development of the so-called socialist construction in Soviet Russia. They were soon afterwards denounced by the Bolsheviks themselves as a mere "negative form" of communism temporarily thrust upon a reluctant Bolshevik leadership by the emergencies of war and civil war. Thus the great historical experiment of the so-called War Communism, which in fact represented a far more positive move toward a Communist society than the measures of any NEP, NEO-NEP, or other variances of the no more socialist and proletarian policies which were later inaugurated by the various combinations of the post-Leninist and Stalinist bureaucracy, became a forgotten and abandoned episode of past history in the very country which even today claims to match in front of the international proletariat by the so-called construction of socialism in a single country.

Even before this new turn of the Bolshevik economic policy, on December 4, 1919, two years after the full seizure of the state power, Lenin in a speech delivered to the *First Congress of Agricultural Communes and Agricultural Artels* gave the following description of the results until then achieved by the Bolshevik struggle for communism: "Communism, when people work because they realize the necessity of working for the common good. We know that we cannot establish a socialist system now—God grant that it may be established in our children's time, or perhaps in our grandchildren's time."[4]

"To serve the history of the revolution" is the program which is invisibly written on the front page of the above cited faithful and comprehensive report on the positive results achieved in the economic field by the revolutionary workers of Barcelona and by the industrial and agricultural laborers in many a small Catalonian town or remote and forgotten village. "To serve history" means for the writer as well as for us, revolutionary workers of a dismal world laboring in the crisis and decay of all forms of the "old" socialist, communist, and anarchist labor movements, to learn from the deeds and from the mistakes of past history the lesson for the future, the ways and means for the realization of the goals of the revolutionary working class.

Notes

1. This and the following quotations are taken from J. Bunyan's and H. H. Fisher's documentary history, *The Bolshevik Revolution 1917–1918*, Hoover War Library Publications, no. 3 (Stanford: Stanford University Press, 1934).

2. We quote here for the benefit of those hitherto Stalin-worshipping Communists who have recently begun to learn the lesson of great "purges" in Russia, a sentence from Pravda testifying to what the Stalinist "friends" did and intended to do in a thoroughly "Bolshevized" Spain. Says Pravda from December 17, 1936: "The purging of Catalonia from all Trotskyist and anarcho-syndicalist elements has already begun; this task is pushed on with the same energy with which it has already been performed in USSR."

3. *Collectivizations*—L'oeuvre constructive de la Révolution Espagnole—Recueil de Documents—Editions CNT-FAI, 1937.

4. Quoted from vol. 8 of the *Selected Works*, ed. Marx-Engels-Lenin Institute, Moscow (English translation, New York: International Publishers: p. 205).

8. Fascism and Counterrevolution

Introduction

One of Korsch's central thematic concerns from the 1930's through World War II was fascism and counterrevolution. We recall that Korsch was concerned with the rise of fascism in the early 1920's and paid close attention to the development of this phenomenon, which he rightly saw as a dire threat to the working class movement.[1] In "Theses Toward a Critique of the Fascist Conception of the State," published in the left journal *Gegner* in 1932,[2] Korsch polemicizes against the interpretation of fascism as a regression to an earlier pre-bourgeois type of state. Rather, fascism should be seen as a modern form of oppression of the working class that would secure the existence of capitalist relations of production and crush the working-class movement.

Korsch saw German fascism as an epochal phenomenon that was part of a world-wide counterrevolution. Hence, he was not interested in analyzing the specific features of German fascism (as, say, Franz Neumann in *Behemoth*),[3] but rather wanted to conceptualize fascism as a moment of the counterrevolution. The two-fold contribution of Korsch's theory is his emphasis on the need for a Marxist theory of the counterrevolution, and a Marxist theory of the state as an instrument of suppression of the working class. In both "State and Counterrevolution" and "The Fascist Counterrevolution,"[4] Korsch shows the dubious interpretations of counterrevolution in the Marxian tradition. For Korsch, the counterrevolution is capital's counteroffensive against the working class movement, and should not be seen as part of an evolutionary process toward socialism, for a specific counterrevolutionary movement may well spell a decisive defeat for the working class. Korsch cites passages from Marx, Proudhon, Lassalle, and others who enthusiastically greet various counterrevolutions as steps on the way to progressive social change—as if counterrevolution was a moment in an emancipatory historical process. This position was repeated by those members of the KPD and Comintern who thought that Nazism would immediately collapse and prepare the way for socialism. What was needed, Korsch believed, was a theory of counterrevolution that showed how capital used the state as a new weapon of working-class oppression and that emphasized the serious threat this phenomenon involved.

Korsch's theory of the counterrevolution moved from a first formulation of fascism as part of an emerging counterrevolution to an emphasis on the Soviet Union as part of the counterrevolution—a shift visible in the essay "State and Counterrevolution." Korsch indicated the "gradual degeneration" of the Russian state into an "anti-democratic" and "totalitarian" counterrevolutionary state, that internally utilized a reign of terror to the extent that "today the punishments meted out in Russia for the smallest deviations from the prescribed patterns of conduct and opinion exceed in violence the measures applied against nonconformity either in fascist Italy or Nazi Germany."[5] On the international scene, the Soviet Union was engaged in the same game of imperialist politics and relentless pursuit of its own state interests as the bourgeois states, thus surrendering the Marxist proletarian internationalist perspective. Korsch's critique of the Soviet Union takes its most radical form in this context.

In "The Workers' Fight against Fascism," Korsch includes the bourgeois democracies in his rubric of the counterrevolution.[6] The bourgeois democracies, he writes, have lost their self-confidence and are seriously considering adopting fascist methods to wage war and contain the working class. Korsch warned the workers about the "quasi-fascist character of the New Deal" and the possibility of fascism in America.[7] Underlying the crisis of bourgeois democracy is the transition from competitive capitalism to monopoly state-capitalism, where more and more wealth and power is concentrated in ever fewer hands. Korsch outlines in detail the new concentration of wealth and power in America and concludes that "There is very little difference between that economic 'coordination' that is achieved, and sometimes not achieved, by the political decrees of victorious nazism, fascism, and bolshevism, and this new 'corporate community' that has been created by a slow but relentless process in this country through the system of 'interlocking directorates,' through the activities of the major financial institutions, through particular interest groupings, through firms rendering legal, accounting, and similar services to the larger corporations, through 'intercorporate stockholdings,' and a number of other devices."[8] Korsch then analyzes the end of competition and the market in the American economy, dominated by monopoly capital, concluding that this centralization of the means of production creates the conditions for a totalitarian political and ideological dictatorship. Under the increasing growth of monopoly, Korsch warns the workers to disregard all their illusions about the system and to prepare to fight for a new system.

The political thrust of Korsch's concept of the counterrevolution is directed against the united front policy supported by both the Communist and Social Democratic parties. Korsch sees fascism, soviet communism, social democracy, and liberal democracy as part of the same counterrevolutionary front that serves to oppress and exploit the working class. His rejection of the united front comes out clearly in an essay, "The Fight for Britain, the Fight for Democracy, and the War Aims of the Working Class," where Korsch notes his "invincible distrust of all forms of 'sacred unions,' " which he has maintained since the first World War, and urges the working class instead to pursue an "independent revolutionary policy" not subordinate to any bourgeois dominated united front.[9] The underlying rationale for the rejection of the united front is Korsch's concept of the counterrevolution which posits bourgeois democracy and Soviet communism as vehicles of domination of the working class as well as the fascists.

Hence the counterrevolution is an expanding category for Korsch that came to encompass all those systems that served to oppress and dominate, rather than to emancipate the working class. In a strange way, Korsch radicalizes Rosa Luxemburg's slogan "socialism or barbarism," and seems to conclude that wherever there is no genuine socialism there is barbarism. One might ask whether Korsch is exaggerating the "worldwide triumph" of the counterrevolution and whether such different systems as nazism, Soviet Russia and the New Deal can accurately be subsumed under one "counterrevolutionary" rubric. Moreover, such a general concept of counterrevolution sacrifices the principle of historical specification which works out in detail the specific historical features of a given society or situation. In a sense, then, Korsch's concept of the counterrevolution serves more as a short-hand symbol to sum up a string of working-class defeats than as an explanatory concept that illuminates the current world historical situation. It also serves as an indicator of Korsch's revolutionary pessimism. For Korsch is very pessimistic about the possibility for radical change in the face of "ultra-imperialist and fascist world revolution."[10] He ended his paper evaluating a new left-wing American workers party with the paranoic conclusion that their program was but "an ideological glorification of a much more limited practice" which would reduce "the voluntary proletarian party to a bourgeois opposition party," such that "its final destruction through the American Mussolini or Hitler can be accomplished the more readily."[11] Korsch's pessimism lasted through the war, and even afterwards he saw the bourgeois restoration in the Soviet Union as part of "a potentially world-wide totalization"—suggesting a continued reign and expansion of totalitarian counterrevolution.[12]

Korsch's theory of the counterrevolution thus reflects both the devastating defeats of the working-class movement and his own political frustrations. The 1930's were an incredibly depressing decade for socialist radicals, and Korsch's concept of the counterrevolution reflects the dashed hopes and brutal scars of the process of the fascistization of Europe and Stalinization of the world Communist movement. The counterrevolution also refuted Korsch's previous somewhat optimistic faith in Marxism: that socialist revolution was the motor of history and prime actor on the historical scene. Korsch was forced to become more critical of Marxism through his experiences of counterrevolution, and to seek new strategies of social change that could reverse the string of working-class defeats that had plagued the once revolutionary movement.

Notes

1. See my discussion in "Korsch's Revolutionary Marxism."
2. Karl Korsch, "Thesen zur Kritik des faschistischen Staatsbegriffs," *Gegner* 6, nos. 4–5 (March 1932). Reprinted in *Politische Texte.* Translated in this anthology as "Theses toward a Critique of the Fascist Concept of the State," by Karl-Heinz Otto and Andrew Giles-Peters.
3. Franz Neumann, *Behemoth* (New York: Oxford University Press, 1944).
4. Karl Korsch, "State and Counterrevolution" and "Fascist Counterrevolution."
5. Korsch, "State and Counterrevolution."
6. Karl Korsch, "The Workers' Fight against Fascism."
7. Karl Korsch, "On the New Program of the 'American Workers Party,' " *International Council Correspondence*, no. 4 (January 1935), p. 25.
8. Korsch, "Workers' Fight against Fascism."
9. Karl Korsch, "The Fight for Britain, the Fight for Democracy and the War Aims of the Working Class," pp. 36–49.
10. Korsch, "State and Counterrevolution."
11. Korsch, "On the New Program of the 'American Workers Party,' " p. 25.
12. Karl Korsch, "Restoration or Totalization? Some Notes on Trotsky's Biography of Stalin and on the Revolutionary Problem of Our Time," *International Council Correspondence, Quarterly* 1, no. 2 (July 1946): 13.

Theses toward a Critique of the Fascist Conception of the State

I. Exposition

"The modern state, whatever its form may be, is essentially a capitalist machine, the state of the capitalists, the ideal aggregate capitalist" (Engels, *Socialism: Scientific and Utopian*).

1. The fascist state is a modern state. It does not signify a return to pre-bourgeois state structures. The corporative state has nothing to do with the "state of estates"—fascism as "counter-reform."

2. The fascist conception of state is grounded in the negation of the early bourgeois ideal of the state. It signifies disillusionment vis-à-vis the political ideals of liberalism and socialism of all directions. It takes over the criticism by the restoration, Marxism, and syndicalism (Proudhon/Sorel) of the political institutions and ideals of the early bourgeois epoch.

3. This does not contradict but rather corresponds to the conscious statement of a new state-mythos. Fascism unites in Pareto's sense a sober, illusion-free, rational goal-directed state practice (carried out by the "elite") with a completely irrational state mythology (represented by the state's people, the race, and the mass).

II. Immanent Critique

"Monopoly begets competition, competition begets monopoly. . . . the synthesis is of such nature that monopoly can only maintain itself by constantly entering into the competitive struggle" (Marx, *The Poverty of Philosophy*).

1. As the stabilization of intercapitalist contradictions by the state shipwrecked in the previous period on the basis of competition in the form of parliamentarism and democracy, so now it shipwrecks upon the inevitable breaking through of capitalist group and individual interests and falls into the form of dictatorship and corporative constitution on the basis of monopoly. The monopolization of state power by the monopolistic grand bourgeoisie takes the place of the "ideal aggregate capitalist."

2. The production of the "ideal aggregate capitalist" on a national basis is at the present phase already being thwarted by the direct international tendency of capitalism. Thus one has to understand the present reformation of fascism as an "export commodity," the expansion of the opposition Italy-France to the opposition Europe-America.

3. The monopolistic claim of the fascist state authority enters into competition with the old authoritarian forces, particularly with the claim to authority by Catholicism which is independent of that state authority.

III. Transcendental Critique

"But the struggle of class against class is a political struggle" (Marx, *The Poverty of Philosophy*).

1. The fascist remodelling does not mean an economic revolution or radical dissolution of the old relations of production or the freeing of new productive forces. This is the main difference between fascism and Bolshevism—apart from given distinctions of material possibilities and order of magnitude.

2. The fascist state signifies the union of the economic and political power of the bourgeoisie against the proletariat; thus not the overcoming of the class-state, but the restoration of the class-state in the form of the class-state.

3. The new form of union of the economic and political class power of the bourgeoisie in the fascist "total state" demands new forms of combining the economic and political action of the proletariat.

Translated by Karl-Heinz Otto and Andrew Giles-Peters

State and Counterrevolution

I

More than any preceding period of recent history, and on a much vaster scale, our period is a time not of revolution but of counterrevolution. This is true whether we define this comparatively new term as a conscious counter-action against a preceding revolutionary process or whether we describe it, as do some Italians and their ideological forerunners in pre-war France, as an essentially "preventive revolution." It is counter-action of the united capitalist class against all that remains today of the results of that first great insurrection of the proletarian forces in war-torn Europe which culminated in the Russian October of 1917. At the same time it embodies a series of "preventive" measures of the ruling minority against such new revolutionary dangers as have been most conspicuously revealed by recent events in France and Spain and which are actually contained in the whole European situation, be it in "red" Soviet Russia or fascist Italy, Nazi Germany, or any of the old "democratic" countries.

The heightened consciousness of the counterrevolutionary drive, in contrast to the merely conservative and reactionary tendencies, desires more than the curtailment of the workers' resistance to increasing suppression and pauperization. The common goal of such figureheads of the present-day European politics as Hitler, Mussolini, Daladier, and Chamberlain is the creation of conditions which will make impossible any independent movement of the European working class for a long time to come.

To attain this goal the leading statesmen in the so-called democratic countries of Europe are prepared to break every hallowed tradition and to abandon every cherished "idea" of the past. To this objective they will sacrifice not only, as they always have done, the freedom and welfare of their peoples, but even part of the privileges hitherto enjoyed by their own class. They are even willing to surrender some of the material and ideal advantages of their traditional positions, including personal dignity, in order to participate as minor partners in the benefits expected from the increased exploitation forced upon the workers by the new counterrevolutionary forms of complete political, social, and cultural enslavement.

II

The foregoing description deals with the general aspects of the present-day European counterrevolution as they have developed after the crushing defeat of every attempt to extend the Revolution of 1917 and thus to furnish the new proletarian society in Russia with a suitable parallel environment in other European and extra-European countries. All but the most willfully blinded partisans of the Communist party recognize the fact that for a considerable time even the new workers' state emerging from the first proletarian victory in Soviet Russia has ceased to possess an unequivocally revolutionary character. By a historical process which I shall tentatively describe as a gradual "degeneration," the Russian state has abandoned more and more its original revolutionary and proletarian features. Through the comprehensiveness of its anti-democratic and totalitarian development it has often anticipated the so-called fascist characteristics of the openly counterrevolutionary states of Europe and Asia. Even today the punishments meted out in Russia for the smallest deviations from the prescribed patterns of conduct and opinion exceed in violence the measures applied against nonconformity either in fascist Italy or in Nazi Germany. On the international scene the new Russian common-wealth has increasingly participated in the game of imperialistic politics, in military alliances with certain groups of bourgeois states against other groups of bourgeois states, and contributed its full share to what in the highly deceptive language of modern bourgeois diplomacy is called a furtherance of "peace," "collective security," and "non-intervention." Thus the leading bureaucracy of the so-called workers' state has become irretrievably enmeshed in the counterrevolutionary aspects of present-day European politics.

Under the widely changed conditions of the class struggle today what Lenin wrote in the opening paragraphs of his pamphlet on the "State and Revolution" in August, 1917, concerning the increased importance of the question of the state both in theory and from the point of view of practical politics takes on renewed importance. The imperialist war and its aftermath have greatly accelerated and intensified both the trans-formation of monopoly capitalism into state-monopoly capitalism and the monstrous oppression of the laboring masses by the state which becomes increasingly intertwined with the all-powerful capitalist com-bines. The apparently transitory and war-conditioned effects of this post-war development have become enduring and indeed normal features of present-day capitalism as a whole. There is no doubt today of the perma-nent nature of the process described by Lenin twenty years ago by which "the foremost countries are being converted into military convict labor prisons for the workers."

Yet under the conditions of an existing counterrevolution it is by no means sufficient at the present time merely to repeat those powerful state-ments of which Lenin in 1917 elaborated the revolutionary Marxian theory of the state and the relation of the proletarian revolution to the state. It is strange that the Trotskyites should refer today to "Lenin's magnificent formulation" as a work written on the eve of October "in order to explain to the masses not merely of Russia but of the world and for the future (as a guide if the Bolsheviks that time fail in achieving their aims) the meaning of workers' democracy." This was never the aim of that translator into action of the traditional Marxian theory. When the outbreak of the political crisis "intervened" with the conclusion of his theoretical work he cheerfully added to his pamphlet the exultant remark that "it is more pleasant and useful to go through the 'experience of the revolution' than to write about it."

III

Today the whole situation has profoundly altered. There is no point in continuing in the unreal ideological sphere, the materialistic and entirely practical philosophy of the revolutionary state as worked out by Marx and restated by Lenin. We might as well philosophize with Plato on the most perfect form of the ideal state and the extent to which the counterrevolutionary empire of Hitler is the true earthly fulfillment of Plato's lofty dream of the transition from debased democracy to *"the noble tyranny, from all preceding forms different, the fourth and last disease of the state."*

It was very well for the Russian proletariat and its Bolshevik leaders in 1917 to "go through the experience" of the developing revolution rather than to philosophize about it. But the Russian and non-Russian workers today cannot confine themselves to experiencing the steadily advancing counterrevolution without making every effort to interpret its significance. By a careful examination of the past they must find out both the objective and the subjective causes for the victory of fascist state capitalism. They must closely watch its unfolding in order to discover the old and new forms of contradiction and antagonism appearing in that development. Finally they must find out a practical way to resist, as a class, the further encroachments of the counterrevolution and later to pass from an active resistance to an even more active counteroffensive in order to overthrow both the particular state capitalist form recently adopted and the general principle of exploitation inherent in all old and new forms of bourgeois society and its state power.

Thus, what is needed first of all is a comprehensive analysis of the new phases which the general theory of the state assumes in face of an existing counterrevolution. There is no doubt that this particular task has been hitherto almost entirely neglected. This is true in spite of the tremendous work done in the field by Marx, Engels, and their most consistent followers up to Luxemburg, Lenin, and Trotsky on the one hand, and by Bakunin, Proudhon, and the later spokesmen of revolutionary anarchism and syndicalism on the other.

IV

Of course, there would be no need for a specific investigation into the counterrevolutionary state if the sweeping generalizations of the anarchists, that every state at all times, including the workers' state resulting from a proletarian revolution, is by its very nature opposed to the proletarian aims, is accepted. Yet this abstract principle did not prevent the great proletarian thinker, Proudhon, from acclaiming the coup d'état of December 2, 1851, as a historical victory of the social revolution.

In looking back upon that first historical appearance of quasi-fascist counterrevolution following the failure of the French revolution of 1848, there appears a striking resemblance between the recent utterances of some assumedly progressive and revolutionary writers on Hitler and Mussolini and the first reactions of practically all progressive schools, not excluding Marx and Engels, to the coup d'état of Louis Napoleon in 1851. Just as on the news of the coup d'état the moderate bourgeois progressive ex-minister, Guizot, burst out into the alarmed cry, "This is the perfect and final triumph of socialism," so Proudhon philosophized about the *"Révolution sociale démontrée par le coup d'état du 2 décembre."*[1]

Even Marx, although he was aware of the personal unfitness of Louis Bonaparte for the quasi-revolutionary role usurped by him for a short time, indulged in the same self-deception. Witness his paradoxical statement that this time "revolutionary progress made headway not through its immediate tragi-comic achievements, but on the contrary through the creation of a powerful, united counterrevolution, through the creation of an opponent, by fighting whom the party of revolt first ripened into a real revolutionary party."

There is, indeed, only a small step from this Marxian (and for that matter, Guizotian and Proudhonian) self-deception to the remarkable illusions after Hitler's accession to power in 1933, which possessed the German Communists and their Russian masters. They welcomed the victory of an acknowledged fascism over what they had until then described as a disguised but even more hateful form of "social fascism," that is, the political rule of the Social Democratic party in post-war Germany. They predicted a speedy collapse of the new counterrevolutionary government which would be superseded by a proletarian revolution and thus hailed their own defeat and, incidentally, the lasting defeat of all progressive tendencies in Germany and, indeed, all over Europe, as a "victory of communism."

V

It seems to the writer that the apparent unawareness of the particular nature of counterrevolutionary events shown on those two occasions by the older and newer schools of the Marxists is not a mere personal accident. It is rather bound up, in a hidden way, with the whole historical character of the Marxian theory of the proletarian revolution which, in many respects, still carries the birthmarks of bourgeois revolutionary theory, of Jacobinism and Blanquism.[2] This applies particularly to the political aspects of the Marxian theory, to the Marxian doctrines of the so-called permanent revolution and the "dictatorship of the proletariat," and to Lenin's doctrine of the leadership of the revolutionary political party before, during, and after the conquest of the bourgeois state, as embodied in the "Guiding Principles on the Rule of the Communist Party" adopted by the second Communist World Congress of 1920.

From this point of view it becomes possible to approach, in a rational manner, those vexing problems which, during the last twenty years, have over and over again assailed and tormented the best Marxian revolutionaries who had become aware of the striking contradictions between the uninterrupted existence of the so-called proletarian dictatorship and the increasing suppression of all proletarian and socialist, nay even of the most modest democratic and progressive tendencies, in Soviet Russia: How did it happen that the workers' state emerging from the 1917 revolution in Russia was slowly and without any "Thermidor" or "Brumaire" transformed from an instrument of the proletarian revolution into an instrument of the present-day European counterrevolution? What is the reason for the particularly close resemblance between the Communist dictatorship in Russia and its nominal opponents, the fascist dictatorships in Italy and Germany?

VI

Within the limit of a short article I cannot deal in detail with the factual side of this historical development. I merely wish to trace that uncanny ambiguity by which a revolutionary dictatorship contained, as it were, from the very beginning its possible future transformation into a counterrevolutionary state, and a corresponding ambiguity in the revolutionary Marxian theory itself. If the political concepts of Marxism were derived from the great tradition of the bourgeois revolution, if the umbilical cord between Marxism and Jacobinism was never cut, it seems less paradoxical that the revolutionary Marxist state in its present development should reflect that great historical process of decay by which today the leading sections of the bourgeoisie in every country of Europe abandon their previous political ideals. It ceases to be inconceivable that the Russian state in its present structure should act as a powerful lever in the fascization of Europe.

Nevertheless, this inherent ambiguity of the political doctrines of Marx contains in itself nothing more than an abstract possibility of that radical degradation. Just as the proletarian revolution, according to the materialistic principle of Marx, is not exclusively or primarily a consciously willed action of isolated groups, of parties or even "classes," so the present capitalistic counterrevolution is primarily the result of an objective economic development of society—though, of course, neither a revolutionary nor a counterrevolutionary action will necessarily spring from the mere fact that it has become economically feasible. Thus, the real source of the actual transition of the revolutionary workers' state in Russia into its present counterrevolutionary condition cannot be found in any particularities of its political form, be it the principle of "revolutionary dictatorship" itself or, for that matter, the dictatorship of a (single) party as opposed to a dictatorship of the revolutionary Soviets or of the proletarian "class" as a whole. We must rather look for the causes of this gradual metamorphosis of the political superstructure in the underlying economic development of the class forces.

There is, according to this materialistic view, little wonder in the fact that the Russian workers' state could not maintain its original proletarian revolutionary character when, after the frustration of all revolutionary movements outside Russia, it was reduced to a mere driving-belt, transmitting the curbing and destructive effects of capitalist world economy to the exceedingly small beginnings of a true socialist economy built up in Soviet Russia during the years 1918–1919, called the period of "War-Communism." The really remarkable fact consists in the circumstance that just those new assumedly anti-bourgeois features of the Russian state which had been devised as a means to defend the proletarian content of the revolutionary society should have served (along with the "new" counterrevolutionary states shaped on the very model of the Russian "dictatorship") as an instrument not only of the reversal of revolutionary transformation of the whole traditional framework of European capitalist society. "Though this be madness, yet there's method in it."

To solve this bewildering problem by sober materialistic research is one of the main tasks of a Marxian analysis. In attempting this task we may expect with Hobbes (when in his *Behemoth* he retraced the course of the English revolution and counterrevolution of 1640–1660) that we too, looking back as from Devil's Mountain upon the historical development of the last twenty years, shall have "a prospect of all kinds of injustice, and of all kinds of folly, that the world could afford, and how they were produced by their damn hypocrisy and self-conceit, where of

the one is double iniquity and other double folly"; but at the same time
a full insight into the actions which then took place and into "their
causes, pretensions, justice, order, artifice and event."

Notes

1. Title of a comprehensive pamphlet written by Proudhon at the time and
contained in *Oeuvres Completes* VII, Paris, 1868.
2. See the author's discussion of "Unitarian versus Federal Principles in the
French Revolution," in *Archiv für die Geschichte des Sozialismus* XV, Leipzig, 1930; two essays on "Revolutionary Commune," in *Die Aktion* XIX &
XXI, Berlin, 1929–31; "Theses on Hegel" and "Theses on the fascist state"
in *Gegner*, Berlin, 1932; and the pertinent passages in a recent book *Karl
Marx*, London & New York, 1938.

The Fascist Counterrevolution

What hope have we revolutionary Marxists, remnants of a past epoch,
inheritors of its most advanced theories, illusions, ideologies—what hope
have we left for a revolutionary turn of the sweeping counterrevolutionary
movement of victorious fascism? The fate of France has finally proved
that the old Marxist slogan of "world revolution" has in our epoch
assumed a new meaning. We find ourselves today in the midst not of a
socialist and proletarian but of an ultra-imperialistic and fascist world
revolution. Just as in the preceding epoch every major defeat—the defeat
of France in 1871, that of Russia, Germany, Hungary in 1905, 1917,
1918—resulted in a genuine revolution, so in our time each defeated
country resorts to a fascist counterrevolution. Moreover, present-day war
itself has become a revolutionary process, a civil war with an unmistakably
predominant counterrevolutionary tendency. Just as in a horse race we do
not know which horse will win but we do know that it will be a horse,
so in the present war the victory of either party will result in a further
gigantic step toward the fascization of Europe, if not of the whole European, American, Asiatic world of tomorrow.

I

There seem to be two easy ways for the "orthodox" Marxist of today to
handle this difficult problem. Well-trained in Hegelian philosophical

thought, he might say that all that is, is reasonable, and that, by one of those dialectical shifts in which history rejoices, socialism has been fulfilled by the social revolution implied in the victory of fascism. Thus Hegel himself at first followed the rising star of the French Revolution, later embraced the cause of Napoleon, and ended by acclaiming the Prussian state that emerged from the anti-Napoleonic wars of 1812–1815 as the fulfillment of the philosophical "idea" and as the "state of reason" corresponding to the given stage of its historical development.

Or, for that matter, our orthodox Marxist might not be willing, for the present, to go so far as to acknowledge the fascist allies of Stalin as the genuine promoters of socialism in our time. He would then content himself with feeling that the victory of fascism, planned economy, state capitalism, and the weeding out of all ideas and institutions of traditional "bourgeois democracy" will bring us to the very threshold of the genuine social revolution and proletarian dictatorship—just as, according to the teachings of the early church, the ultimate coming of Christ will be immediately preceded by the coming of the Anti-Christ who will be so much like Christ in his appearance and in his actions that the faithful will have considerable difficulty in seeing the difference.

In so reasoning, our orthodox Marxist would not only conform with the church but would also keep well in line with the precedents set by the earlier socialists and "revolutionary" Marxists themselves. It was not only the moderately progressive bourgeois ex-minister Guizot who was deceived by the revolutionary trimmings of Louis Napoleon's coup d'état of 1851 and, when he heard the news burst out into the alarmed cry, "This is the complete and final triumph of socialism." Even the leading representative of French socialism, P. J. Proudhon, was taken in by the violently anti-bourgeois attitude displayed by the revolutionary imperialist, and he devoted a famous pamphlet to the thesis that the coup d'état of the Second of December did in fact "demonstrate the social revolution."[1]

Indeed, in many ways that counterrevolutionary aftermath of 1848 is comparable to the infinitely more serious and more extended counterrevolutionary movement through which European society is passing today after the experience of the Russian, the German, and the other European revolutions which followed in the wake of the First World War. Every party and every political tendency had to go through a certain period of bewilderment until it had adapted itself to a totally changed situation. Marx himself, although he utterly despised the imperialist adventurer because of his personal inadequacy, was inclined to believe in the revolutionary significance of the counterrevolutionary coup. He described the historical outcome of the two years of revolutionary defeat from 1848 to 1849 by the paradoxical statement that "this time the advance of the revolutionary movement did not effect itself through its immediate tragicomic achievements but, the other way round, through the creation of a united and powerful counterrevolution, through the creation of an antagonist by opposing whom the party of revolt will reach its real revolutionary maturity."[2] And even after the fateful event he most emphatically restated his conviction that "the destruction of the parliamentary republic contains the germs of the triumph of the proletarian revolution."[3] This is exactly what the German Communists and their Russian masters said 80 years later when they welcomed the advent of Nazism in Germany as a "victory of revolutionary communism."

This ambiguous attitude of Proudhon and Marx toward counterrevolution was repeated ten years later by Ferdinand Lassalle, a close theoretical disciple of Marx and at that time the foremost leader of the growing socialist movement in Germany. He was prepared to cooperate with Bismarck at the time when that unscrupulous statesman was toying with the idea of bribing the workers into acceptance of his imperialistic plans by an apparent adoption of the universal franchise and some other ideas borrowed from the 1848 revolution and the Second Empire. Lasalle did not live to see Bismarck at the end of the 70's, when he had subdued the liberals and the ultra-montane Catholic party, revert to his old dream of enforcing a kind of "tory-socialism" based on a ruthless persecution and suppression of all genuine socialist workers' movements.

There is no need to discuss the wholesale conversion of internationalists into nationalists and proletarian Social Democrats into bourgeois democratic parliamentarians during and after the first world war. Even such former Marxists as Paul Lensch accepted the war of the Kaiser as a realistic fulfillment of the dreams of a socialist revolution, and the about-face of the socialists they themselves glorified as a "revolutionization of the revolutionaries." There was a "national-bolshevist" fraction of the German Communist party long before there was a Hitlerian National Socialist Party. Nor does the military alliance that was concluded "seriously and for a long time" between Stalin and Hitler in August, 1939, contain any novelty for those who have followed the historical development of the relations between Soviet Russia and imperial, republican, and Hitlerian Germany throughout the last twenty years. The Moscow treaty of 1939 had been preceded by the treaties of Rapallo in 1920 and of Berlin in 1926. Mussolini had already for several years openly proclaimed his new fascist credo when Lenin was scolding the Italian Communists for their failure to enlist that invaluable dynamic personality in the service of their revolutionary cause. As early as 1917, during the peace negotiations in Brest Litovsk, Rosa Luxemburg and Karl Liebknecht had been aware of the dreadful danger that was threatening the proletarian revolution from that side. They had said in so many words that "Russian socialism based on reactionary Prussian bayonets would be the worst that still could happen to the revolutionary workers' movement."

It appears from this historical record that there is indeed something basically wrong with the traditional Marxian theory of the social revolution and with its practical application. There is no doubt, today less than at any former time in history, that the Marxian analysis of the working of the capitalist mode of production and of its historical development is fundamentally correct. Yet it seems that the Marxian theory in its hitherto accepted form is unable to deal with the new problems that arise in the course of a not merely occasional and temporary but deep-rooted, comprehensive, and enduring counterrevolutionary development.

II

The main deficiency of the Marxian concept of the counterrevolution is that Marx did not, and from the viewpoint of his historical experience could not, conceive of the counterrevolution as a normal phase of social development. Like the bourgeois liberals he thought of the counterrevolution as an "abnormal" temporary disturbance of a normally progressive development. (In the same manner, pacifists to the present day think of war as an abnormal interruption of the normal state of peace, and physicians and psychiatrists until recently thought of disease and more especially the diseases of the mind as an abnormal state of the organism.) There is, however, between the Marxian approach and that of the typical bourgeois liberal this important difference: they start from a totally different idea about just what is a normal condition. The bourgeois liberal regards existing conditions or at least their basic features as the normal state of things, and any radical change as its abnormal interruption. It does not matter to him whether that disturbance of existing normal conditions results from a genuinely progressive movement or from a reactionary attempt to borrow revolution's thunder for the purpose of a counterrevolutionary aggression. He is afraid of the counterrevolution just as much as of the revolution and just because of its resemblance to a genuine revolution. That is why Guizot called the coup d'état "the complete and final triumph of the socialist revolution" and why, for that matter, Hermann Rauschning today describes the advent of Hitlerism as a "revolt of nihilism."

As against the bourgeois concept, the Marxian theory has a distinct superiority. It understands revolution as a completely normal process. Some of the best Marxists, including Marx himself and Lenin, even said on occasion that revolution is the only normal state of society. So it is, indeed, under those objective historical conditions which are soberly stated by Marx in his preface to the "Critique of Political Economy."

Marx did not, however, apply the same objective and historical principle to the process of counterrevolution, which was known to him only in an undeveloped form. Thus, he did not see, and most people do not see today, that such important counterrevolutionary developments as those of present-day fascism and nazism have, in spite of their violent revolutionary methods, much more in common with *evolution* than they have with a genuine revolutionary process. It is true that in their talk and propaganda both Hitler and Mussolini have directed their attack mostly against revolutionary Marxism and communism. It is also true that before and after their seizure of state power they made a most violent attempt to weed out every Marxist and Communist tendency in the working classes. Yet this was not the main content of the fascist counterrevolution. In its actual results the fascist attempt to renovate and transform the traditional state of society does not offer an alternative to the radical solution aimed at by the revolutionary Communists. The fascist counterrevolution rather tried to replace the reformist socialist parties and trade unions, and in this it succeeded to a great extent.

The underlying historical law, the *law of the fully developed fascist counterrevolution of our time*, can be formulated in the following manner: After the complete exhaustion and defeat of the revolutionary forces, the fascist counterrevolution attempts to fulfill, by new revolutionary methods and in widely different form, those social and political tasks which the so-called reformistic parties and trade unions had promised to achieve but in which they could no longer succeed under the given historical conditions.

A revolution does not occur at some arbitrary point of social development but only at a definite stage. "At a certain stage of their development the material productive forces of society come into contradiction with the existing production-relations (or property-relations) within which they hitherto moved. From being forms of development, those relations turn into fetters upon the forces of production. *Then a period of social revolution sets in.*" And again Marx emphasized, and even to a certain extent exaggerated, the objectivistic principle of his materialist theory of revolution according to which "a formation of society *never* perishes until *all* the forces of production for which it is wide enough have been developed." All this is true enough as far as it goes. We have all seen how evolutionary socialism reached the end of its rope. We have seen how the old capitalistic system based on free competition and the whole of its vast political and ideological superstructure was faced by chronic depression and decay. There seemed no way open except a wholesale transition to another, more highly developed form of society, to be effected by the social revolution of the proletarian class.

The new historical development during the last twenty years showed, however, that there was yet another course open. The transition to a new type of capitalistic society, that could no longer be achieved by the democratic and peaceful means of traditional socialism and trade unionism, was performed by a counterrevolutionary and anti-proletarian yet objectively progressive and ideologically anti-capitalistic and plebeian movement that had learned to apply to its restricted evolutionary aims the unrestricted methods developed during the preceding revolution. (More particularly, both Hitler and Mussolini had learned much in the school of Russian Bolshevism.) Thus, it appeared that the evolution of capitalistic society had not reached its utter historical limit when the ruling classes and the reformistic socialists—those self-appointed "doctors at the sickbed of capitalism"—reached the limits of their evolutionary possibilities. The phase of peaceful democratic reforms was followed by another evolutionary phase of development—that of the fascist transformation, revolutionary in its political form but evolutionary in its objective social contents.

The decisive reason that the capitalistic formation of society did not perish after the collapse of the First World War is that the workers did not make their revolution. "Fascism," said its closest enemy, "is a counterrevolution against a revolution that never took place."[4] Capitalistic society did not perish, but instead entered a new revolutionary phase under the counterrevolutionary regime of fascism, because it was not destroyed by a successful workers' revolution, and because it had not, in fact, developed all the forces of production. The objective and the subjective premises are equally important for the counterrevolutionary conclusion.

From this viewpoint all those comfortable illusions about a hidden revolutionary significance in the temporary victory of the counterrevolution, in which the earlier Marxists so frequently indulged, must be entirely abandoned. If counterrevolution is only extremely and superficially connected with a social revolution by its procedures, but in its actual content is much more closely related to the further evolution of a given social system, and is in fact a particular historical phase of that social evolution, then it can no longer be regarded as a revolution in disguise. There is no reason to hail it either as an immediate prelude to the genuine revolution, or as an intrinsic phase of the revolutionary process itself. It appears as a particular phase of the whole developmental process, not inevitable like revolution yet becoming an inevitable step within the development of a given society under certain historical conditions. It has reached its up-to-now most comprehensive and important form in the present day fascist renovation and transformation of Europe, which in its basic economic aspect appears as a transition from the private and anarchic form of competitive capitalism to a system of planned and organized monopoly capitalism or state capitalism.

III

It would be the greatest folly and, for people even slightly imbued with the great discoveries of Marx in the field of the social sciences, a total relapse into a prematerialist and pre-scientific manner of thought if one were to expect that the historical progress from competitive capitalism to planned economy and state capitalism could be repealed by any power in the world. Least of all can fascism be defeated by those people who, after a hundred years of shameless acquiescence in the total abandonment of their original ideals, now hasten to conjure up the infancy of the capitalist age with its belief in liberty, equity, fraternity, and free trade, while at the same time they surreptitiously and inefficiently try to imitate as far as possible fascism's abolition of the last remnants of those early capitalist ideas. They feel a sudden and unexpected urge to celebrate the French Revolution's fourteenth of July and at the same time dream of destroying fascism by adopting fascist methods.

In opposition to the artisan and petty-bourgeois spirit of early utopian socialism, the first word of scientific and proletarian socialism stated that big industry and the machine age had come to stay, that modern industrial workers had to find a cure for the evils of the industrial age on the basis of a further development of the new industrial forces themselves. In the same manner the scientific and proletarian socialists of our time must try to find remedies for the wrongs of monopoly capitalism and fascist dictatorship on the basis of monopoly and state capitalism itself. Neither free trade (that was not so free for the workers after all) nor the other aspects of traditional bourgeois democracy—free discussion and free press and free radio—will ever be restored. They have never existed for the suppressed and exploited class. As far as the workers are concerned, they have only exchanged one form of serfdom for another.

There is no essential difference between the way the *New York Times* and the Nazi press publish daily "all the news that's fit to print"—under existing conditions of privilege and coercion and hypocrisy. There is no difference in principle between the eighty-odd voices of capitalist mammoth corporations—which, over the American radio, recommend to legions of silent listeners the use of Ex-Lax, Camels, and neighborhood grocerys, along with music, war, baseball and domestic news, and dramatic sketches—and one suave voice of Mr. Goebbels who recommends armaments, race-purity, and worship of the Fuehrer. He too is quite willing to let them have music along with it—plenty of music, sporting news, and all the unpolitical stuff they can take.

This criticism of the inept and sentimental methods of present-day anti-fascism does not imply by any means that the workers should do openly what the bourgeoisie does under the disguise of a so-called anti-fascist fight: acquiesce in the victory of fascism. The point is to fight fascism not by fascist means but on its own ground. This seems to the present writer to be the rational meaning of what was somewhat mystically described by *Alpha* in the spring issue of *Living Marxism*[5] as the specific task of "shock-troops" in the anti-fascist fight. *Alpha* anticipated that even if the localized war-of-siege waged during the first seven months of the present conflict were to extend into a general fascist world war, this would not be a "total war" and an unrestricted release of the existing powers of production for the purpose of destruction. Rather, it would still remain a monopolistic war in which the existing powers of production (destruction) would be fettered in many ways for the benefit of the monopolistic interests of privileged groups and classes. It would remain that kind of war from fear of the emancipatory effect that a total mobilization of the productive forces, even restricted to the purpose of destruction, would be bound to have for the workers or, under the present-day conditions of totally mechanized warfare, for the shock-troopers who perform the real work of that totally mechanized war.

This argument of *Alpha's* can be applied more widely and much more convincingly. First of all we can disregard for the moment (although we shall have to return to it at a later stage) the peculiar restriction of the argument to the "shock-troops" and to the conditions of war. The whole traditional distinction between peace and war, production and destruction, has lost in recent times much of that semblance of truth that it had in an earlier period of modern capitalistic society. The history of the last ten years has shown that ever since, in a world drunk with apparent prosperity, the American Kellogg Pact outlawed war, peace has been abolished. From the outset Marxism was comparatively free from that simple-mindedness which believed in an immediate and clear-cut difference between production-for-use and production-for-profit. The only form of production-for-use under existing capitalistic conditions is just the production-for-profit. Productive labor for Marx, as for Smith and Ricardo, is that labor which produces a profit for the capitalist and, incidentally, a thing which may also be useful for human needs. There is no possibility of establishing a further distinction between a "good" and a "bad," a constructive and a destructive usefulness. The Goebbelian defense of the "productivity" of the labor spent on armaments in Germany by referring to the amount of "useful" labor spent in the United States for cosmetics had no novelty for the Marxist. Marx, who described the working class in its revolutionary fight as "the greatest of all productive forces" would not have been afraid to recognize war itself as an act of production, and the destructive forces of modern mechanized warfare as part of the productive forces of modern capitalistic society, such as it is. He, like *Alpha*, would have recognized the "shock-troops" in their "destructive" activity in war as well as in their productive activity in industry (armament and other industries—war industries all!) as real workers, a revolutionary vanguard of the modern working class. Historically it is a well-established fact that the soldier (the hired mercenary) was the first modern wage-laborer.

Thus, the old Marxian contradiction between the productive forces and the given production relations reappears in the warlike as well as in the peaceful activities of modern fascism. With it there appear again the old contrast between the workers, who as a class are interested in the full application and development of the productive forces, and the privileged classes, the monopolists of the material means of production. More than at any previous time the monopoly of political power reveals itself as the power to rule and control the social process of production. At the same time this means, under present conditions, the power to restrict production—both the production of industry in peace and destructive production in time of war—and to regulate it in the interest of the monopolist class. Even the "national" interest that was supposed to underly the present-day fascist war waged by Hitler and Mussolini is revealed by the war itself and will be revealed much more clearly by the coming peace as being ultimately an interest of the international capitalist and monopolist class. Much more clearly than at the end of the First World War it will appear that this war is waged by both parties—by the attacking fascists as well as by the defending "democrats"—as a united counterrevolutionary struggle against the workers and the soldiers who by their labor in peace and war prepared and fought the truly suicidal war.

What, then, is the hope left for the anti-fascists who are opposing the present European war and who will oppose the coming war of the hemisphere? The answer is that, just as life itself does not stop at the entrance of war, neither does the material work of modern industrial production. Fascists today quite correctly conceive the whole of their economy—that substitute for a genuine socialist economy—in terms of a "war economy" (*Wehrwirtschaft*). Thus, it is the task of the workers and the soldier to see to it that this job is no longer done within the restrictive rules imposed upon human labor in present-day capitalist, monopolist, and oppressive society. It has to be done in the manner prescribed by the particular instruments used; that is, in the manner prescribed by the productive forces available at the present stage of industrial development. In this manner both the productive and the destructive forces of present-day society—as every worker, every soldier knows—can be used only if they are used *against* their present monopolistic rulers. Total mobilization of the productive forces presupposes total mobilization of that greatest productive force which is the revolutionary working class itself.

Notes

1. *Oeuvres Completes de Proudhon*, vol. VIII, Paris, 1868.
2. First article on *Class Struggles in France. Neue Rheinische Zeitung*, January 1850.
3. *The Eighteenth Brumaire of Louis Bonaparte*, February 1852.
4. Ignazio Silone, *School of Dictators*, 1938.
5. *Living Marxism*, vol. V, no. 1, pp. 44–58.

The Workers' Fight against Fascism

"Democracy"—a self-styled name for the traditional set-up of present day capitalist society—is fighting a losing battle against the attacking forces of fascism (nazism, falangism, iron guardism, and so forth). The workers stand by. They seem to say again what their predecessors, the revolutionary workers of Paris in 1849, said in regard to the final struggle between the leaders of a self-defeated liberal democracy and the quasi-fascist chief of a new Napoleonic imperialism, Louis Bonaparte.

They say (as interpreted by Marx and Engels), *"C'est une affaire pour Messieurs les bourgeois."* (This time it's a matter to be settled among the bosses.)

The "secret" underlying the verbal battles between "totalitarianism" and "anti-totalitarianism" and the more important diplomatic and military struggle between the Axis and the Anglo-American group of imperialist powers is the historical fact that the worst, and the most intimate foe of democracy today is not Herr Hitler, but "democracy" itself.

Yet this is not a problem of "split personality" nor can it be explained as an "inferiority complex," or a "father complex," or any of the other lofty creations of Freudian psychology. It is not even a conflict between old age and youth, or, as Mrs. Lindbergh puts it, between "the forces of the past and the forces of the future."

The real facts underlying all these high-sounding phrases are to be sought nowhere else but—re-enter Marx—in the material basis of all ideological conflicts, that is, in the economic structure of contemporary society or in the impasse that modern capitalism has reached in the present phase of its historical development.

Ambiguities of Democracy

We must not, however, jump to conclusions. Before we explain the basic reasons for the ambiguities of "Democracy" in its present "fight" against the fascist challenge, we must deal somewhat more closely with the phenomenon itself. We must show that the assumed split, though it does not exist in any psychological, anthropological or cosmic sense, does yet exist as a very real split in what, for want of a better term, we shall continue to call the "class consciousness" of the ruling strata of present-day society.

We shall not waste our time with a discussion of the more conspicuous forms in which this condition manifests itself—a world-wide war between two equally capitalistic parts of that one big capitalistic power that rules the world today, and the open division of each of the fighting parties into mutually opposed factions. In spite of the fact that in our truly "Chinese" age every party and every faction endeavors above all to "save face" by hiding its own and borrowing its opponents' slogans and by pretending "not to offer any solution," it is sufficiently clear today that the same divisions that became visible in the collapse of Norway, Holland, Belgium, and France exist and develop in various forms both in the actually fighting, and the so-called neutral "democracies." This alone is sufficient to prove that the present "war" is fundamentally a "civil war," and will be decided in the future, just as it has been up to now, not by the relative military, or even the economic, strength of the fighting countries, but by the help that the attacking force of fascism will get from its allies within the "democratic" countries. The main task of the following paragraphs is to deal with the less conspicuous manner in which this internal strife pervades the "conscience" of every group, of every institution, and, as it were, of every single member of present-day "democratic" society.

The American public today hates and fears the growing threat of fascism. It takes a fervent interest in the various official and non-official forms of the search for "Trojan horses" and "fifth columnists." It girds itself for the defense of the democratic traditions against the attack that is brought nearer our shores by the progress of the Nazi war in Europe, Africa, and Asia. At the same time, an increasing part of this American public is secretly convinced of the several material benefits that could be derived for the so-called elite and, to a lesser extent, for the mass of the people as well, from an acceptance of fascist methods in the field of economics, politics, and, maybe, even for the promotion of the so-called higher cultural and ideological interests. It is apt to regard the very institutions and ideals for which it is prepared to "fight" as a kind of "*faux frais*" of production, of conducting the business of an efficient modern administration, and of fighting a modern war. It never seriously considered "democratic" methods as an adequate means of running an important private business, or, for that matter, a business-like trade union. It would prefer, on the whole, to have its cake and eat it too, that is, to apply those amazingly successful new methods to the fullest advantage, and yet at the same time, somehow retain a workable "maximum" of the traditional "democratic" amenities.

It is easy to see that this more or less platonic attachment to the great democratic tradition, in spite of the assumedly greater material advantages of the fascist methods, offers small comfort for the real prospects of democracy in times of a serious and hitherto unconquerable crisis. In fact, an increasing number of the foremost spokesmen, the most vociferous "experts," and the truest friends of democracy begin to express some grave doubts as to whether their unyielding allegiance to the "underlying values of the democratic American tradition" has not already degenerated into a costly hobby that the nation may, or, in the long run, may not be able to afford. (This sentiment became most evident in the all too ready response of the greater part of the American "democratic" public to Anne Lindbergh's booklet.)

There are some definite fields in which even the most fervent opposers of the ruthlessness of the fascist principles admit an undeniable superiority of totalitarian achievements. There is, for example, universal admiration for the splendid work done by the Nazi propaganda. There is widespread belief in the full success of the Nazi attack against the most incurable plagues of modern democratic society. Fascism is supposed to have abolished permanent mass unemployment and, by one bold stroke, to have released the brakes put on free enterprise by wages disputes and labor unrest. There is a tacit agreement that an all-round adoption of fascist methods will be necessary in time of war.

An Economic Pythia

The most striking testimony to present-day democracy's implicit belief in an overwhelming superiority of fascist methods is to be found in an official document published in June, 1939, by the National Resources Committee, that deals with the basic characteristics of *The Structure of the American Economy*.[1] We shall make ample use of this report when we approach the main question of our present investigation. For the moment, however, we shall disregard the momentous discoveries made by Dr. Gardiner C. Means and his staff with regard to the present state of American economy. We shall deal exclusively with the forecast of the chances for a survival of the democratic principle that is revealed in the general statements contained in the introduction and conclusion.[2]

The authors of the report start from impressive description of the well-known "failure" of the present economic system to use its gigantic resources effectively: "Resources are wasted or used ineffectively as parts of the organization get out of adjustment with each other, or as the organization fails to adjust to new conditions; as individuals fail to find, or are prevented from finding, the most useful field of activity; as material resources are unused, or as their effective use is impeded by human barriers; and as the most effective technology is not used or its use is prevented."

They attempt to estimate and picture the "magnitude of wastes" that resulted from this failure both during the depression and the preceding non-depression years. According to this estimate the depression loss in national income due to the idleness of men and machines from 1929 to 1937 was "in the magnitude of 200 billion dollars worth of goods and services." This extra income would have been enough to provide "a new $6,000 house for every family in the country." At this cost " the entire railroad system of the country could have been scrapped and rebuilt five times over." It is equivalent to the cost of rebuilding the whole of the existing "agricultural and industrial plant" of the nation.[3] Even in the peak pre-depression year, 1929, both production and national income could have been increased 19 percent by merely putting to work the men and machines that were idle in that year, even without the introduction of improved techniques of production.[4]

The authors then go on to deal with the "impact" of this waste upon the community as reflected in the development of a "sense of social frustration" and in "justified social unrest and unavoidable friction." They begin, however to show a wavering in their democratic convictions when they proceed, in the following paragraph to discuss the "tremendous opportunity" and the "great challenge" that this very waste of resources and manpower presents for the American nation today. The "great challenge" for democracy assumes at once the sinister features of an impending tragedy: "How long this opportunity will be open to the American democracy involves a serious question. The opportunity for a higher standard of living is so great, the social frustration from the failure to obtain it so real, that other means will undoubtedly be sought if a democratic solution is not worked out. The time for finding such a solution is not unlimited." And they reveal their inmost sentiment as to the probabilities of a "democratic solution" of that tremendous task by the very language in which they finally "state the problem" arising from the results of their investigation:

> This problem, the basic problem facing economic statesmanship today, can be stated as follows: How can we get effective use of our resources, YET, AT THE SAME TIME preserve the underlying values in our tradition of liberty and democracy? How can we employ our unemployed, how can we use our plant and equipment to the full, how can we take advantage of the modern technology, YET IN ALL THIS make the individual the source of value and individual fulfillment in society the basic objective? How can we obtain effective organization of resources YET AT THE SAME TIME retain the maximum freedom of individual action?

This same defeatistic sentiment pervades, as it were, the whole of this otherwise most valuable official document. There is nowhere an unambiguous attempt to claim for the democratic principles any material value or usefulness for restoring the good old days of capitalism or for bringing about an even greater expansion for the productive forces of the American economic community. There is nothing but a sentimental craving for a policy that would not be altogether incompatible with a more or less verbal allegiance to a few remanants of the "democratic" and "liberal" traditions and what might yet work as well as the fascist

methods, which they never question. Thus the whole of the proud attempt to conquer a new world of prosperity and of full use of resources
and manpower for American democracy boils down to a pronouncement
about the result of the impending struggle between democracy and fascism that in its sinister ambiguity rivals the well-known oracle of the
priestess of Delphi. "If Croesus sets out to conquer the country beyond
the Halys, he will destroy a great empire," said the oracle of ancient
Greece. "If the present government of the USA sets out to conquer the
problems of unused resources and mass unemployment, it will destroy an
important form of government," echoes the economic oracle of our time.

A New Fighting Ground

It appears from the preceding observations that the workers are quite
right if they think twice before they listen to the generous invitations extended to them from every quarter, including most of their former leaders, to forget for the time being about their own complaints against capital and to join wholeheartedly the fight against the common enemy. The
workers cannot participate in "democracy's fight against fascism" for the
simple reason that there is no such fight. To fight against fascism means
for the workers in the hitherto democratic countries to fight first of all
against the democratic branch of fascism within their own countries. To
begin their own fight against the new and more oppressive form of capitalism that is concealed in the various forms of pseudo-socialism offered
to them today, they have first to free themselves from the idea that it
might still be possible for present-day capitalism to "turn the clock back"
and to return to traditional pre-fascist capitalism. They must learn to
fight fascism *on its own ground* which, as we have said before, is entirely
different from the very popular, but in fact self-destructive, advice that
the anti-fascists should learn to fight fascism by adopting fascist methods.

To step from the ground on which the workers' class struggle against
capitalism was waged in the preceding epoch to the ground on which it
must be continued today presupposes full insight into a historical fact
that is not less a fact because it has served as a theoretical basis for the
claims of fascism. This historical fact that has finally arrived today can be
described, as a first approach, either negatively or positively, in any of the
following terms: End of the Market, End of Competitive Capitalism,
"End of Economic Man"; Triumph of Bureaucracy, of Administrative
Rule, of Monopoly Capitalism; Era of Russian Four Year Plans, Italian
Wheat Battles, German "Wehrwirtschaft"; Triumph of State Capitalism
over Private Property and Individual Enterprise.

The tendency toward this transformation was first envisaged by the early socialists in their criticism of the millennial hopes of the bourgeois apostles of free trade. It was later more and more neglected by the socialist writers in their attempt to adopt their theories to the needs of the progressive fractions of the bourgeoisie. When it was finally revived, around the turn of the present century, it was already destined—as we can see today— to serve not the purposes of the socialist revolution, but rather the aims of the imperceptibly growing counterrevolution. We shall presently see that today any further denial of the accomplished fact has become impossible even for hard-boiled defenders of the traditional dreams of bourgeois economy.

The Corporate Community

For a more detailed description and factual confirmation of this general statement we turn again to the above discussed document which contains, as far as the writer can see, by far the most comprehensive, the most reliable and, at the same time, the most dramatically presented information on the subject. When this government report on the structure of the American economy first became known to the American public, the chief sensation was created by its careful statistical proof that even the boldest estimates previously made were far below the degree of monopolistic concentration actually reached by American economy. According to the statistics given and explained in Chapters 7 and 9 and Appendices 9–13 of the report—that bring up-to-date the figures published in 1930 by Berle and Means in *The Modern Corporation and Private Property*—the one hundred largest manufacturing companies of this country in 1935 employed 20.7 percent of all the manpower engaged in manufacturing; accounted for 32.4 percent of the value of products reported by all manufacturing plants; and contributed 24.7 percent of all the value added in manufacturing activity.

Although there are some cases in which these large corporations comprise almost the whole of a particular industry (steel, petroleum, refining, rubber and cigarette manufacturing), manufacturing industries on the average cannot compete with the much higher degree of concentration that has been reached by the railroads and public utilities. Of the total number of the two hundred "*largest non-financial corporations*" that are listed in the report, approximately half are railroads and utilities; the railroads included in this list in 1935 operated over 90 percent of the railroad mileage of the country, while the electric utilities accounted for 80 percent of the electric power production, for most of the telephone and telegraph services of the USA, and a large part of the rapid transit facilities of New York, Chicago, Philadelphia, Boston, and Baltimore. No less striking are the figures relating to the fifty *"largest financial corporations"* including thirty banks, seventeen life-insurance companies, and three investment trusts, each with assets of over 200 million dollars. The thirty banks together hold 34.3 percent of the banking assets of the country outside of the Federal Reserve Banks, while the seventeen life-insurance companies account for over 81.5 percent of the assets of all life-insurance companies. There is an equally high degree of concentration in the field of government activities. The twenty *"largest government units"* together employ 46 percent of all the manpower employed in government, excluding work-relief programs. The largest of these, the federal government, is by far the largest single "corporation" in the country; the post office alone employed in 1935 nearly as many persons as the largest corporate employer.

All these figures, however, do not tell half the story of American business concentration. Much more is shown by a breakdown of the total number into major industrial categories and by an investigation into the growth of the relative importance of all non-financial corporations in 1909 to over fifty four percent in 1933. And the whole picture begins to reveal its true significance when the report endeavors to show the tremendous degree of interrelationships through which "the managements of most of the larger corporations are brought together in what might be called the *corporate community"* [emphasis by K. K.]. This is indeed a picture that might cure the illusions of the most innocent believers in that "spirit of free enterprise" that must be protected by "all means short of war" from the sinister threat of "totalitarianism." There is very little difference between that economic "co-ordination" that is achieved, and sometimes not achieved, by the political decrees of victorious nazism, fascism, and bolshevism, and this new "corporate community" that has been created by a slow but relentless process in this country through the system of "interlocking directorates," through the activities of the major financial institutions, through particular interest groupings, through firms rendering legal, accounting, and similar services to the larger corporations, through "intercorporate stockholdings," and a number of other devices.

After a careful study of the working of all these different devices, the report reaches its climax by disclosing that no less than 106 of the aforesaid 250 largest industrial and financial corporations and nearly two-thirds of their combined assets are controlled by only "eight more or less clearly defined interest groups." (Even this estimate, as pointed out by the authors themselves, falls far short of reality: "No attempt is made to include the assets of smaller corporations falling within the same sphere of influence, though many such could be named." Other and more important shortcomings will be discussed below.) To give an idea of the significance of this fact, we must restrict ourselves to a few data concerning each of those eight mammoth groups.

(1) *Morgan-First National.* Includes thirteen industrial corporations, twelve utilities, eleven major railroads or railroad systems (controlling 26 percent of the railroad mileage of the country), and five banks. Total assets:

(Millions of dollars)	
Industrials	3,920
Utilities	12,191
Rails	9,678
Banks	4,421
Total	30,210

(2) *Rockefeller.* Controls six oil companies (successors to the dissolved Standard Oil Co.) representing 4,262 million dollars, or more than half of the total assets of the oil industry, and one bank (Chase National, the country's largest bank; assets: 2,351 million dollars).

(3) *Kuhn, Loeb.* Controls thirteen major railroads or railroad systems (22 percent of the railroad mileage of the country), one utility, and one bank. Total assets: 10,853 million dollars.

(4) *Mellon.* Controls about nine industrial corporations, one railroad, two utilities, two banks. Total assets: 3,332 million dollars.

(5) *Chicago group.* Controls on the basis of interlocking directorates four industrial corporations, three utilities, four banks. Total assets: 4,266 million dollars.

(6) *Du Pont.* Comprises three top rank industrial corporations and one bank. Total assets: 2,628 million dollars.

(7) *Cleveland group.* The Mather interests control through the Cleveland-Cliffs Iron Co. the four so-called independent steel companies; control two other industrial corporations and one bank. Total assets: 1,404 million dollars.

(8) *Boston group.* Includes four industrial corporations, two utilities, one bank. Total assets: 1,719 million dollars.

In interpreting this list, the reader should have in mind that it is far from complete. As we have seen, the authors, on principle, have only considered interconnections between the 250 largest non-financial and financial corporations. Even within these limits, many corporations that are "fairly closely related with one or another of these groups" have been left out for technical reasons. For example, the giant *International Paper and Power Corporation* that is equally closely related to Boston and Rockefeller was therefore assigned to neither the Boston nor the Rockefeller groups. Ten equally important links between the eight big interest groups are considered in the appendix but are only slightly touched upon in the body of the report.

Even with these restrictions, the *corporate community* as described in this report appears as a momentous concentration of economic and thus also of political power. The report does not deny the importance of the controls that the corporate community "exercises over the policies of the larger corporations, through them affecting the whole American economy." It is equally aware of their political significance. Just as the controls exercised by the organized interest groups—the big associations of capital and labor, by organizations of farmers and of consumers—operate through government, so also do "some of the controls exercised by the corporate community operate through government." Yet, says the report: "it is not intended to imply that these aggregations of capital ever act as a unit under the rule of individual or oligarchic dictatorships. The social and economic content of the relationships which bind them together is far more subtle and varied than this." It would not be easy to determine just what degree of subtlety and variety separates a democratic from a dictatorial exercise of an uncontrolled power. We have to trust, instead, the judgment of our experts when they tell us that the corporate community as existing in the USA today is not a dictatorship; it is only a "concentration of the economic leadership in the hands of a few."

The End of the Market

The foregoing description of the degree of concentration reached by American capitalism does not by itself answer the crucial question as to whether the present structure of this economy still conforms to the traditional principles of "democratic" capitalism, or whether it already assumes the characteristic features of present-day Nazi, fascist, and Bolshevik economies. Recent history has shown that a "totalitarian" form of government could just as well be imposed upon the comparatively backward economies of Russia, Italy, Spain, and so on as upon that most highly concentrated type of capitalist economy which existed in Germany. On the other hand it would be "theoretically" possible to imagine a development by which a highly concentrated capitalist economy would still retain, in an unaltered form, the whole of the internal structure of nineteenth-century capitalism.

The actual truth that is revealed in another and, to the writer, most significant part of Dr. Means' report is that this miracle has not happened and that, on the contrary, the external change of the structure of the American economy has been accompanied by an even more incisive transformation in its internal structure and operating policies.

American economy today no longer receives its decisive impulses from the competition of individual enterprises in an uncontrolled ("free") market, but has become, by and large, a manipulated system. Goods are still produced as commodities. There is still something that is called "prices," and there are still the three capitalist "markets"—goods, labor, and securities. There even remain some sizable areas in which the "price of an article can still act, after a fashion, as a regulator of production." "The proportion of cotton and corn planted on Arkansas farms varies from year to year with changing relationships in the prices of those crops, and reflects the operation of markets as an organizing influence." Yet outside of those increasingly restricted areas—agricultural products and listed securities—the bulk of "prices," including labor rates, are no longer established in free markets. They are manipulated by administrative decisions that are influenced to a varying extent, but no longer—as of old—strictly and directly determined by market conditions. This appears, for example, in the wholesale price of automobiles and agricultural implements that are set and changed from time to time by the respective manufacturers, and thus result from "administrative" decisions.

The reader should be careful here to distinguish between those elements within the "administrative" organization of production that have long existed and have changed in degree of importance only, and that other aspect that is entirely new and is still widely ignored by traditionally minded economists.

The mere fact that administrative rule replaces the mechanism of the market in the coordination of economic activities within the limits of a single enterprise has no novelty for the Marxist. It is true that even this fact assumes a new importance under conditions of modern concentration when, as in the case of America's largest enterprise, A.T.&T., the activities of over 450,000 persons are coordinated within one administrative system. It is also true that there has been a great increase in the proportion in which the economic activities of the producing community are administratively coordinated (within single enterprises) as against that in which they are still coordinated through the shifting of prices and the interaction of a large number of independent sellers and buyers in the market.

The decisive problem, however, that has to be investigated if one wants to grasp the process that has recently undermined the traditional democratic character of American society is contained in the question of how far that change of proportion reflects itself in the whole structure and operation of present-day American economy. It is the great merit of the authors of this report that they have investigated that decisive problem to the full and that they are absolutely unambiguous and outspoken about the results of their investigation. According to them American economy as a whole has been transformed "from one regulated by impersonal competition to one in which policies are administratively determined."

They never tire of repeating this most important result and of describing in most impressive terms the "significance of the extensive role of administrative prices" that appears to be "inherent in the modern economy" and forms "an integral part of the structure of economic activity." They insist again and again that "however much of a role price administration may have played in the earlier years of this century, there can be little question that it plays a dominant role today."[5]

There is no space here to describe in detail the 101 methods and devices by which prices, apparently settled by the law of supply and demand in an open market, are in fact manipulated and controlled by very definite "price policies" of the decisive strata of the "corporate community." These controls may originate from one or from different foci of control. "The threads of control over labor policy may be divided between the corporation and a labor union, some threads focusing in the corporate management and some in the union officials; threads of control over some aspects of policy may rest with the government bodies, as in the case of minimum working standards or public utility regulations; still other threads may rest with some dominant buyer, or a supplier of raw materials or of services, etc." They may, furthermore, be direct and immediate or indirect and intangible. "They may operate simply through establishing a climate of opinion within which policies are developed."

They may be entirely informal or may be accomplished by a formal setting, and in many cases the formal and the actual lines of control will differ. They arise from three main sources: possession of one or more of the "factors of production," possession of liquid assets, and most important, position in relation to a functioning operation.

The main thing to understand is that the new "structure of controls" that emerges from these various forms of non-market control (1) is entirely a child of modern times, and (2) it has come to stay for a very long time.

The controls thus exercised over prices and markets on a nation-wide scale by the leading members of the industrial community far surpass in importance the well-known non-market controls heretofore exercised by financial institutions through the handling of investment funds—the so-called supremacy of finance capital. In fact, as shown by recent investigations not yet included in this report, most of the largest business firms are today "self-financing" and no longer depend on the aid of the money-lender and his organizations. The strictly "private" controls exercised by the administrative acts of the members of the corporate community are even more important than the old and new forms of non-market controls which are exercised by government (federal, state, and local) through its fiscal policies, through the protection of property and enforcement of contracts, and so forth.

Nor can the influence exerted on the market by the action of some powerful pressure groups any longer be regarded as a transitory and un-"normal" encroachment on the normal activities of trade—any more than the influences exerted on the U.S. Congress by political pressure groups in Washington can be considered an anomaly. The constitution of the corporate community has become the real constitution of the U.S.

There remains the question of the working of this new system. How can "administration-dominated prices" that are changed from time to time replace the practically unlimited flexibility of market prices both in their reaction to the different phases of the industrial cycle (prosperity and depression) and to the technologically-conditioned structural changes? Dr. Means and his staff are inclined to take a very optimistic attitude toward the working of the new type of administration-dominated prices. They clearly see certain "violent distortions" that arose during the years of the last depression and the succeeding "recovery" from the differential behavior of the two kinds of prices co-existing in American economy: "Between 1929 and 1932 there was a considerable drop in the wholesale price index, but this drop was made up of a violent drop in the prices of market-dominated commodities, and there was only a very small or no drop at all for the bulk of the prices which are subject to extensive administrative control. In the recovery period of 1932 to 1937, much of this distortion was eliminated [perhaps new distortions were created?—K. K.] by the large increases in the market-dominated prices and the relatively small increase in the bulk of administration-dominated prices."

Yet they do not blame this disturbance on the new phenomenon of administration-control of prices. They rather take it for granted that the market, though "theoretically" still able to act as an organizing influence, does in fact no longer act in that beneficial manner. On the other hand, they have proved to their own satisfaction that the degree of flexibility which results from the administrative regulation of the bulk of the prices of goods, labor and securities "appears sufficient to allow the gradual readjustment of price relationships to reflect the gradual changes in wants, in resources, and in techniques of production, *if the level of economic activity were reasonably well maintained*" [emphasis by K. K.]. Thus to the authors of this report, "the serious distortions in the price structure resulting from the differential sensitivity of prices to depression influences reflect a disorganizing rather than an organizing role that the market can play" (p. 152).

This statement might be acceptable to us who are equally convinced—though from an altogether opposite viewpoint—of the impossibility of retaining or restoring the traditional forms of capitalist economy. It seems, however, that they take a lot for granted if they assume that the level of economic activity could be reasonably well maintained under existing conditions of the "democratic" society. They do not tell us in what way they think that this condition will be better fulfilled in the near future than it has been during the recent past. It is quite possible that this omission betrays on the part of the authors an unconscious anticipation of a future dictator who will fill this apparent gap in the structure of the American economy. The only hint of a solution of this crucial problem that we were able to discover in the report is its pathetic appeal to "an increased understanding of the problem on the part of leaders of business, labor leaders, farm leaders, political leaders, and other leaders of public thinking."

The Viewpoint of the Workers

We do not propose to discuss the "task" of the workers. The workers have already too long done other people's tasks, imposed on them under the high-sounding names of humanity, of human progress, of justice, and freedom, and what not. It is one of the redeeming features of a bad situation that some of the illusions, hitherto surviving among the working class from their past participation in the revolutionary fight of the bourgeoisie against feudal society, have finally been exploded. The only "task" for the workers, as for every other class, is to look out for themselves.

The first thing then that the workers can do is to make absolutely clear to themselves that the old system of "free trade," "free competition," and "democracy" has actually come to an end. It does not matter so much whether we describe the new system that has replaced it in terms of "monopoly capitalism," "state capitalism" or "a corporate state." The last term seems most appropriate to the writer for the reason that it recalls at once the name that was given to the new totalitarian form of society after the rise of fascism in Italy twenty years ago. There is, however, a difference. The corporate community of the US represents as yet only the "economic basis" of a full fledged totalitarian system, and not its political and ideological superstructure. On the other hand, one might say that in backward countries like Italy and Spain there exists as yet only the totalitarian superstructure, without a fully developed economic basis.

As to "monopoly," there is no doubt that every increasing concentration of capital is tantamount to an increase in monopoly. The term itself, however, has changed its meaning since a predominantly competitive economy has been superseded by a predominantly monopolistic system. As long as "monopoly" was regarded as an exception, if not an abuse, the emphasis was on the "excessive" and "unfair" profits derived from a monopolistic position within an otherwise competitive economy. An observation made by Marx at an early time in his critique of Proudhon has recently been unconsciously accepted by an increasing number of bourgeois economists. "*Competition,*" said Marx, "*implies monopoly, and monopoly implies competition.*" Thus the terms "monopoly" and "competition" have recently been redefined to refer to the "elements of a situation" rather than to the situation itself, which as a whole is neither entirely monopolistic nor entirely competitive. In a sense it can be said today that all (or most) profits are essentially monopolistic profits, just as the bulk of prices have become monopolistic prices. Monopoly has become not an exceptional but general condition of present-day economy.

Thus it is quite correct to describe the historical process here discussed as a transition from competitive to monopolistic capitalism; but the term monopoly has, by the very generalization of the condition to which it refers, become an entirely descriptive term, no longer fit to arouse any particular moral indignation.

Similarly, there is no serious harm in describing American economy as a system of "state capitalism." Yet this description does not fit American conditions so well as it does the general pattern of German and other European societies. In spite of the special powers of coercion invested in the political authorities alone, the administrative decisions emanating from various economic enterprises controlled by the government have become the most important influences exerted by the government on the functioning of the U.S. economy. They are co-ordinated with all other forms of non-market controls which, together with the still-existing remainders of market controls, constitute the essential features of the "control structure" of the present economic system. The authors of the report use the terms "administration," "administrative rules," and so on indifferently with reference to all kinds of non-market controls whether they originate from governmental agencies, from different kinds of organizations based on business interests (or for that matter on labor, farmer, consumer interests) or from private firms and combines. There is no doubt that the position of the government will be considerably strengthened in the case of war. But even this would not be a decisive reason to call the existing system of American economy a "state capitalism" as the same condition will occur in all countries at war whether they are backward or fully developed, "competitive" or "monopolistic," whether they are based on a scattered or a concentrated system of capitalist production.

The second thing the workers may be expected to do, once the importance of the change in the basic conditions of capitalist economy has been fully experienced and grasped by them, is to reshuffle their hitherto most cherished revolutionary and class ideas. When Marx described capitalist society as being fundamentally a "production of commodities" this term included for him—and was meant to include for all those who would be able to understand the peculiar "dialectical" slang of the old Hegelian philosophy—the whole of the suppression and exploitation of the workers in a fully developed capitalist society, the class struggle and its increasingly stronger forms, up to the revolutionary overthrow of capitalism and its replacement by a socialist society. This is all right as far as it goes, except that today it should be translated into a less mysterious and much more distinct and outspoken language. But Marx's emphasis on "commodity production" included something else and, this time, something that may well have become inadequate for the workers' fight against the two species of the "corporate state" that exist in the fascist and the so-called democratic countries today.

The emphasis on the principle of commodity production, that is, production for exchange for an anonymous and ever-extended market, was at the same time an emphasis on the positive and progressive functions that capitalism was to fulfill by expanding modern "civilized" society all over the world and, as Marx said, "transforming the whole world into one gigantic market for capitalist production." All kinds of illusions were inevitably bound up with that great enterprise that was conducted, as it were, by humanity itself. All problems seemed to be solvable, all contradictions and conflicts transitory, and the greatest happiness for the greatest number ultimately obtainable.

The workers, in all their divisions, had a big share in those illusions of commodity production and their political expression, the illusions of democracy. They shared them with all other suppressed minorities and progressive strata of capitalist society—Jews, Negroes, pacifists. All "reformism" and "revisionism" that distracted the workers' energies from their revolutionary aims have been based on those illusions. The very advent of fascism in the world and its intrusion into the inner sanctums of traditional democracy has at last destroyed the strength of those illusions. We shall attempt in a later article to trace the positive features of a new program for the workers in their fight against the class enemy in his new and more oppressive form which, at the same time, is more transparent and more exposed to their attack.

Notes

1. For sale by the Superintendent of Documents, Washington, D.C.; vii; 396 pp.; $1.00.
2. Cf. pp. 1–5, 171. All quotations in the following paragraphs, if not otherwise marked, are taken from these pages. [Emphases by K. K.]
3. Cf. p. 27.
4. Cf. *America's Capacity to Produce*, Brookings Institution, p. 422. Quoted—p. 3.
5. Cf. pp. 116, 145, 155, 333, etc.

9. Korsch and Marxism

Introduction

I have reconstructed in detail Korsch's complicated relationship to Marxism in the introduction to the anthology. Here I wish to make a few remarks summing up Korsch's interpretation-critique of Marxism to introduce some of his later work. His post-1940 writings consist of a few published essays, some notes and unpublished manuscripts, and a large collection of letters.[1] The central focus of his later work is the theoretical and political status of Marxism. The selection of documents and letters here should indicate the remarkable ambiguity contained in the later Korsch's attitude toward Marxism.

During the 1930's, after his expulsion from the Communist movement Korsch was concerned to define the essence of Marxism and to spell out "what is living and dead in Marxism." In a series of essays, and in his last book, *Karl Marx*, Korsch attempts to elucidate those ideas that are of continuing validity in Marxism and to criticize those dogmatic versions of Marxism that are at least in part responsible for the debacle of the working-class movement. In "Why I am a Marxist" and *Karl Marx* Korsch defines the core of Marxism in terms of (1) the principle of historical specification; (2) the principle of change and transition; and (3) the principle of revolutionary practice.[2] The principle of historical specification articulates Marx's practice of comprehending "all things social in terms of a definite historical epoch."[3] Marxism for Korsch is a theory of the capitalist mode of production that forms the skeleton of bourgeois society.[4] Marx's achievement was to uncover and analyze those historically distinct and specific features of capitalism and bourgeois society.

Korsch is thus denying that Marx's theory is basically a general theory of the fundamental features of society and history in general.[5] For in Korsch's view, Marx was primarily concerned with the specific features of capitalism, and the specific forms of bourgeois society in such places as Europe, the United States, and Russia.[6] Bourgeois political economy and theory, on the other hand, dealt with the categories of bourgeois society as if they were universal, eternal, and unchanging relationships, rather than merely historically specific features of a system that was full of contradictions and was thus subject to radical transformation. The principle of historical specificity also tells us that truth is concrete: that problems of economy, politics, and culture cannot be solved through a general abstract description of "economics as such," and so on, but requires rather "a detailed description of the definite relations which exist between definite economic phenomena on a definite historical level of development and definite phenomena which appear simultaneously or subsequently in every other field of political, juristic, and intellectual development."[7]

Marxism, in Korsch's view, is also a theory of change and transition which sees reality as a process of flux and change. Marx was especially interested in those aspects of bourgeois society that would propel the system toward radical change.[8] It deflates the pretenses of bourgeois theory to represent the existing society "as a general and unchangeable form of all social life."[9] Marx's dialectical theory of contradiction, negation, and *Aufhebung* ferrets out those antagonisms and conflicts which would require radical transformation. Marxism is a *critical theory* that criticizes the given society in terms of its unresolved contradictions and conflicts, and its higher possibilities.[10] Hence Marxism is a theory of *social revolution*. Marx recognizes the reality of social change and treats bourgeois society and thought as phenomena *to be changed*.[11]

Finally, for Korsch, Marxism is above all a theory of *revolutionary practice*. By analyzing the ruptures, fissures, and crises of capitalist society that provide the foundation and justification—the blueprint—for proletarian revolution, Marxism represents the interest of the proletariat in emancipation from capitalism. Korsch summarized his description of the basic principles of Marxism in *Karl Marx*:

> Marxian theory, viewed in its general character, is a new science of bourgeois society. It appears at a time when within bourgeois society itself, an independent movement of a new social class is opposing the ruling bourgeois class. In opposition to the bourgeois principles it represents the new views and claims of the class oppressed in bourgeois society. It is, so far, not a positive but a critical science. It "specifies" bourgeois society and investigates the tendencies visible in the present development of society, and the way to its imminent practical transformation. Thus it is not only a theory of bourgeois society but, at the same time, a theory of the proletarian revolution.[12]

As we have seen, Korsch also developed a sharp critique of Marxism, particularly of its political theory and theory of revolution. The documents collected in "A Non-Dogmatic Approach to Marxism" illustrate that Korsch believed that the "critical, pragmatic, activistic element" of Marxism provided its living core (and one might add, the core of Korsch's own theory).[13] The documents accompanying the article contain "Theses on Hegel and Revolution" and "On an Activistic Form of Materialism and on the Class and Partisan Character of Science" which Korsch penned in 1931, as well as short pieces by Sorel and Lenin that in his view present important insights into the materialist theory of history. Korsch once called for a "Sorelization" of Marxism, by which he meant a concrete historical analysis of the existing society to prepare the ground for revolutionary theory. The selection by Sorel supposedly illustrates such a materialist approach to history. The selection from Lenin illustrates the political thrust of historical materialism as a theory of proletarian revolution.

The "Ten Theses on Marxism Today" are probably Korsch's most radical critique of Marxism. The "Theses" were delivered as a lecture on Marxism in Zurich in 1950 and have been widely republished.[14] They contain the most radical and striking summary of Korsch's critique of Marxism which I have developed in detail throughout the introductory sections. They should not be seen, however, as Korsch's rejection of Marxism.[15] For Korsch continued to reflect on the Marxian theory and in one of his later letters he writes, "As always, I have good plans to activate my theoretical and political tendencies, but hold on at the same time to another dream: to theoretically restore the 'ideas of Marx' that today are seemingly annihilated after the conclusion of the Marx-Lenin-Stalin episode."[16] To the end Korsch was obsessed with the Marxian theory and its relevance for political practice.

This continued involvement with Marxism is evident in Korsch's letters where he is endlessly projecting plans to write definitive works on Marxism. I have chosen four letters from Korsch's correspondence to illustrate his developing theoretical reflections. Many of his later ideas and keenest insights are expressed in his correspondence, and often never found expression in his published essays. Hence the crucial importance of his letters for reconstructing the complicated position of the later Korsch vis-à-vis Marxism.[17]

In conclusion, Korsch can be seen as one of the most important representatives of a non-dogmatic critical Marxism. His entire life was a meditation on and participation in Marxist theory and practice. Korsch had strong activist tendencies that were frustrated by the course of history. But he continued to develop revolutionary theory and to reconstitute Marxism to provide, if possible, a viable weapon of revolutionary practice. Korsch's failure to develop a revolutionary Marxism that would

serve as an instrument of emancipation reflects the failure of the European
working class to throw off the yoke of capital. But as long as the need
for radical change exists, Korsch's life-work will remain a challenge and
stimulus to revolutionary theory.

Notes

1. Korsch's manuscripts and letters are collected in the Institute for Social
History in Amsterdam.
2. Karl Korsch, "Why I Am a Marxist," in *Three Essays on Marxism* (New
York: Monthly Review Press, Korsch, 1972), and *Karl Marx*.
3. Korsch, *Karl Marx*, p. 24.
4. Ibid.
5. In "Why I Am a Marxist," p. 63, he writes, "The contention set forth
in my edition of Marx's *Capital* that all the propositions contained in this
work, and especially those concerning 'Primitive Accumulation' . . . represent
only an historical outline of the rise and development of capitalism in Western
Europe and 'have universal validity beyond that only in the same way in which
every thorough empirical knowledge of natural and historical form applies
to more than the individual case considered,' was unanimously rejected by
spokesmen of both fractions of German and Russian orthodox Marxism."
6. Korsch, *Karl Marx*, pp. 25–26.
7. Korsch, "Why I Am a Marxist," pp. 64–65.
8. Korsch, *Karl Marx*, chap. 4.
9. Ibid., p. 44.
10. Korsch, "Why I Am a Marxist," pp. 61–66.
11. Korsch, *Karl Marx*, p. 55.
12. Ibid., p. 86.
13. Korsch, "A Non-Dogmatic Approach to Marxism," *Politics* 3, no. 5
(May 1946).
14. Korsch, "Ten Theses on Marxism Today," translated in this anthology
by Douglas Kellner. The "Ten Theses" were first published in French,
Arguments 3, no. 16 (1959), and later in German, *Alternative* 41 (April
1965).
15. Leonardo Ceppa claims in "Korsch's Marxism," p. 118, that the "Ten
Theses on Marxism Today" are an example of "Korsch's total rejection of the
Marxian perspective." Nothing could be more false.
16. Karl Korsch, Letter to Erich Gerlach, December 16, 1956; first published in *Politische Texte*, pp. 392–394; translated in this anthology by
Douglas Kellner.
17. There are many unpublished letters—including a series of correspondence with Roman Rosdolsky 1950–1954—that will no doubt shed further light
on the hitherto little known work of the later Korsch and its relation to

Marxism. My discussion merely intends to introduce this material and stimulate further research. See my review of Korsch's letters published in *Jahrbuch Arbeiterbewegung 2*, in *Telos* 27 (Spring 1976).

A Non-Dogmatic Approach to Marxism

The documents here assembled are not meant as a contribution to the discussion for or against Marxism that has been conducted in this magazine for so many months. There is no use in discussing controversial points in any social theory (not even in that social theory which is commonly described as religion) unless such discussion is part of an existing social struggle. There must be several possibilities of action for the party, group, or class to which the social theory in question refers. The difference may concern social aims, tactics, forms of organization, or the definition of the enemy, of allies, neutrals, or the master plan (if any) to be based on one or another way of judging a given social situation or development. Yet the result of any such materialist discussion must in all cases "make a difference" in respect to the actual behavior not of an individual nor of a small group of people, but of a veritable collective, a social mass. In this materialistic sense, it is not even sure that the particular social theory called Marxism has ever been the subject of a discussion in this country.

Various people have been asked from time to time why they are, or why they are not, Marxists, just as they might have been asked why they believe, or do not believe, in God, in science, or morality; in race, class, democracy, victory, peace, or the impending destruction of all civilization by the atom bomb. There has also been some philological and interpretative effort spent on settling the question of "what Marx really meant." Last but not least, there has been far too much of that most senseless of all discussions which aimed at deciding which particular shade of the theories of Marx, Engels and the several generations of their disciples up to Lenin, Stalin, or, let us say, Leontov, represents the most orthodox version of the Marxist doctrine. Or, one step higher, which of the various methods used at different times by Hegel, Marx, and the Marxists truly deserves to be called the genuine "dialectical" method.

As against that altogether dogmatic approach which had already sterilized the revolutionary Marxist theory in all but a few phases of its century-long development in Europe, and by which the attempted extension of Marxism to the U.S. has been blighted from the very beginning, it is here proposed to revindicate the critical, pragmatic, and activist element which for all this has never been entirely eliminated from the social theory of Marx and which during the few short phases of its predominance has made that theory a most efficient weapon of the proletarian class struggle.

The documents reprinted below result in part from an earlier attempt at reemphasizing just this element of Marxist theory—an attempt that was made by the present writer and a group of associates in Germany in the early thirties and which was then temporarily interrupted by the anti-Marxist violence of the Hitler government. Of the four documents, two date still further back to similar attempts that had been made in 1894 and 1902 by such non-dogmatic Marxists as Lenin and Georges Sorel. They were used as models and as points of departure by the group of 1931 when it started on its new attempt at de-dogmatizing and reactivating the Marxian theory.

The Lenin piece of 1894 (Document III) was directed against a book in which the economic and sociological theories of the famous Narodniki theorist, Mikhailovski, had been critically attacked by the then "Marxist" (later, bourgeois) writer, Peter Struve. Of this important work of Lenin, unfortunately only a small part has appeared in English (*Selected Works of Lenin*, vol. I) and that part does not include the chapter from which we have taken the piece printed below. The particular interest of our document lies in the fact that just on that occasion Lenin, himself a materialist critic of the idealist "subjectivism" of the Narodniki, found himself in a position in which he had to extend his materialist criticism, with equal fervor, to the abstract and lifeless "objectivism" of Struve. In order to make Lenin's argument fully understandable, we quote the sentence of Struve which aroused Lenin's ire. Struve had found fault with Mikhailovski's opinion that there are "no unsurmountable historical tendencies which serve as starting points as well as obligatory limits to the purposive activity of the individual and the social groups." Lenin is quick in discovering the non-revolutionary implications of this Struvean comment on Mikhailovski. "This," says Lenin, "is the language of an objectivist, and not that of a Marxist (materialist)." And from this point of departure, Lenin embarks on his demonstration of the important differences which separate the principles of the "objectivists" on the one hand, from those of the "Marxists" (materialists) on the other hand.

Document IV tries to bring out more distinctly the non-dogmatic character of Lenin's antithesis to Struve's objectivistic version of the traditional Marxist doctrine. For this purpose and for a series of further experiments in loosening up and de-dogmatizing certain parts of the Marxist theory, the group of 1931 made use of the similar experiment made by Sorel in 1902. According to Sorel, the six theses reproduced in Document II below result from a process of "extracting the strictly scientific elements of history from the theory of historical materialism." In this critical reformulation of historical materialism by one of the most scientific and most pragmatically minded interpreters of Marxism in modern times, the least important point is, in the view of the writer, Sorel's special emphasis on the role of legal concepts and the legal profession. What really matters is the attempt to clarify the various concatenations that exist between the general terms of the materialist theory and of which the law and its professional exploiters seem to be only one of a number of possible illustrations. Most important, however, is the form in which Sorel has changed into a positive inspiration for unfettered scientific research what till then must have seemed to many historians a somewhat authoritarian laying down of the rules of writing history. (A different impression might have been derived, perhaps, from a closer acquaintance with the remarkably free application that had been made of the new "critical and materialist method" by Marx himself. Yet the new weapon of the revolutionary class struggle had already lost much of its critical edge in the hands of the first generation of the Marxist scholars at the time of Sorel's writing. And it is no secret that since then revolutionary Marxism has lost out completely against the "stabilizing" influences that were expressed theoretically in the growth of the old and the new Marx orthodoxy—from Kautsky to Stalin. So the Sorelian operation has to be performed once more.)

Finally, we had added a document which is meant to do for the famous "dialectical method" what Sorel and Lenin did for historical materialism. The "Theses on Hegel and Revolution," translated in Document I were first written in German for the centenary of Hegel's death, in 1931. As will be seen, they approach from a totally opposite direction the whole tangle of difficulties which beset the problem of the Hegelian dialectic and its (modified or unmodified) use by Marx and Engels. Dialectics is here considered not as a kind of super-logic, that is, not as a set of rules to be applied by individual thinkers in the process of thinking—just like ordinary logic, and distinguished from the latter only in the sense in which so-called higher mathematics is distinguished from those simpler and, in fact, long out-dated rules which are taught as "elementary mathematics" in our schools today. It is treated rather as a number of characteristic phenomena that can be observed from without in the sequence and development of thoughts in a given historical period.

The first "non-dogmatic" result of this changed approach is that a man does not become a revolutionary by studying dialectics but, on the contrary, the revolutionary change in human society affects among other things also the way in which the people of a particular period tend to produce and to exchange their thoughts. Materialist dialectics, then, is the historical investigation of the manner in which in a given revolutionary period, and during the different phases of that period, particular social classes, groups, individuals form and accept new words and ideas. It deals with the often unusual and remarkable forms in which they connect their own and other people's thoughts and cooperate in disintegrating the existing closed systems of knowledge and in replacing them by other and more flexible systems or, in the most favorable case, by no system at all but by a new and completely unfettered movement of free thought passing rapidly through the changing phases of a more or less continuous or discontinuous development.

Secondly, it appears by implication (from theses II and III) that there is no reason to boast of the fact that both Marx and Lenin, after a first violent criticism and repudiation of the old Hegelian "dialectic," have returned at a later stage, in a mood of disenchantment and partial frustration, to a very little qualified acceptance of that same philosophical method that, at its best, had reflected the bourgeois revolution of an earlier period. Here as in many other respects, the unfettered development of the Marxian theory does not point backwards to old bourgeois philosophies and ideas, but forward to a non-dogmatic and non-authoritarian, scientific and activistic use of the Marxian as well as all other theoretical formulations of the collective experience of the working class.

DOCUMENT I
Theses on Hegel and Revolution
(Karl Korsch, 1931)

I. The Hegelian philosophy and its dialectical method cannot be understood without taking into account its relationship to revolution.
   A. It originated historically from a revolutionary movement.
   B. It fulfilled the task of giving to that movement its conceptual expression.
   C. Dialectical thought is revolutionary even in its form:
      1. turning away from the immediately given—radical break with the hitherto existing—"standing on the head"—new beginning;
      2. principle of contradiction and negation;

        3. principle of permanent change and development—of the "qualitative leap."

  D. Once the revolutionary task is out of the way and the new society fully established, the revolutionary dialectical method inevitably disappears from its philosophy and science.

II. The Hegelian philosophy and its dialectical method cannot be criticized without taking into account its relationship to the particular historical conditions of the revolutionary movement of the time.

  A. It is a philosophy not of revolution in general, but of the bourgeois revolution of the seventeenth and eighteenth centuries.

  B. Even as a philosophy of the bourgeois revolution, it does not reflect the entire process of that revolution, but only its concluding phase. It is thus a philosophy not of the revolution, but of the restoration.

  C. This twofold historical nature of the Hegelian dialectic appears formally in a twofold limitation of its revolutionary character.

      1. The Hegelian dialectic, though dissolving all pre-existing fixations, results in the end in a new fixation: it becomes an absolute itself and, at the same time, "absolutizes" the whole dogmatic content of the Hegelian philosophical system that had been based on it.

      2. The revolutionary point of the dialectical approach is ultimately bent back to the "circle," that is, to a conceptual reinstatement of the immediately given reality, to a reconciliation with that reality, and to a glorification of existing conditions.

III. The attempt made by the founders of scientific socialism to salvage the high art of dialectical thinking by transplanting it from the German idealist philosophy to the materialist conception of nature and history, from the bourgeois to the proletarian theory of revolution, appears, both historically and theoretically, as a transitory step only. What has been achieved is a theory not of the proletarian revolution developing on its own basis, but of a proletarian revolution that has just emerged from the bourgeois revolution; a theory which therefore in every respect, in content and in method, is still tainted with the birthmarks of Jacobinism, that is, of the revolutionary theory of the bourgeoisie.

DOCUMENT II
Theses on the Materialistic Conception of History
(Submitted to the 1902 Convention of the Societé
Française de Philosophie, by Georges Sorel)

1. For investigating a period (of history) it is of great advantage to find out how society is divided in classes; the latter are distinguished by the essential legal concepts connected with the way in which incomes are formed in each group.
2. It is advisable to dismiss all atomistic explanations; it is not worth while to inquire how the links between individual psychologies are formed. What can be observed directly are those links themselves, that which refers to the masses. The thoughts and activities of individuals are fully understandable only by their connection with the movements of the masses.
3. Much light is thrown on history if one is able to clarify the concatenation between the system of productive forces, the organization of labor, and the social relations that rule production.
4. Religious and philosophical doctrines have traditional sources; yet in spite of their tendency to organize themselves in systems totally closed to all outside influences, they are usually somehow connected with the social conditions of the period. From this viewpoint, they appear as mental reflections of the conditions of life and often as attempts to explain history by a doctrine of faith.
5. The history of a doctrine will be fully clarified only when it can be connected with the history of a social group that makes it its task to develop and apply that particular doctrine (influence of the legal profession).
6. Assuming that revolutions do not have the effect to make possible a greater extension of the productive forces that are obstructed in their development by an outdated legislation, it is still of the greatest importance to examine a social transformation from this point of view and to investigate how the legal ideas are transformed under the pressure of a universally felt need for economic emancipation.

DOCUMENT III
Materialism versus Objectivism
(Lenin, 1894)

The objectivist speaks of the necessity of the given historical process; the materialist (Marxist) determines exactly the given economic form of society and the antagonistic relations arising from it. The objectivist, in proving the necessity of a given series of facts, always runs the risk to get into the position of an apologist of those facts; the materialist reveals the antagonisms of classes and thereby determines his own position. The objectivist speaks of "unsurmountable historical tendencies"; the materialist speaks of the class which "directs" the given economic order and thus, at the same time, brings forth one form or another of resistance by the other classes. Thus, the materialist is, on the one hand, more consistent than the objectivist and reaches a more thorough and more comprehensive objectivism. He is not satisfied with pointing to the necessity of the process, but clearly states the economic form of society underlying the content of just that process, and the particular class determining just that necessity. In our case, for example, the materialist would not content himself with referring to "unsurmountable historical tendencies"; he would point to the existence of certain classes which determine the content of the given order and exclude any possibility of a solution but by the action of the producers themselves. On the other hand, the materialist principle implies, as it were, the element of party, by committing itself, in the evaluation of any event, to a direct and open acceptance of the position of a particular social group.

DOCUMENT IV
On an Activistic Form of Materialism and
on the Class and Partisan Character of Science
(Karl Korsch, 1931)

1. There is little use in confronting the subjectivist doctrine of the decisive role of the individual in the historical process with another and equally abstract doctrine that speaks of the necessity of a given historical process. It is more useful to explore, as precisely as possible, the antagonistic relations that arise from the material conditions of production of a given economic form of society for the social groups participating in it.
2. Much light is thrown on history by countering every alleged necessity of a historical process with the following questions: (a) necessary by the action of which classes? (b) which modifications will be necessary in the action of the classes faced by the alleged historical necessity?
3. In the investigation of the antagonistic relations existing between the various classes and class fractions of an economic form of society, it is advisable to consider not only the material but also the ideological forms in which such antagonistic relations occur within the given economic form of society.
4. The content of a doctrine (theoretical system, any set of sentences and operational rules used for the statement and application of a theory or belief) cannot be clarified so long as it is not connected with the con-

tent of a given economic form of society and with the material interests of definite classes of that society.

5. There is no need to assume that the objectivity of a doctrine will be impaired by its methodical connection with the material interests and practical activities of definite classes.

6. Whenever a doctrine is not connected with the material interests of a definite class by its own proponents, one will often be justified in assuming that the proponents of such doctrine aim at defending by it the interests of the ruling classes of the society in question. In these cases the theoretical uncovering of the class function of a given doctrine is equivalent to a practical adoption of the cause of the classes oppressed in that society.

7. From this state of affairs, and from its theoretical recognition, springs the objective and subjective partisan nature of science.

Ten Theses on Marxism Today

1. Today, it is senseless to ask to what extent the teaching of Marx and Engels is still theoretically acceptable and practically applicable.

2. Today, all attempts to restore the Marxist doctrine as a whole and in its original function as a theory of the working-class social revolution are reactionary utopias.

3. For good and for bad, however, the significant components of the Marxist teaching remain efficacious today, although with a transformed function and in a different arena. Also, important impulses from the practice of the earlier Marxist working-class movement have now entered into the practical conflicts of peoples and classes.

4. The first step in re-establishing a revolutionary theory and practice consists in breaking with the monopolistic claim of Marxism to revolutionary initiative and to theoretical and practical leadership.

5. Marx is today only one of the many precursors, founders, and developers of the socialist working-class movement. The so-called utopian socialists from Thomas More to the present are equally important. So are the great rivals of Marx, such as Blanqui, and his sworn enemies, such as Proudhon and Bakunin. And no less important, finally, are such more

recent developments as German revisionism, French syndicalism, and Russian bolshevism.

6. The following points are particularly critical for Marxism:
(a) its practical dependence on the underdeveloped economic and political conditions in Germany and all the other countries of central and eastern Europe where it was to acquire political importance;
(b) its unconditional adherence to the political forms of the bourgeois revolution;
(c) its unconditional acceptance of the advanced economic conditions of England as a model for the future development of all countries and as objective preconditions for the transition to socialism; to which one should add:
(d) the consequences of Marxism's repeated, desperate and contradictory attempts to break out of these conditions.

7. The results of these conditions are:
(a) the overestimation of the state as the decisive instrument of social revolution;
(b) the mystical identification of the development of the capitalist economy with the social revolution of the working class;
(c) the later ambiguous development of this first form of Marxist revolutionary theory through artificially grafting a two-phase theory of the Communist revolution onto it. This theory, directed in part against Blanqui, and in part against Bakunin, whisks away the real emancipation of the working class from the present movement and into an indefinite future.

8. The Leninist or Bolshevik development entered at this point, and it is in this new form that Marxism has been transferred to Russia and Asia. Thus Marxian socialism has been changed from a revolutionary theory to an ideology which could be—and has been—used for a variety of different goals.

9. The two Russian revolutions of 1917 and 1928 are to be critically comprehended from this point of view. And from this point of view one must determine the varying functions fulfilled by Marxism in contemporary Asia and on a world-wide scale.

10. The workers will not attain control over the production of their own lives by occupying the positions on the international and world markets that have been abandoned by self-abolishing, so-called free competition between monopolistic owners of the means of production. This

control can only result from planned intervention by all the presently excluded classes into production which already today tends to be regulated in a totally monopolistic and planned fashion.

Translated by Douglas Kellner

Letter to Paul Mattick
New York, November 20, 1938

I am here on the third day of my sad journey to explore the present possibilities of work and influence on the Institute for Social Research.[1] Up to now, it is clear that my two contributions, *if at all*, will appear in the *Zeitschrift für Sozialforschung* with such deletions and distortions that they will completely lose their real meaning. I would have taken them back long ago if I did not think that it would still be a certain advantage for both Pannekoek and Spain if they were taken by the journal in whatever distorted form.[2]

By the way, are you *completely* sure that one could name Pannekoek in print as the author of the Harper piece? If not, I would be glad to ask him directly, right away. With *Living Marxism*, it is not so bad, but the *Zeitschrift* is still read by bourgeois people in Holland. After conversations with the comrades around Canne Mejer and Sneevliet in Amsterdam in 1928, I had the impression that Pannekoek had given the Dutch government some sort of pledge not to engage in political activity (or not in Holland, not publicly, or something like that). Did he, then, sign the article on the organization question for *Living Marxism* with his own name or with a pseudonym?

After the first couple of long discussions with Horkheimer about plans to collaborate on a great book on dialectics, I am very skeptical. It appears that they want to use me, approximately as they used you recently with your report on economics. They treat me with almost exaggerated respect, but that is only another form, corresponding to my "high" class position and the respect due to me in virtue of it. When nothing financial results from this, I shall probably in some way break off this partnership that is now viewed very positively from all sides (an anonymous partnership in so far as I am in question, and that suits me fine!). This is all in the deepest confidence completely between us. You can speak about it with Hans if you convey to him my request for the strictest absolute discretion.

Pollack is truly kind and is positively interested in utilizing my power of production in some form, which would also be useful for me. But he is completely immersed in the private capitalist business of the Institute and doesn't even take part in the discussions.

Horkheimer is subjective (*innerlich*), as I already noticed in our discussions in Seattle,[3] and in the last years has come very close to my, our, political standpoint. But he is in no way ready to come out with his views publicly.[4] The entire Institute has always been and still is completely grounded in a *double book-keeping* (*doppelten Buchführung*) in politics and revolutionary theory.[5] It is not so bad as others (for example the "New School")[6] who instead of offering their teaching positions to qualified and needy political emigrants (like A. Rosenberg, Hallgarten and—Korsch?) hire rich people like Reizler from Frankfurt or outspoken reactionaries like the Dollfuss-Weiner Mayor *Winter* (there is a grotesque book by Winter that deserves a review in *Living Marxism*)— and all financed by American Jews and anti-fascists. These people are the most disgusting scum that one can imagine. But the people from the Institute for Social Research think that because they are merely cowardly and egotistical and limited, and not openly counterrevolutionary, that they are in some way revolutionary and ready for struggle (in secret!).

Wiesengrund (Adorno) is one of the most capable heads in philosophy, as *Grossman* is a luminary of economics. *Wittfogel* too, despite his boredom with his field, may accomplish something scientific. Politically he is externally still a Stalinist, while the others only want to avoid a direct hostility with the Stalinists. Internally, they are all without exception, in various degrees, anti-Stalinist.

Marcuse is a sort of orthodox Marxist who might even still be a Stalinist, and is bureaucratically authoritarian in matters of bourgeois philosophy and Marxism (which today has become one and the same). Theoretically, he has somewhat more character and solidness than the others, whose greater "freedom" consists only in a greater fluctuation and uncertainty. But he is not especially sympathetic as a person.

Lowenthal and *Neumann* are on the whole talented, personally decent, writers, one in the field of literature, the other in jurisprudence.

That is approximately the situation. They work but little, and talk a lot. This they call "collective work." In a definite hierarchy, each gives the other some chatter and then they conclude. This they call Community.

I talked to Grossman briefly for the first time yesterday at a Horkheimer university lecture (whose circle of hearers was for the most part the people in the Institute and their wives, and a few confused students—more or less Stalinist influenced, far under the intellectual level of your circle in Chicago).

I haven't yet been able to discuss your economic manuscript or *Living Marxism* with him. In regard to support for the latter, it looks bleak. I mentioned it often in conversations, but have the impression that no one reads it, and that all of them have anxiety about it (at bottom they have anxiety over it in general, although in fact no danger at all exists that they would be influenced or shaken in any way through reading our articles!).

According to a communication from Chapman & Hall, my book (*Karl Marx*) is to appear in London on *November* 7! Concerning the American edition, they have *submitted* the work to Wiley & Son and are waiting for their decision. . . .

I can receive copies for 4 shillings apiece (bookstore price is 6 shillings), and have already ordered 6 copies.

Perhaps you can already announce in this number of *Living Marxism* that the book has appeared and is available (for the bookstore price expressed in dollars). If you think that is all right and would not prefer to wait until Wiley has made his decision, so as to eventually deal with him, let me know. I shall then order a number of copies from Chapman and will have him send them to me in Chicago at your address.

I shall speak with [Sidney] Hook Friday evening and think that I shall also call [Lewis] Corey and some others to make appointments. Boelke is still doing well and I'll look him up;[7] maybe he'll call me in the meantime . . . ; I am always at home until 10:00 a.m. He can also leave a message for me with Frau Lucy Bernhardi where I live. Greetings to all friends. If I still had money I would probably come to Chicago very soon. In fact, I am thinking of coming in a month or so for a couple of weeks. Write! When is *Living Marxism* appearing?

Yours, KK

[P.S.] I received *Modern Quarterly* in Boston before my trip. Thanks a lot. *Garrat*[8] understands nothing about class struggle; from the materialist standpoint, it is not a question of what people are thinking in their heads ("struggle against religion, etc."), but what they are and do. From Garrat's presentation it follows that the sole *counterforce* to Franco + Negrin, Mussolini, Hitler, Chamberlain, etc. is the proletariat (that is active in Spain, that is latent internationally; and in Russia ambiguous!); the church and order in Spain represent a great part of capital (*more directly* than elsewhere) and thus "struggle against religion, etc." is a more direct struggle against capital. And so on.

Translated by Douglas Kellner

Notes

1. For background on the history of the Institute for Social Research and Korsch's relation to it, see my article, "The Frankfurt School Revisited," *New German Critique* 4 (Winter 1975), and the introduction to this anthology.

2. Korsch is referring here to his article on Pannekoek's book *Lenin's Philosophy* and his article "Economics and Politics in Revolutionary Spain" (published in this anthology). Both essays were published in Mattick's journal *Living Marxism* and a truncated version of the essay on Spain appeared as a review in the *Zeitschrift für Sozialforschung* 7: 469–474.

3. Korsch speaks of Horkheimer's visit to him in Seattle in a letter July 26, 1938, cited in *Jahrbuch Arbeiterbewegung 2*, p. 243.

4. The article where Horkheimer comes closest to Korsch's political position is "Authoritarian State," which he originally published under a pseudonym. Translated in *Telos* 15 (Spring 1973).

5. The term "double bookkeeping" was used by the Comintern to condemn the politics of Ruth Fisher and her group and signifies a two-faced ambiguity and opportunism.

6. For a discussion of the New School for Social Research and its relation to the Institute for Social Research, see J. Radkau, *Die deutsche Emigration in den USA* (Dusseldorf: Bertelsmann Universitatsverlag, 1971). This book has information on the people discussed by Korsch here.

7. Sidney Hook was a student of Korsch's in Berlin and in his 1933 book *Toward an Understanding of Karl Marx* (New York: John Day, 1933) cites his debt to Korsch. Lewis Corey was the author of *The Decline of American Capitalism* (New York: Covia Fried. 1934) and many articles on Marxism. Boelke was a member of the council's Communist group.

8. Korsch is referring to a book by G. T. Garratt, *Mussolini's Roman Empire* (London: Harmondsworth, 1938), reviewed in *Living Marxism* 4, no. 7 (June 1939): 221–222.

Letter to Bertolt Brecht
Boston, April 18, 1947

Dear Brecht:

It will soon hardly seem true that we are both living on the same continent and in the same country. Hence I want to report to you today on "The Present Situation and Perspectives." Sort of in the sense of one of

Marx's young Hegelian friends, who wrote a pamphlet, "The Good Cause of Freedom and My Cause."

Since I saw you last, things have not been going well for me. I have been working little, and what I have done has led to nothing, or at best, like the study I had begun earlier of the Phillipines and the other struggles between the new colonialism and the new struggles for independence in the Far East, to a new "self-realization." After that, I broke off this work as well, and occupied myself with various minor projects, among them the study of Toynbee, in whom, unlike earlier, nothing now seems to me to be great except his weakness. Precisely for that reason he is becoming popular, and, in the May issue of *Politics*, I will perhaps discuss critically the new condensation of his works into one volume (six-in-one; formally not badly done, and perhaps to be recommended to you for reading after all).

Meanwhile it has become quite clear to me that on the world-wide scale we are in an era of regression. The retrogression in intellectual and cultural matters can be traced almost from day to day. It is also useless to point to the continuing "progress" of technology. On the contrary, the intellectual decline will reach an extent in the foreseeable future which will bring even the progress of technology to a halt—and even now the already threadbare foundations for nearly equating the progress of technology with that of material production are disappearing more and more. Nothing is changed in this overall picture by the regions of the world where material progress is still continuing or only really beginning, on the one hand, Russia, on the other, China and (with several question marks) India. It is as in the Roman Empire, from roughly the second or third century on, where even in the most remote province a certain resistance was waged against the loss of culture, and beyond the borders the construction of a new world had begun amongst the "barbarians"—but how difficult it was already for Engels (even for a much later time!) to "prove" that feudal society represented a "progressive epoch of the formation of economic society" vis-à-vis ancient society, that is, a higher development from slave labor to serfdom. (Today we know that slavery existed in all historical forms of society, and that it played a very different role in each, for example, in Chinese society, a very small one in relation to the statute-labor (corvées) required by the state, on the one hand, and the various free and semi-free forms of labor in the fragmented rural economy, on the other. In many other ways, the old Marxian, really Hegelian, model has fallen into disorder today; even earlier, however, it did not fit the relationship between medieval and ancient society.)

In this general retrogression, I have finally decided to take a step backward also and begin anew with Marx. His activity in the *period from 1848 to 1867* (*Communist Manifesto* to *Capital/* or Revolution 1848 to First International) now seems to me in fact to be *the classical form* for the development of Marxian theory (and action) as well as for the entire bourgeois era, which began in the sixteenth century and in part even earlier in Europe and attained its culmination at this time.

Having taken this step, I am overflowing with new thoughts and plans for work. There seems to be a way of presenting Marxism which I have not yet properly tried out. If, for example, I wanted to write something for the one-hundredth birthday of the *C(ommunist) M(anifesto)*, written in December, 1847, published in February, 1848, it would no longer be of importance to present its genesis exactly, as has been done by many good scholars on other memorial days, and as I myself, for example, did rather extensively for the theory of "Capital" in my last book.

The important thing now is presenting *the Century of the CM*—or perhaps even: *The first Marxism Century.*—Proceeding from the classical form: the various challenges which this finished theory subsequently met and how it reacted to them. Here belong also the new problems appearing within the theoretical work of Marx himself: (1) The details of "classical" bourgeois economics and its "positive" extensions, particularly by the English theorists, peaking in Richard Jones, who nearly matches Marx. They are, however, treated under the heading "Antithesis to the Economists on the Basis of the Ricardo Theory," in the third volume of the so-called "Theories on Surplus Value," edited by Kautsky. (2) Similarly, the problems of (Hegelian and post-Hegelian) dialectics, recurring in the work on economic theory and previously declared "overcome" by Marx, but not solved concretely at all up to that point. (3) Later, especially problems of agricultural economy: America, Russia, Asian society. (4) Perhaps less important for Marx than for Engels: prehistory. (5) Very late, and, unfortunately, attested in the main only in Engels' formulations, the problems of monopoly capitalism and so-called state capitalism—whose clarification and solution was, in my opinion, possible in large part at the time on the basis of the Marxian theory of "commodity fetishism."

In addition:

II. historical, III. practical challenges, which to a greater extent than the theoretical ones (I.) have led, not merely to a further development, but also to a kind of *disintegration* of the Marxian theory. Here belong:

The experiences of the First International—in England:

The dissociation of the labor unions from all direct or indirect *necessary* connection with the revolutionary movement;—in southern France, Switzerland, Italy, Spain: anarchism;—analogous and in part overlapping, the *nonsuitability* of classical Marxian theory for the non-industrialized countries, which was not merely negatively symbolized, but made clear for positive further development in the struggle against Bakunin; Slavic countries of Europe, Asia;—analogous nonsuitability for America.

The Commune revolt, the American Civil War, the potentially revolutionary crisis of the '60s in Russia—then the renewed bogging-down of all these impulses and the reaction against them: Third Republic in France; Marx's democratic foreign policy; national wars; foundation of the German Reich. The emergence of national Social Democratic parties in France and Germany, and temporally somewhat earlier, Marx's overwhelmingly *reformist* reaction to the English factory legislation; proletarian dictatorship or democracy; "withering-away of the state"; role of the "party"; struggle for the reception of revolutionary theory by non-revolutionary movements, organizations and "elites"; differing developments in Germany, France and Russia; end of this epoch at beginning of the '80s.

The new epoch, since 1890, is perhaps best not treated in this book. Or?

Additionally, I would like to say that some things have now changed in my own position toward Russia and thus, indirectly, towards the Communist party. In spite of the frightful brutalities in the occupied areas and, even more, in Russia itself, all in all the perspectives for the economic and political regions in the Russian sphere of influence seem better, or at least less desperate, than for those in the areas of Western dominance. Even the "United States of Europe" would come into being, under this leadership, only in the form drastically represented by Franco-Spain on the one hand, and the present Greek government on the other. After all, I have seen quite clearly from my careful studies of the Far Eastern movements that Russia is the best and, at the same time, the only ally for these countries—even if it actually does nothing for them and forces their independent movements, without equivalent concessions, into its own forms, which serve quite different purposes. A world-wide hegemony of the Yankees would be not only the worst thing I could imagine for this world, but, beyond that, merely a reactionary utopia. "Imperialism" has to be learned, and for a long time, the Americans, in contrast to the Britons, would only bumble around with this task, and the rest of the world would have to suffer, not only from American imperialism, but also from the deficient development of this imperialism. Put another way, previous U.S. imperialism in the Caribbean region, in Central and South America, and probably also in its impending forms in Japan, will not even serve the interests of U.S. capitalism as a whole, but instead only a relatively small group of colonial-pretorian exploiters. In all these respects Russian imperialism is better for the world today than Yankee imperialism, and there is hardly a third chance. The forms in which the non-ruling, secondary, peripheral "national minorities" within the Russian empire are likewise subjected to a special (quasi-colonial) repression and exploitation are obviously still very little developed, and show more a factual than a systematic discrimination. The coercive measures applied against the entire citizenry (e.g., mass deportations, forced-labor camps and other physical and social measures against insufficiently dependable segments of the population) are of course more effective, that is, more destructive, when they are applied against such externally segregated, less densely populated, and professionally and socially less differentiated regions, where, for example, entire states can be annulled as such and their populations moved away. The repressive and exploitative element in the rule of *bordering* areas (Balkans, Czechoslovakia, etc., Poland, occupied zone of Germany) is easier to show, but so far has constituted only a subordinate, and not necessarily the *dominant* factor in the character of these forms of government.

These reflections I have just inserted here have only a little to do with my return to the study of Marx. They serve more as a supplement to the first part of the letter, where I dealt with the situation of the world as a whole, and in the historical comparison with the decline of the Roman Empire did not expressly take into account the fact that the Russian world today is in a quite different position from that of the "barbarians" outside the Roman imperial boundaries back then. But it is true for both times that the construction of the new world was begun crudely, and it cannot even be said as definitely today, for the future, as we can presently say it for the past era, that this new world, no matter how it may be in other respects, will really develop as a "new" world in contrast to the old one, and that it will not be brought back again into the old one (like the East Roman Empire in relation to West Roman Empire).

Finally two more personal points: Please write and tell me how long you plan to stay in the west this year. I would perhaps come to Los Angeles for a short time in August, partly to visit you, partly to visit the gentlemen from the Institute, who have been developing an ever more "western" orientation (first of all geographically). And, as much as I would enjoy seeing the rest of the Brecht family (if I take away Steff, whom I have here, and you, in case you were gone by then), whether I

would still find you there has some importance for my decision. Hanna
and I want to fly to Mexico in the beginning of September; I could, however, come to Los Angeles before then.

The second point leads me back to the *Communist Manifesto*. It seems
to me that it would be nice if you could get your *didactic poem* finished
by October or November of this year, so that it could be published in time
for the one-hundredth anniversary of the CM.[1] I would like to cooperate
in one way or another. Since it would probably be more correct not to
print the text of the Manifesto along with it, perhaps a small introduction
would be in order—which you could [crossed out; hand-written addition
illegible] alone or together with me. And secondly, I would very much
like to write a concentrated presentation in German of the thoughts just
discussed; but expanded upon everywhere, and suited to the occasion,
with a smaller dose of explicit criticism, which could be published as the
second part of the new book. [Hand-written marginalia illegible.] To
appear in this good company would be so important to me that I would,
if necessary, write anonymously or under a pseudonym. At the same time,
I am writing the work discussed above, more in detail and probably in
English, and if at all possible, so that it will be ready for print at the end
of this year. Just now, however, it is difficult for me to go beyond the
stage of good thoughts and all the other forms of pure "brain-work"
to the real writing. [crossed out: Also, it is not possible] to gather the
completeness I previously considered necessary, and I can only adapt with
difficulty to these further consequences of the current regressive development of the world. But even in Moscow, where formally everything is
assembled, I fear that it would firstly not be available at all, and, secondly,
no longer for me in the same way as it was in an earlier period. Stalin's
recent statement that "even the classics can err," and expressly including
"the socialist classics" as well, opens of course everything but the prospect for a greater tolerance towards historical criticism, which, after all,
did not begin for the holy scriptures of the Bible until the nineteenth
century, and then only for Europe, but has not yet begun even today for
America. With many cordial greetings from one house to another

Your old K. K.

P.S. I won't even read my stenogram through, but will send it immediately to Hanna, with the request to send you and me one copy each.
P.P.S. As may have occurred to you by yourself while reading, I will soon
be needing again my copy of Engels' catechism of October, 1847 ("Principles of Communism"). Luckily, however, I can refer you to the fact
that this work is printed, with all the more or less important corrections
and deletions of the original manuscript, in the *Marx-Engels-Gesamtaus-*

gabe 16, pp. 501–22. Both of the omitted answers to the questions 22 and 23 are not to be found there either; according to the editor's assertion on p. 682, they are "not extant."

Translated by Mark Ritter

Note

1. Brecht's versification of the "Communist Manifesto" can be found in *Gesammelte Werke* (Frankfurt: Suhrkamp, 10: 1967), 911ff. Korsch's commentary on this project and suggested improvements have been published in *Alternative* 41 (Berlin: 1965).

Letter to J. A. Dawson
Boston, Mass., USA
May 3, 1948

Dear Friend:

Though it might have been wiser to look through the last issues of your paper first, I decided not to postpone any longer my long-delayed plan of writing to you directly. Up to now I heard from you only indirectly, and I read with interest such issues of your paper as were given to me either by my friend Paul Mattick or by the Boston friends who publish the *Western Socialist*. You need not be told, I think, that my connection with the latter is merely personal, and is not based on any theoretical or political agreement. What separates us can perhaps be most easily expressed by a phrase which I keep repeating to my dear friend, George Gloss—that his group represents, at best, the ideas of the revolution of the nineteenth century, while I am only interested in that of the twentieth century.

Maybe I should state first in detail who I am, and give you a historical analysis of the long development through which I changed from a member (though an oppositionist member even then) of the English Fabian Society in 1912–14 to a member of the German Independent Social Democratic party during the first World War, and from there through a short enthusiastic adherence to the party of Lenin to an "ultra-leftist" opposition, first from within, afterwards from without the party, and from there further on, during the last twenty years, to a new position which seems to me in many ways similar to your present tendency as reflected by your issue of December, 1947—the last, so far, that I have seen. I think, however, that you are more or less aware of all the relevant shades of the present development, and thus probably know more about me than I could tell you in a short letter. I should not neglect, though, to tell you that I enjoyed your reprinting my review of Trotsky's book, and so many pieces by Mattick and Pannekoek. Just now I should be busy writing a review of the English edition of Pannekoek's excellent criticism of Lenin's philosophy for the *Western Socialist*. Yet I find it difficult to do so, since I said most of the things I had to say in my earlier review of the German text that appeared in vol. IV, no. 5, of *Living Marxism*, in 1938. If I wanted to improve on that now, after ten years, I would have to deal with the newest attack of positivism against Marxism that is contained in K. R. Popper's two volumes on *The Open Society and Its Enemies* that appeared in London (George Routledge and Sons Ltd.) in 1945, and which I got only now, after it had been reprinted in 1947. I find this book very loathsome, however, though it is ably written and has made a deplorably strong impression on some former leftists of the Pannekoek-Mattick stamp. Thus I find it difficult to make me read it through, and this again, up to now, has kept me from writing the review I had promised both to Mattick and the *W.S.* for the purpose of promoting the sale of Pannekoek's valuable book. If and when I write the review I shall send you a copy forthwith, since it is quite possible that the *W.S.* will find my review "too academical and too confused" again— as they did in regard to my review of Trotsky's book, and I really cannot blame them for thinking so from their own particular viewpoint.

I am absorbed, at present, in two different kind of studies, which will appear first in the German language, and in which I try to trace both the final results of the "Marxist" era of the workers' movement to the original *theory and practice* of Marx: (1) before, during and after 1848; (2) during the period of the W.M.I.A. in the 60's and 70's. I'll send you copies of what is ready as soon as I manage to translate it into English. (In case you can get German MSS translated down under, I'd send you quite a selection of new and old writings which might be of interest to you—but I am afraid that cannot be done, and it is well nigh impossible for me to get copies of my English writings of the last 10–15 years myself.)

In connection with the above-described studies I plan to write on the theories of Bakunin, and more particularly on his theory of the state as presented in a book of 1873 which is widely unknown and does not exist in any non-Russian edition except in one of the Spanish editions which is nearly unobtainable, too. Thus it will take some time before I overcome the linguistic difficulties. I learnt Spanish now, and can read the Spanish translation myself, but I need help for the original Russian version, and I have to get photostatic copies of it because I can borrow the book itself only for a limited period, which is nearly exhausted. There are a few articles in which I dealt with the subject in the German periodical *Die Aktion* in 1928 and 1931, but they have not been translated. So I was quite glad when Lain Diez sent me his article on the *Interpretation of the Paris Commune*, and I translated it into English myself, first from a French translation, and now from the Spanish original version, which turned out to be far better than the French version. I also made a few changes, with the consent of the author (whom I do not know in person). I enclose a copy of this article with a view to publication in your paper if you think that you can do so. In spite of certain obvious shortcomings, I think that the little article is well written and approaches certain important questions in a manner which might interest people who have not yet freed themselves from the Marx-Lenin-Trotsky legend to the same extent as you or I might claim it for ourselves.—Comradely greetings,

Karl Korsch

Note

The letter is to J. A. Dawson, editor of *Southern Advocate for Workers' Councils*, and was published in the July–August issue (Melbourne, 1948), pp. 9–10.

Letter to Erich Gerlach
December 16, 1956

I am ashamed that I have not written you for such a long time after our conversations in Hanover, and after receiving the two issues of "Sozialistische Politik" of July and August, 1956. I have immediately read in detail here both issues and found almost everything within extraordinarily good and useful as preparation for the new socialism of a German and European workers' movement that appears to me completely non-utopian. I would thus be glad to write occasionally for the journal. But that which in this activity could precisely be most important for us— a continuous comparison and synthesis between the workers' movement here, that has already developed further, and your European experiences—I could not carry out for a long time in the disappointed and depressed condition after my return from the trip to Europe; even though I produced some contacts and really tried every day to see the possible connections between the developments there and here. What happened is that I came up with an immense amount of material here, which had been gathered during my absence and has since increased more, before I could work through the earlier material. Further, my old habit of forty years of going back and forth from theory to practice has been considerably reinforced by the present events in Russia, Poland, and the other so-called satellites.[1] Even in order to "see together" these last events in the context of a great middle-European development, I need a renewed, purely theoretical, study of this entire epoch, and especially its present development that has been so violently mutilated before its maturity. I shall report again to you on these questions after some time when my "self-understanding" has progressed further. . . .

Despite my previous neglect, I am very excited about your answer to the statements in this letter, and the present position and perspective from the standpoint of socialist politics. In the meantime, I send you, along with Hedda's, our warm greetings—naturally to your wife also. Is there any chance that you might come to America sometime?

Yours, Karl Korsch

[In a letter written on the same day to Ruth Fisher, which Korsch included in the letter to Gerlach, he writes:]

I travelled to Detroit, after a quick decision, to participate in a massmeeting of auto workers. I had a good reception from old and new friends, but the time was too short to build anything further. For me in my U.S.-desert, it is already a lot when I am once again among real workers. As always, I have good plans to activate my theoretical and political tendencies, but hold on at the same time to another dream: to theoretically restore the "ideas of Marx" that today are seemingly annihilated after the conclusion of the Marx-Lenin-Stalin episode.

Translated by Douglas Kellner

Notes

1. Korsch is referring to the demonstrations and strikes in Poland in 1956 and the uprisings in Hungary and East Germany that were forcefully crushed by Russian troops.

Index

Thanks to Pam Goldberg for help in compiling the index.—D.K.